WITHDRAWN FROM
MACALESTER COLLEGE
LIBRARY

Tourism and the Globalization of Emotions

Today, an increasing number of people from all over the world travel to Buenos Aires to dance tango. To accommodate these intimate voyagers, tourist agencies offer travel packages, including classes in tango instruction, dance shoe shopping, and special city maps pointing out the tango clubs in town. Some of these agencies even provide "taxi dancers"—mainly Argentine men, who make a living by selling themselves as dance escorts to foreign women on a short term stay. Based on a cheek-to-cheek ethnography of intimate life in the tango clubs of Buenos Aires, this book provides a passionate exploration of tango—its sentiments and symbolic orders—as well as a critical investigation of the effects of globalization on intimate economies. Throughout the chapters, the author assesses how, in an explosive economic and political context, people's emotional lives intermingle with a tourism industry that has formed at the intersection of close embrace dances and dollars. Bringing economies of intimacy centre stage, the book describes how a global condition is lived bodily, emotionally and politically, and offers a rich, provocative contribution to theorizing today's global flows of people, money, and fragile dreams. As the narrative charts a course across a sea of intense, emotional sensations, taken-for-granted ideas about dancing, romance and power twist and turn like the steps of the tango.

Maria Törnqvist is a Senior Lecturer in Sociology at the Department of Education, Uppsala University. She has previously published on Swedish gender equality politics and has written an award-winning teaching book in feminist theory (with Katharina Tollin).

Routledge Advances in Feminist Studies and Intersectionality

CORE EDITORIAL GROUP: DR. KATHY DAVIS (INSTITUTE FOR HISTORY AND CULTURE, UTRECHT, THE NETHERLANDS), PROFESSOR JEFF HEARN (MANAGING EDITOR; LINKÖPING UNIVERSITY, SWEDEN; HANKEN SCHOOL OF ECONOMICS, FINLAND; UNIVERSITY OF HUDDERSFIELD, UK), PROFESSOR ANNA G. JÓNASDÓTTIR (ÖREBRO UNIVERSITY, SWEDEN), PROFESSOR NINA LYKKE (MANAGING EDITOR; LINKÖPING UNIVERSITY, SWEDEN), PROFESSOR CHANDRA TALPADE MOHANTY (SYRACUSE UNIVERSITY, USA), PROFESSOR ELŻBIETA H. OLEKSY (UNIVERSITY OF ŁÓDŹ, POLAND), DR. ANDREA PETŐ (CENTRAL EUROPEAN UNIVERSITY, HUNGARY), PROFESSOR ANN PHOENIX (INSTITUTE OF EDUCATION, UNIVERSITY OF LONDON, UK)

Routledge Advances in Feminist Studies and Intersectionality is committed to the development of new feminist and profeminist perspectives on changing gender relations, with special attention to:

- Intersections between gender and power differentials based on age, class, dis/abilities, ethnicity, nationality, racialisation, sexuality, violence, and other social divisions.
- Intersections of societal dimensions and processes of continuity and change: culture, economy, generativity, polity, sexuality, science and technology;
- Embodiment: Intersections of discourse and materiality, and of sex and gender.
- Transdisciplinarity: intersections of humanities, social sciences, medical, technical and natural sciences.
- Intersections of different branches of feminist theorizing, including: historical materialist feminisms, postcolonial and anti-racist feminisms, radical feminisms, sexual difference feminisms, queerfeminisms, cyberfeminisms, posthuman feminisms, critical studies on men and masculinities.
- A critical analysis of the travelling of ideas, theories and concepts.
- A politics of location, reflexivity and transnational contextualising that reflects the basis of the Series framed within European diversity and transnational power relations.

1 **Feminist Studies**
A Guide to Intersectional Theory, Methodology and Writing
Nina Lykke

2 **Women, Civil Society and the Geopolitics of Democratization**
Denise M. Horn

3 **Sexuality, Gender and Power**
 Intersectional and Transnational Perspectives
 Edited by Anna G. Jónasdóttir, Valerie Bryson and Kathleen B. Jones

4 **The Limits of Gendered Citizenship**
 Contexts and Complexities
 Edited by Elżbieta H. Oleksy, Jeff Hearn and Dorota Golańska

5 **Theories and Methodologies in Postgraduate Feminist Research**
 Researching Differently
 Edited by Rosemarie Buikema, Gabriele Griffin and Nina Lykke

6 **Making Gender, Making War**
 Violence, Military and Peacekeeping Practices
 Edited by Annica Kronsell and Erika Svedberg

7 **Emergent Writing Methodologies in Feminist Studies**
 Edited by Mona Livholts

8 **Gender and Sexuality in Online Game Cultures**
 Passionate Play
 Jenny Sundén and Malin Sveningsson

9 **Heterosexuality in Theory and Practice**
 Chris Beasley, Heather Brook and Mary Holmes

10 **Tourism and the Globalization of Emotions**
 The Intimate Economy of Tango
 Maria Törnqvist

Tourism and the Globalization of Emotions

The Intimate Economy of Tango

Maria Törnqvist

NEW YORK LONDON

First published 2013
by Routledge
711 Third Avenue, New York, NY 10017

Simultaneously published in the UK
by Routledge
2 Park Square, Milton Park, Abingdon, Oxon OX14 4RN

*Routledge is an imprint of the Taylor & Francis Group,
an informa business*

© 2013 Taylor & Francis

The right of Maria Törnqvist to be identified as author of this work has been asserted in accordance with sections 77 and 78 of the Copyright, Designs and Patents Act 1988.

All rights reserved. No part of this book may be reprinted or reproduced or utilised in any form or by any electronic, mechanical, or other means, now known or hereafter invented, including photocopying and recording, or in any information storage or retrieval system, without permission in writing from the publishers.

Trademark Notice: Product or corporate names may be trademarks or registered trademarks, and are used only for identification and explanation without intent to infringe.

Library of Congress Cataloging-in-Publication Data
Törnqvist, Maria.
 Tourism and the globalization of emotions : the intimate economy of tango / by Maria Törnqvist.
   p. cm. — (Routledge advances in feminist studies and intersectionality)
Includes bibliographical references and index.
 1. Tango (Dance)—Social aspects—Argentina—Buenos Aires. 2. Tango (Dance)—Economic aspects—Argentina—Buenos Aires. 3. Tourism—Argentian—Buenos Aires. 4. Women travelers—Argentina—Buenos Aires. I. Title.
 GV1796.T3T65 2013
 793.3'3—dc23
 2012038789

ISBN13: 978-0-415-89220-9 (hbk)
ISBN13: 978-0-203-38622-4 (ebk)

Typeset in Sabon
by IBT Global.

Printed and bound in the United States of America on sustainably sourced paper by IBT Global.

For Maja and Märta

Contents

Preface and Acknowledgements   xi

PART I
Introduction

1   Intimate Voyages in Global Times   3

PART II
Argentine Tango Dancing

2   The Production of Belief   31

3   An Intimate Dance Economy   58

4   Voyages out of the Ordinary   89

5   Trading Tango   104

PART III
Negotiating Tango Tourism

6   Tourists and Other Tourists   139

7   Commercialized Intimacy   162

8   Sex, Romance and Tango   177

9 Dancing Geographies 195

PART IV
Conclusion

10 Tango Tourism: Between Market Adaption and Cultural
    Resistance 215

Appendix: Notes from a Dancing Researcher 247
Notes 259
References 277
Index 289

Preface and Acknowledgements

When I first encountered tales about tango life in Buenos Aires I was a couple of weeks into a beginner course in tango dancing. New acquaintances from the San Francisco and Berkeley dance-floors told me about the *milongas* open until seven o'clock in the morning and the old *milongueros* who had lived the tango since its golden age, when orchestras flourished in the cafés of Buenos Aires. Some of my recent friends also spoke of the intimate bonds created by Argentine dance teachers and women from all over the world who had come to Argentina to realize a dance dream. I had early on decided not to make a research project out of my new hobby, but the more I heard about kitschy tango hostels harboring westerners on two-week dance holidays, Argentine men who sold their company to lonesome tourists without a dance partner and the growing market for all kinds of dance services and tango consumption items, the closer I was to brake the promise I had given myself. The Argentine dance-floors were simply too tempting for a sociologist like myself. What was really going on behind velvet curtains in the old dance venues of the proud tango capital? What did the dance voyagers come looking for and what did they find? What about the local dancers—those Argentines who made a monthly revenue out of their dancing skills and cultural heritage—and what about those *porteños* who claimed that the gringos had stolen their tango and taken away everything authentic about it? Tango tourism in Buenos Aires seemed to embrace it all: exoticism, romantic longing, economic hardship, escapist adventure, sexism, postcolonial fantasies and resistance in the shape of dancing movements.

As I laid out the first sketches of an ethnographic study I was influenced by a number of well-known social scientists who have studied the effects of globalization and neo-liberalism on the intimate life. Zygmunt Bauman, Arlie Hocschschild, Wendy Brown and other scholars have come to the conclusion that the logic and rationale of capitalist markets are corrupting the body and soul of late-modern (wo)man. No matter whether the object of study is Internet dating, sex tourism or the trading of migratory care labor from the Global South to the North, one common feature is that the values connected with intimate relations are being sold out as commercial items and being mixed up with a consumption logic. Also as lovers, mothers and friends we are socialized to become clients and providers, adapting our behavior to suit a market of endless choice.

These studies have been crucial for my work. In fact, I have been curious to find out how such claims would fit the case of dancing and the expanding number of people travelling to Buenos Aires in search of the tango. Was the culture subject to a Disneyfication process, taking away the intimate promises and making tango yet another exotic souvenir ready to be consumed by wealthy westerners? Were private dance classes in the tourists' hotels actually a cover for transactions of romance? Did the dance travelers aim for goals similar to those of female sex tourists in Jamaica and Ghana? As I plunged deeper into the world of tango and slowly made myself at home in the Argentine dance venues and tango hostels, partly with my notebook hidden in my shoe bag, I discovered that the impact of globalization and commercialization was more diffuse and complex than I had assumed. The tango, in the form of all those dancers dedicated enough to spend their savings and most of their leisure time on a wooden dance-floor—Argentines, Swedes, dancers from San Francisco, Paris and Tokyo —proved, in part, to constitute resistance to the attempts to put a price tag on the culture. Not least, this resistance manifested itself in the organizing of social dancing as an intimate economy. As it turned out, money proved to be an ambiguous credential within this symbolic economy. The Argentine dance-floors were populated by a group of unwilling or at least restrictive consumers. In tango, many dance tourists claimed, they wished to be recognized as dancers, not as clients. The conflicts and interdependencies between the intimate dance economy and the market of goods and services, primarily targeting tango tourists, makes up one important focus in this book.

However, this study is not another contribution to the rich and flourishing celebration of tango. It aspires to do quite the contrary of what most literature on tango does; it wishes to make sociological sense of a world that is obsessed with its own legendary existence. Throughout the chapters I seek to map out the *practical reason* of tango, embodied by the dancers as an ability to move across dance-floors as well as sensing, captivating and justifying the world. More precisely, this book inquires into the ways in which tango-tuned dancers respond to the tourist experience. How do they manage being "outsiders" in a world that they wish to become one with, and how are they affected by the upper-class journey implicit in travel to a much poorer country? Part of the contemporary Argentine tango culture will hence be put in dialogue with a world that is selectively distributing its wealth and safety measures. This book wishes to explore the intimate encounters and conflicting relations within such a context, acknowledging structural restraint, radical promises as well as dancing pleasure to be equally important ingredients in the tango voyages.

* * *

Preface and Acknowledgements xiii

During the ethnographic work on and off dance-floors throughout the world, and the process of writing and rewriting this book, I have had the pleasure of being surrounded by many thoughtful and generous people. My own tango journey, involving both a dancing exercise and an academic project, began at UC Berkeley on a nine-month postdoc visit in the fall of 2006. I am very thankful to Marion Fourcade and Barrie Thorn at the Department of Sociology, who kindly invited me. Without their generous offer and the inspiring academic milieu to which they welcomed me, this study would never have begun. I am also deeply grateful to Brian Lande, who supported the project with thoughtful conversations and readings during its very first steps. I owe him special thanks for encouraging me to leave the bookshelves and throw myself into ethnographic endeavors.

Upon my return to Sweden, the project found its new home at the Center of Gender Excellence (GEXcel) in the Gender Department at Örebro University. I am tremendously grateful to GEXcel for providing funding and emotional support for this study. Many thanks to Anna G. Jónasdóttir, Kathleen B. Jones and Nina Lykke, who have encouraged the project and provided helping hands at various stages. Thanks also to all my colleagues in the Gender Department at Örebro, and a special acknowledgement to Lena Gunnarsson. I also wish to mention Kathy Davis at Utrecht University, who on several occasions enriched the work with valuable comments.

Like the tango, this project has constantly been on the move. After it left Örebro, the project was based in the Sociology Department in Stockholm for one and a half years. I am deeply grateful to the Ahlströmer and Terserus Stiftelse, who financed part of the study, and my former advisor Barbara Hobson, who, over the years, has encouraged my sociological explorations and provided generous feedback at many different stages. Acknowledgements also go to my Stockholm colleagues Göran Ahrne, Magnus Haglunds, Rebecca Lawrence and Mikaela Sundberg, who read and commented on different chapters of this book. Several seminars have proven important during the process. I wish to mention and express my gratitude to the participants in the Swedish Cultural Sociology working group (a special acknowledgement goes to Anna Lund, who closely interrogated Chapter 9, and Tora Holmberg, who read early drafts of Chapters 6 and 7), the SCORE seminar and the Gender and Politics seminar at Stockholm University. Many thanks to Mats Franzén, Kerstin Jacobsson, Raoul Galli and Katharina Tollin, who contributed significant comments at the very last minute. Acknowledgements also go to the colleagues at my present workplace, the Department of Education at Uppsala University, for their encouragement and patience. Many thanks also to the Routledge editors Max Novick and Jennifer Morrow, and the "book production team", for their support during the process of turning this study into a book. My deepest acknowledgement is, however, reserved for my father, Tommy Törnqvist, who has thoughtfully and energetically engaged with this project. He has served as a sociology coach, encouraging me to continue when

xiv *Preface and Acknowledgements*

my will has been weak and finding the main thread for me when I have lost it. Many warm thanks to the rest of my family and friends for all your love and encouragement. Without your emotional support and practical care this book would never have been realized.

Last but not least, I wish to thank all you wonderful tango dancers out there—in Buenos Aires, San Francisco, Stockholm, Örebro, Uppsala, Barcelona, Paris, Lisbon, Valparaiso and elsewhere. Thank you for sharing your heartbeats and your reflections on tango with me. In particular, I wish to express my affection and gratefulness to Nicolas Lieste (who also helped me collect additional material in Buenos Aires in the spring of 2012), Micaela Bertolotto, Alicia Bonvini, Ylva Elzén and Marta Fallgren, with whom I have shared my own tango tears and pleasures. These would have been much lonelier and less exciting years without you.

* * *

I have learned a tremendous amount during my years as a dancing sociologist, at times more than I wished to. The embodied ethnography used in this work has many analytical advantages, but it can be rather challenging on a personal level. The borders which allow academics to approach the world with critical distance dissolve as we engage with and become one with the world. This is both an amazingly rewarding and quite a frightening exercise. The vulnerabilities and fears expressed by the dancers in this study, over time also became my dreads. The field-work left me with feet fractures and body memories of how constant rejections affected my posture and gaze. Besides the bodily and emotional scratches, the predominant effect of this study is, however, the delight generated through tango dancing. This book is dedicated to the memory of my grandmothers Maja Berglund and Märta Törnqvist, for whom dancing was a true pleasure. For reasons having to do with the religious convictions and family duties during the early twentieth century, restricting primarily women, they were not able to throw themselves onto the dance-floors as much as they would have liked. I am sure they would be happy to know that their granddaughter, at least, had the opportunity to do so.

Stockholm, 4 September 2012

Part I
Introduction

1 Intimate Voyages in Global Times

INTRODUCTION

Why study tango dancing? And why make a sociological case out of the streams of dancers who go on tango holiday to Buenos Aires?

The answer proposed by this book is that tango dancing constitutes a sensual metaphor for the mutually constitutive relations between intimacy and globalization. The Argentine tango provides a striking example of an unsettled internationalized culture that was carried across national borders long before social scientists invented the word "globalization". The tango is danced on the edge of a vulgar and immoral intimacy, forming its steps into a dangerous play revolving around sexualized representations and exoticism as well as artistic values and rigorous dance training. At center stage in tango is the emotional experience transmitted through the intimate dance embrace, the improvised dancing style and the dramatized Argentine music. When framing the tango in terms of a dance voyage to Buenos Aires, however, the nexus of intimacy and globalization shifts slightly and changes color. In fact, adding elements of the holiday experience evokes a number of dilemmas at the heart of our time. How is the quest for emotionality affected by the economic realities exposed through the relations in tourism? How is tango intimacy affected by the fact that the dancers are no longer *only* dancers but also wealthy and poor, clients and service providers within a market of intimate services and cultural goods? And what happens when a tourist industry attempts to annex feelings and symbolic values such as authenticity?

Today, an increasing number of people from all over the world travel to Buenos Aires to dance and explore tango culture.[1] According to an Argentine survey from 2001, between ten and fifteen thousand people travel to Buenos Aires to dance tango every year. Most likely, the numbers have doubled, or more, over the past decade. According to reports from the World Travel and Tourism Council together with tourism studies and travel magazine surveys, Buenos Aires and Argentina are showing strong growth in the area of tourism and top several lists of the world's most popular tourist destinations. This might be related to the fact that Argentina became a fairly cheap travel destination—and site for tourist investments—in the aftermath of the economic crisis in 2001. Although Argentina has one of the strongest economies in Latin America, and is normally spoken of as a "European" nation with a luxurious lifestyle compared with other Latin-American countries, it is still coping with the adverse effects of the economic collapse (Fiszbein et al. 2002; Whitson 2007). Besides spurring unemployment and migration streams to Europe, the crisis has created a national attempt to attract foreign capital, particularly through international tourism, and has resulted in requisites to create all kinds of job opportunities. Tango has thus become a source of income and an expanding market in the informal tourist sector.

Among those travelers who are coming specifically for the tango, a broad repertoire of practices and experiences related to tango make up the core of the holiday journey. Besides taking private classes taught by some of the world's best tango dancers and exploring past and present tango culture—its music, poetry, people and places—most tango tourists dance their nights away in the dimly lit dance-halls, the so-called *milongas*. To accommodate these intimate voyagers, a market of tango services and goods has emerged. More advanced dancers pick and choose from a selected number of services, whereas beginners can purchase travel packages which include classes in tango instruction, dance-shoe shopping and special city maps pointing out the tango clubs in town. In fact, the dance tourists' desire to access the "deep emotions" of the dancing culture has turned tango into an expansive business.

Drawing on a cheek-to-cheek ethnography of so-called tango tourism in Buenos Aires, this book explores some of the imprints of globalization and market adjustments on local cultures. It seeks to offer a passionate exploration of Argentine tango dancing through the lens of its sentiments and symbolic orders, and a critical investigation of international tourism's effects on intimate economies. Through comprehensive fieldwork in Argentina as well as in two local dancing communities in the U.S. and Sweden, this project maps a complex social, emotional and political landscape. Throughout the chapters, the book assesses the ways in which people's emotional lives intermingle with a tourism market made up of close-embrace dances and dollars as well as of an explosive economic and political Argentine reality. The intimate tango voyages evoke a world beyond the steps of the dance-floor, stretching into social formations and embracing multiple conflicts and dilemmas. By bringing economies of intimacy center stage, and exploring the macro–and micro–power dynamics at work, this book seeks to identify a global condition that is lived on and through the body.

Moreover, tango tourism represents an intriguing case for exploring intimacy as a social form. The tango harbors promises of a heart-to-heart communication that evokes existential dwelling at the same time that the social organization of the dancing offers easy exits based on the primate of emotional thrills. Tango dancing seems in fact ostensibly well suited for what is sometimes described as late-modern societies, characterized by individualism, flexibility and emotionally centered cultures (Bauman 1998, 2003; Giddens 1992; Illouz 2007). In addition, tango includes a provocative association with sex. The dancing, with its close-embrace movements involving the dancers' legs wrapped around each other, is often used as a metaphor for sexualized feelings. Adding various aspects of tourism to the study of this edgy intimacy evokes a number of questions. In fact, one particular aim of this book is to explore and make sense of a stream of tourism that blurs the boundaries between affectionate and economic relations. Although the relationships in tango tourism, emerging in the Argentine dance-halls, rarely lead to sexual affairs or temporary romances, they are still part of a globalized skin-to-skin intimacy. In addition, the relations between local hobby dancers and tourists initiated at the *milongas* rarely involve economic transactions; still, they are affected by an expanding market of intimate dance services and the consequences of economic hardship. In that sense, tango voyages put at stake not only how gender, race and class are intersecting in the making of a tourism geography, but also sheds light on the implications of a globalized world for our intimate lives. The intimate practices, discourses and sets of emotions produced in this particular context unfold into a complex landscape of market forces, dollars and close-embrace dancing.

THEORIZING TANGO TOURISM

The growing academic interest in dancing must be related to the body-turn in the social sciences and humanities. In a theme issue in the international journal *Ethnography* on so-called "physical cultures", John Hughson describes this as another term for catching "the human body as a site of social meaning" (2008: 422). There are increasing attempts to embrace the social significance of dancing. Some scholars relate it to traditions such as cultural theory (Thomas 2003), postcolonial theory (Sawyer 2006) and phenomenology (Parviainen 2002). Among them is a strong interest in dancing, not least couple dancing, from the angle of gender and sexuality studies. In work targeting various dance forms and cultural contexts, researchers are approaching the bodily movements of individual dancers and larger group dynamics as an arena for resistance and reproduction of dominant ideologies. One example, drawing on Leslie Gotfrit's (1988) study of women and the so-called "politics of pleasure" in a Canadian dance-club, is Jonathan Skinner's follow-up case within the Belfast salsa community. Skinner argues for a shift in focus from seeing the dance as a "cathartic activity" and courtship to seeing it as "a choreographic play between resistance and self-regulation" (2008: 76). In a similar fashion, Lisa Wade argues that there is an emancipatory promise in couple-dancing. She explores a lindy-hop dancing community which is actively "re-shaping the collective body towards feminist ends" (2011: 224) through negotiations of power in the lead-follow dynamic. Looking into the literature on tango, we find that it often targets the rich culture of poetry and music, national history and tango as a lifestyle, especially around the turn of the last century (Denniston 2007; Goertzen and Azzi 1999; Guy 1995; Romano 2005; Rypka et al. 2005; Savigliano 1995a, 1995b; Taylor 1976; Thompson 2005). Still, a rather limited, though possibly expanding, group of studies has focused on the dance scene and its practices (Goodwin 1998; Hess 1998; Manning 2003; 2007; Taylor 1998), and among them few place the particular world of tango dancing within a broader context of social and political concerns (Olszewski 2008; Savigliano 1995a, 1995b; Viladrich 2005). We might also notice that some of the most prominent academic work on tango was written during the nineties and primarily targets the history of tango throughout the twentieth century. One example is Marta E. Savigliano's fascinating work *Tango and the Political Economy of Passion* (1995), which traces the development of tango from its birth in Buenos Aires to the Parisian fin de siècle cabarets through the lens of feminist and postcolonial theories. The subtitle of this book—*The Intimate Economy of Tango*—creates a bond with Savigliano's important work, but frames the study within the contemporary tango culture and focuses on the imprints of tourism. I also wish to mention a beautiful essay by Julia Taylor, *Paper Tangos* (1998), which fuses the personal life of tango to a political chart of the Argentine military regime and historic economic hardship. However, much has happened since then. This book attempts to turn a page in the literature on tango and move on to the magnetism and antagonism making up the early twenty-first century's tango world.

Whereas the tango orchestras hit their golden age during the forties and fifties, today's brightest shining stars seem to be the internationally recognized tango dancers, constantly on tour around the world. In addition, tango is an everyday practice which finds more and more dedicated aficionados all over the world. As a consequence, Buenos Aires has become an expanding tourist site for cultural consumption. This book wishes to place the dancing and the culture within this broader geographic terrain and in the crosscutting intersections of tourism, embracing both commodification and the endeavor to retain tango as an autonomous art form. Throughout the chapters we will encounter a group of tango practitioners born far away from Rio de la Plata but with a strong commitment to the culture. Therefore, one difference between this and other studies on tango is that it is not tango *per se*, nor the history or the Argentine embeddedness of the tango, which is in focus, but rather the phenomenon of tango tourism. Moreover, my interest in tango does not revolve solely around the dancing experience, the bodily condition inscribed in tango as an art form and the social regulations shaping the dancing culture, but also addresses the nexus between tango dancing as an intimate social form and tourism as an expression of globalization. Hence this study wishes to build upon previous traditions in dance research and studies on tango as well as to provide new research angles, allowing a dance-floor ethnography to resonate with larger sociological and political questions.

A limited number of studies have investigated the implications of globalization for tango. In a chapter in the *1999 Yearbook for Traditional Music*, Chris Goertzen and María Susanna Azzi address the shifts in tango music and discuss its adaption to a global music scene. They touch upon the process through which "outsiders" in Argentina have become an important target group for the musicians and therefore also a possibly transformative force which might change the music and the working conditions for the musicians. They write: "Much of the modern support of the tango in its birthplace comes from outsiders, especially tourists, whose images of the tango must therefore be accommodated. The favourite music of today´s poor in Buenos Aires is no longer the tango" (1999: 69). Another example is Anahí Viladrich's (2005) study of so-called Argentine tango immigrants in New York and the reciprocities of values exchanged between Argentine tango dancing artists and North-American hobby dancers. Also, the Argentine dance journeys are part of the globalizing of tango and might in fact add to the tendency of fracturing the culture. Implicit both in tango migration (out of Argentina) and tango tourism (to Argentina), is an intriguing relation between culture and geography. The spread of the tango and the increasing dance tourism in Argentina seem both to strengthen and challenge the territorial bonds between tango culture and Argentina. Although tango's national identity is stressed in the name—*Argentine* tango—the successful export demonstrates that the culture has made itself adoptable in various social and cultural environments throughout the world. As Erin Manning puts it in her captivating book on the "politics of touch", in which tango dancing is used as an empirical prism, the tango is "at once fiercely nationalistic and startlingly inventive [. . .] a transcultural improvisation and a national artifact" (Manning 2007: xvii).

Although the global spread of tango is a crucial component of the expansion of Argentine dance tourism, the main purpose of this book is not to add another case to the study of "export-tango" through mechanisms of globalization. Instead, the scope is the holiday framing. Coupling tango dancing and tourism creates a number of dynamics which will be explored throughout this book. This intersection comprises practices and discourses, all of which both strengthen and challenge the alliance between tango and tourism. Starting with the similarities, we find an escapist framing to be present both in tango dancing and holiday travelling. In fact, both tango and tourism involve promises of a break with everyday routines, a voyage out of the ordinary. In addition, the cases of both dancing and travelling illustrate how spatial and bodily displacement evokes cultural and emotional dislocation. This is emphasized by the verbs "to move" and "being moved", which imply that physical movements have an emotional dimension. This we might, in turn, relate to what some describe as the etymology of tango, being the Latin word *tangere*, meaning "to touch" (Manning 2003: 1). In that sense, dancing and travelling take place equally on earthly and existential terrains. They transport the subject through memorial, imaginative and emotional landscapes—as well as through geographic and political terrains. Furthermore, both dancing and tourism shape narratives for social metamorphosis, tempting its practitioners with radical transformations of selves.

However, the nexus between tango dancing and tourism also evokes conflict. One example of this is that the profane economic logic of a tourist market is, by some dancers, believed to create hindrances for a voyage out of the ordinary. Within the Argentine *milongas* and through the gazes of service laborers within the tango market, foreign dancers are not only passionate tango aficionados but also wealthy westerners and potential clients. Throughout this book, we will address the shift in public mirroring and self-image in relation to a number of dilemmas facing the tourists. It will in fact be argued that the context of holiday travelling makes the micro-politics of tango dancing an indicator of certain aspects of a fragile global order. The relations in tango tourism can help us to think more carefully not only about gendered aspects of this contested terrain, but also about how class and racial regimes pave the way for larger cultural and economic changes, as when dance tourism shapes new job markets and turns dancing into an economic relation. Such a focus suggests that the dancers are not only dancers, but also women and men, Argentines and Swedes, rich and poor, as well as to various degrees exoticized and sexualized bodies in an ongoing trade of dance partners and money. Far from representing a meditative embrace, the case of tango draws out the conflicting elements in both dancing and tourism. The dancers are bound to interact with class-related, gendered and racialized structures, and are hence far from one-layered carriers of the heterosexual emotionality associated with the tango. Moreover, the dance voyagers are part of ongoing negotiations which aim at evaluating, legitimizing and discrediting practices, artifacts, bodies and feelings in the nexus of intimacy and globalization.

To sum up, the overall aim of this book is to explore tango tourism as a lived reality which makes the dancers—locals and foreigners, market actors and clients—visible as significant players within a larger global scene. This focus emphasizes the highly political nature of both tango dancing and tourism. In order to capture these processes, we need perspectives sensitive to the production of gender, race and class and to the structure and function of an intimate dance economy. The complexity of the object of study calls for an engagement with various empirical and theoretical frameworks. In the following subsections, the study will be situated within several academic research areas, starting with the fields of *intimacy* and *globalization* studies, and followed by a conceptualization of *tourism*. Thereafter we will move on to theorize tango tourism as a conflict between different *economic logics* and we will close this section by discussing the negotiations of *spaces* and places in tango tourism.

Intimate Relations in Late-Modern Societies

One assumption underlying this book is that the search for intimacy has taken new directions and forms in late-modern societies. Recent shifts in western family life show that the number of people living in traditional nuclear families is decreasing, that relationships are more unstable and fluid and that both women and men seek out casual sexual relations, free from long-term commitments. Studies also show that people's intimate lives are reflected in new constructions of self in which autonomy and reflexivity are at center stage (Bauman 2003; Bawin-Legros 2004; Beck 2000; Giddens 1991, 1992; Illouz 2007; Jamieson 1998; Lewis 2001; Roseneil and Budgeon 2004; Roseneil 2007). In contrast to the majority of intimacy studies, this book suggests an opening up of the research area to include not only non-heteronormative ways of practicing sex and kinship, but also relations defined outside of the traditional realm of family life and sexuality. I will argue that Argentine tango dancing is an intriguing phenomenon that enables us to rethink intimacy and the ways in which we organize and make sense of personal life together with others.

As a consequence of the postponement of marriage, higher living standards and greater interest in self-development and -expression, leisure-time activities, such as tango dancing, make up an increasingly important social dimension in many western societies. Far from being a once-weekly hobby, tango takes up large amounts of the practitioners' free time and encompasses an entire social and emotional universe for many. Dancing communities throughout the western world consist of dedicated practitioners who visit dance clubs, take classes and participate in all kinds of tango-related events several nights a week. In general these people are not part of professional dance groups, but rather enjoy the social dancing, through which people meet and share a passionate interest. This is a milieu where friends and strangers share heartbeats and experience the emotional longing captured in melodies of sentimental tango songs. Moreover, the tango is a subculture that seems to fulfill some basic human needs: differing from leisure pursuits such as literary circles and language courses, the world of tango offers a social arena in which physical and sensual aspects of intimate relations are in focus. Tango dancing is a lived body-to-body and heart-to-heart experience revolving around physical touch and intimate connections.

In order to incorporate these experiences into the framework of intimacy, the conventional concept must be broadened. In the social sciences intimate relationships are often restricted to "whom to choose as a partner, and how to live harmoniously together" (Plummer 2003: 14). The case of tango dancing illustrates the need to reconceptualize intimacy in ways that also include non-sexual experiences and relations that lie outside the expectations of commitment in marriage and partnership. Hence, I use the term intimacy to identify a range of practices and emotional states of being with others that is characterized by an affective connection and, with respect to the tango, incorporates a bodily and sensual dimension. In Jessica Mjöberg's terms, the intimacy at stake in this study might be approached in terms of a particular kind of relational presence regarding the subjective experiencing of "oneself in relation" (2011: 85). Intimacy is here approached as a kind of interaction that involves forms of bodily, emotional and social comportment and a sense of belonging that includes both sensual and non-sensual factors (cp. Jamieson 1998). In effect, the case of tango dancing can be used as a paradigm case to rethink intimacy across and beyond dichotomies such as the following: sexual/non-sexual, bodily/verbal, stability/fluidity, monogamy/polygamy and heterosexuality/homosexuality.[2] In addition, this book addresses the social structuring of intimacy. Like demonstrated in several studies on romantic love (Featherstone 1999; Giddens 1992; Collins 1992), the tango provides an intricate social arrangement of practices, emotions, discourses, identities and institutional arrangements which produce a particular kind of intimacy. The dancers engage in certain practices, such as transforming their bodies to adapt to the movements of tango. Furthermore, they invest in certain emotions, they label themselves tango dancers and familiarize themselves with the institutional arrangements of tango dancing, i.e. the formal and informal rules of the dancing communities. In this book we will look into the production of a tango intimacy. We will interrogate dancers' embodied practices as well as the sense-making processes, forming tango dancing into an intimate universe.

Global Intimacy

In academic literature intimacy and globalization are often considered distinct from one another. Whereas *intimacy* is referred to as those relations taking place in a narrow world, characterized by familiarity, similarity and mutual understanding (Jamiesson 1998; Plummer 2003), *globalization* is often represented in terms of the anonymous flows of capital and ideas across dispersed and deterritorialized geographies (Castells 1996; Mishra 1999; Sassen 1999). The enclosed, bodily and slow-moving world of intimacy is contrasted with the fast and fluid movements of capital and technology. This book suggests, on the contrary, that intimacy is often bound up with processes of globalization and that the search for intimate relations has become more and more interconnected with a global time-space compression. To an increasing extent our intimate lives seem to take place in a vast geography of traversed national borders, not the least through the use of Internet. One example of this is that cultural imaginaries of other places and people are at the heart of the western cultural production of intimacy. Globalization is expressed in the blending of the exotic and the erotic in commercials, Hollywood movies and war journalism (Fanon 1956/1986; Nagel 2003; Said 1995; Yuval-Davies 1997).

Consequently, tango tourism is not only about gendered imaginaries linked to individual bodies, but also builds upon images of entire countries and continents: so-called exotic places (Mohanty 2003; Skeggs 2007; Spivak 2002).[3] With the increasing stream of (dance) tourists, the tango capital—Buenos Aires—has been turned into a market space for emotional consumption. Dancers and other visitors demand interactive settings that allow them to participate in the sensual play associated with the city. Tourist companies, in turn, construct spatio-temporal markers and boundaries meant to focus consumers' attention on emotional aspects of their holiday. In the case of tango tourism, foreign visitors have laid the ground for a market space in which a kind of emotional labor, together with a range of emotionalized experiences, is being traded (cp. Hochschild 2003/1983). For example, tourist pamphlets from Argentina contribute to an emotionalized mythology by attracting tourists with phrases such as "visit Buenos Aires to experience the passion, sensuality and nostalgia of tango." In other words, the tourist industry tempts potential consumers by using and possibly expropriating images of a place and its culture: its sights, smells, sounds and metaphors—such as the tango—which are being both sexualized and exoticized.

In this respect, the tango voyagers and other emotional tourists might be understood in relation to Europeans of former centuries who travelled the world in search of exotic foreign cultures. Faraway places were associated with and are still believed to harbor people deeply connected with their own emotional lives and bodies—but are also portrayed as uncivilized and in conflict with modern values (hooks 1999; Nagel 2003; Said 1995; Yuval-Davies 1997). Today we find versions of the same imaginary when westerners travel to countries in Africa, Latin America and Asia in search of authentic cultures and particular "ambiances" based on presumptions of local people's emotionality. In tourist pamphlets, magazine covers and tourist rumors, "the generous mildness" of Thai people, "joyful Africa" and "passionate South America" are brought forward to promote travelling. In that sense the images of a people—in our case, the Argentine people—make up a larger global economy in which presumed emotional capacities become objects of consumption.

One important area of research in the field of intimacy and globalization studies is the stream of literature exploring the "new gold" of Third World zones. Today's Global South is no longer (only) exploited in terms of natural resources, but also in regard to love and affection. This argument has been explored through case studies of the global sex trade and nannies in international care chains (Ehrenreich and Hocschild 2003; Gavanas 2010, Sanchez Taylor 2006). Rather than providing a neat case of an intersectional analysis in which wealthy white westerners travel the world in an attempt to conquer foreign cultures, however, tango tourism adds complexity to the field of critical globalization studies. It is not so much an example of how various power structures are reproduced and enforce each other—as when white middle-class men exploit poor women and children in the Global South through various forms of sex labor (Kempadoo 1999; Opperman 1998; Pettmann 1999; Ryan and Hall 2001). Instead it reveals a rather contradictory reality. Similar to cases of women's so-called romance tourism in Jamaica and the Dominican Republic, the market of intimate dance services primarily targets women as clients and men as providers and hence turns a traditional gender order upside down (O'Connell Davidson and Sanchez Taylor 1999; 2005; Sanchez Taylor 2006). Like these examples, tango voyages involve a search for emotional connection and bodily closeness, experiences sometimes accessed through payment. For example, lonely tourists can contact so-called *taxi dancers*, mainly Argentine men who make a living out of selling themselves as dance partners in the tango clubs. However, as will be discussed in this book there are also differences between the dance travels and the romance tourism studied by Jacqueline Sanchez Taylor (2001; 2006) and other scholars in the field. Unlike Sanchez Taylor's essays on female romance tourism, which emphasize rather one-sidedly women occupying positions of power, this book adds a multilayered case to the exploration of domination. Unlike participants in up-front cases of sex tourism, most tango dancers wish to experience the body-to-body connection in tango without a sexual continuation beyond the dance-floor and without the involvement of economic transactions and other material goods.

Therefore, the case of tango tourism adds complexity to a polarized debate in the globalization literature. Optimistic scholars, on the one side, often argue that the rise of global cultures and new forms of political action resulting from information technology and a time-space compression create new possibilities for equality and deepened human relations across economic and cultural borders. The skeptics, on the other hand, claim that injustices in class, gender and ethnicity are increasing in the new global order. Feminist scholars are among those who have pointed to sex tourism and the ongoing labor migration of care workers from the Third World as examples of postcolonial exploitation (Ehrenreich and Hochschild 2003; Kempadoo 1999; O'Connell Davidson and Sanchez Taylor 1999). As will be discussed throughout this book, dance travels to Buenos Aires both fit and do not fit these worldviews. On the one hand, tango tourism takes place in an economic landscape of hardship, power imbalances and exotic projections. Furthermore, tango tourism involves examples of commercialized services of intimacy, implying that local dancers trade their body work and emotional labor to foreign dancers. On the other hand, the voyages to Buenos Aires illustrate how people make use of the intimate dance to resist structural exploitation of the Global South. Many dancers see the journey to Argentina as a way to create exchanges—social, cultural and economic—across continents, and perceive the sensual dance as a means to redress racist ideologies and power imbalances. Thus, tango tourism indicates that intimacy holds a key both to radical forces in times that increase the divergences between people and to a reproduction of an unequal and divided world.

Conceptualizing Tourism

Tango tourists show similarities not only with other intimate travelers (cp. Bialski 2012) but with a range of people on holiday. In the following section we will conceptualize the travels in terms of a market of "commercialized hospitality" (Cohen 2005: 52), a diffused social category being shaped and re-shaped through structural shifts and travelers' identity work. We will also address tourism as a social form, a sociality revolving around the adventure, made up by a particular "form of experiencing" (Simmel 1911/1971: 197). In addition we will inquire the imprints of tourism on local cultures and particularly the issue of how tango, in the aftermath of the economic Argentine crisis, has become magnet for foreign capital.

In the famous opening of Lévi-Strauss' autobiographical book *Tristes Tropiques*, the world-renowned anthropologist declares that he hates travelling and travelers (1976: 15). This seems rather symptomatic for the topic. The academic interest in tourism was for a rather long time undiscovered—or even despised—terrain in the social sciences (Crick 2005). In an historic account of the subject's slow introduction to academic studies, Jeremy Boissevain notes that classic anthropologists tended not to see the tourists, although they existed in the empirical field, whereas neo-Marxists "avoided tourism as distasteful", and still others regarded tourism as a "light" subject "unworthy of academic attention" (2002: x). It was in the late 1980s that tourism began to attract serious interest among academics; later on, it generated its own academic departments, research journals and book series within the larger publishing houses. At that point international tourism was already a massive global industry.

Turning to matters of definition, tourism appears as a diffuse and shifting concept which is often loosely defined as international post-industrial travelling for the sake of pleasure and leisure. The World Tourism Organization defines tourism as "the activities of persons travelling to and staying in places outside their usual environment for not more than one consecutive year for leisure, business and other purposes" (1995: 1). Others have made adjustments to the concept, such as the remark that tourism requires one overnight stay in domestic or international sites (Weaver and Opperman 2000: 28). In spite of such attempts to define the phenomenon, the wide range of travelling the world for the sake of pleasure and leisure makes tourism far from a neat analytical category. Rather, it calls for further distinctions to be made in relation to motives, destinations, practices and identities (cp. Cohen 2005; Crick 2005). Some people are looking for slow days under a clear blue sky (Dielmans 2008), whereas others travel to realize a transformation of self through connecting with history in so-called dark tourist sites such as slave castles (Mowatt and Chancellor 2011) or through the experiencing of "remote and risky locations at the geographic as well as cultural peripheries of our world" (Laing and Crouch 2011: 1516). As for the dance journeys to Buenos Aires, we will encounter several examples of how the category of (tango) tourism dissolves. For example, one group of foreign dancers strongly identify with Argentine culture and embrace Buenos Aires as their "second home" (see for instance the autobiographical tango novels by Cusumano 2007, Palmer 2006 and Winter 2008). Within the context of tango we might also consider how to approach those voyagers who return on a yearly basis, some with part-time jobs in the Argentine tango market. As will be discussed in Chapter 5, there are European and North-American dancers who take on semi-professional positions as dance teachers and tourist organizers, but who are also involved in typical "tourist" practices (housing in touristy areas, recreational lifestyles, "European" preferences in cafés and restaurants). Dance voyages also involve the somewhat delicate matter of nationality and national belonging. There is a group of Argentine dancers and other Latin-Americans residing in foreign countries who, just like other dance tourists, enjoy the tango venues and dance services once they are in Buenos Aires to visit family and friends. These dancers conceive of themselves both as tourists and locals, normally depending on the social context.[4] Moreover, as will be discussed in more detail in Chapter 6, tourism and tourists are far from value-neutral descriptive terms; rather, they are often inscribed with positive connotations (recreation, adventure, personal development) and negative meaning (exploitation, cheap travel, shallowness). In fact, the content, significance and values connected to tourism are negotiated and (re)defined by those travelers whom we identify as tourists—together with market agencies and local people in the tourist sites.[5]

Although travelling the world for the sake of recreation and excitement is not a new phenomenon, the number of travelers has expanded dramatically during the post-industrial era. As several scholars have pointed out, international tourism is intimately tied with some major developments of the twentieth century: industrialization, urbanization and modernity (Löfgren 1999). The workers' monthly salaries together with new ideologies, blending discipline and liberty, paved the way for the making of remote coastal towns into large resorts hosting millions of temporary visitors. Part of this transformation is bound to colonialism and the dependent relations between the tourists' home countries and the sites of destination (Jonsson 2012; Urry 2002). Today the hosting of temporary guests is fully commercialized and has been turned into a full-scale industry: a market of so-called "commercialized hospitality" (Cohen 2005: 52).

Addressing contemporary travelling requires that we put tourism not only in relation to industrialization and urbanization, but also to the significance ascribed to emotional experiences. When buying travel passage with the Swedish railways company you are no longer encouraged to have a pleasant journey, but to have a pleasant experience. Implicit in this turn of phrase is the idea that every moment of life can—and moreover should—become a memorable event, an emotional happening. Contemporary western culture feels its way through the world and makes sense of life through the language of emotions, partly helped by the expanding market of therapists, personal coaches and self-help books promising to improve people's emotional lives (Illouz 2007; cp. Bauman 2003). As recognized by various social scientists, this increasingly makes emotions and emotional experiences objects of consumption (Ahmed 2004; Bernstein 2007; Hochschild 1979, 1983/2003; Holbrook and Hirschman 1982; Holyfied 1999). Whether it takes the form of "buying time" to spend with friends and family, cultural or culinary experiences (dining at fine restaurants, watching movies, listening to music) or travelling to foreign countries, much of today's consumption is directed towards emotional sensations. Like climbing mountains, sky diving and raft guiding (Lois 2001; Lyng 1990, 2004), tango dancing is a leisure activity which is a target for global tourism and which provides intense and visceral challenges for the consumer—what some call a manufactured adventure (Holyfield 1999).

Although tourism appears as a diffuse category, there have been attempts to break it down into a social form, a kind of sociality, somewhat similar to what Simmel addresses as an adventure. "The most general form of adventure is its dropping out of the continuity of life. [. . .] An adventure is certainly a part of our existence, directly contiguous with other parts which precede and follow it; at the same time, however, in its deeper meaning, it occurs outside the usual continuity of this life", he writes (1911/1971: 187–188). Drawing on Simmel, Jeremy Boissevain, for instance, describes tourism as representing "a liminal period removed from the constraints of normal, everyday routine" (2002: x), whereas Paul Beedie and Simon Hudson address traveling, in their study on mountaineering tourism, in terms of a "dislocation of self from the ordinary to the extraordinary" (2003: 625). These matters are sometimes discussed with a focus on the social and historical contours of holiday travelling. In a pioneer study in tourism research, Dean MacCannell (1976) portrays the driving forces behind people's wishes to travel abroad as the anomalies of modern life. People go on holiday to foreign countries as a response to alienation growing out of industrialization and social fragmentation. In his view, contemporary tourism—such as dance travels to Buenos Aires—fulfills the functions of secular pilgrimage.

Besides emotional experiences and a time-out-of-time adventure, many scholars claim authenticity to be an important, yet multilayered and sometimes contradictory, dimension in tourism (Larsen et al. 2011; MacCannell 1976; Moaz 2007; Cohen 1988; 2011). MacCannell speaks of staged versus real authenticity (1973), Selwyn (1996) refers to "cool authenticity" (knowledge) as opposed to "hot authenticity" (feelings), and John Urry distinguishes the authentic experiences evolving from "romantic tourism", exemplified by travels to "non-touristy" destinations, from those experiences involved in so-called "mass tourism" (1990). Others make distinctions between various elements of an authentic connection with a place, such as spiritual, cultural, environmental, secular and educational authenticity (Andriotis 2009; 2011; cp. Wang 1999) or with regard to the actual tourist places, as in Cohen's (2011) distinction between *in situ* tourist sites (primary sites such as Auschwitz) and *in populo* venues aiming at creating knowledge about an *in situ* site (secondary sites such as Holocaust museums). Implicit in some of these distinctions is the assumption that authentic values are bound to particular places, so-called "untouched grounds", and that these values are both exploited by tourism and threatened by the very same exploitation. Among backpackers in Asia, travelers who undertake so-called knowledge expeditions to a variety of African countries, and among hobby dancers who travel to Ghana or Cuba to practice salsa or African dancing, a frequent belief is that the level of "realness", when connecting with a foreign culture, is affected by the engagement in so-called "tourist" activities. Hence, some travelers try to avoid places that are experienced as "touristy" and venues such as souvenir shops, expensive hotels and restaurants serving modified versions of national dishes to suit the foreigners' taste (cp. Maoz 2007).

Conceptualizing tourism in terms of an authentic adventure has been confronted with critique. As pointed out by several scholars, even tourists with the explicit goal of avoiding the commoditized décor are often involved in the tourist industry, particularly in Third World zones in which locals depend on a tourist-based revenue (Coleman and Crang 2002; Sanchez Taylor 2006). MacCannell (1976) conceptualizes this in terms of a continuum from front stage to back stage in which the "back stage" region promises to take the visitors to the *real* Buenos Aires, Paris or Bangkok. However the back stage is often just one step down the tourism continuum, staging a rougher scene to meet the tourists' needs. Other scholars question the claim that tourism offers conversions and a "time-out-of-time" existence. Edward Bruner (1991), for instance, argues that quite the opposite is often the case. A two-week holiday hardly brings about a total transformation of self, whereas the constant impact of tourists and a tourist industry profoundly changes the sites of destinations—their natural and/or urban geography—and hence the everyday life of many people. For such reasons he argues that researchers should make a distinction between tourist discourses, produced by the industry as well as by individual tourists, and actual tourist experiences together with their impact and consequences.

This critique addresses the question of how to contextualize the "form of experiencing", that traveling might imply (Simmel 1911/1971: 197). Rather than assuming that a two-week travel can hardly bring about "transformations of self", I wish to turn to the other aspect of Bruner's argument. Besides the motives and imprints on the level of individual tourists, the fact that tourism is today a global industry has consequences—not only for tourists—but for those who live in what has become tourist destinations. Several studies have revealed the negative impact of international tourism on those places which become tourist sites. Adjustments to holidaymakers' demands has resulted in the damaging of unique natural places—as when beaches are exploited for hotel complex and recreation areas—and the commodifying distortion of cultural art expressions (Boissevain 2002; Britton 2005; Dielemans 2008). Accounting for this in terms of David Harvey's work on neo-liberalization, tourism makes possible a cultural expropriation of the human condition. As Harvey writes: "The creativity [is] embedded in the web of life appropriated by capital and circulated back to us in commodity form so as to allow the extraction of surplus value. This is appropriation of creativity and affective cultural forms" (Harvey 2005: 71). In the case of Argentina it is symptomatic that the economic crisis has functioned as a positive driving force to develop the tourism industry. It even made necessary the promotion of the earlier secretariat of tourism to a cabinet ministry with its own minister of tourism in June 2010. In tango, the hardships and struggles to create new jobs are part of the expanding market of tango hostels, dance schools, city tours and shoe and clothing stores—primarily targeting foreign capital in the form of dance tourists.

This suggests that international tourism must be analyzed from various dimensions of how class operates in a globalized world, primarily in the obvious sense that the unequal distribution of economic wealth determines our degree of geographic mobility. Far from all people are allowed access to the *free movement* across national borders implied by the term "globalization", whereas some groups are faced with an obligatory mobility. Large groups of people—possibly larger each year as a consequence of global warming—are forced to leave their home countries because of natural disasters, famine, war, political persecution and poverty. Mobility is hence an equality issue. To quote John Urry: "the power to determine the corporeal mobility of oneself or of others is an important form of power in mobile societies" (2002: 262). In the larger scope of globalization, leisure travelling stands out as a result of its privileged nature—and its simultaneous manifestation of unequal living conditions. Whereas the tourists stage a western middle-class lifestyle, very few people living in the Latin-American, Asian and African sites visited by tourists can afford similar recreational travel to faraway places. In fact, the unequally distributed wealth can be described as one of the engines behind international tourism: some people (are forced out of scarcity to) create tourist value out of their natural resources and cultural heritages, whereas others pay money to access these places and experiences.

Drawing on the discussions in this section, I suggest that we approach tourism not so much as a matter of particular destinations, but rather as a set of practices and identities. As Baerenholdt et al. put it: "tourist places are not bound to specific environments or place images. Rather it is the corporeal and social performances of tourists that make places 'tourist'" (2004: 2). Or in the words of Simmel: "The adventure, in its specific nature and charm, is a form of experiencing. The content of the experience does not make the adventure" (1911/1971: 197). In that sense, Buenos Aires becomes a tourist site—or an adventure—in relation to the ways in which people inscribe it with tourist—or adventurous—meaning. When it comes to the scope of this study, tango tourism makes up a web of *spaces* (Buenos Aires, tango hostels, shoe stores), *bodies* (dancing in the *milongas*, walking the streets), *practices* (visits at historic sites, sharing anecdotes with other tango tourists), *imaginaries* (memories, expectations, novel narratives, tourist pamphlets) and *objects and artifacts* (tango shoes, money, dance clubs), subjected to a constant evaluation process, reflecting and providing significance to these spaces, bodies and practices. In addition, we must theorize traveling within a broader political and economic context, recognizing the impact of class, gender and racialized structures. In that sense, tango tourism comes to fore as a multilayered phenomenon conveying transformative meaning as well as arenas for reproducing global inequality. Rather than downplaying the one or the other dimension, this book suggests that we attempt to explore these aspects in dialogue. By integrating an analysis of tourists' motives with the possible imprints of tourism, we are able to recognize how these dimensions both conflict and interplay.

We will end this subsection by returning to Bruner's critique and by addressing the question of how to study tourism. Let us start by acknowledging that the analytical distinction he proposes between discourse and practice, also suggested by other tourist researchers (see for instance Larsen et al. 2011), is difficult to make. What, for instance, are experiences outside of discourse, i.e. outside people's ways of making sense of them? And how can we, as researchers, access peoples' experiences outside of meaning-making processes, i.e. outside language and discourse? Still, Bruner's critique points towards something important. With respect to tango tourism, we should be careful not to accept the narratives of the voyages as accounts of what the dancers spent their days in Argentina doing. As Torun Elsrud suggests in a study on backpackers' narrating practices, the consequences of a "cultural grand narrative of travel" (2011: 613) are connected with a particular form of identity work with potentially rewarding effects. Hence, rather than solving the epistemological inquiry raised by Bruner, I suggest that we approach it as an empirical matter and that we study tourism from various angles, acknowledging the simultaneous existence of several discourses and experiences—at times peacefully overlapping, at times in conflict. Rather than engaging with a vocabulary of *real* experiences and *fake* discourse, however, I propose that we make an analytical point of exploring identity work, related both to everyday holiday practices and tourist narration, while acknowledging that dislocations and contradictions—as well as the discursive shaping of the world through narratives and mythmaking—are instances of the conflicting forces of tourism.

Conflicting Economies

Readdressing the issue of authenticity, some scholars claim that the bodily nature of dancing makes such cultures fairly resistant to the negative impacts of tourism and commercial market forces. Bryan Turner argues, for instance, that dancing, in contrast to other art forms, is particularly resistant to "manufactured authenticity" and the loss of magnetism (Turner 2005; cp. Larsson and Svensson 1992). In an article in *Body & Society* on the kinetic and social fundamentals of tango, Brandon Olszewski follows up on Turner's argument and claims that this is particularly true for tango. "Due to the social, improvised and intimate nature of the dance, tango—more so than other social or performance dances—withstands artistic degradation and retains an authentic and auratic character, despite the global wayfaring and hybridization the dance continues to experience. The kinetic connection—the passionate, musical and dynamic relationship between leader and follower—sustains this vitality", he writes (Olszewski 2008: 64). This book provides several examples of how tango culture meets the forces of commercialization and the impact of globalization. In the last chapter of this book we will return to this claim, asserting for a modified version. Rather than arguing that the resistance lies within the dancing *as such*, the kinetic and intimate connection—the politics of touch—together with the improvised nature of the dance form, I suggest that we should approach this in terms of an ongoing negotiation and balancing act which must be understood in relation to tango as a value system with its internal belief structure and economy.

In addition to the conceptual terrains discussed so far, tango tourism will be explored in terms of an encounter—or clash—between two different economic logics. On the one hand we find a *market space* of tango services and commodities, trading symbolic tango values to tourists in exchange for money. On the other hand, the traditional honor culture of tango forms the world of dancing into an *intimate economy*, structuring the social order of tango dancing according to the distribution of a symbolic tango capital, and partly through the disavowal of economic interest. The sociological classics have approached similar phenomena in terms of a fundamental dimension in society—at times involving conflict—between solidarity and self-interest, sentiment and materiality, an erotic and an economic value sphere and *gemeinschaft* and *gesellschaft* (Durkheim 1893/1994; Simmel 1907/1971; Tönnies 1887/2001; Weber 1915/1995). More recently, the conflict has been considered in terms of a capitalist system's use and corruption of people's emotional life. It has been argued that the commercialization of various aspects of human life is exploiting people's intimate lives (Bauman 2003; Ehrenreich and Hochschild 2002; Habermas 1992; Hardt 1999; Hochschild 1983/2003; Illouz 2007). Similar value conflicts appear in tango tourism. What happens, for instance, when a milieu known for its sensuality and intimate encounters becomes subject to commercialization? What happens when a price tag is put on experiences that the dancers wish to live authentically and out of free will? Which experiences, bodies and forms of knowledge conflict within the realm of practices that make up tango tourism? Why does it *feel* wrong to pay for certain services but not others, and how are such emotional responses manifested and managed?

Before we can answer such questions we must explore the intimate dance economy in more detail. In order to do so, I wish to point out the normative ideologies and hierarchies produced in dancing cultures such as tango.[6] At first glance the Argentine tango evokes images of emotional encounters characterized by sensuality and nostalgia along with a romantic narrative of affectionate connections that just seem "to happen". For most people involved, however, tango is far from a randomly organized world made up by "free-floating feelings". The romantic narrative is contrasted by reports of the many rules at the *milonga* together with evidence of the strict hierarchies in which people recognize their exact status position within a relational chart of dance partners. Besides dancing tango, the dancers at the Argentine tango clubs are negotiating identities and creating a social space in which values and credentials are redistributed and traded. Argentine tango covers an entire symbolic and social order in which people orient themselves towards others in relation to embodied codes of conduct. In order to elaborate theoretically on what I call an intimate dance economy, this book explores tango dancing in terms of a relational field of intersecting resources (Bourdieu 1990a, 1991, 1993, 1998, 2000; cp. Schiling 2004; Viladrich 2005).[7] In a *first stage*, this study will explore the values at stake: the recognized identities, practices, bodies, skills and sets of knowledge; the transactions at work (i.e. trading money for dances or dancing company for social networks); the role of ethnicity, gender and class as discursive and lived categories; and the play of romantic expectations and a heterosexual matrix in the shaping of this symbolic economy. In Bourdieu's terminology, the dancers are embodying not only the movements and body styles which allow them to participate in the dance-floor exercise, but also the symbolic economy and a particular kind of conviction, providing them with a naturalized "feel for the game" (Bourdieu 1998: 77; 2000).[8] However, like other economies, traditional or capitalist, material or symbolic, the tango is not enslaved to a law of interest. The dancers are not bound to maximize profit (economic or otherwise)—although the striving for recognition is important. Rather, we will find that other elements, such as the devices following from a (hetero)romantic honor code and a discourse of emotionality, also prove important when understanding the dancers' actions and ways of relating to one another. In fact, economy is here used as another word for a social system which creates social relations and solidarity as well as antagonism and competition (cp. Wacquant 2008: 265). Hence, this book theorizes tango dancing as an organized emotional space which includes intimate relations and solidarity in equal measure with symbolic struggles and economic trading. It will be argued that the close-embrace dancing and the strict hierarchies make up two sides of the same coin, generating and enforcing tango *illusio* within the dancers.

In a *second stage*, this book will explore the relation between the intimate dance economy and the logic of a money market, made up of tourist agencies and various tango goods and services. The study explores the mechanisms that turn the values and resources in tango, together with the exotic imaginaries of Buenos Aires, into objects of consumption and a specific form of body labor. As will be discussed throughout this book, this produces a number of dilemmas, partly having to do with the feature of the intimate dance economy. One such conflict targets the tourists' search for authentic experiences and intimate relations, on the one hand, and the market addressing them as tourists and clients, on the other hand. Exploring such potential value clashes, this book engages with a stream of economic sociology which focuses on the cultural configuration of economic capital—primarily money—and its impact on social life (Aspers 2006; Bourdieu 1994, 1996, 1998, 2000; Zelizer 2005; Fourcade 2007). One aspect relevant for this study is the tense relation between different kinds of values, of which economic capital is one, and how the negotiations around these values are bound up with complex justification processes. In that sense, this book provides an empirical case of what Patrik Aspers and Jens Beckert (2011) describe as the function of moral values in markets, at times "blocking markets", as in the traffic of human bodies for sexual pleasure and slave work, and at other times contributing to the creation of economic value, as when ecological ethics increase the demand for fair-trade products. We will also turn to the work of Vivianne Zelizer (2005) and of Pierre Bourdieu (1984, 1998) on how societies create taboo against the use of money within intimate relations and family networks. Like the informal rule that a husband is not supposed to pay his wife for the household services she performs, the honor code of tango evolves into a sophisticated and partly misrecognized gift exchange revolving around the dancing invitation (cp. Mauss 1923/1997).[9]

Negotiating Space

Returning to the globalization debate, tango tourism addresses an argument made about space in late-modern societies. Globalization and the development of the digital net is often said to have reduced, or at least to have radically changed, the importance of actual places. Manuel Castells (1996), together with other sociologists (Bauman 2011; Negri and Hardt 2008), claims that today's economic and political life primarily takes place in the anonymous spaces of flow, far from the scrutinized practices and social responsibilities which are bound to actual places. Financial transactions with implications for millions of people occur in seconds, far from national borders and outside national regulation. Parallel to such tendencies, however, manifold spatial negotiations regarding actual places are occurring. The struggles over spatial borders, national anchoring and governmental institutions show that the regulation and definition of actual places are highly significant matters in our time (Brown 2010; Harvey 2005; Urry 2002). Tourism is just one of many examples which illustrate the economic, political and symbolic values connected with physical places. Tango tourism is intriguing because it puts the body at the heart of these spatial negotiations. Rather than being about faceless individuals behind anonymous computer screens (cp. Knorr Cetina 2012), the global condition in tango tourism "puts the body into the analysis of the social organization of mobility" (Urry 2002: 258). Throughout this book, both tango dancing and tourism are foregrounded as highly sensual movements in space. Translated into the language of urban geographers, tango tourism emerges into a micro-cosmos of slowly moving bodies stretching into cities and entire countries as Buenos Aires and Argentina are targeted by an expanding stream of dance tourists—and reaching other places as the tango spreads and is adopted into local communities throughout the western world.[10] Dancing tango stirs up motions which pave the way for larger political movements across the borders of national states and time époques. The semiotic connection between emotion and movement is striking in English as well as in Latin; to be moved or to move someone means to create emotional affect. The dancing takes its practitioners throughout the twentieth century, from the days of tango's birth in the simmering melting pot of Buenos Aires, where European emigrants tried to make a living side by side with Americans and African slaves, to the present day, when the city finds itself in the aftermath of a gigantic economic crisis and with open scars from the dirty war of several military regimes. Moreover, the tango spurs its aficionados back and forth through territorial, sensual, emotional, class-based and gendered landscapes. As Henri Lefebvre writes, the body is the starting point for such movements and hence implicit in considerations of social relations and spatiality.

> Space—*my* space—is [. . .] first of all my body, and then it is my body's counterpart or "other", its mirror-image or shadow: it is the shifting intersection between that which touches, penetrates, threatens or benefits my body on the one hand, and all other bodies on the other. Thus we are concerned, once again, with gaps and tensions, contacts and separations. (Lefebvre 1991: 184)

Taking Lefebvre's suggestion seriously, we might approach tango—and tango tourism—as a captivating case for studying the relational and multilayered constitution of space. Couple dancing, such as tango, provides a bodily and emotional geography of the self and the "other", negotiating spatial relations in terms of "gaps and tensions, contacts and separations". Moreover tango dancing highlights the dialogue, not only between different dancing bodies ("my body and the 'other'"), but also between the bodily (material) *and* the imaginative (symbolic) dimensions of a place. On the one hand, the sensual dance movements ultimately express the materiality of a room as legs, arms and chests stretch out to make space in a given place: a dance-hall or a crowded city street. On the other hand, the imaginative nature of tango dancing implies an escape from the actual placement of the dancing body. As Angela McRobbie puts it in a study on disco-dancing: "Like the cinema, the dancehall or disco [. . .] creates a temporary blotting-out of the self, a suspension of real, daylight consciousness, and an aura of dream-like self-reflection. [. . .] Dance affords the opportunity for fantasy" (1984: 144). This might be captured in a rather cliché *as-if* exercise, suggested by some tango teachers. It is taught that the tango should be danced *as if* a temporary dance partner was a secret lover, *as if* there was no tomorrow and *as if* the dance-floor did not belong to a gloomy community center in January-cold Stockholm but rather to a velvet-covered café in early twentieth-century Buenos Aires. In other words, the break with spatial and temporary conventions is part of the seductive nature of tango dancing. The body—with its layers of sensual, emotional and imaginative perception—is the ultimate condition and basis for such transgressions.

This duality, which in fact represents a unity in tango tourism, provides a particular framing to the attempts to break with a dualistic thinking which divides the myth-making of cities from their lived realities. Moreover, the use of tango implies a critique of a common privileging of material dimensions in the constitution of a place (cp. Davis 1990; Malkki 1995). This critique is an important departure for this study, in which a place—primarily Buenos Aires—is analytically approached in terms of a dialectical relation between material spaces and multiple lived and imagined realities, involving projected fantasies, feelings and commercialized representations.[11] Understanding the emergence of tango tourism, together with its local and global impact, urges us to relate various forms of spatial praxis to the impact of medial and commercialized representations (see Franzén 2004, Franzén 2005 and Johansson 2004 for a comprehensive discussion of various responses to this in urban geography).[12] Implicit in both tango and tourism is the significance inscribed in actual physical places and bodies which require a geographic terrain in order to exist. Buenos Aires is a city which lives as much in the broken-down capital pavements as in the mythology: in the endless stream of songs and poetry the tango capital comes to the fore as both a projected longing—an imagined and possible future space—and a material condition lived through the body.

EMBODYING ETHNOGRAPHY

To understand tango tourism we need to take into consideration the fact that the tango is ultimately an economy of the *body*. Part of what people are trying to achieve through these voyages is not only intimate experiences, but also the techniques of the body that will allow them to enter into what some dancers describe as "tango magnetism": an artistic and musical flow, transmitted through the body. To fully participate, dancers must engage in the intensive work of investing themselves with the appropriate movements, sensitivities and habits. This implies that the body cannot be understood only as yet another textual sign, but that it must be seen also as the condition and ultimate point of departure for the dancers' being-in-the-world (cp. Aalden 2007; Beauvoir 1949/1995; Bourdieu 1990b; 2000; Heinämaa 1998; Lande 2007; Merleau-Ponty 1945/1999; Young 2005; Wacquant 2004, 2005; Øygarden 2000). To enter the world of tango requires that people not only position themselves within the right gendered categories but that they also "know how" to move, express themselves and interact with their bodies. This implies that I, like Bourdieu and various sociologists of the body, wish to break with a notion of rational action and instead explore the field of tango tourism through an "embodied theory of practice", which holds that people act from a practical and embodied sense of the world (Bourdieu 1998: 76; cp. Wacquant 2008; Galli 2012). Recognizing that participating in tango tourism is itself a bodily enterprise implies that the body is not only the object of study but that it can also be used as a methodological tool helping us to grasp incarnate understandings. A study of tango tourism focusing solely on discursive practice, using material made up only of interviews and written narratives, would be shortsighted. A lack of ethnographic understanding of the embodied everyday practices in tango, would—for instance—most likely lead us to see domination where other explanations are more relevant and expressions of free will where there are none. However, this book suggests that the dancers also engage in rather complicated discursive practices through which the bodily experiences are being made sense of. At times the narrating practices relate to the belief system of tango; at times they relate to gendered and class-related discourses of sex, money and tourism. By inscribing tango and the dance journeys within a particular language and by acknowledging certain practices and experiences as legitimate, the dancers engage in a boundary work which both reproduces and destabilizes the borders of tango.

Acknowledging these two aspects—embodied practice and discursive narration—as equally important has implications for the design of the study. Designing a methodology sensitive both to the embodied nature of tango dancing and the discursive processes which shape and reshape the field requires different kinds of material. This study wishes to bring together ethnographic work focusing on the embodied practices of tango tourism, an interview-study exploring the dancers' sense-making processes and a text-analysis of recurrent tango narratives found in autobiographical novels, blog posts and Argentine tango magazines. In the Appendix—"Notes from a Dancing Researcher"—I discuss the material in more detail. The promises and challenges of an embodied ethnography will be inquired as well as the selection principles directing the interview-study and the collection of written material.

This combined methodology has several advantages. *First*, it enables us to encounter multiple and conflicting meaning of a particular practice, such as the intimate tango embrace. Solely observing this practice—or even embodying it oneself—will not reveal the many interpretations it might actually have for different dancers. In addition to studying what people "do", studying how they make sense of their actions and negotiate meaning in context adds more layers. *Secondly*, a combined methodology enables us to interrogate, when necessary, the inconsistencies between practice and discourse, as a way of exploring the contradictory field of meaning in tango tourism. At times these inconsistencies appear as dislocations between the stories people tell about their lives, particularly their intimate lives, and the practices that are shaping their everyday lives (cp. Jamieson 1998: 158). Exploring such inconsistencies is not a way of describing discursive narratives as "false" and lived practice as "authentic". Rather, discrepancies are interesting as they point to how the dancers manage a range of emotional dilemmas and conflicts. *Thirdly*, the combined methodology aims at creating a dynamic in the analytical process. We might approach this in terms of an interpretative interplay between closeness and distance in the researcher's relation with the field of study (see Törnqvist 2006 for an expanded discussion on this topic). The embodied ethnography that makes up an important part of this study is characterized by a chest-to-chest connection between me, the researcher, and the "cosmos under investigation" (Wacquant 2004: viii). This connection has provided me with a somewhat non-reflective understanding of the logic of the world. As such, the embodied ethnography has brought intimacy and sensitivity to the analyses, regarding values and vulnerabilities at stake. A methodological embodiment enables access not only to bodily dispositions—in this case, the requisites for dancing tango—but also a particular perspective on the world, a language for making sense of it from the vantage point of an "insider", as well as an emotionalized sense of reason, a "feel for the game" (Bourdieu 1998: 77). However, we should notice that the emotional involvement, the empathy and compassion in relation to the field of study, potentially poses a threat to analytical work. The possible lack of critical distance can "blind" the researcher. As Geir Angell Øygarden writes in regard to his so-called "full-contact sociology" of a Swedish boxing community, in order "to see", the ethnographer must partly remain an outsider:

> The fact that he brings with him something alien creates an inner distance, and distance is a necessary condition for observing. You see because you do not see. [. . .] Without such an element you will be

26 *Tourism and the Globalization of Emotions*

absorbed by the culture. And being absorbed by the culture is to not see the culture (2000: 33–34, my translation).

In order to avoid such blindness, the analytical process that is the basis for this book involves ongoing shifts from an embodied understanding of the object of study to a more distant, deconstructivist reading. The larger degree of distance implied in the interview study and in the textual analysis of blog posts and tango magazines has aided such analytical shifts. Addressing the multifold of interpretations made by other dancers, has helped me to confront my own embodied understandings of the world. In addition, the break with interpretations made through my own bodily and emotional investments in the field has been aided by constant engagement with theoretical works and an ongoing dialogue with different streams of academic research(ers). The analytical interplay between closeness and distance implies a shift from being an insider, a tango dancer and a tourist, embodying the pleasures, fears and dilemmas implicit in tango tourism, to becoming a researcher, engaging with such experiences through field-notes, interviews and blog posts, approached as sociological data. Time is a crucial element in this kind of empirical work. Letting the culture possess you, embody you and infuse all its behaviors and emotions within you takes time. Breaking with the culture, with all that has become part of you—a necessary second step in the research process—takes even more time. Methodological mobility is hence a matter of allowing oneself the time required to move between inside and outside, the familiar and the foreign, between dancing and writing, sensing and analyzing, observing and going blind.

OUTLINE OF THE BOOK

This book is divided into an introduction, presenting the scope of study, two main empirical parts and one concluding section. The relation between the two empirical parts requires a brief clarification. The first part aims primarily at describing the main features and values at stake in tango dancing as well as in tango tourism. Throughout four chapters the following themes are being discussed: the belief system creating social relations and solidarity among the dancers together with the social organizing of the tango (Chapter 2), the intimate economy creating order and difference within the world of dancers (Chapter 3), the motives and expectations associated with a tango voyage (Chapter 4) and the trading of tango goods and services within the Argentine market space targeting primarily tourists (Chapter 5). This part of the book might in fact be described in terms of a triad made up by three M's: the *milonga*, the market and the motives ascribed to the voyages. In the second empirical part, "Negotiating Tango Tourism", we will explore how these dimensions—the three M's—are put in motion and come to work in the intersection of tango dancing and holiday traveling. Throughout the empirical chapters in this part of the book, we will investigate the encounters between the belief system of tango, with its intimate economy, and the logic of a tango market targeting tourists. This relation will be explored throughout four contested terrains. We will investigate the ways in which dance tourists, primarily, negotiate the relation between a dancer identity and a tourist or a client identity (Chapter 6), the commercialized intimacy provided by taxi dancers (Chapter 7), the ambiguous search for romantic and sexual intimacy in tango (Chapter 8) and the relation between cultural art forms, such as tango, and the significance of space, such as the city of Buenos Aires (Chapter 9). The concluding chapter, "Tango Tourism: Between Market Adaption and Cultural Resistance", frames the study within a discussion on how tourist markets meet cultural resistance. In this chapter we will explore the relation between tango as an art form and the market forces targeting the dance tourists. It will be argued that the impact of tourist markets on cultural art forms is constituted through ongoing negotiations which direct those forms (in this case, tango tourism) into an unsettled arena of commercialized and affective relations. In this chapter we will also theorize tango tourism in relation to a larger economic and political terrain by broadening the focus of the study to include the intersection of gendered subjectivities, social class, ethnicity, sexuality and emotional power modalities. The travels to Buenos Aires aim at the enjoyment of the tango music and dance movements, but they are also political voyages that carry both the promises and dilemmas of freedom in our globalized era.

Part II
Argentine Tango Dancing

2 The Production of Belief

INTRODUCTION

As will be argued throughout this book, the exploration of social processes such as globalization can be fully conducted only in their locally embedded practices and discourses, i.e. within the social situations in which they are meaningful to people. When exploring Argentine tango as yet another globalized market of emotional experiences, sold to western tourists by local dancers, we need to take seriously the particularity of the field: the belief structures embodied by the dancers, the processes through which they become integrated as dancers and the function of a structured dance economy. In order to fully understand dance voyages to Buenos Aires and the possible impact of this kind of tourism, we must simply understand the embodied driving forces of the travelers. In many situations appearing in the nexus of tango and tourism—perhaps a majority—dedication to the culture is what explains actions as well as attitudes. In the present chapter we will look more closely into the belief system, the practices and relations which make tango dancing a partly autonomous cultural field with its own logics and its own practical reason. Using the vocabulary of Pierre Bourdieu, this belief system functions as a set of "dispositions of the body" (1998: 54), which creates social bonds among the dancers. The dancers are socialized into a tango-tuned embodiment of cognitive frames which, due to the fact that they are shared with others, create a sense of a common world: a social *field*, characterized by its distinctive logic, which sets it apart from other charts of social relations.

When dedicated tango dancers are asked about their hobby, in dinner conversations or at work, they often get a sparkle in their eyes. With dramatic gestures or the characteristically low voice of a close conversation, they speak of magical late-night dancing, the intimate embrace shared among strangers on a crowded dance-floor, the particular sentiment expressed within the music, the nostalgic history transmitted into dancing communities within and beyond Argentina, the new friends, the heartbreaks, the addictive drug that is running through their veins. "Magic connection", as some dancers call it, is portrayed as conveying intense feelings of joy, harmony and sense of meaning, for some people close to the sensation of falling in love: a mind-blowing escape from time and space. That way, the dancers' investment in tango is intertwined with other meaning systems that provide a sense of existential depth and serve as a cohesive social force bringing groups of people together.[1] By analogy with what Charles Lindholm notes regarding romance, we might state that tango dancing is "akin to religious experiences—a vision of the beloved as the other as a unique, transcendent and transformative being who can 'complete' one's own life" (1999: 248). As with other subcultures, such as punkers or stamp collectors, the social world of tango is "established through the division of the world into the sacred as opposed to the profane" (Hannerz 2012: 4). In fact, religious metaphors which focus on transformative capacities are often present in the dancers' own descriptions of their hobby, not least when differentiating tango from other dances. Kate from San Francisco, for instance, describes the tango as a "rich" and "deep [. . .] conversation about existentialism" (Kate, 38-year-old, U.S.). On the home page of a Uruguayan-Swedish dancing couple, the tango is expressed in terms of a sacred promise: "The dancing and the music possess magic powers. When the expression is deeply personal and the dancer connects with her own existence, the dancing brings out magic qualities. The reality of tango is beyond language."[2] Using similar language, some dancers speak of their first year of dancing as a time of having "found salvation" and "seen the light". One Argentine dancer in his late forties, Ezequiel, describes the tango as "very deep, in all aspects: socially, emotionally, culturally. Today I can't imagine living without tango" (Ezequiel, 48-year-old, Argentina).

These accounts indicate that tango dancing, like other leisure activities, is far from being a mere diversion in the outskirts of life. The strong belief in the values transmitted by tango implies that dancing takes center stage in many dancers' lives. In their understanding, the tango is far more than a dance. Some of them describe tango poetry as their new bible; the dancing movements as a force which has reshaped their bodies and ways of being in and through their bodies; and the musical connection in the dancing as a new language, richer and more sensual than verbal communication.[3] In fact, many dancers describe the tango as an existential conversion that dramatically influences their self-image and daily routines. For many active dancers, the tango determines which people they see, what they spend evenings and weekends doing, which travels they make and which music they listen to. In addition, the tango creates an emotional universe which affects the dancers' moods and proves decisive with respect to whom they make friends with and whom they love. Whether the dancers are Argentine by origin and grew up with the tango in the ancient cafés of Buenos Aires or practice steps and posture in an eldercare center in Stockholm, what brings them together is their common dedication and emotional, economic and time investment in a cultural art expression. Although the global spread of Argentine tango has multiplied both the number of dancing communities throughout the world and its many interpreters, tango dancing involves a fairly consistent *belief system* which keeps its members together by the significance and values assigned to tango.[4]

Like the belief systems of other cultural pursuits, the tango conviction is embodied within the participants. Becoming a tango dancer implies going through a process whereby the body is tuned, not only for dancing movements, but for a larger set of practices and habits encompassed by the social world of tango. We might in fact suggest that the devotion to tango is a consequence of practice. To take an example, religious belief might be approached as an effect of religious practice, meaning that institutionalized routines—involving prayer, going to church, engaging with holy texts and other believers—is ultimately what creates belief (cp. Bourdieu 2000; Collins 1992). With respect to tango, this implies that the belief is not primarily experienced as a cognitive frame but rather as an embodied practice that tunes the dancers for the social world of tango dancing—and that allows them to cultivate an implicit devotion strong enough to recognize the point in doing so. As will be discussed throughout this chapter, the belief in tango is fused with a bodily conversion, necessary for the dancers to participate in the social world of tango dancing. Therefore, we will approach the tango in terms of an embodied belief structure, which brings the dancers together by an incarnate faith in the game and its stakes. In this chapter we will inquire into the conversions and values implicit in these processes. What are the practices, institutionalized routines and feelings that make up the social world of tango dancing? What are the values at stake? What is the glue that holds the dancers together, not only in dance-floor couples but in larger tango communities reaching across the world? What sacrifices and adaptions—bodily, emotional, social and economic—are required to become a tango dancer? What happens at the dance clubs? What is the significance of the intimate dancing and the close proximity of bodies in tango? How do the dancers manage romanticized feelings towards a dance partner? How do dancers ask each other up and what are the social functions of the rules and regulations framing the invitation process? What kinds of relationships and modes of sociality are enforced by the social organizing of tango dancing?

In this chapter we are not looking specifically into tango tourism, but rather into more general qualities of tango dancing and the requirements addressed in the process of becoming a tango dancer. However, the discussion is situated primarily within an Argentine tango geography and is given voice by tango dancers—Argentines and others—based on their experiences in Buenos Aires. The chapter is divided into two parts. In order to understand the logics, practices and values at stake in tango, we will start by approaching the intricate level of intimacy and emotionality in the dancing, conceptualized in terms of a set of embodied practices, cultural rules and discourses. The first section takes up the process of embodying tango dancing, i.e. the socialization and bodily adaption required by the process of learning to engage with and master the intimate communication in tango. The second part addresses the institutionalization of tango dancing in the form of the *milonga*, a social venue or event created for social tango dancing. In this part we will encounter the tango clubs where dancers meet and examine the rules and regulations restricting—and thereby paradoxically enhancing—the kind of dancing intimacy that arises in tango. We will explore the features of the social bonds, the function of dance-floor honor and the promises associated with tango intimacy.

GETTING INTIMATE: EMBODYING THE TANGO

The afternoon dance at the *Confitería Ideal* has just started. Visitors are being seated at the tables closest to the dance-floor, while tango songs from the 1940s fill the air. This is one of the traditional tango venues in the middle of town, known for its lush velvet curtains and marble pillars that support the roof and the weight of sentimentality that tango carries with it. Regular customers wait to be taken to "their" table. Argentine dancers, primarily in their fifties and sixties, arrive fully dressed in suits and elegant dresses. A group of first-time tourists from West-Coast America just got into town and stare expectantly, with big eyes, at the peculiar details, the indoor decoration, the shoes and the clothing, in the hall. When the second *tanda* of the evening—a dance set of three or four songs—starts to play, a woman and a man get up on the floor. They belong to a group of tourists, sitting in the back of the room. She is dressed in a tight red dress, with a split that exposes more and more of her legs as they move around the hall. He is casual, wearing a pair of jeans and a t-shirt. An older Argentine couple swaps gazes across the room, inviting each other's company through the sublime *cabeceo*. She accepts his invitation, adjusts her shoe-buckle, stands up and approaches the dance-floor. Their dancing style is intimate. A tight embrace and small but intense movements play along with the sadness and the shifting tempo of the music. Some of the newly arrived tourists are transfixed by the woman's grace: "imagine having her legs and dignity at seventy!", a blond woman whispers to a friend.

Hours later, the marble-hall ambiance has reached a crescendo. Most people in the room have been up dancing, including foreign beginning dancers with their newly bought first pair of dance shoes, trying out their purchases on the floor. The dancer in the red dress has ordered her third glass of wine and is talking a little too loudly. As the scene winds down, a man in his early fifties walks in the door. He greets the staff with a familiar kiss and proudly takes a seat next to the dance-floor. He attracts attention with his typical *milonguero* style: a neat ponytail, black trousers and a well-ironed black shirt, supported by a large amount of self-esteem. He turns to one of the blonde women in the back and asks her "up" with a mixture of a flirty gaze and a few select English words. As she gets up on the floor, a little embarrassed, he gently puts his arms around her back and asks her to close her eyes. As the slow-moving dance set ends he discreetly offers her his card and explains to her that he is a tango taxi dancer, offering his dancing company for ten dollars an hour.

The description above derives from ethnographic work at *La Confitería Ideal* conducted on a sunny afternoon in the early Argentine summer (field-note: 26 November 2007).[5] The mixed crowd points to the diversity typical for the tango scene in contemporary Buenos Aires, involving "older" local dancers who have been regular customers for many years, the newcomers—the tourists—who are visiting the *milonga* for the very first time, together with those dancers who are trying to make a living out of tango, in this case a taxi dancer who attempts to attract clients by providing a taste of his dancing skills and charms. Moreover, striking in this field-note, and representative of all Argentine *milongas*, is the level of intimacy and the different ways of acting out the challenges and pleasures evoked by the close-embrace dancing. We find the discreet flirting on the part of the local taxi dancer and the slight embarrassment on the side of the invited foreign woman; there is evidence of *el cabeceo*, the traditional head-nod used to ask another dancer up in a manner that is discreet and carries little "risk"; and there is dancing, music and a mixture of feelings such as enjoyment, nervousness, fear and courage together with the warm ambiance appearing between friends. Turning to the level of bodily closeness between the partners, this is a striking feature, present in my field-notes as well as in the dancers' own descriptions. One example of how tango intimacy might strike a beginner is found in the autobiographical book *Long after Midnight at the Niño Bien* (2008), in which the author, a male journalist from Texas, travels to Buenos Aires to discover and eventually fall in love with the tango. His first encounter with the culture is described as a promise—and challenge—of the flesh. On his first visit to an Argentine dance-hall, the *Niño Bien*, one of the largest and one of the fancier clubs in town, he is emotionally knocked out by "the sea" of embracing bodies moving as one over the dance-floor, the cheeks glued together while legs and feet are free to execute steps and adornments.

> I turned the corner into a blinding white light and realized I hadn't *touched* anyone in a month. Here before me was a sea of people, all locked in an intimate embrace. There were about two hundred people dancing, slowly rotating around the room, two by two, as if on a grand carousel. The men stood up straight, their chests puffed out, their arms encircling the women protectively. The women leaned in ever so slightly, pressing their chests tightly up against their partners', their legs lightly tracing figure-eights on the hard wood dance floor. (Winter 2008: 40)

In my interviews with tango dancers in Buenos Aires and elsewhere, they often stress that the physical, non-verbal communication is a key to the seductiveness of tango. In most tango styles the lead is literally transmitted chest-to-chest and involves movements which require the dancers to let go of their own axis and trustfully lean on a partner. This partly has to do with the improvised basis of the dance form. The fact that ready-made choreographies and dancing figures do not belong to the social dancing of the *milonga* requires leaders and followers to be bodily and emotionally attentive to one another and to the shifts in the music. This implies engaging fully with a partner's bodily comportment, musical interpretation, way of executing steps and figures, together with her or his breathing and way of holding an arm and putting down a foot.[6] All those subtle pieces of information about a dance partner are necessary for tango communication to be successful. The tango implies a "thick co-presence" (Urry 2002: 259), involving not only words—or hardly ever words—but body movements, facial expressions, humming, breathing and touch. The bodily condition in tango is, together with the dramatic and sentimentally tuned tango music, what many dancers describe as the reason they "fell for" the tango.

One Swedish tango dancer, 50-year-old Daniella, stresses that it was the unique combination of expressive tango music and the intimate dance embrace which caught her. She has been dancing for five years, made two travels to Buenos Aires and extended her initial dancing interest into an exploration of the orchestras and music recordings. For a couple of years, she has been an appreciated *milonga* organizer and tango DJ who visits festivals and clubs in Sweden and elsewhere. She describes the tango as "an art form" which is expressed and interpreted through the body and the human senses.

> For me tango is an art form which appears in highly bodily manner. It's like playing an instrument but I do it with my own body. That is the way it has been all along when I have been dancing. This is the important interest. It's a rather fascinating movement dynamics in tango, the fact that it is made up by improvisation and the way the body moves and the close embrace which might itself exude oxytocin and endorphins (. . .) To me the art form of the movement is the thing. And the music, of course. It really fascinates me. The tango is so nuanced. These different orchestras express such an experimental joy. When you manage to connect the music and the dancing in a way that makes you forget time and space, you are in a flow which might be rather consuming because you let go of everything else. (Daniella, 50-year-old, Sweden)

What makes many dancers, Argentines and others, return to the *milongas* night after night is the promise of "flow" described by Daniella. Much like what Loic Wacquant (2004) and Geir Angell Øygarden (2000) report about the rather brute trade of boxing, and what ethnographer Helena Wulff

(2008) concludes about hard-training professional ballet dancers, hobby dancers in tango are driven by the promise of flow. As Wulff describes it, flow is "a peak point when action and consciousness blend" and can hence be described as a "transcendental state" (2008: 526). Those dance sets which make the dancers "forget time and space" are often described as excellent in communication and bodily dialogue with a partner, framed by a favorite tango song, that additional personal chemistry and the flow of movements and musical interpretation seemingly connecting all couples on the dance-floor. In the following statement by North-American Kate, who has been dancing intensively for two and a half years and who is now visiting Buenos Aires for the first time, the tango is described as a deep and intimate dialogue:

> The level of intimacy in the connection between you and your partner, because you have to. There are just layers and layers and layers of communication. [. . .] Tango is a conversation about existentialism, so much more rich and deep than what you would find in salsa for example. [. . .] It's partly because it's improvisational, it's just an endless possibility for exploring everything and anything, to me that's just alluring, addictive and rewarding. But you also get vulnerable. (Kate, 38-year-old, U.S.)

Although existentially "rewarding", as Kate states, the intimate communication is one of the challenges in tango, not least for beginning dancers. Many describe the bodily closeness, especially with new dance partners, as "awkward" and "disturbing", as such practices normally correspond with a rather different kind of social and emotional relation. In order to become more attentive to the music shifts and a partner's movements, without being disturbed by "irrelevant" facts such as the surrounding audience, many dancers use techniques such as closing their eyes while dancing. Although the physical intimacy can still evoke embarrassment and feelings of disgust among those who dance regularly, they often describe it as a natural part of the dancing experience. As a function of continuous practice, the dancers incorporate the ways of interacting with others and hence dissociate tango intimacy from similar intimate situations outside the social world of tango. Through repetition, they *embody their bodies* in ways that adjust them and make them suitable to the intimacy implicit in tango dancing. This involves actual steps and movements, body posture, a way of breathing and falling into the dancing embrace, together with the successive embodying of aesthetics and taste regarding body styles, clothing, hairstyle and decorative accessories.

One striking example of this is the learning process undertaken to master dancing in shoes with heels measuring at times up to ten centimeters or more. For many women who have not worn high-heeled shoes, learning the tango comes down to mastering their attributes. This example dramatically shows how material artifacts become decisive parts of the ways in which we embody culture. The high-heeled tango shoes change body posture and the way of walking and moving, accentuating a straight posture and slender legs, what is sometimes described as "the tango profile". Moreover, the shoes do bring about emotions such as fear (of falling) and pleasure associated with sensuality and femininity. The Swedish dancer Anna-Lena describes how the "hard work" of learning to manage high-heeled tango shoes was aided by the fact that she was going to Buenos Aires with a tango-dancing friend. At that point she was a beginner in tango. Visiting the capital of tango, however, strengthened her training and supported her advancement. Although she accepted that she would not become a great dancer in a couple of months, she wished—at least—to be able to participate in the Argentine tango life with a tango-tuned body, i.e. a body adapted to the movements and postures of tango, which involved the incorporation of its artifacts: the shoes.

Anna-Lena: Just walking in those shoes. When I started dancing I was wearing a pair of shoes with this tiny heel [Anna-Lena draws a three centimeter heel in the air] and had such problems just walking across the room and now I'm running in my tango shoes with much higher heels [she measures a ten centimeter heel]. You can actually train yourself to do this. I wasn't sure but it's actually possible. (Anna-Lena, 58-year-old, Sweden)

Maria: Yes, it kinds of sticks to you like when you're learning to ride a bike.

Anna-Lena: But it's hard work. I tried so hard and also made improvements. It was because I had decided to go to Buenos Aires with a tango-dancing friend and I wanted to be able to dance at least a little once we got there.

Experiences like the ones described by Anna-Lena, Kate and Daniella suggest that the tango-dancing body cannot be reduced to a sign or piece of text, but rather constitutes the condition and ultimate point of departure for the dancers' being-in-the-world (Aalden 2007; Beauvoir 1949; Bourdieu 1990b; Heinämaa 1998; Lande 2007; Young 2005; Wacquant 2004, 2005). To enter the tango—the dancing movements and social worlds—requires that the dancers know how to move, stand, sit and interact through subtle bodily and emotional acts. This implies bridging the discursive imaginaries of tango—the mythology and poetry—with an array of embodied structures. Becoming someone who comfortably moves around the dancing venues requires much more than mastering steps and figures. It requires adjustment of an entire range of bodily and emotional dispositions. As expressed by Anna-Lena, becoming a tango dancer is recognized among dancers as a difficult process. It is a process which requires not only technical mastery taught in dance classes, but a deeper knowledge involving bodily transformations, achieved only through endless hours of practice and presence within tango environments. Most dancers will not become professionals and have no intentions of transforming their hobby into work. Still, many dancers devote enormous amounts of hard dance work to the tango. Part of what drives the dancers to make extraordinary investments, dedicating their bodies, minds and leisure time to the adoption of new postures, movements and aesthetics, is the sensual rewards, experienced bodily. This is what many tango dancers describe as the driving force behind their investments in and dedicated practice of tango. As the dancers embody the tango step-by-step, a conscious motivation—in terms of what the dancer will actually achieve through the dance training—is not needed for practicing posture and adornments. Over time, tango movements become a natural way of moving outside the tango dance-halls as well. The body style adapted for tango dancing, implying a particular way of walking, sitting and breathing, become incorporated into a way of being and acting, decisive for pushing a shopping cart as well as killing time at a bus stop.

Those dancers who stay long enough to make tango music and the dancing movements part of "the system" often describe their relation to tango in terms of an addiction. Carolina, a Swedish dancer on tango holiday in Buenos Aires, states: "Once I started dancing, I became fanatic" (Carolina, 53-year-old, Sweden). Another dancer, Argentine Allan, describes tango as a drug, powerful enough to make people give up on their ordinary lives and as difficult to quit as other drugs:

> When people ask me if I can teach them tango, although I only know a little, I ask them several times if they really are sure. Because for us who are already down there, we know that once you get inside there is no way out. It's the worst of drugs because so far no one thought of a rehab clinic. Even worse when oneself is the dealer. (Allan, 24-year-old, Argentina)

For some dancers, visiting Buenos Aires implies an emotional peak which takes the dedication to a new level. The Swedish dancer Daniella reports that she "went mad" the first time she got there, spending every day and night on her high-heeled shoes.

> The first time I went there [Buenos Aires] I didn't leave the city center, it was absolutely absurd. An entire month I was locked up in the tango ghetto. I went mad. I lost three to four kilos. Every night I was out at the *milonga* and I took two classes each day. I wasn't that good of a dancer at that time, I just knew that I would go crazy if I didn't go to Buenos Aires. It was the only thing on my mind. (Daniella, 50-year-old, Sweden)

Feeling Tango

The quotes by Daniella, Allan, Carolina and Kate indicate that the embodied tango belief revolves around feelings and a particular kind of emotionality. For anyone who approaches the culture the songs and poetry are striking as strong declarations of dark nostalgia. From its birth and onwards, the tango provides a lasting metaphor reflecting an intimate longing. The poetry is often about absent lovers rather than present ones and plays in melancholic registers of yearning, desperation and loss (Savigliano 1995; Taylor 1998). The emotionality of tango comes to the fore when the culture is manifesting its particularity and when dancers are creating an in-group by distinguishing the tango from more "happy", "sexy" or even presumably "shallow" dances such as jitterbug, salsa and ballroom dancing. At times this is described as a reason the dancers fell for the dancing and the music. Some describe the encounter with the dramatic music as a way of "coming home" and finding a space for dealing with feelings of loss and pain. When asked in an interview in one of the Argentine tango magazines what she feels when she is dancing, one recognized star dancer—Alejandra Zavala—replies: "As it happens, what Enrique Santos Discépolo once said, 'Tango is a sad feeling that is danced', and starting out from there you have a shower of feelings whilst you're dancing and that is poured out together with the personality of each one" (*La Milonga Argentina*, March 2012: 34). Moreover, the process of becoming a tango dancer implies the embodiment and mastery of a broader emotional repertoire. Similar to Frantz Fanon's (1952/1986) report on affective responses to a racist ideology, the intersecting landscape of Argentine tango triggers emotional responses which inform the aficionados coming into being as dancers. In that sense feelings are not only discourse and décor in tango, but also lived experience.

Although all social worlds are grasped and made sense of emotionally, some milieus seem to make stronger claims on our emotional engagement than others. Tango provides one such *emotional space,* in which the social organizing of relations in the form of ritualized practices reflects emotionality. Randall Collins' (1992) studies of romantic love suggest that it is the institutional character of romantic couple-making, the ritualized construction of love together with a concept of free markets, which creates the feeling "love". Similarly, the actual routines and acts involved in tango dancing are part of creating emotional responses. This is to say that emotions emerge from social arrangements, rather than the other way around. In conversations with tango dancers, stories are often told of strong feelings of bliss when bodily communication works well, and of jealousy, sadness and anger when dance invitations are rejected. In that sense, feelings in tango might be approached as responses to expectations bound to the culture (the tango *should* be emotional) as well as ritualized acting. As the Swedish dancer Ida explains it, tango has always brought about emotional sensations. From her first nervous steps in the primary dance classes to late-night dancing in the clubs of Stockholm and later on Buenos Aires, the particular rooms with their lightning, music and perfumes, together with the clothing and muted conversation in the back corners, touched her emotionally. When describing how tango emotionality comes to work, she recalls a concert given by Argentine tango orchestra Fernández Fierro and the informal dancing session which followed it. She explains that her strong bodily reaction was evoked by the intense musical experience and the memories brought about by the intimate dancing.

> At that time I hadn't been dancing for some months and was out of balance, literally—and emotionally. I didn't feel at ease while dancing. Soon before I had broken up with a boyfriend in tango and now I saw him for the first time dancing with some girl. All of a sudden it hit me—the sentimental tango music, that striking smell of dancing bodies, my own physical weakness and the painful memories. I got a bad stomach pain, all blood was drained from my head and I started leaning forward, like I was covering myself from the other's gazes. One minute later I left the room, running. For my friend who had joined me [a non-dancing friend] my reaction was so dramatic. She caught me outside as I was leaning towards the wall. I explained that I had a stomach problem. My friend looked at me with concern but accepted my apology. (Ida, 35-year-old, Sweden)

As the story suggests, the trajectory of Ida's reaction was from the outside in. The tango music and the particular tango environment made her respond emotionally in the form of a stomach pain. The scenario that Ida describes reflects a response not (only) to biological processes of emotional reactions but rather to what Silvan Tomkins (1963) calls a person's *affect theories*, the composite of affective experiences registered and embodied within the individual. Rather than stating that tango is a more emotional world than others, however, I wish to make the slightly different claim that the tango is an emotional space which functions through embodied repertoires of recognition. Whereas Ida was emotionally struck by the ambiance at the concert venue, having "lived" the tango for a number of years, her non-dancing friend was left with reactions no stronger than a slight concern regarding Ida's mental well-being. This reflects a relational understanding of emotions, implying that the object that is thought to evoke a particular emotion never simply exists before the subject. As Sara Ahmed puts it, a bear is not fearsome *in itself*, but rather becomes fearsome *to* someone who is always situated in relation to various meaning structures (Ahmed 2004: 7). Furthermore, emotions are never merely a matter of human relations. As Ida's story illustrates, our emotional lives involve places, music, smells, gestures, artifacts and collective memories. This suggests that feelings are relational in nature, that emotions, which are sometimes seen as personal matters and as arising from within unique individuals, have a significant social and political dimension. In line with Durkheim, we might approach emotions to be a social force which ties people together and creates the social body we call society. This involves boundary making and regulations through feelings of joy, shame and fear (Durkheim 1893/1994).

This perspective helps us to create an argument against cultural essentialism, at times present in explaining the Argentine tango. Rather than relying on explanations of blood, temperament or race, quite common in discourses on tango (the temperament of the tango is sometimes referred to as that of the "hot" Argentine people), I suggest that we explore the organization of social relations in tango. Instead of claiming that an Argentine "mentality" brings passion to the tango, I propose that the organization of relations in the world of tango dancing transmits certain feelings into its practitioners, Argentine or not. One example of how this occurs is the techniques used for intensifying feelings, sometimes taught by tango teachers as an "as-if" device; tango students are asked to dance *as if* they were in love with the partner, *as if* there were no tomorrow etc. Such imaginative practice aims at intensifying the feelings evoked by the dancing and transmitted between dancers. As a further example, the intimate physical closeness of the dancing sometimes evokes memories of emotional intimacy shared elsewhere (with former lovers, children or family members), and hence evokes feelings of connection—although those feelings might touch upon other relations than the present one with a temporary dance partner. Another example is the constant fear of being rejected, as an immediate response to the rigid dance hierarchies and the delicate distribution of partners. For some dancers, the most dramatic turn of an evening does not take place so much in the actual dancing, but in the break *between* dances. The selection process and the forming of new dance couples is the moment when some dancers proudly walk towards the floor with a favorite dancer—while others continue to wait alone in their chair. Some dancers, like Ida, suggest that the level of intimacy in the tango makes the rejection harder to manage than in other couple dances with a "looser" embrace: "Not being invited to dance is like being rejected as a person, it hits your emotional self. Tango dancing comes down to a hug. Being rejected a hug hits you by the heart" (Ida, 35-year-old, Sweden). The continuous process of exclusion in tango creates a particular vulnerability which people respond to emotionally and which affects the culture at large. Many dancers describe tango as extremely emotionally demanding. Some even consider giving up the dancing due to the hardships of constantly being rejected and having difficulties interpreting the floating and "unreliable" intimacy.

Hence tango is an emotionally loaded subculture in which the dancers search for "flow" and emotional "kicks" –at the same time that they manage feelings of fear, sadness and anger. This brings us to the question of what the emotionality and intimacy of tango *do*, in terms of structuring a social world. In line with the theorizing of Durkheim (1893/1994), one could argue that the strong feelings in and for tango are what constitute the social fabric of its world. Emotions function as a cohesive force bringing people together. The expectation of emotional experiences—the "kicks" of the "flow" being the result of perfectly tuned dance communication—is ultimately what brings the dancers back to the clubs and dance schools. The tango feeling is a key motive that all dancers accept and recognize as one of the main values at stake. In that sense feelings function as a legitimizing force with explanatory power. Feelings are a legitimate reason, at times the only legitimate reason, that couples—on and off the dance-floor—refer to when they split up or when dancing friendships come to an end. As in the sphere of romantic relations—and possibly more and more spheres of social life—feelings win over verbal argumentation; or rather, referring to a feeling becomes a wining argument in itself: "It just doesn't feel right". In that sense tango emotionality comes across as a set of embodied feelings as well as a powerful discourse with justificatory capabilities.

Sexualizing Tango

Related to the tango's presumed emotionality is the associative tie between sex and tango. In popular narratives tango dancing is often represented as a metaphor for heterosexual desires and eroticism. Man meets woman and sparkling passion arises. This partly has to do with those historical accounts of the tango that claim the culture was born in the Argentine brothels. The dance is said to have been introduced in the poor Argentine harbor neighborhoods where dancing was traded for money as a way of attracting clients to brothels. It was hoped that the "sexy" dance movements would awaken the men sexually and ready them to pay for the intimacy of flesh behind closed doors (Guy 1995). When looking into the actual practices and conveyed understandings of contemporary tango life, the associative ties with sex are still present but negotiated in a variety of ways. Instead of being constructed as a means of spurring erotic desire, most dancers perceive the tango as a delicate mixture of fine dance expression and sociality based on a bodily and musically transmitted intimacy, which at times grows into friendship, restrained dance-floor flirting or even attraction, romance and sex. The sharing of an axis, the fact that the dancers are forced to breathe together and instantly respond to one another's bodily movements, creates a particular kind of trust which at times is described as evoking feelings of belonging or even attraction. In the following conversation between me and two Swedish dancers on a tango holiday in Buenos Aires, Magdalena reflects upon the significance of a particular attraction, stemming from the close-embrace dancing.

Maria: What is this *tango feeling* that all dancers refer to?
Elisabeth: It is a kind of feeling you get when you manage to interpret another person's intentions in the dance, the fact that you are feeling, you just know, you follow and it's easy. (Elisabeth, 48-year-old, Sweden)

Magdalena: Well, for me it's related to some kind of attraction. You can fall in love with almost anyone on the dance-floor, I mean during the dancing. It can be a man that you would never choose as a man, you would never want to see this man in another situation. Without the dancing you would never get close to this person. But while dancing, you can still feel that it becomes very . . . well, yes, it becomes passionate in some way, or sensual. But actually this is not what it's about, the magic is limited to the meeting. It could be a fat old man or a tall tiny one, I mean it could be whoever, it's about the expression you find together, you find each other's bodies in some way together with the interpretation of the music. (Magdalena, 50-year-old, Sweden)

As Magdalena puts it, tango involves romance and attraction, although the magnetism is restricted to the dance-floor. This means that the feelings she might have for a partner are not evoked by the person *per se* but rather by the complete tango experience: the intimate embrace, the music, the dance-hall ambiance and the surrounding dancing couples. In that sense the intimate potential of tango implies a transgression of conventional preferences. Magdalena states that the tango makes it possible to "fall in love with almost anyone", if the dancing is right. As other dancers put it, the reason they—especially as newcomers—so easily fall in love with their dance partners has to do with body memory. The intimate tango embrace reactivates memories of romantic or sexual experiences, lived bodily and emotionally (Törnqvist 2010a: 43–44). As one Swedish dancer interestingly puts it on the Internet page Tangoportalen, this might be a matter of language. The lack of a richer and more nuanced vocabulary to describe physically intimate experiences makes many dancers, consciously or unconsciously, interpret the dancing embrace framed by the dramatic Argentine music within a romantic or sexualized narrative rather than as a kind of communicative touch necessary for the transmittance of musicality and dance movements.[7]

The travels to Buenos Aires are ascribed different meanings in relation to sex and romance. On the one hand, as we will discuss in greater detail in Chapter 8, the tourist context makes some dancers wish to de-sexualize tango. On the other hand, the travel is expected to pull emotional trigger intensifying feelings of connection and attraction. Some dancers believe that the actual place, the sensual city of Buenos Aires, evokes romantic feelings within the temporary visitors. A North-American dancer and teacher, now living part-time in Buenos Aires, reflects on the lack of intimacy in the tourists' home countries as a circumstance which makes the Argentine experience special, particularly for women:

> I wonder if people believe that tango will offer them an avenue to things that they cannot get where they live. In the United States people

are very sexually repressed and I wonder if the warmth, the hugging and kissing . . . they can't do that over there, they just can't. [. . .] So I wonder if that doesn't mean that in some sense something is missing and they are looking for that connection here [Buenos Aires]. And I find that especially in women, they are more sensitive. (Steve, 58-year-old, U.S./Argentina)

Also, Argentine dancers convey a belief that tango tourists come both for dancing pleasures and possible romantic adventures. In response to my question about why Europeans and North-Americans come to Argentina to dance, the Argentine dancer Martin states the following: "They want to become better dancers. We have better teachers in Buenos Aires. But at the same time as they are making improvements of their dancing they also wish to meet someone, they want to live!" (Martin, 58-year-old, Argentina).The fact that the tango is often described as a highly romantic dance form, at times even evoking feelings of sexual attraction, does not have to do only with the framing of Buenos Aires as a "sexy" and sensual city—or with the intimate dance form itself. The emotional framing of the dance also seems to be evoked and transmitted through the *social organizing* of the dancing (Collins 1992). In fact a traditional notion of heterosexual romance might be described as part of the institutionalization of traditional Argentine tango, being inscribed in rituals (the asking-up procedure), the spatial organization of the old fashioned *milongas*, in which men and women occupy opposite sides of the room, the romantic tango lyrics, the clothing aesthetics which serve to mark gender difference and the script of acts.[8] At times the alluring passion of tango is said to be brought to the dance-floor in the form of a heterosexual courtship. One aspect of this play is the significance of the dance-floor flirting (*chamuyar, piropos*). Many Argentine *milongas* consist of the chivalrous play blending polite questions with up-front compliments and at times romantic invitations. Most often the dance-floor flirting is a way of socializing while using a romantic and flirtatious language. However, the function of flirtations and flattery should also be related to the production of heterosexuality and the absolute difference between men and women, marked by clothing, body styles, manners etc. Being a man, in this particular context, is defined by the conquest of women (Archetti 1999): a conquest which does not necessarily involve a sexual "finale," but rather a broader spectrum of social and symbolically charged practices such as heterosexual recognition from other men.

Among the tourists, the Argentine dance-floor courtship is at times experienced as a "fun part of tango life" (Lisa, 39-year-old, U.S.), or at least a flattery that few men at home would offer. Others see the flirting as part of a social convention, something that people do without putting too much meaning to the acts. As Swedish Elin puts it: "Flirty, that is what it is. But on a rather superficial level, it's part of the culture. That is how you are supposed to act. I was only there for two weeks so I'm not an expert but that was my feel to it" (Elin, 35-year-old, Sweden). Still others find the dance-floor flattery tedious and "cheap"; as the Swedish dancer Magdalena puts it: "I don't get impressed by this 'ah *milonguero*', I only care about what goes on in the dancing. What they say and what they do in between dances is just childish and silly. It actually makes me feel awkward, it's hard to manage" (Magdalena, 50-year-old, Sweden). In other words, although many visiting dancers acknowledge tango as an intimate and romantic interaction which makes it easy "to fall in love", the up-front sexualization or attempts to impress with a flirtatious manner is sometimes described as "awkward". In fact, the romantic promise of tango might even make the "superficial" romantic attempts disturbing. Once again, it seems as if the dancing itself is the key to the legitimate and "right" feelings, practices and rules, also in regard to romance.

The diffused relation between tango and sex might, however, also enable new approaches to sexuality and sexual identities—outside a heterosexual matrix (cp. Wade 2011). In the following passage, Kate describes herself as "straight" and mostly taking on the role of a follower in dances with men. However, during her stay in Buenos Aires she frequented the queer tango festival and discovered new enjoyments with women.

> I have had a couple of really good dances with women lately. I'm straight but I noticed that there is a sort of energetic intimate connection not with all women but with the women I enjoy dancing with, with the magical dance partners there is certainly some heartfelt connection or body connection and it is sensual [...] it isn't just moving to the music it is this skin-on-skin and chest-to-chest and all of that stuff but it doesn't seem to be dependent on somebody that you would go home and have sex with. So even when I have that connection with a woman I'm not thinking that I will go home and do her but it's really at that moment really energetically sexy. (Kate, 38-year-old, U.S.)

As Kate describes it, dancing with other women made her susceptible to a sensual attraction that diverged from her general sexual orientation. However, she still defines herself as "straight" and emphasizes that she would "not go home and do" a female dance partner. Although she does not want to transfer the ambiance into a "lesbian" identity or "lesbian" practice, she admits that the "energy" is sexual. In her understanding, it is actually the nature of the tango intimacy—restricted to the tango environments—which makes possible feelings and desires that she would normally renounce. However, and rather ironically, the attraction she felt for a female dance partner might also be a consequence of her own de-sexualizing of tango, or of what she describes as a shift in her understanding of tango, from a simplistic notion of "tango as sex" to a more complex understanding of the dance as a sensual way of connecting with the music and others. When the dancing intimacy is discursively kept apart from a sexually framed intimacy, sexualized feelings which diverge from normative heterosexuality might actually be more easily accessible. In that sense, we might suggest that the heterosexual framing of the tango does not necessarily bring about heterosexual feelings for a dance partner. The partly anonymous dance-floor actually seems to allow for destabilizing fantasies. As Angela McRobbie puts it:

> the dancehall or disco offers a darkened space where the dancer can retain some degree of anonymity or absorption. This in turn creates a temporary blotting-out of the self, a suspension of real, daylight consciousness, and an aura of dream-like self-reflection. [. . .] Dance evokes fantasy because it sets in motion a dual relationship projecting both internally towards self and externally towards the 'other'; which is to say that dance as a leisure activity connects desires for the self with those for somebody else. (1984: 144)

Following McRobbie's claim about fantasy and dancing, the heterosexual framing of the tango does not necessarily evoke heterosexual feelings or even interpersonal intimacy. The sensuality might be experienced in same-sex dancing formations as well as in autoerotic settings. Embodying the tango enables dancers to discover an intimate and pleasurable relation with their own bodies. In that sense the tango seems to offer yet another case of what Leslie Gotfrit (1988) explores in a study of a Candian dance-club, and of what Jonathan Skinner in his report from the Belfast salsa scene speaks of as "the politics of the pleasure of memory and the moving [. . .] body", which offers a safe space for "self-discovery, self-expression and experimentation, as well as a preamble to other bodily pleasures" (Skinner 2008: 67–68).

LIFE AT THE *MILONGA*: INSTITUTIONALIZING THE TANGO

Once the newcomer has started the bodily and emotional process of becoming a tango dancer, an entire social world opens up with new places to visit, new friends to make and new aesthetics, manners and ethics to incorporate. In Buenos Aires and elsewhere the social dancing is instituted in the *milonga,* a dancing event and the label for those venues where social tango dancing takes place. In Buenos Aires, various *milongas* are offered all days of the week—during certain weekends around fifty different clubs can be frequented at almost all hours of the day. In the old dance-hall *Confitería Ideal*, the afternoon *milonga* starts around three p.m., whereas late-night dancers can go on until seven o'clock in the morning at *la Viruta*. A scenario of a typical evening in one of the many clubs is an early start at six or seven p.m. with a class for beginners and intermediate-level dancers. A couple of hours later, the lights are lowered and a DJ begins playing in a corner of the room, or on rare occasions a live orchestra. This signals dancers to start asking each other up for dancing by searching the room with gazes, and soon the floor is filled with couples moving counterclockwise throughout the hall. The later the hour, the more experienced dancers find their way to the floor, whereas newcomers rest their feet around the tables framing the *pista* (dance-floor). Whereas the rules framing the *milonga* urge dancers on the floor to keep silent as long as the music plays, the tables encircling the floor provide a social spot where discreet talking is encouraged. If they are not too engrossed in studying the dancing styles and postures of more advanced *tangueras* and *tangueros,* those at the tables can take advantage of this moment to chat with friends and acquaintances and enjoy the food and drinks served in the bar.

On the social map of the milongas in Buenos Aires, one dividing line runs between the traditional clubs such as the Niño Bien, Confitería Ideal and Club Gricel and the newer venues such as Pratica X and La Cathedrale.[9] First, in the traditional venues only traditional tangos and classic orchestras, mostly from the "golden age" (1935–1952), are being played, whereas the up-and-coming clubs mix traditional tango music with electronic tangos played by groups such as Gotan Project and pop music. Secondly, the dancing style of the former is generally characterized by a closer embrace and more discreet steps and figures adjusted to a crowded dance-floor, a style sometimes called tango milonguero or tango salon. In the newer venues the dancing is often performed in an open or semi-open embrace which allows for larger and more acrobatic movements, a style sometimes called tango nuevo. As the name Practica X indicates, it is also more common to see couples who practice on the "younger" dance-floors even though the evenings are still structured along tandas and cortinas. Thirdly, the crowd differs. Although all of these venues attract a mixture of international tourists and local dancers, the average age is usually from twenty to forty in the newer venues and from forty to sixty in the traditional ones. The crowds also differ in how they make sense of the tango. Dancers who frequent the "younger" venues are more often critical of the traditional rules of the older venues, such as the expectation of dancing in man-woman formations. Most of these dancers are less invested in a romantic and semi-historical tango mythology and more focused on the actual dancing—its techniques, forms of bodily comportment, communicative forms etc. At the more traditional milongas, the rules are stricter and the dancers, not least the international ones, appreciate the conformity to what is referred to as the "old tango culture". All of the clubs mentioned above, together with most of the well-known inner-city *milongas,* are frequented by a mixture of Argentine and foreign dancers, particularly during the tourist season stretching from the Argentine spring in early November to the autumn season beginning in May. At times it is even hard to tell the difference between tourists and locals, as when professional dancers from Germany, Japan and Australia dominate the dance-floors (at times for the sake of attracting dance students to their schools and private dance classes), while beginning Argentine dancers watch from the seats. In addition, today's market space of dance teachers and tourist agencies contains a growing number of foreigners who live full- or part-time in Buenos Aires to make a career out of tango.

The structuring of a tango evening and the many formal and informal rules create a sense of belonging among the practitioners, an institutionalized sense of shared belief. Although local variations do exist, tango communities in different parts of the world are surprisingly alike and stable over time. The general vocabulary of dance steps and body styles is the same all over the world, although local variations do exist. This involves the distinct body language, the codes of conduct, the structuring of a dance evening as well as the music. Dancers who have fully embodied the dancing together with the social code of the *milonga* are able to move not only between different partners' embraces during a night, but also in and out of larger dancing communities throughout the world. The ability to act according to the formal and informal social scripts of tango quickly makes a temporary guest in a dancing community feel at home. Dancers who have embodied the movements and rules of tango will also easily decipher the social orders within a new community—its hierarchies and groupings—based on the members' dancing: their level of dancing, their dancing style and, moreover, their choice of dance partners—which implies an implicit evaluation made by other dancers.

Restricted Intimacy

Besides functioning as a cohesive force, the structuring of the *milonga* aims at regulating—and thereby actually also enhancing—the level of intimacy. Part of what is specific about the social forms of tango is that they enable a kind of intimacy which would hardly find the same social acceptance in other settings. The intimate dancing is enabled through limitations. As in swingers' sex-clubs or private gatherings of S/M practitioners, the many formal and informal rules of the *milonga* provide a sense of liberty from expectations about intimacy found in other places (cp. Bernstein 2001). This is partly due to an unspoken agreement—both parties know that the level of intimacy is restricted to the specific *room* of tango and the shared *time-frame* of a three-minute-long tango song.[10] An account of this playing with regulation and liberty might be illustrated by the following passage from a weblog for tango dancers, reaffirming a traditional (male) fantasy of women and heterosexual romance:

> She allows herself to be taken, to be transported, she is not afraid to surrender and express her deepest sentiments because she knows that she is protected by the rituals of the *milonga*. She can do all that without any further consequence because she knows that the real world and

the world of the *milonga* are totally separated. The rituals that take place here are courtship: represented by staring, nodding, then comes the union or communion: the embrace, then the separation, the music stops, the magic ends, he keeps her in his arms for an instant more and then takes her back to her table, but stops about three feet before her table to fulfill the last ritual of not invading her space. A love story in one tango. Birth, life and death.[11]

As this account suggests, romantic fantasies—portrayed in this blog post in terms of a rather masochistic femininity, allowing "herself to be taken"—can be lived out safely because of the walls of the *milonga* which imply that the dance-floor reality is strictly separated from life outside. Parallel to the seemingly free-floating world of sensual movements, the rules and regulations serve various social functions in relation to the intimate social tango environment. One example of this is the organizing of the dancing by *tandas*, which are dance sets of three to four tangos separated by a *cortina*, a short musical interlude consisting of pop music, salsa or parts of a classical piece, played to divide each dance set from the next and make time for people to find a new dance partner. One social function of the *tanda* is to give new partners enough time to get intimate enough to dance well together (becoming familiar with a partner musically and bodily), and to be short enough to keep dancers from "getting caught" with one person for too long and thereby possibly also deepening the level of intimacy. In addition, the restrictions partly target the associative tie between sex and tango. Although the dancing can involve "sexy" movements and clothing styles which reveal and accentuate the dancers' bare skin, most dancers accept the unspoken rule of not transgressing the level of bodily integrity. This implies that you almost never find people kissing in public in a *milonga* although their dancing might be extremely intimate and sensual.

Most dancers learn to share heartbeats and embraces with many different people during a night, and see their dance partners doing the same, although some people tend to stay with the same partner for longer periods. The fact that the dancers normally share heartbeats with many different dancers during a night affects the strength of the bonds. This is a culture in which the enticement of strong emotional "kicks" and easy exits is institutionalized. The partner shifts aim at making the dancers comfortable engaging in chest-to-chest communication with people that they would not normally get close with, knowing the time-limits. The delimitation enforced by the tanda restricts a set of relations which could potentially generate significant tensions, partly because of the level of intimacy. In fact, like practitioners of other forms of couple-dancing, such as salsa dancers in Belfast (Skinner 2008), many tango dancers report that their dance form is a rather safe space for exploring intimacy. Although tango intimacy is restricted by the *milonga* and its social code, the level of intimacy can become part of making certain dancers rather picky regarding their partners. Some dancers describe the bodily and emotional closeness as an obstacle to "dancing with whomever". The chest-to-chest intimacy implies that followers (often women) lean into the lead's (often a man's) embrace. This creates a bodily vulnerability which is further enhanced by the fact that many women dance with naked arms and backs. This reminds us that intimacy is not solely about positive feelings (cp. Zelizer 2005). In tango the intimate embrace sometimes creates vulnerability as well as fear and anger, especially among female dancers. As described by various gender scholars, such as Iris Marion Young in her work on female body experiences (2005), opening up one's bodily space, inviting the other, is bound to different sets of meaning in the different situations characterized by men and women. Also, the bodily risk taking in tango dancing seems to be different for women and men. Some women avoid dancing with unknown partners as they have experienced dancers who take advantage of the intimate connection. Many women lodge complaints about male partners who have violated their comfort zones by putting their hands and legs in inappropriate places or squeezing the woman too close. Violation of a dancer's bodily and emotional integrity is most often explained in the intimate vocabulary of tango itself, and might hence be justified as an arousal evoked by the dancing. However, dancers who repeatedly break this implicit rule are normally caught with bad reputation. In that sense the culture controls and disciplines its members by means of rumor and stigma.

The Tango Family

Although partners are shifted in and out on the dance-floor, facilitating social exits, the tango is also a world of social bonds and responsibilities. Some dancers, in Argentina and elsewhere, even describe the tango community as "a family". North-American Steve, for instance, accounts for tango as an escape from oneself, a path out of "your ego": "The *milonga* is not about the individual. It is about the individual within a group. This is something that you should identify with. (. . .) That's when you get out of your ego and share culture with everybody. That's why people say this is my family. (Steve, 58-year-old, U.S./Argentina) Many dancers would probably agree with Steve's emphasis on the social aspects of tango. Many spend their leisure time on the dance-floors and in tango-related activities such as practicing dance steps with partners or friends, listening to tango music, watching exhibitions and practical dance devices on YouTube, preparing social events or seeing friends from the tango world to have coffee and "chat about tango". Some dancers outside Argentina even decide to sell their houses and all belongings to move to Buenos Aires to spend all their days on the dance-floor; more often, though, people report that their monthly schedules and vacation plans are decided on the basis of tango-related activities. For such reasons, some dancers declare that they have everything they need in the community: a social network, a passionate hobby and, moreover, the comforting bodily intimacy shared among dance partners.

One reason so many dancers are able to dedicate so much time and effort to tango has to do with their life situation. The tango—generally speaking—attracts with some consistency a group of dancers primarily located in Buenos Aires, the larger cities of the U.S., Europe, Australia and some parts of Latin America and Asia, most of them with "cosmopolitan" routines.[12] The dancers normally belong to an economic and cultural middle class, although the implications of being middle class vary dramatically between different countries. The practitioners range from twenty to eighty years of age, with a majority of dancers in their thirties to late fifties. Another circumstance that affects the significance of the tango in the dancers' lives is their family situation. A majority of the dancers I interviewed were singles at the time of the interview or in short-term relationships, often with another tango dancer. Some of them describe a divorce or breakup as the starting point for their interest in tango. Susanna from the Bay Area formulates it rather poetically: "I started dancing tango because my heart was broken. I wanted to have an avenue to forget" (Susanna, 50-year-old, U.S.), while Kate, from the same dancing scene, tells a similar story of a search for distraction: "I started dancing tango two and a half years ago when my marriage ended unexpected and abruptly. I went down to the Allegro Ballroom to take any class they were offering because I didn't want to be home alone" (Kate, 38-year-old, U.S.). Later on in their dancing careers, both Susanna and Kate explain that they have developed a love relation with tango which actually makes it difficult to engage romantically with someone who is not a dancer—and equally difficult to engage romantically with another dancer since the constant partner-shifts and what they describe to be an individualist culture with a strong focus on emotional kicks make long-term commitments difficult maintain. This is also how Rebecca, an Australian dancer on tango holiday in Buenos Aires, describes it.

> Anyone who wants to have a long-term relationship has to give up certain things. Putting yourself on the dance floor, chest to chest with another person, will eventually destroy the relationship. You can't have both. It's either dance tango or have a relationship. [. . .] But the people you meet in tango are not very fulfilling, you won't wake up next to that person in the morning. You can't trust them, because of the nature of tango. A three-minute love affair sometimes went out of the dance floor. (Rebecca, 43-year-old, Australia)

Although other tango dancers might be approached as "not very fulfilling" romantically, due to the "nature of tango", "a three minute love affair", tango dancing makes up a socially structuring principle in many dancers' lives: an embodied way of being in the world with consequences far beyond the walls of the dance-hall. If, for a short time, we leave Argentina and look into how tango dancing melds with other parts of the dancers' social lives, we might investigate the Bay Area tango scene in particular, one of the empirical "home" case studies. It is illustrative that the tango venues in this area holds open during family-and-friend-based holidays such as Christmas, New Year's Eve and Thanksgiving, suggesting that the tango community fills such needs in the dancers' lives. It is also indicative that the community serves purposes other than dancing. The tango, just like other organizations and activities within U.S. civil society, is a provider of social welfare. As an illustration, during my fieldwork one of the main teachers, Christina, got ill from a disease which turned out to be both difficult and expensive to cure. Because dance teachers with low incomes find it difficult to cover health insurance, Christina and her husband depended on the local dance community for economic support and benefits. Money was raised through specific *milongas* where entrance fees and donations were set to pay her medical bills. This shows how the dancing community laid the foundation for a social belonging that prompted the dancers to help each other out in difficult times (cp. Viladrich 2005).

Dance-Floor Honor

The social structuring of tango dancing, particularly in Argentina but also elsewhere, revolves around a play of honor. As some dancers explain it, pride is an essential tango feeling. In an historic piece by Julia Taylor, on early tango poetry, she states that "el tipo tanguero refers to someone who is "always watching out so that he may not pass for a fool" (Taylor 1976: 277). In that sense, tango life at the *milonga* has similarities with everyday life among Kabylian farmers, explored in some of Bourdieu's work (2001). These games take the form of a quest for recognition, which entails the risk of losing face in front of others (cp. Øygarden 2000: 76–79). Proudly entering the *milonga* and presenting oneself as a tango dancer—hence making oneself vulnerable to this risk—is part of the social game. The structure of the *milonga* mitigates this vulnerability and eases the situations in which the dancers' honor is at risk. This is particularly noticeable in the socially and emotionally delicate invitation procedure. It asks for the dancers to be sensitive to their own and their counterparts' dancing status and dancing interests and might be described as a balancing act of neither giving away too much (not accepting invitations from dancers below one's level) nor asking for too much. The invitation process, however, is constructed in such a way that the dancers do not risk losing face in public. In traditional venues women and men are seated on opposite sides of the dance-floor. Formally it is the man who asks the woman up by capturing her gaze from across the hall, then raising an eyebrow, hardly noticeable but hopefully apparent to the woman. The woman accepts by holding eye contact with the man and subtly indicating her interest with a slight nod. Only at this point will the man stand up and walk towards the woman to escort her to the dance-floor. In practice, though, both parts are active in the invitation process as they both try to capture the attention of other dancers—and avoid gazes from unwanted partners. This way of asking up is called *el cabeceo*, from the Spanish word *cabezo* (head), and refers to the discreet head nod. One social purpose of this ritual is to make the dance rejections discreet and to minimize the embarrassment and dishonor to which rejected dancers are vulnerable. In various discussions among dancers, the significance of this ritual is associated with the heterosexual play in tango. In the following passage from an Argentine home page, which aims at explaining the historical roots of the tango, *el cabeceo* is described with reference to the protection of "tender women" and "male ego".

> The traditional *cabeceo* was developed for important sociological reasons—the protection and preservation of male ego and female vulnerability. How else can one guarantee a man's protection from public ridicule if he is to walk across a crowded dance floor to ask a woman to dance risking potential refusal? How else does one protect the tender nature of a woman who may not have the strength of character to refuse a dance with a man she does not want? The answer is the *cabeceo*—the mantle of protection that allows both genders a choice![13]

Accounts from contemporary dance-floors indicate that a similar notion of honor is still at play today. In the following questions posed by a male North-American dancer on an international tango webpage, tango masculinity is described as closely interconnected with an honor code serving to protect male dancers from losing face in front of others.

> What could be more mortifying to a man than to cross a crowded room to invite somebody to dance, only to be turned down? What could be more embarrassing to both parties than to turn somebody down who had made that trek? What could be more brusque than a man walking up to a woman and peremptorily extending his hand to her, as if demanding a dance . . . often without even looking at her at all?![14]

As illustrated in these accounts, the honor culture of tango is highly gendered and heterosexualized. In the more traditional *milongas*, a woman who is sharing table with a man might be experiencing that possible dance partners ask the man at her table for a dance with her, instead of asking her directly—or to treat her as already "occupied". The heterosexual structuring of the dancing—not least the fact that a majority of dancers take part in man-woman constellations—creates a milieu in which dancers are strongly urged to create alliances with the opposite sex. As many female dancers note, they quickly learn the names of most men in the *milongas* they visit, but few of the women's names. On the one hand, this might be explained by the fact that most dancers spend the majority of their nights in the arms of the opposite sex; hence it is more likely that they will have a chat with a member of the opposite sex. Out of traditional politeness or actual interest, dancers ask each other for names, dance experience, musical preferences, country of origin etc. in the break between dances. On the other hand, the alliances between men and women are also a result of the competition over dance partners. In many dance-halls and tango schools men are still a scarce resource, and hence it is important for women to "claim them" for future dancing.

Also when dance partners have been distributed and accepted, the presence of an honor code is striking. If an invitation is accepted, it is understood that the partnership lasts throughout a dance set of three or four tangos. Breaking a partnership before the dance set has ended is a way of dishonoring the partner. This might happen if the dancing dramatically deviates from a dancer's level and preference—or if a dancer is violating the bodily integrity of another dancer. It is not considered acceptable to interrupt a dance or a dance set. Like the customs in other dance scenes, such as the salsa scene (Urquía 2004), receiving a dancing acceptance involves a promise not to be broken. If legitimate reasons do not back up the breaking of a *tanda*, the act is interpreted not only as rude to the partner but also as an insult to the culture. Such an act is associated with risk and cannot be resorted to very often, as dancers who are known for rejecting partners on the dance-floor will end up with a stigma. Instead of interrupting the dancing, the dancers can indicate their disapproval of a partner's dancing style or level by staging emotional distance. Publicly declaring dislike is a way to resist an inappropriate partner and thereby protect one's own dancing honor.

CONCLUSION: TANGO DANCING AS AN EMBODIED BELIEF STRUCTURE

The title of this chapter—*the production of belief*—is in fact the title of an article by Pierre Bourdieu from 1980 targeting the art business, with the subtitle "Contribution to an Economy of Symbolic Goods". Later on in this book the theme at stake in Bourdieu's article—the misrecognition of economic interests within an economy trading "things that have no price" (1980: 261)—will be discussed. In this chapter the title serves to highlight tango as a belief system with its internal practical reason and embodied practices. In line with the discussion of tango in this chapter, a *tango habitus*—or what I will call an *embodied belief structure*—is produced and given meaning through various practices, primarily in direct relation to the dance-floor. The notion of embodied structures comes to fore in relation to the highly body-oriented world of dancing. In tango, just as in other dance forms, a main part of the communication and the social mapping of relations takes place without the interference of verbal language. Being part of a social world like that of tango requires and creates not only bodily dispositions, but also cognitive models and beliefs in certain values. In other words, only the dancers recognize the absolute value and beauty emerging from rigorous bodily training—the refined sweep of a foot over the dancefloor, the exact timing with which a dancer puts his or her arm around a partner, the subtle responses to the rhythm in the music. If an outsider could at all recognize and evaluate such acts, it would still be a mystery for most non–tango dancers how and why people put such effort into apparently insignificant details. The insiders, however, sense that learning to recognize and master the details—precise movement and musicality—is part of a distinction process: between the sacred and the profane, the outsiders and the insiders, and dancers at different levels of excellence. In that sense, exploring the belief system of tango might be described as a search for the *practical reason* behind people's actions, in this case within the framework of tango dancing (Bourdieu 1998: 76). A belief in the values associated with tango dancing is generated partly as a response to a set of benefits and promises associated with the culture. This involves the thrilling and comforting close-embrace dancing, the new friends and lovers and the investment in a cultural art form made up of music, poetry and dancing.

Furthermore, the embodied dispositions allow the dancers to navigate not only within the complicated structure of dancing movements, but also in a complex network of social relations. To enter into the world of tango dancing one must procure and embody the right credentials as well as the requisite knowledge to act in ways defined as appropriate. In that sense, tango dancing is far from a floating sphere of feelings. Rather, the dancing represents a demanding social form which asks the practitioners to master a bodily engagement with complicated movements, refined musicality and the capacity to tune their bodies in to a close-embrace communication. In addition, the *milonga*, the dancing venue, provides a regulated space in which the intimate dancing is performed under the constraints of a social code. Hence, tango dancing appears as a rather regulated social form in which people engage in close bodily and musical communication with others.

We might, however, reconsider the use of Bourdieu's concept of *habitus* when exploring the social formations tango dancers occupy. Bourdieu's concept often refers to a more complete constitution of self, covering a full range of dimensions in social life, at times referred to as an "order of beliefs, that is, at the deepest level of bodily dispositions" (Bourdieu 2000: 177). The concept is often situated within an economic structure, as when various social or economic classes provide similar modes of cultural preferences in regard to music and food . For most dancers in this study, however, tango offers a somewhat loosely defined—and flexible—relation between "the objective structures of social space" (Bourdieu 1998: 77) and the mental and bodily dispositions shaped by and for life at the *milonga*. For many, being a tango dancer is but one of many social formations constitutive of life. Most tango dancers are not only tango dancers but also family members, with their particular social backgrounds, and employees of various workplaces.

The ways in which tango dancers embody not only dance steps and body styles, but also a worldview with its implicit cultural distinctions, tastes, evaluation schemes and cognitive frames, are rather specific to the field of tango dancing. This implies that some dancers are able to walk in and out of this belief system. For example, the female lawyer who enters the *milonga* leaves behind her the work code, aesthetics and practices bound to her profession at court and enters a quite different social world with radically different expectations. This, however, is not so much a conscious shift—what some people would call "fake" or a sign of inconsistency—but rather the embodied response to different sets of belief structures. Inside the tango world the female lawyer appreciates and embodies an aesthetic that she in other contexts would evaluate as "cheap" and vulgar, such as stiletto shoes, slit skirts and a body posture and movements which exaggerate a particular kind of femininity. Although she would not wear this kind of clothing—or act this way—at work, at family dinners or out in the street, the *milonga* activates a set of bodily dispositions with its particular aesthetic and tastes. As this book suggests, however, this is not to say that the tango belief plays only a minor role in dancers' lives, being an insignificant parenthesis. On the contrary, the tango has a strong impact and actually proves to be a dominant force in structuring dancers' lives. This might be put in dialogue with theories of the flexible identities and deconstructed subjects at times described as typical of social life in late-modern societies (Bauman 2007; Giddens 1992). For many dancers it seems as if tango makes up an important belief structure and a practical *raison d'être*—although it is not the only belief structure which shapes their actions and choices in life.

In fact, the design of this study—addressing the intersection between tango and tourism together with the multiple social structures the tango tourists embody—is meant to highlight such possible conflicts and overlapping processes. As will be discussed in more detail in the next part of this book, different belief systems and regimes of justification come into conflict in the study of tango tourism. This implies that the bodily dispositions required for participating in tango are quite different from the ones the dancers activate when entering other parts of life. Being a tourist, for instance, involves certain practices and temporary identities which at times go hand in hand with the embodied tango belief; at other times clashes occur and dance tourists are forced to face and manage various dilemmas.

3 An Intimate Dance Economy

INTRODUCTION

Like all micro-universes which thrive on affective mythologies, the tango revolves around values and practices other than a meditative intimacy that connects people. And much like most social groupings, be they diving clubs, workplace organizations or friendship networks, tango dancing involves hierarchies and a play of status. To simplify matters somewhat, tango dancing might in fact be divided into two general narratives. The first one, which was discussed in the previous chapter, draws from the embodied belief structure revolving around tango intimacy: the bodily proximity between dancers, the liberty and escapism made possible by the well-regulated spaces of the *milonga*, the emotionality, the romantic magnetism and the similarity with family life. The other narrative, which is the focus of this chapter, takes on the darker sides of the tango: the hierarchies and the conflicts within the culture, the logic of a game with its implicit rationality, the striving and struggles over scarce resources, the function of an economy generating recognition and symbolic rewards.

At first sight these two narratives appear to conflict with one another. As I will argue, though, they make up two sides of the same coin: both the belief in the values associated with close-embrace tango dancing and the strict dancing hierarchies keep the world together. Rather than contrasting individual pursuits of status with solidarity and cohesion, tango culture includes prestige as part of its collective structure. When looking closer into the social organizing of the *milonga*, difference comes across as one of the primary structuring principles: differences between men and women, Argentine dancers and temporary tourists, dancers of different skill levels, professionals and beginning dancers. Also significant are those differences associated with various dancing styles: *milongueros* and *nuevo* dancers, traditionalists and inheritors. Such distinctions are reaffirmed in and enforced by the spatial arrangements of the *milonga*, indicating social status through the placement of the dancers: women on one side, men on the other; recognized dancers close to the dance-floor, beginners and newcomers seated in the back of the hall. One important aspect of the social life at the *milonga* is the managing of these distinctions and the consequences of a competitive world inside which people strive not only to become "fine dancers", but also to be acknowledged as such by other dancers (cp. Broady 1991: 169; Galli 2012: 14).

In contrast to the narrative of tango as a sentiment produced at the level of the dancing couple, it is also a highly competitive and self-aware culture. Also, social dancers without ambitions of becoming professionals are mindful of their status, which involves their "looks" and manners, as well as their selection of dance partners for the sake of protecting their dancing honor or upgrading their status. The play of recognition is mirrored on the dance-floor, through the distribution of dance partners, and affects the dancers' chances of participating in the collective dance body. This forces tango dancers to reflect upon their status within the group, whether they wish to or not, and additionally makes the dance-floor a methodological arena, which renders visible the ongoing play of recognition. The map of status and stigma comes to fore in the form of a selection process, coupling the dancers in social formations which affirm—and at times destabilize—an existing social order. Who gets to dance and with whom? At what hour of the evening and for how long? Who spends an entire dance evening sitting, without being invited or without having her or his invitations accepted? Answering such questions gives a rough sense of the relational map of a particular dancing community.

However, the status play is not only a means to access dance invitations but becomes a value in itself. What brings dancers back to the *milonga* is not only the promise of bodily connection and intimacy, but also the game itself, although it is often unrecognized as a game. Bourdieu speaks of this in terms of *illusio*, an embodied belief that compels the agents of a particular field—in this case tango dancing—to play the game and eventually to become good at playing it. This is to say, in the somewhat twisted words of Bourdieu, that "you cannot get a tango dancer (philosopher) moving by tempting with the rewards strived for by a geographer" (1991: 127–128). This does not imply, however, that dancers strategically reflect upon their actions and choices; rather, the game is part of the unintended consequences of becoming a tango dancer.

> *Illusio* is the fact of being caught up in and by the game, of believing the game is "worth the candle", or, more simply, that playing is worth the effort. [...] If your mind is structured according to the structures of the world in which you play, everything will seem obvious and the question of knowing if the game is "worth the candle" is not even asked. In other words, social games are games that are forgotten *qua* games, and the *illusio* is the enchanted relation to a game that is the product of a relation of ontological complicity between the mental structures and the objective structures of social space. That is what I meant in speaking of interest: games which matter to you

are important and interesting because they have been imposed and introduced in your mind, in your body, in a form called the feel for the game. (Bourdieu 1998: 77)

Before moving on to describe the actual "game" in tango, we should reflect upon the importance of the struggles and the existential contours of Bourdieu's work. Regarding a common (mis)reading, Loïc Wacquant states that: "this is not a utilitarian theory of social action in which individuals consciously strategize to accumulate wealth, status, or power. In line with Blaise Pascal, Bourdieu holds that the ultimate spring of conduct is the thirst for dignity, which society alone can quench. For only by being granted a name, a place, a function, within a group or institution can the individual hope to escape the contingency, finitude, and ultimate absurdity of existence" (Wacquant 2008: 265).[1] In a similar fashion, Raoul Galli returns to Bourdieu's anthropological work in order to capture the origin and complex significance of his later on developed concept symbolic capital. In Bourdieu's earlier studies on the Kabylian honor economy, participating in these games is acknowledged as a "fundamental dimension of the social existence" (1990: 22). As Galli frames this existential struggle: "For individuals or groups who do not possess the assets and qualifications that those people, on which they depend, do recognize as valuable, is potentially equal to not existing in this specific social context. [. . .] 'One of the most unequal of distributions and possibly the cruelest is the distribution of symbolic capital, i.e. social reason for existence' [Bourdieu 2000: 241]" (Galli 2012: 16). This framing is important for this study on tango. As will be discussed more carefully in the concluding section, the dancers' strive to be recognized as dancers partly has to do with the honor codex, being an important aspect of the traditional Argentine tango culture (Savigliano 1995a). However, it also has to do with the intimate relations and subjectivities at stake. For some dancers, not being recognized within the legitimate terms of the field dramatically reduces their "social reason for existence", within and outside the *milonga*.

Whereas the previous chapter focused on the production of belief, in terms of an embodied intimate promise which creates solidarity and social cohesion between dancers, the present one takes on the production of recognition as a "major principle" both of "uncertainty" and "assurance" (Wacquant 2008: 265), divergence and cohesion. The social existence of tango dancers, generated through belief and recognition, might be captured in the notion of a *field*, defined as "a structured space of positions, *a force field* that imposes its specific determinations upon all those who enter it" (Wacquant 2008: 265). Throughout this book, the relational field of tango will be approached primarily in terms of an *intimate symbolic economy* which structures the social order of dancers. Entering the social world of tango dancing requires, and equally produces, the recognition of a particular set of values and resources, defined and temporarily fixed as a result of ongoing struggles among dancers

(Bourdieu 1990, 1998, 2000; cp. Galli 2012; Schilling 2004; Wacquant 2008).[2] When laying out the sociology of tango, the production and function of this economy is highly significant.[3] Studying life at the *milonga* in terms of an ongoing negotiation of symbolic values indicates that dancing experiences, tango relationships, acquired skills and bodily attributes are being evaluated and that they affect the social structuring of dancers. This structure, based on the distribution of resources, determines the dancers' status within the field and hence their possibilities to participate in the social world of tango. Most noticeably, it affects their chances of getting to dance but also their likeliness of becoming successful actors within the tango market (as dance teachers, *milonga* organizers etc.). Approaching tango as a field with its own symbolic economy makes intelligible the dancers' praise of capacities such as moving backwards in high heels or the possession of detailed knowledge in tango orchestras. Such knowledge is recognized as valuable resources only within the world of tango, i.e. only among tango dancers is such knowledge associated with transformative capacities. As Bourdieu writes, symbolic capital is in fact an "ordinary property" which, within a restricted social configuration, is loaded with sacred meaning and magical capacities.

> Symbolic capital is an ordinary property (physical strength, wealth, warlike valor, etc.) which, perceived by social agents endowed with the categories of perception and appreciation permitting them to perceive, know and recognize it, becomes symbolically efficient, like a veritable *magical power*: a property which, because it responds to socially constituted "collective expectations" and beliefs, exercised a sort of action from a distance, without physical contact. (Bourdieu 1998: 102)

In order to analytically approach and conceptualize the endowment of symbolic capital in tango, this chapter aims at presenting those "ordinary properties", i.e. those skills, practices, experiences and body styles which are loaded with symbolic and sacred meaning and hence recognized and used as resources in tango. The first of those properties is *dancing skills*, which represent, for obvious reasons, one of the most important resources in tango. Dancing qualities involve bodily adjustment and technicality, musicality, artistic expression in the dancing and communicative talent to engage within the lead-follower dialogue; in short, dancing qualities include all those skills that tango dancers acknowledge as necessary components for tango dancing to be effectuated. Closely related to the dancing credentials is the level of *emotionality*, manifested through the embodied schemes which help the dancers to engage with, manage and perform intimacy and the appropriate "tango feeling". The tango economy also involves the ambiguous significance of *social capital* concerning the simultaneously rewarding and restricting tango friendships, family ties and loose relationships such as dance-partner acquaintances made at the *milonga*. Greeting the "right" visitors in a tango club might increase a person's chances of getting to dance with acknowledged dancers, as do kinship relations with so-called star dancers. In this chapter we will also explore the significance of *sexual capital* involving physical characteristics such as "beauty" and sexual attractiveness—framed within the aesthetic cosmos of tango dancing—as well as social features such as communicative skills in the area of charms and flirting. In the context of tango in Buenos Aires and the expanding number of international tango tourists, we must also take into account the significance of *authenticity* credentials. Performing Argentine culture through looks (hairstyle, clothing) and manners (language, upright body style, courtship) functions as a resource, particularly in tourist-dense tango environments. However, tourists also engage in a play surrounding *exotic attributes*, reporting that their blond appearance attracts attention among certain local dancers and makes it easier for them to get to dance in Argentina than at home. Also, *economic capital* serves as a credential within the tango economy. Material resources are needed in order to access the tango in the form of *milonga* entrance tickets, tango classes, dance shoes and, for tourists, travel to Buenos Aires and the housing and food required for a dancing holiday. Within the framework of tango tourism, economic capital has also become a currency which certain dancers aim for by converting and trading their symbolic tango capital (dancing skills, authenticity credentials and "looks"). Just like sexual capital and social networks, money is an ambiguous currency within tango and is at times perceived as a partly illegitimate resource. The use and negotiations of economic capital will be dealt with separately in Chapters 5, 6 and 7.

Put simply, we might conclude that symbolic capital in tango implies that the dancers are endowed with or rather embody a successful combination of the resources listed above. A technically advanced dancer without social networks in tango or authenticity credentials might be rejected by other dancers, whereas social charms and charisma together with the staging of Argentine culture can make an average dancer a highly popular partner.[4] In addition, we should be careful to note that the particular qualities and capacities discussed above must be theorized within the field of tango dancing, and with respect to the function of what Bourdieu labels "symbolic alchemy" and "symbolic violence" (Bourdieu 1998: 102). The recognition of "looks", for instance, cannot be fully captured from an isolated descriptive analysis of a particular body style or manner. Rather, the relations in tango, characterized by domination and subordination, transform dancers and their bodies into desirable and loveable subjects, endowed with sexual capital, due to their position within the field of forces. A tango dancer acclaimed as a star might be surrounded by a swarm of admirers finding her or him attractive, beautiful, sexy, charming—due to the dancer's position within tango and, implicitly, her or his capacity for exerting symbolic power. In that sense, the "magical power" allows for the field to create values as well as affective relations of attraction and love.

Many dancers are capable of tracing the "logic" behind some of the conversions taking place on the dance-floor, as, for instance, when recognized star dancers invite beginning tourist dancers with important tango networks in their home country or when apparently charming and charismatic dancers without dancing skills manage to access advanced dancers. This is to say that those dancers invested with the tango have an embodied sense for the structuring of the world and also incorporate a "feel for the game" (Bourdieu 1989: 77). In fact, the tango comes to fore as *a* regime of justification (cp. Boltanski and Thevenot 2006), indicating which kinds of dance-partner choices are fair and just. This partly builds upon a meritocratic principle drawing primarily on dancing skills. The notion of justice in the trading of dance partners—and conversions of credentials—is not formalized like the academic meritocracy, but rather lived and sensed as an embodied category. In fact, the dance economy is far from a rationally structured game in which the actors make strategic moves. As previously discussed, we should approach dancers' navigation throughout this social order with its implicit justificatory logic as embodied and instinctive—as well as rational. The dancers might be described, in the words of Edgar Morin, as guided by a "principle of rational uncertainty" (Morin 2008: 48). As he puts it: "We are infantile, neurotic, frenzied beings and yet we are rational. That is truly the stuff that human beings are made of" (2008: 48). In this chapter, the "rational uncertainty" involved in the intimate dance economy is explored in relation to a number of resources useful in tango. We will start by exploring the impact of negotiated dancing skills and the function of recognition and dancing sacrifices. In the subsequent sections we will discuss the importance of social networks as well as a play balanced between the attributes of sex and flirting. We will also interrogate the emotional play in tango together with the values associated with authenticity. In the final section we will discuss the significance of a partly unrecognized symbolic economy, exemplified by the tango, in which the exchange rate, the "price", is left implicit. In addition, we will discuss the relation between symbolic economies and social cohesion. It will be argued that the hierarchies create motives for further bodily and emotional investments in the culture, and hence generate a belief which unites the dancers. However, the fact that the values at stake are perceived as closely related to dancers' emotional selves creates a particular vulnerability which makes some dancers unwilling to pay the price for achieving recognition and dance-floor intimacy. In this last section we will recognize that the logic of the game, with its implicit heterosexual matrix, makes certain dancers more vulnerable than others. Particular attention will be paid to the group of middle-aged western women who experience rejections within this (hetero)romantic economy and how the cohesive function—the play for recognition—at times risks creating dividing lines strong enough to tear the world apart.

DANCING SKILLS AND BODILY SACRIFICES

To understand the social field of tango dancing we need to recognize that this is ultimately an economy of the flesh. The main value recognized and negotiated in tango is dancing skills and values linked to dancers' bodies. Part of what people are trying to achieve are the bodily and musical techniques that will allow them to enter into the intimate tango encounters. For those who learn to master the dancing—with all its dimensions and depths—there are rewards to be had. As the Swedish dancer Carolina states in a comment regarding the striking age differences on the Argentine dance-floor: "All these young women who press their bodies so close to these old men, these fat old men with no hair. Just because these men are dancing so tremendously well" (Carolina, 53-year-old, Sweden). Achieving a level of dancing so high that people who would not normally interact fall intimately into each other's arms requires successive and far-reaching transformations. The tango is mastered through bodily training and sacrifice. Like practitioners of other physical cultures such as ballet (Wulff 2008) and boxing (Wacquant 2004, 2005; Øygarden 2000), tango dancers report on the painful consequences of their intense training, such as feet fractures and sore backs. To fully participate—and in order to be a successful player within the field—dancers must engage in a long labor of investing the body and the emotional self with the appropriate sensitivities and habits. This makes tango a highly achievement-based world. Parallel to the sentiment that tango is all about "the right feeling" and "the right connection" this is an elitist culture that worships excellence. Meanwhile, in their search for breathtaking tangos almost all dancers struggle to develop their dancing technique, body posture, artistic expression and musicality. High on the list of concerns for many of the dancers who travel to Buenos Aires is the improvement of their dancing. Most international guests on a short-term stay spend their days taking private dance classes with reputed Argentine teachers, practicing figures, steps, body posture and the more elusive skills of connecting with partners and transmitting emotional presence while dancing. In fact, holiday dancers make significant sacrifices to tango by investing not only bodily training but also large amounts of money and vacation weeks in order to improve their dancing skills.[5]

The fact that the complicated dance offers a non-stop track for continuously refining one's steps and artistic expression is by some said to be part of the attraction. This is captured in a conversation between three tango dancers, Allan, an Argentine dancer, and two North-American dance teachers living in Buenos Aires, Steve and Monique. The verbal exchange starts with an evaluation of the time Allan has spent dancing tango.

Allan: Some people don't believe me when I say that I have been dancing for six months. (Allan, 24-year-old, Argentina)

Steve: No I can see that. You look more like a two-year dancer. (Steve, 58-year-old, U.S./Argentina)
Allan: But I always want to get better. There are so many things to learn.
Steve: You always get better because you have to get better . . .
Monique: For people who really get good they feel that they never stop learning. (56-year-old, U.S./Argentina)
Steve: Ever, they never stop learning.
Monique: Because we the professionals we always want to get better. We take a class, we take a private, I mean we always wanted to study. You can't just sit back and think "now I've done it". Very few people do that, very very few people.

The essence of this conversation lies within the importance of constant development. The dancers confirm the cultural requirement of improvement as well as the pleasures of taking the dancing "to the next level". In that sense we might return to the previous chapter, and claim that the tango is constituted as an honor culture in which the hardship of dancing practice functions to assign merit to dancers. A meritocratic narrative of hard work helps to explain why some dancers have developed an outstanding technique or musicality—and why they are rewarded. The years invested in tango are also used to legitimate the sometimes rough rejections facing many newcomers in tango. However, the conversation also suggests that the dancing skills together with the hardship and sacrifice invested in the culture must be recognized by other dancers. Like other dancers, Allan, Steve and Monique are preoccupied with trying to capture the dance practice—in the quote pinned down in years and months—required to achieve a particular level of dancing. As the discussion indicates, at times dancers wish to "cheat" the system and be recognized as more advanced dancers than they actually are; the cult of genius and street-smartness has a strong presence in tango culture. One particular focus in such discussions is directed towards dancers' way of walking. According to a tango saying, the finest dancers can be distinguished not through their excelling in rapid movements and high kicks, but rather through their way of walking the dance-floor. The distinctions lay within the subtle way of putting down a foot, knowing the exact balance between tension and relaxation when starting the movement. This is another way of saying that only those dancers who fully embody the rich spectra of dancing expressions are capable of perceiving artistic exclusivity and hence drawing a line between newcomers and experienced dancers. The key to tango lies not within the grand gestures, possible for anyone to discern, but rather in the subtle and sophisticated details requiring an insider's embodied feel for the dancing.

In tango, as in other symbolic economies, value is connected with scarcity, and the more exclusive a value is, the higher its status. This implies that the top-ranked dancers are envied for several reasons. For obvious reasons, more advanced dancers are likely to offer a more comfortable embrace and a more elegant dancing style than beginners. Striving to access the company of a recognized dancer, though, is also bound up with the transmittance of status. For those dancers who wish to climb the social tango ladder, it is more rewarding to have one set with a star dancer than to dance an entire evening away in the arms of a beginning dancer. Dancing with a recognized dancer at times functions as a mark of quality which makes other recognized dancers more likely to invite or accept an invitation. In return, not "giving away" your dancing company too easily is a way of protecting virtue, as dancing "below" one's level might function to discredit one as a dancer. In that sense, dancers can use the processes of coupling up with other dancers as a means to move up—or at times down—the social hierarchies of tango. Hence, the "pickiness" in choosing dance partners is not only a consequence of the level of intimacy and artistic preferences, but also a response to the strict hierarchies and the play of honor.

This indicates that dancing skills, just like other symbolic goods, are far from hard facts, easy to rank and evaluate independently. Rather the actual dancing becomes subject to ongoing negotiations within the tango communities. This implies that rumors involving critical judgements and tributes, not least the small-talk taking place around the tables encircling the dance-floor, are equally important to actual tango training and dance-floor performances in ascribing status and stigma. Some dancers are lifted up and glorified for their "pure and classic" dance style whereas other "exhibitions" are taken down with reference to a "stiff embrace", a bad posture or the use of illegitimate shortcuts (money or sex). In fact the constant talk of better and worse, professionals and beginning dancers, functions as an important brick in the structuring and governing of the social world of tango. However, the impact of judgements is partly linked to a person's status within the world. Just as in the fields of art or literature, the function of consecration is intimately associated with the relational hierarchies. Legitimate judging—meaning evaluations which are recognized as such—is only possible from the inside, by dancers who themselves are acknowledged as honorable dancers. As suggested by a North-American dancer and tango teacher on an international tango webpage, "the best dancers in Buenos Aires" are in the position of defining the tango and the values ascribed to it—by virtue of their level of dancing. According to this account, it is partly the improvised nature of the dancing that allows for certain dancers to exert symbolic power, in its ultimate expression of defining the tango.

> Argentine tango dancing has many similarities with jazz music in that there are no institutionalized rules for its improvisation, but there are common practices or idioms. Those who study jazz music or Argentine tango dancing learn the respective idioms. In that sense, the common practices become the parameters by which the art form is loosely defined by its practitioners. [. . .] Given what we have described for

Argentine tango—a subculture with unwritten standards of practice—an informal group of insiders, probably the best dancers in the city most central to Argentine tango, Buenos Aires, are likely to exert the greatest influence over what and what is not considered Argentine tango. The standard for admission to this inner circle of influence is the high respect of the other practitioners. Those who have not earned a position in the inner circle have substantially less influence on the parameters, if any at all. For the majority of tango dancers, conforming to the accepted practices laid down by one or more of the masters will determine whether they are dancing Argentine tango or doing something else. And perhaps surprisingly, these informal cultural parameters of acceptance can often be more strictly enforced than written laws enforced by police.[6]

To conclude, the relational field of tango dancing—together with the social life at the *milonga*—is important in the evaluation of tango credentials. Although many dancers claim not to take an interest in others' view of their dancing, the gazes of other dancers actually make up an important part of the social life in tango. Being part of this world involves coming into being through the acknowledging gazes of others. This means that the dancing is experienced not only from within the dancer or the dancing couple, but also from the outside—as an exhibition of skill level and dance style for other dancers to view, evaluate and use as measurements to assess and make sense of their own dancing.

SOCIAL NETWORKS AND THE FUNCTION OF A GIFT ECONOMY

The intimate economy of tango can be described as partly an ongoing process of gift exchanges. In it most obvious form, this exchange is structured around the dance invitation. The level of intimacy in the dancing, and the protection of virtue, turns the dance invitation—and the acceptance—into a *gift*. As Marcel Mauss (1923/1997: 90–94) writes, the gift both honors and obligates. Accepting a dance invitation comes with an obligation to return the gift, i.e. to accept future dance invitations as well. This is not particularly true of the first set of dances: the first *tanda* with a new partner is more of a trial in which the dancers are evaluating each other. But once a dancer has accepted two dance sets or more with the same partner, an expectation of future dancing grows. Many dancers have "obligatory" sets to deliver each night. This might involve dancing with a partner who "took care" of her or him during a beginner phase, offering dancing company and advice, and who now awaits a certain number of dances in return. Other times the gift exchange involves dancing with a close friend's sister or the car driver among a group of dancers who co-ride to the *milongas*. Gift-dancing is not the reason dancers return to the *milonga*; these dances are not expected to offer the "tango magic", but play a necessary role of easing social life, and not least the shifts between the tango world and worlds outside of the dancing. This implies that the reciprocity of gifts cannot be reduced to mere self-interest. Rather, it is part of the social fabric of tango dancing, serving the creation of bonds and alliances.

The taboo of making things explicit ascribes a time dimension to the gift exchange.[7] Although tango poetry worships the past, social life at the *milonga* creates a temporality in tango which points primarily towards the future and is structured around the promise and the expectations implicit in previous gifts. In contrast to business commitments with absolute time frames, the tango is structured along a notion of *uncertainty*. It is not made explicit when a gift will issue in an equivalent exchange. Hence, it is possible to reject a dance invitation from an "obligatory" partner for a night or two. If the dancing exchange is not completed within a longer time frame, however, the bond dissolves and the dancer risks being stamped as "snobby". If a dance gift is not returned and an informal contract is broken, it happens that former dance partners stop talking to each other and eventually even stop greeting one another.

The gift exchange in tango makes *social relations* both valuable and difficult to manage. At times the gift economy results in conflicts between the logic of the game, worshiping tango and justifying actions in relation to dancing values, and the logics of other social spheres, such as expectations ascribed to friendship relations. On the one hand, large social networks and close friendship bonds are a resource within tango, facilitating access to the dance-floor and friendship with other dancers. In addition, friendships with experienced and well-regarded dancers transmit tango recognition. On the other hand, social bonds obligate dancers in ways that most dancers perceive at times as difficult to handle; this is true especially when the levels of dancing differ. One example of such a conflict is when a beginning dancer appears in the *milonga* after three beginner classes and assumes that a tango-dancing friend from work will be her or his partner for the night. The stickiness of friendship relations—with their implications of loyalty and accessibility—conflicts with the competitive honor logic of tango. As a consequence many dancers are careful about engaging even in small talk with dancers "below" their level: some fear that the intimacy of such situations might turn into a dance invitation which would be difficult to reject without losing face or making others lose face. The same goes for all kinds of social invitations, such as the sharing of taxis, paying for another dancer's *milonga* entrance ticket etc. Anything that might function as a gift can potentially result in a debt to be paid back in the form of a dance.

One consequence of this is that the culture—in Buenos Aires and elsewhere—is known for its "cliques" of dancers, formed on the basis of dancing levels and dancing interests, which stick together and rarely open up for newcomers. Although some dancers entered the culture for social reasons, wishing to make new friends or find a romantic partner, many of them actually tend to develop a social restrictiveness over time and approach and make friends primarily with those people they wish to turn into dance partners. Others make compromises with new friends and lovers in tango, particularly when there is a large difference in dancing level. They might declare that the new friend or lover should have no expectations of becoming a privileged dance partner, and that a dance-floor rejection should not be understood as a romantic rejection. Relations which go beyond the dancing—like romantic relationships and friendships outside the tango—tend to involve constant negotiation regarding when and how gifts in relation to different parts of life can be expected to be returned.

SEXUAL CAPITAL AND GENDERED VULNERABILITY

Although tango is an economy with a taboo of making the "price" for dancing explicit, most dancers are equipped with a feeling for equal and just deals. This is to say that those dancers who frequently dance "beyond" or "below" their level generally attract comments from other dancers. One assumption is that a "better" dancer is offering her or his dancing company in exchange for something else, be it flirtation, friendship relations or, within the context of dance tourism in Buenos Aires, money. This assumes that one of the dancers in an unequal dancing couple is looking for something in addition to tango. One example of the functioning and dilemmas of a gift economy draws on the delicate relation between sex and tango. When it comes to the impact of sexual expectations, even those dancers who have no romantic interest at all in their dancing are forced to play along with and manage a game partly based on dance-hall courtship—at least in the sense of avoiding flirtatious situations. This implies that a form of sexual capital functions as a credential which affects dancers' chances at the *milonga*. Following Catherine Hakim's (2010) categorization of so-called erotic capital, we might recognize that the tango economy involves body images such as "beauty" and sexual attractiveness—defined along a tango-tuned aesthetic at times mixed up with authenticity markers and signs of exoticism—as well as social skills and practices in the area of romance, such as transmitted charms and verbal flirting.[8] Within the tango scene, as in other parts of social life, popular physiognomic features partly structure and determine the relational field of status. This implies that "the body, especially the face, is a reflection of the self: that a person's inner character or personality will shine through the outer appearance. [. . .] Status and social acceptability depend on how a person looks" (Featherstone 2010: 193). The fact that dancers enter into the tango with and through their bodies, implying that the practice is primarily an economy of the flesh, stresses the significance of appearance. As an example, the significance of the *cabeceo*, they eye-play of dancing invitations, proves that tango revolves around the gaze and the ways in which the dancers come into being through evaluation. This might be exemplified with an account by the Argentine dancer Ezequiel, in his late forties, who also runs a tango agency primarily targeting foreign dancers. He describes the economy rather frankly as a mixture of values of which the essential ones are "good dancing" and "good looks".

> All people in tango are trying to dance with the best-looking women or men and the best dancers. Perhaps they are making a sacrifice, dancing a *tanda* with someone old, or fat or short but they are not going to invite those dancers for more than a *tanda*. And they would not invite them to their table. A group of young good-looking Argentine dancers inviting a tall tourist woman with glasses to their table—impossible. (Ezequiel, 48-year-old, Argentina)

Being recognized as "beautiful" and "sensual" functions as a reward in tango as elsewhere, and as follows: being a "tall tourist woman with glasses", in this account used as an example of a non-desirable body in tango, evokes rejections. This implies that there are expectations for the body, particularly for women's bodies, besides what they actually do and perform on the dance-floor. This is how we might understand the variety of gendered tango services on the market. Besides classes in tango dancing, the advertising pages in the Argentine tango magazines feature agencies which offer makeup classes and plastic surgery, particularly to female dance tourists. Hence, the body appears as one of the main sites for the gendered constitution of tango. Starting with the embodying of the traditional tango movements, we find this to be a highly gendered process in which expressions and the shaping of bodies relate to traditional ideals of femininity. Dancers acquire particular ways of moving in the room, being and communicating through a body style which marks gender difference. One example of this is the advice given to female dancers to continuously draw their feet together, hence keeping their bodies compact. Other movements aim at extending the female leg, making it more sensually visible, and adornments made with the feet are used to make the movements more beautiful—feminine—and to charm a dance partner. Female dancers should also make bodily space for themselves and initiate movements and steps, but not in an overly aggressive way.

When it comes to the relation between sexual capital and age in tango, the reality seems partly to conflict with the mythology praising tango as a dance form that suits all kinds of bodies, particularly older bodies, because of the walking element and the slow and restricted movements (requiring musicality and dancing responsiveness rather than athletic body types). The 61-year-old North-American dancer Irene, who has three years of dancing experience and is now on her first trip to Buenos Aires, states that she is often left sitting during a *milonga* because men choose younger dancers and because the female surplus provides men with an advantage in the selection process. She claims that the "age discrimination" in tango is the same in the

U.S. as in Argentina. For instance, she describes an evening when she travelled to downtown San Francisco from her hometown to dance, a two-hour journey, only to sit in a chair watching younger dancers being invited:

> Many men are not willing to take a chance on women they don't know. I found myself travelling two hours and back all night at a *milonga* where the men are not fantastic but they have so much choice and they have so many younger women for them to choose so it feels a little depressing. (Irene, 61-year-old, U.S.)[9]

For Argentine women as well, age seems to affect the chances of getting to dance. As Martin, an Argentine dancer with many female friends in tango, states, "a sixty-year-old woman is not going to dance".

> A sixty-year-old woman, that's difficult. A woman of sixty is not going to dance. When they go to the *milonga* they know that they will be surrounded by women in their forties, thirties, twenties. The men are saying: "I will dance with these women [in their forties, thirties, twenties] because they are young or because they have a better ass. But dancing with these women can be awful. [. . .] It is horrible, but it's like that. My friend Cristina who told me to start dancing tango in 1998 is a wonderful dancer but she is just dancing in the tango classes, she doesn't go to the *milonga* anymore because the only people who ask her up to dance are her old friends. She is really tired of this discrimination. She hates the tango for this reason, for the game. (Martin, 58-year-old, Argentina)[10]

In order to understand the (gendered) vulnerabilities expressed by Martin's friend Cristina, we might turn to some work by Simone de Beauvoir (1949) and Iris Marion Young (2005). They claim that the female situation in male-dominated societies is characterized by a tension between immanence and transcendence. We might modify their words and claim that hierarchical cultures, recognizing sexual capital in the form of certain "looks" and bodies, place the status of tango dancers ambiguously between that of subjects and that of objects. As Young writes:

> The three modalities of feminine motility are that feminine movement exhibits an *ambiguous transcendence*, an *inhibited intentionality*, and a *discontinuous unity* with its surroundings. A source of these contradictory modalities is the bodily self-reference of feminine comportment, which derives from the woman's experience of her body as a thing at the same time that she experiences it as a capacity. [. . .] The woman lives her body as *object* as well as subject. [. . .] An essential part of the situation of being a woman is that of living the ever-present possibility that one will be gazed upon as a mere body, as shape and flesh that presents itself as the

potential object of another subject's intentions and manipulations rather than as a living manifestation of action and intention. The source of this objectified bodily existence is in the attitude of others regarding her, but the woman herself often actively takes up her body as a mere thing. She gazes at it in the mirror, worries about how it looks to others, prunes it, shapes it, molds and decorates it. (Young 2005: 35, 44)

Although women seem to be a more frequent target of bodily evaluations than men, in tango as elsewhere, the contradictory modality in tango is played out as a general ambiguousness. On the one hand, dancing implies an experience and a coming-into-being characterized by transcendence, movement and the reaching out of one's own body in order to communicate with others.[11] On the other hand, the body is not just a site for movements and agency, but also an object to be evaluated, desired and rejected. The accounts by Irene and Martin suggest that the body constitutes an object in tango, which locks certain dancers together in immanence. The body is not just a site of subjectivity, a lived reality in itself, but also an item which is desired and despised—a resource or a burden.

An Ambiguous Play with Sex

The function of sexual capital in the traditionally honor-coded culture of tango also has to do with performed accessibility. This means that the company of a friend of the opposite sex with whom a dancer shares a table, arrives and departs or dances the first *tanda* drastically delimits the approaches made by other dancers, particularly in traditional *milongas*. This implies that the dancer is not romantically accessible and, as follows from the heterosexualized play in tango, less accessible as a dance partner. Within the masculine honor code of tango, this delimitation is particularly true for female dancers (with male company), whereas men with female company might attract even more attention from other dancers than they would otherwise. In some cases female company functions as a trigger or an assurance that the man is a decent dancer. In other situations the presence of another woman signals less risk of being approached sexually. The potentially positive function of a female companion should be put in dialogue with the discussion in the previous chapter regarding the *milonga* restrictions serving to regulate the dancing intimacy. The perceived risks—physical and moral—following from the associative ties between sex and tango create a need, particularly among women, to set up guidelines for how, where and with whom to share the intimate dancing. As in other social contexts, women are often forced to take on the responsibility of managing emotions (cp. Hocschild 2003). For instance, it happens that female dancers take the blame for violated intimacy. As Magdalena states, she believes that she needs to manage her emotional expression in order not to awaken a sexual drive within a male partner and hence to avoid facing awkward situations or up-front sexual harassment.

> Sometimes I wondered if I transmitted things that I didn't wanted to transmit. Sometimes the men came with offers besides the dancing and then I understood that they were out picking up women. They started dancing with more sexual movements than the tango movements and that was just awful and I thought that I probably transmitted some kind of passion that I didn't want to signal. If you give a lot and let yourself go they might interpret it into a lot of things. (Magdalena, 50-year-old, Sweden)

Situations of overly intimate dancing could arise also in the women's home countries. However, the context of Buenos Aires is said to slightly change the significance of a flirtatious manner and make new strategies possible. Some female tourists explain that the Argentine tango world is partly made up of a play surrounding sensuality, in which the tourist, a foreign woman, can flirt with men to win dances with them. Sexual capital, involving looks, body language and verbal flirting, can be used by both men and women. In tango as elsewhere, though, sex is a dubious credential, particularly for women. The presence of a sexual illusion—acted on or not—makes some women careful. The importance of not getting *too* intimately involved is at times explained as a measure to avoid "messing up the dancing experience", which results in the loss of dance partners and, eventually, a bad reputation. A female tango hostel owner and tango teacher—herself a North-American who settled down in the tango capital some years ago to make a business out of her passion—speaks of tango tourism as evoking new kinds of risks in tango. In advising some newly arrived women from her home country, she tells them to be "careful with the tango guys", to "look out for their intentions" and to guard against being "fooled by their dark brown eyes" before they go out on their first night in town (Sarah, 52-year-old, U.S.). Her moral advice to foreign women is to avoid sexual adventures with local men in order to reach the cultural and artistic heights of tango.

One example of the potentially problematic consequences of playing with sex in tango is found in the autobiographical book *Kiss and Tango: Diary of a Dance-Hall Seductress*, written by Marina Palmer, a North-American dancer on tango adventure in Buenos Aires. In this book—somewhat of a chick-lit bestseller and presumably soon to be a movie with its own interactive webpage with additional features[12]—the author describes how she ends up in sexual affairs with a number of well-known Argentine dancers. Her own explicit agenda is to become a professional dancer, and she hopes for the male dancers to become her professional partners. In fact, she describes how sex slips into some of her dancing relations. In one episode, she accounts for her ambiguous sexual relation with dance partner Diego in the following words.

> Yesterday, Diego changed tactics. He switched off the physical and turned on the psychological pressure. He said that if I didn't feel like

going to bed with him, then he didn't feel like practicing with me. [. . .] I was about to send him to hell, then something held me back. [. . .] I prefer to think of it as 'Love of Tango.' And so for the 'Love of Tango,' I was polite for a second time. But of this you can be sure: there will not be a third. Because no matter how much I love tango, I don't love it that much (Palmer 2006: 211).

Although manifesting agency, in terms of an active response to Diego's "threat", the compromise seems to be in his favor. As a result of his insisting, Palmer agrees to "be polite", as she frames having sex with him. Just like the relation with Diego, a majority of her dance-partners become stranded in short-term affairs. As she describes it herself: "In the eyes of men, I'm not wife material. I'm not even girlfriend material. They take one look at me and think: SEX!" (Palmer 2006: 304). As long as the relations revolve around flirting and a restricted dance-hall intimacy, however, Palmer manages to keep her dance partners, and actually gains dancing knowledge and social networks through her charm and "looks". In these cases she manages to play with sex as an unfulfilled promise. However, as soon as the dance-floor intimacy turns into sex outside the *milonga* Palmer is often cut off from the relations and marked with a "bad reputation". Whereas she wishes for the intimacy created by sex to pave the way for a deeper and long-lasting dancing relation, her male counterparts tend to regard sex as the end point of their dance affair.

One level of morality in this story has to do with the use of sex as a means to access tango values. As Sarah suggests in the passage quoted above, the honor culture of tango teaches that there are no shortcuts to becoming a fine and fully recognized dancer. In that sense, restricting the level of dance intimacy to the dancing movements and the walls of the *milonga* encourages dancers to honor and cultivate the dancing. Punishing dancers who "sleep their way" to the dance-floor with a bad reputation might be an even more important disciplinary measure in tango—with its strong associative ties with sex—than in other cultural pursuits. However, the story of Marina Palmer is clearly also a story about gender. In small talk and rumors throughout Buenos Aires, similar stories are told of women—almost never men—who went on romantic dates (or just went to bed) with well-recognized dancers in order to build a tango career. True or not, and whatever the reasons behind such affairs actually are,[13] these stories come with a moral—for individual dancers and the community at large. The story of Marina Palmer is just one of many targeting women who are believed to have "slept their way" to management and top positions—and are being punished.[14] As Susan Bordo (1993) notes, women's social honor is caught up in affirming a notion of pure "femininity" and, moreover, a restricted heterosexually coded sexuality.[15] The case of tango further strengthens Bordo's claim. As in other traditional honor cultures, the protection of virtue is particularly restrictive when it comes to women's sexuality. Throughout history, the protection of bodily and moral integrity has proved to be a female concern and responsibility. Women have had greater reasons than men to fear both physical abuse in close relations with the opposite sex and the risk of being morally devaluated when acting in an overtly sexual manner (cp. Pateman 1988). Consequently, male tango tourists' thoughts on the "dangers" of the intimate dancing generally differ from those of female dancers. Although both male and female tango tourists describe the aim of their trip as the experiencing and developing of tango dancing—not searching for casual sex and temporary affairs—only women, both foreign and locals, highlight the risks. The men I interviewed and came across during the field-work rather described the situations in which a partner did not respect the limits of the dance-floor intimacy as "at times awkward, but not a big deal" (Lars, 55-year-old, Sweden).

Returning to the contradictory modality forcing the tango dancers to live their bodies both as object and subjects, the use of sexual capital comes to fruition as a delicate balancing act. In fact, the heterosexualized play generates a gendered vulnerability which different groups of women experience, but in different ways and with different kinds of sanctions as possible consequences. As discussed in relation to Marina Palmer's autobiographical book, she—a thirty-something North-American dancer trying to break into the Argentine tango world—is approached and despised as someone representing *only sex*. In this case, the fact that she enters the tango in the form of a desirable body becomes an obstacle in relation to her dancing ambitions. The fact that she is objectified as a "sexy" foreigner, and hence partly deprived of her bodily subjectivity in tango, hinders her from building a serious "tango career". Opening up one's bodily space, inviting the other, is a larger risk for women than for men in relation to the threat of bodily abuse and sexual harassment, as well as in relation to moral sanctions with respect to (female) sexuality. However, the ideals of femininity represent hindrances also for those women who are not (hetero)sexualized.[16] As some dancers declare, they spend most of their time at the Argentine *milongas* sitting, rarely being invited to dance. This, 63-year-old Ruth from the U.S. states, is partly a result of her being an "old" woman who does not try to "make myself beautiful as to please men" (Ruth, 63-year-old, U.S.). For her, however, the fact that she is not objectified does not imply that she is permitted a larger degree of subjectivity. On the contrary, the fact that Ruth is not acknowledged for her appearance hinders her tango subjectivity from emerging. Her body is not received in its full potential for agency; rather, the lack of objectification threatens her inclusion within the world of dancers. For dancers like Ruth, experiencing rejections turns into a tension which over time becomes difficult to handle. For her and other women, their bodies—the ultimate condition for dancing and their being in the dancing world—become an object that they carry and are restricted by. As told by some informants, this might be even more difficult to handle when happening far away from home and far away from comforting networks outside tango.

However, men—and particularly Argentine men—are also criticized for their use of charm and flirtation, i.e. the play with sexual capital. Traditional flirting manners (*chamuyar*) are sometimes viewed as "old-fashioned", "outdated" and even "sexist" by some of the younger dancers, both Argentine and foreign, in the more open-style clubs and *practicas*. In addition, flirting is sometimes perceived as a way of "fooling" tourist women. The Swedish dancer Daniella, for instance, speaks of how erotic play is used by some Argentine men in order to fool foreign women into dancing with them, going to bed with them and "steal[ing] away" their money.

> The Argentine *abrazo* [the dancing embrace in tango], this is probably what many people find so alluring. This might be where the Argentines can pull in their victims, this is where they succeed. The *abrazo* is a technique for seducing women. They trap foreign women who are in Buenos Aires for the first time and who get to experience this amazing embrace that no one has ever showed them in Europe. Then the women fall and they [the Argentine men] can steal away everything they have. (Daniella, 50-year-old, Sweden)

To sum up, the tango conveys a somewhat contradictory sexual morality, both condemning and rewarding engagements in a sexual play. Balancing these devices is a matter of having an absolute feel for the tango culture. Embodying a rewarding erotic capital involves an incarnated sense of how to play the dubious game of tango and sex, a feel for the borders not to be transgressed (the overtly sexual), as well as knowing how, in which situations and with whom to perform romance and flirting. Moreover, the play of sex and tango proves to be a gendered situation which women and men enter on different premises. As will be discussed in more detail, this is also a game revolving around racial expectations and prejudices based on age.

EMOTIONALITY VALUES

In tango, feelings and emotional experiences are part of what dancers strive to access through their dancing—equally this is an important aim of tango journeys to Buenos Aires. In that sense emotions are an important value within the symbolic economy of tango. Mastering emotional presence and expression together with the knowledge of how to transmit feelings to a partner constitutes credential knowledge. This implies that the role of emotions in tango exceeds that of spontaneous feelings evoked on the dance-floor. In fact, we might approach the tango culture in terms of an *emotional imperative*. When looking into the micropolitics of the *milonga* one finds it to be a social world which visitors are forced to feel their way through—however intense the feelings actually are. Some frequently replicated discourses from within the world itself claim the tango is a dance stemming from the heart, and furthermore that feelings are "all that matters" and that only "passionate people" can truly become involved with the dancing. Although such statements are sometimes criticized and made fun of among dancers as being superficial clichés, the emotional imperative shapes dancers' engagement with the culture. To mention one example, some dancers structure their dancing and its frequency according to their emotional status. They state that they do not go tangoing on evenings when they are feeling sad or, on the contrary, happy in an overly energetic sense: "those evenings I'd rather go disco-dancing", claims Ida (35-year-old, Sweden). For Ida, tango dancing requires a balanced emotionality, not influenced by negative feelings of sadness or anger or, on the contrary, overly cheered-up feelings. To comment on another example, emotionality is at times framed in terms of a number of guidelines imposed on beginning dancers by tango teachers or more advanced dance partners. These might involve recommendations for *how to feel* in certain dance-related situations, often suggesting that a dancer "let go" of herself, using relaxation and breathing to open up for a new level of emotional and artistic engagement with the music and a dance partner. In that sense, the rewarding body capital in tango is not limited to images, the performed looks ("not just the clothes you wear, but the way you wear them"; Featherstone 2010: 196), but also involves emotional schemes, expressed in the form of touch and the transmittance of feelings. Those dancers who learn to master their emotional expression and tune their faces and bodies according to the rewarding schemes are more likely to be successful in the social play at the *milonga*. In that sense the art of tango dancing is partly about tuning the body not only to achieve and experience a certain level of emotionality but also to master and stage particular feelings and to make them publicly visible.

What is recognized as an appropriate or even rewarding feeling takes time for beginning dancers to identify. Quite far from the grand gestures of love and hate expressed in tango poetry, the affective play at the *milonga* is often rather subtle. For example, it is true at least in many of the traditional clubs that most dancers perform a serious facial expression, manifesting total focus on their partner and the music during the dancing. Outright laughing during a dance set, as well as talking, chewing gum and searching for things in a jeans pocket, signals emotional distance. Such acts normally indicate that a dancer is a beginner—or a dancer with credentials enough to act outside of the script and express a lack of interest in a partner. As the dance set ends, the dancers often relax into a smile or laughter as they leave the floor. In fact, those dancers who stick with a serious facial expression off the dance-floor are less likely to be invited to dance. Expressing feelings of solitude, grief and anger—feelings elevated to the sublime in tango poetry—often leads to distance and loneliness at the *milonga*. This is reflected in the following conversation between me and the Swedish dancer Magdalena on tango holiday in Buenos Aires:

Magdalena: This woman who keeps sitting, *tanda* after *tanda*, she might be a really good dancer. Nobody knows. (Magdalena, 50-year-old, Sweden)

Maria: How come, why isn't she asked to dance?

Magdalena: Well, it has to do with attraction and charisma, I don't know, the feelings that you transmit, that must be it. [. . .] I was in Paris once and I didn't get to dance at all and I felt sick, I turned sick because I felt really bad about not dancing. [. . .] If you've been sitting for too long you express absolutely nothing. You just communicate that you are disappointed and bored and you're not going to dance with that expression.

Magdalena brings forward the complicated *play of emotions* through which the evaluation of expressed feelings makes up an element in the partner-selecting process. North-American Steve agrees. He claims that the level of transmitted emotionality is a matter of judging potential partners' level of "tango depth": "It is not to see how she dances, but rather to see *how she feels* when you dance with her. It's a difference. In one case it's academic the other case it's not. One case comes from within" (Steve, 58-year-old, U.S./Argentina). Having embodied the tango feeling, he adds, is what distinguishes Argentine dancers from the European and North-American visitors. Most foreigners in Buenos Aires maintain an emotional distance and are less interesting dance partners, according to Steve.

In contrast to Steve's account, however, many dancers acknowledge tango to be a world that teaches people to *manage* their emotions—rather than unleashing them—and channel them into expressions which are legitimate and rewarding within the culture. This can be exemplified by returning to Magdalena, who recognizes that there are situations in which the social relations in tango require a more up-front management of feelings, as when the dance expression risks to threaten social bonds and conventions. As she explains it, when she is dancing with someone's boyfriend she restrains her dancing expression and controls the feelings she is transmitting. "I might not look like the happiest woman on earth. This is done in respect because you know that this relation is different from when you're dancing with someone who is 'everyone's property'. When dancing with those men you can express whatever without considering another person." (Magdalena, 50-year-old, Sweden). Magdalena indicates that an unrestrained emotionality would threaten the bonds and dissolve the cohesion of the world. One additional aspect of the mastering of feelings is that it provides protection from negative and harmful consequences of feelings in tango. The ability to distance oneself from dance-floor rejections—as well as from "falling in love" with every new dance partner—is necessary in order to be a long-term practitioner. This process might be described in the terms of Arlie Hochschild's work on the everyday management of feelings, so-called *emotion work* (1975, 1983). Like the social spaces of bridge clubs and academic seminars, those of tango constitute an emotional arena in which dancers manage joy, bitterness and anger, structured as a collective and public matter. In fact "the managed heart", to refer to the title of a book by Hochschild (1983/2003), is a better metaphor to capture the tango dancers, then "the passionate heart". Emotional techniques are used by amateur hobby dancers in order to attract other dancers' interest. In that sense we might suggest that the emotional imperative—at times involving regulation—serves to create and maintain an illusion of tango as a strongly emotional world.

As follows from this discussion, there are rewards for those dancers who manage to embody and respond to the imperative. However, this is not the same as saying that reward-oriented actions are staged and hence "fake", rhyming poorly with a person's "inner feelings". On the contrary, the process of becoming a tango dancer involves embodying certain emotional performances and makes them a natural part of dancing the tango. This might be exemplified by the "as-if" practice sometimes taught by dance teachers. Staging a feeling, for instance nostalgia, can make the dancer "feel" nostalgic. Those dancers who perform a sad face might actually more easily connect with the nostalgic feelings expressed in the tango music (cp. Bergman Blix 2010). Much like the incorporating of particular dance movements and postures, emotionality should partly be understood as an embodied process. This implies that advanced dancers have embodied a legitimate and rewarding kind of emotionality. This implies that the transmittance of certain feelings comes "naturally" and, moreover, that they are experienced as natural by other dancers. Hence, the analytical distinction between emotional sensations and performances blurs. In addition, we might conclude that dancers, most of the time and for various reasons, engage at different stages of an emotional spectrum. In one and the same dance set dancers might engage in an emotional play, consciously staging rewarding feelings, and a minute later be engrossed in an unreflective bodily response to a shift in the music.

TANGO AUTHENTICITY

One aspect of symbolic capital in tango is related to authenticity. Most tango-dancing communities establish distinctions between dancers, clubs, teachers, dance schools, outfits and manners in relation to a perceived connection with the cultural roots of tango and a deep embodiment of the dancing. Travels to Argentina must be related to the significance of such values. As one humorous comment on the Swedish webpage Tangoportalen suggests, the trip functions as a future tango credential in the dancers' home community: "What they say: 'I have been to Buenos Aires'. What they mean: 'my value as a human being is greater than yours'". Technique classes and late-night dancing in the Argentine *milongas* are not only joys for the present; they also create values for use back home.

Authenticity is performed partly in the form of a particular aesthetic. Certain looks and body styles are simply rewarding due to the fact that they transmit cultural heritage. This is particularly true in the context of tango tourism and the ways in which certain "Argentine looks" might attract attention among foreign dancers. When it comes to physical appearance, the racialized expectations involve hair and eye color, but also "outer" attributes such as particular clothing and haircuts acknowledged as "Argentine". Among men a classic well-dressed *milonguero* style includes black trousers and a well-ironed shirt, black or white; for women a dress or a skirt, sometimes with a slit, together with the characteristic high-heeled tango shoes. Among the younger tango crowd a rougher urban style represents a trend noticeable during my field-work, equally associated with "genuine Argentine tango". For men, this style includes a long hair in a ponytail or topknot together with sports clothing. For women a softer leisure style involves low-cut baggy trousers and tank tops, exposing tattoos and piercings, at times combined with flat-heeled dancing shoes. The typical expressions of these aesthetics are primarily adopted and reshaped by teachers and dance performers who wish to create symbolic value and attract dancers to their dance schools. However, regular dancers, not least temporary dance tourists, also normally adopt some of these aesthetics, be it a slit skirt or, as for most dancers (both men and women), a refined interest in the selection and variety of tango shoes. On a regular dance-floor in Buenos Aires, however, one will find these styles mixed up with those of both male and female dancers who appear in jeans and t-shirts, as they stop by the *milonga* after work for a glass of wine and a dance.

Authenticity also involves the adoption of appropriate *milonga* manners and dancing styles, together with linkages to the past. This is what makes age a potential resource, at least for a certain group of Argentine men.[17] Dance couples made up of men in their sixties and seventies and women in their twenties and thirties attract attention, particularly when non-dancing people make contact with the tango. This is partly because of the symbolic significance provided and presumably transmitted by the *milongueros*, older Argentine dancers, supposed to be more routine dancers as well as gentlemen, known for their cultural knowledge, compliments and charm. This is how one Canadian tango tourist in Buenos Aires explains the key to the seductiveness of older Argentine *milongueros*.

> Interestingly, the average age of the *Porteño Milonguero* is about 70, and they all dance wonderfully. One gets a range of good, great and superlative dances here. No bad ones, as older *Porteño milongueros* are musically driven and not given to fancy shmancy stuff, although they do leave plenty of room for adornment on the follower's part. Laura and I decided that they all kind of look the same. Grey/whitish

hair, ample pot belly, Dark pants and button down collar shirt (short or long sleeved), or in a suit, same hairdo. Good sense of humor. First question is always "de donde 'sos?" (Where are you from?)[18]

Moreover, age represents a link with tango history, with places and people perceived as authentic in tango. Hence, providing personal histories from the past creates an interest among other dancers. This is expressed in an interview with the star dancers Gabriel Angio and Natalia Games, who claim to be "nostalgic" about the era in which they made contact with the tango. The nineties were, according to Natalia, "wonderful, because 80% were older people [. . .] and they lived through the age of the glory of tango. That is why we feel nostalgic about it. [. . .] They had experienced the *prácticas*. In other words, the places where men got together to dance and compete." (*El Tangauta*, February 2012: 34)

Just like sex and money, however, authenticity is a dubious credential which requires a perfect ear for the culture as well as for up-and-coming trends. Those dancers who exaggerate the expression of Argentine culture through particular clothing and body styles risk ending up being stamped as "clichés" or "fakes". In addition, those Argentine dancers who are identified as carriers of authentic tango might face exoticization and objectification. There are occasions when Argentine men and women experience the negative consequences of a racialized authenticity discourse. Argentine Martin has been involved in several romantic relations with foreign women he met through tango and describes one of the dangers connected with such affairs in terms of an exoticizing objectification.

Martin: At times I felt this with some foreign women. Like "here I have a dark-skinned (un morocho) Argentino Latin-Americano, a Carlito Gardel". No. (Martin, 58-year-old, Argentina)
Maria: How did this make you feel?
Martin: I felt like an exhibition [. . .] that I was showcased like an exotic thing, an object. But it didn't hurt me that much. [. . .] When I felt that, that she showed me off like a monkey, I said well, this is not a real relationship.

In that sense, the glorification of Argentine heritage in terms of a partly racialized aesthetic and manner is ambiguous. The worshiping of Argentine expression—particularly in the tourists' home dancing communities, as for instance during the visit of a touring Argentine dancing couple—creates a hierarchy between different ways of performing geographic anchoring and cultural belonging, through which certain bodies and body styles are rewarded if performed in a modified way. However, the experiences of the Argentine dancer Martin illustrate that the praise of cultural difference often plays side by side with an objectifying essentialism. In line with the work of Laura Ann Stoller (2002), Paula Ebron (2002) and Lena Sawyer

(2006) regarding the racial production of Africa as an exotic and uncivilized continent, this chapter suggests that those counterarguments serving to "upgrade" Latin America at times reproduce colonial categorizations and reinscribe Argentina as a unified place and people.

Exoticizing the Tourist

The impact of symbolic values such as "looks", sexual charisma and exotic attributes are at times associated with authenticity values, particularly when ascribed to Argentine dancers. There are, however, also certain tourists who attract interest due to their "exotic" appearances and manners, not least foreign women in their twenties to fifties. For instance, embodying and performing a Japanese look or a blond Scandinavian femininity attracts attention among certain local dancers. Just as an "Argentine" look might be sexualized by certain tango tourists, a "foreign" appearance is at times romanticized—or even sexualized. Linn, a 21-year-old Swedish dancer who came to the Argentine tango schools with her tango dancing mother and actually had no initial interest in tango, states that the Argentine teachers—especially male teachers—were curious about her. "All these people asked me about everything, they could tell that I was not from there, from Buenos Aires. I am blond and Swedish and that was interesting to them. So they convinced me to try out the tango and before going home I was absolutely hooked" (Linn, 21-year-old, Sweden/Argentina). Today she is living in Buenos Aires, working as a dance teacher in that same tango school. She is also involved in a love relationship with one of the Argentine teachers. In Sonia Abadi's book on the Argentine *milonga*, the author—herself an Argentine tango dancer and psychologist—notices a similar interest as Linn accounts for. Not only are tourists excited about Argentine dancers, locals are also "charmed" by the visitors. . According to a heterosexualized tango narrative, Abadi describes a resident-visitor dance-floor encounter in the following way:

> The man from Buenos Aires is totally charmed when he gets to embrace a blond woman who is dancing silently because of the emotions stirred up in her or perhaps because of her lack of vocabulary, but ready to engage fully with the fifteen minutes of madness and exoticism. (Abadi 2003: 44, my translation)

Implicit in Abadi's description is not primarily the impact of an exoticized "look", but rather the foreigner's innocent charm, typical for newcomers and outsiders. The "emotions stirred up" in "blond women" are here portrayed as "charming" Argentine men. According to some dancers, we might in fact understand the reciprocal interest between Argentine and tourist dancers as a response to a mutual kind of exoticism. As the Swedish dancer Elin reflects: "Both parts have something to win. I got this feeling that there are those older *porteños* who are trying to deliver the tourist fantasy, an imaginary of what Argentines are like and a promise of happiness. But it is equally something very exotic about all those Europeans who come over [to Buenos Aires] because of a cultural art form" (Elin, 35-year-old, Sweden). Some Argentine dancers even attribute part of the fascination with tango life in Buenos Aires to the streams of tourists. The mixed *milongas* with equal shares of Argentines and tourists open up the world internationally. The Argentine dance-halls and cafés have become places not only where foreigners can meet "real Argentine" dancers, but also where Argentines can make friends with people from other parts of the world. A few men declare that the encounters with tourists are "fun" situations for romance and flirting, because an adventure with a temporary visitor is time-limited and hence "make[s] things less complicated" (Allan, 24-year-old, Argentina). Everyday conversations with Argentine dancers demonstrate that women on a two-week visit are at times viewed as more sexually accessible than Argentines. This is reflected in the following discussion between Argentine Allan and North-American Steve and Monique.

Monique:	Some men from here love dancing with foreigners, that's what they live for. (Monique, 56-year-old, U.S./Argentina)
Steve:	Why? Because they are the only people they will get to dance with. (Steve, 58-year-old, U.S./Argentina)
Monique:	[. . .] Tango is a three-minute-long love affair and it is as if they had a love affair with women from all these different countries. That's like bragging about your lovers.
Allan:	[. . .] My friends ask me, ok tango, tell me about it, you will get to know so many women. And you can meet so many people from different countries. [. . .] You have all these stereotypes and for me, I am South-American, if I start to think about the females from Europe I'm going to think oh yeah, it's a very pretty woman, very attractive. We're going to take a coffee and then we're going to get laid bla bla. And maybe they think the same about South-Americans, they are such good lovers, they are so fascinating bla bla. Maybe if you have this image you transmit it to tango and think oh these dancers are going to hug me and treat me like no other guy in this world . . . Maybe they have this fantasy. That's the reason why they come here, to look for that. (Allan, 24-year-old, Argentina)
Monique:	Everybody wins in that respect, there's nothing wrong with it.

Allan's account of the mutual heterosexual interest between Argentine men and European women—romantically and dance-wise—stresses that it is possibly easier for some tourists to get to dance in Buenos Aires than at home. They are temporary players both on the dance scene and on the romantic market. This is what some tango tourists claim when reflecting upon their dancing situation in Argentina. Swedish Magdalena, for instance, notes that "I got to dance so much more, they were very keen on inviting" (Magdalena, 50-year-old, Sweden). Perhaps, she adds, this has to do with her being a tourist and a foreigner. Although often feeling "invisible" within Swedish dancing communities, she became visible in Argentina, partly because of her different looks and behavior, she says. Steve states that some Argentine dancers are happy to dance with foreigners "because they are the only people they will get to dance with". This suggests that foreigners are appreciated not (only) for their exotic "looks", but rather for their willingness to dance, particularly with Argentine dancers. This might be explained as partly a consequence of the tourists' limited stay and their wish to dance their holiday weeks away and partly a result of their being away from their home community and hence faced with less risk when dancing with partners below or beyond their level. From this it follows that once a tourist has become part of everyday Argentine life and a frequent visitor at the *milongas*, she or he might lose the aura and innocent charms of a "first-timer". One North-American dancer who has been in Buenos Aires five times, Beth, states that the interest from local dancers has "cooled down" over the years. In response to the obligatory questions ("Where are you from?" and "Is this your first time to Buenos Aires?") she no longer gives the timid answers that barely conceal the curiosity and fascination typical for newcomers. As she puts it herself, she might have become "used up" as a tourist—and still not integrated enough to pass as an Argentine woman (Beth-52, year-old, U.S.).

CONCLUSION: EMBODYING THE TANGO ECONOMY

What does it take to live within the tango economy? Who do the dancers become once they embody the logic of the game? What are the stakes? And for whom do the costs implicit in the accessing of potential rewards become too high?

The *homo tanguerus*, a pleasure-maximizing individual who embodies the tango *illusio* and the logic of the economy, is caught up not in a play of free choice but rather in enforced choice-making. The particular distribution of dance partners implies a constant presence of potential rejection and exclusion. In fact, tango is characterized by the constant threat of devaluation. The implicit uncertainty and evaluation processes evoke similarities between the tango world and what Zygmunt Bauman and other sociologists sketch as typical for late-modern intimacy. In his book *Liquid Love*, Bauman deciphers a culture of intimate relations represented by fluid affections and a consumption rationale according to which people search for "the best deal" and quick fixes—meaning physical and emotional connection with clear exits (Bauman 2003: 5–13; cp. Beck 2000; Illouz, 2007). In short, he argues that this culture encourages people to apply the same logic to their emotional and romantic lives that leads to boredom with clothes and objects that are not worn out but phased out by new fashion trends. Encountering resistance or a better catch is what makes people give up on their relations. In his terminology, this phenomenon occurs along a distinction between desire and love; he claims that long-term commitments have been phased out for a restless desire (the craving for a new pair of shoes or a more fulfilling sex partner).

This, we might argue, is a useful framework for approaching the social structuring of tango. In fact, it is possible to approach tango as an example of the individualization of intimate life. Although the tango appears as a conservative culture structured with rules from the past century, the complexity of the economy entails flexibility. The logic and terminology is that of connection—and disconnection. This rhymes well with Bauman's reasoning; he writes: "people speak ever more often (aided and abetted by the learned advisors) of connections, of 'connecting' or being 'connected'". But just like some tango dancers, he asks: "What are the merits of the language of 'connectedness' that are missed by the language of 'relationships'?" (Bauman 2003: xi). Tango is an area in which each individual is in charge of her or his own rewards and failures and in which dancers face a high degree of uncertainty. The *milonga* is made up of a stream of individual choices in which dancers negotiate their own and other dancers' preferences, dancing styles and level of recognition and credentials. The advantages of the specific social milieu are portrayed not only in terms of what is offered (dance connection and intimate encounters), but also in terms of what is easy to avoid: long-term commitments and the caring responsibilities associated with such relations. Kate, a 38-year-old dancer from the U.S., claims that one of the strengths of tango is that you never get bored. The constant stream of partners assures continuous surprises. "The beauty of the tango is that the honeymoon never ends, you just shift the partner. It does end sometimes, because you see someone dancing and you think oh my god you're fabulous and then you dance with him and it doesn't measure up and you never dance with that person again but there are other people" (Kate, 38-year-old, U.S.). In addition, in order to create an endless "honeymoon" with constantly new embraces to discover, the dance economy—involving partner shifts as a means to move up within the relational chart—motivates the dancers to make further investments and sacrifices. The efforts put into tango are necessary for the experience to remain dynamic, i.e. for the dancers to be evaluated as attractive on the dance-floor and the "honeymoon" to continue. However, the economy and the dividing lines actually risk tearing the world apart as they become harmful to individual dancers and the social world as a whole.

Economy and Risk

Implicit in the concept of an economy is the idea that there are rewards as well as prices to be paid. In addition, an economy often contains winners and losers. In symbolic economies like the tango, partly organized around the lack of collectively agreed-upon "prices", the dancers enter the economy with different sets of credentials and with various predispositions for "playing the game". In contrast to the image of tango as a meditative dance through which the dancers neglect the gazes of the outer world, everyday life at the *milonga*—as described in this chapter—accounts for the hierarchies and social surveillance through which every step of the dancers is evaluated by other dancers. For some dancers the price of achieving recognition and dance-floor intimacy in such a world gets too high. Some dancers, Argentines and foreigners, decide to stop dancing because of the rigid hierarchies. They describe the community as a culture of fluid feelings which does not allow for "real love" or friendship bonds to grow strong. The people who give up on the tango for such reasons speak of the intimacy provided on the dance-floor as superficial and the emotional kicks as a means of simple recognition rather than building blocks of a community. This chapter suggests that the emotional risk-taking in tango puts at stake dancers' entire selves: their bodies, senses and self-understanding. The pursuit of recognition, ultimately a quest for human recognition and social belonging, implies an existential dimension as it creates a sense of one's *reason for existence* (Bourdieu 1990: 240; cp. Galli 2012: 16). In that sense the risks in tango are not primarily about the physical pain or death caused by falling down a mountain, as in other kinds of tourism elaborating with risk (although dancers at times fear for their lives as they are being pulled around the dance-floor, particularly female beginners in high-heeled shoes). Rather, the risks involve the facing and managing of emotional and social downfalls, particularly devastating in an honor culture such as the tango.

The accounts in this chapter suggest that the fall is strikingly harder on some dancers. This might be illustrated by the emotional outbursts occurring in many of the interviews I conducted, particularly among female tango tourists. Some women started crying during our conversations; other interview situations involved intense, aggressive outbursts over the ways in which the social world of tango functions. Many informants expressed a passionate relation to tango as an art form—the dancing and the music— but an ambiguous relation to the social world, including the hierarchies and conservative modes of conduct. Some dancers told stories of how they had been subject to constant rejections, how former dance partners abandoned them for a younger "acrobatic" woman and how the tango repeatedly led to heartbreak because the level of intimacy and the constant partner shifts make long-term commitment difficult. Daniella, for instance, explained that to protect herself, she allowed her skin to get tougher and tougher every year. For some dancers the emotional state evoked by tango, and especially tango in Buenos Aires, became difficult and harmful to the point that they looked for avenues out of it. Some described tourist trips outside the capital, visits to Argentine museums and activities disconnected from tango as important outlets that prevented them from "go[ing] crazy" (Irene, 61-year-old, U.S.).

Following the discussions in this chapter, it is not a coincidence that the emotional outbursts occurred in interviews with western middle-aged women, whereas the male tourists and Argentine dancers I encountered during my field-work expressed a more relaxed relation to tango. In the terms of this chapter, this suggests that the nature of the intimate economy and the logic of the game make certain dancers more vulnerable than others. Using the vocabulary of the economy itself we might conclude that those dancers who lack tango credentials have a hard time, particularly those who have invested a great deal of time and emotional engagement in the dancing and who feel that they "merit" more than what they get. One group which experiences shortcomings within the economy is women who do not play along with the (hetero)romantic game, out of their own will or because other dancers do not recognize them as romantic subjects (due to looks, age, sexual accessibility, their willingness to flirt etc.) As discussed in this chapter, age appears to be a decisive category within the bodily dance economy which partly comes with different consequences for women (devaluating) and men (possibly valuating). The older so-called *milongueros,* male Argentine dancers, are perceived, particularly by certain tourist women, as potential carriers of authenticity values. In the heteroromantic economy of tango, women, on the other hand, experience that the function of sexual capital (involving looks, charm and flirting) turns aging into a process which devaluates them as dancers. For women, the body is not only the subjective condition for dancing, but also an adornment which generates—and possibly degenerates—aesthetic and sexual values. This is even more striking in relation to those western women who are no longer appreciated for their exotic looks and sexual accessibility. Whereas seventy-year-old Argentine women are potentially perceived as carriers of tradition, culture and refined dancing skills, many European and North-American women of that age face difficulties at the *milonga*, at home as well as on tango holiday in Buenos Aires.[19] In that sense we might conclude that different kinds of values or credentials are differently important—and differently achievable—for different groups of dancers: authenticity credentials are more important for male dancers, whereas women are more dependent on their position in relation to a heterosexual game.

In some ways the framing of the intimate dance economy actually gives the impression that the tango is a man's world. As previously mentioned, the actual gender structure of the *milonga*—in Argentina and elsewhere–, with its higher proportion of women, provides men with a greater value and larger degree of choice, due to their being a scarce resource. Also, the heterosexualized play in tango ascribes agency and potency to men, as they are supposed to introduce gallantry and play the role of the formal initiator in the asking-up-procedure. In the traditional framing, women are required to wait for men to offer them dances and recognition. As a matter of fact, even the *verso*, the compliment in the heterosexualized tango play, seems to make women vulnerable rather than strengthen them, as the gendered recognition in tango is bound up with certain appearances and actions. The *verso* can be taken back if a woman does not live up to the promises implicit in the compliment. Still, as follows from the discussion in this chapter, the tango economy is layered and nuanced, and not simply a matter of gender.

Despite the competitiveness, however, the economy still functions as a cohesive structure which keeps the dancers together. The dance economy and the tango hierarchies make up an embodied—and emotionalized—social structure which the dancers (those who choose to continue dancing) learn to act within and move along. We might also notice that although the *milongas* contain examples of "shortcuts" and dancing "beyond" what dancers "ought to merit", the economy and the tango hierarchies convey a notion of meritocratic justice. And although the tango makes room for explanatory narratives based on genius, charisma, chemistry and dance magic, the many rules actually support the idea of a justified tango order in which the dancers receive what they have warranted. The belief in the value of tango dancing is generated in relation to the striving to reach perfection in the execution of an art form. Within such a framing, the hierarchies and dividing lines might be approached as visible expressions and marks of dance commitment and tango sacrifice. In addition, the many formal and informal rules, together with the strict dancing hierarchies, create a sense of exclusivity. The *milonga* is an open space for anyone to enter; becoming a member of the social and emotional world, however, is a process which the dancers are required to merit. The economy, generating bodily and mental hardship, involving dance training and the managing of dance-floor rejections, constitutes the basis for such an embodied membership.

4 Voyages out of the Ordinary

INTRODUCTION

In previous chapters we have approached tango voyagers from the perspective of their strong emotional and bodily investment with tango dancing. In the present chapter we will frame dancers' sense-making of tango from the angle of a dance journey to Buenos Aires. As will be discussed throughout this book, the tourist context adds layers of meaning to the tango-dancing experience. In addition, when travelling to Buenos Aires in search of the Argentine tango, dancers are no longer "only" dancers but also tourists and are forced to engage with a conflicting field of travelling, involving a set of identities and practices revolving around the holiday experience together with the interests of an expanding global tourist industry. This chapter aims at theorizing the aspirations ascribed to these voyages. We will situate the journeys within the cultural contours of tango, primarily referring back to the meaning system and symbolic values discussed in the previous two chapters. In doing so, we will inquire into the values and qualities associated with the travels. What are the expectations and driving forces associated with a journey to Argentina?

We should be careful to note, however, that this chapter is about the aspirations associated with a voyage to Buenos Aires. This is to say that the expectations explored in the following sections are not necessarily descriptions of what the travelers actually do once they reach Argentina. It is actually quite common that the holiday aspirations differ from lived holiday experience. We might claim that most leisure travelling departs from a number of expectations linked with recreational aims, cultural objectives or relational motives, such as strengthening family bonds. These are, so to speak, the reasons which motivate people to travel across the world. What these people actually do during their vacation—how the holiday turns out—however, might match these expectations or dramatically deviate from them. Typical for the expectations bound to a journey is the positive framing, stressing the promises of a certain place or a particular holiday activity, whereas the lived holiday normally involves negative aspects, or at least some disillusionment. This suggests that the accounts referred to in this chapter should not be read as proof that tango tourism actually equals a voyage out of the ordinary, offering radical breaks with dancers' everyday life or the restraints associated with late-modern societies. As we will move on, later in this book, to some of the everyday practices in tango tourism, we will find examples showing that the dance holidays at times actually take the form of a voyage into the ordinary. The limited focus of this chapter serves to lay ground for such forthcoming discussions, primarily targeting the negotiated values and identities at stake in tango tourism.[1] This implies that an analysis of objectives and motives ascribed to a particular journey must be related to the cultural worlds inside which they are meaningful and possibly also rewarding. From such a perspective, we can notice that certain aspirations are more or less neglected when the tango tourists speak about the motives behind their journeys. Sexual aspirations and the striving to achieve tango recognition through travel to Buenos Aires are, for instance, normally not addressed by the dancers—although such elements might be relevant during their actual holiday visit. As will be discussed in more detail in Chapters 8 and 10, this can be explained by returning to the practical reason implicit in the world of tango dancing as well as by a "disturbing" associative tie between the intimate tango voyages and other kinds of intimacy tourism.

Following from this general discussion, we will explore four themes in relation to which the main values in tango tourism are discussed. As will be shown, the intimate voyagers in this study have greater aspirations than merely enjoying life at the Argentine *milonga*. In this chapter, the motives ascribed to Argentine dance journeys will be framed in terms of a quest for authenticity, an existential adventure characterized by intimate encounters, an educational and artistic exploration and an emotionally charged voyage.

A QUEST FOR AUTHENTICITY

Among certain groups of tourists the holiday aspirations are intimately bound up with a search for so-called genuine experiences. The quest for authenticity might in fact shape entire voyages, involving choices of where to stay (avoiding fancy hotels and "touristy" areas), what to eat (local dishes at local restaurants), which souvenirs and memories to consume (non-commercial items, personal anecdotes), which people to engage with (locals, preferably outside the tourist sector) etc. (Maoz 2007). When it comes to tango voyages to Buenos Aires, the search for genuine experiences is foregrounded in the dancers' own framing of their objectives. One particular aim is to connect with Argentine culture. Among dance voyagers, Argentina represents a space not only for pursuing carefree dancing excitements, like those to which certain tourist agencies allude in their advertisements, but also for exploring a passionate interest. In fact, the creation of Buenos Aires as the city of tango revolves around its implicit function as a transformative stage to pass through, a ritualized place for dancers who wish to make a deeper connection with tango. Besides a wish to develop dancing skills and have "magic moments" out in the clubs, some visitors actually travel to Buenos Aires with a desire to experience the difficulties bound up with "real" Argentine tango life. As Swedish Daniella puts it, most dancers who have become "passionate tango addicts" are curious to encounter the city of origin, the Mecca of tango and its contemporary scene.

> I believe that if you go to Buenos Aires it's because you have been hit by the big tango passion. I don't think people go there unless they are really, like really hooked on tango, if you're hooked you want to see the origin, at least once. I have a hard time taking those people serious who have been dancing tango for ten fifteen years without ever being in Buenos Aires. If I would be a karate woman I would want to visit Japan. Although the boiling pot is spreading throughout Europe [. . .] it's still Argentine tango. So you want to go there. I was so curious to experience tango in Buenos Aires, to get to see how it all works out there, how people dance, what kind of attitude they have towards tango. [. . .] I was eager to experience all that, the real stuff. (Daniella, 50-year-old, Sweden)

As Daniella puts it, Argentine tango is almost made synonymous with a place—Argentina—"so you want to go there". Experiencing "the origin" and "the real stuff" involves discovering the routines of the *milongas*, "how people dance" and the "attitude" towards tango in its home country. Like Daniella, various dancers acknowledge that authenticity involves various aspects. The significance linked to certain *places* is crucial. Visiting those Argentine cafés and dance-halls in which people have been dancing for decades is viewed as a means to make contact with authentic values. The journeys pave the way for accessing those *emotions* and *ambiances* constructed as typically Argentine and tied to Argentine tango, such as the sentimentality expressed in the tango lyrics and the musical pulse believed to exist also in everyday street-life. Authenticity is also associated with the notion of cultural heritage and is believed to be transmitted by certain *people*. Visiting dancers wish to encounter contemporary tango through the company and dancing experiences of local Argentine dancers. For Daniella, the Argentine *abrazo*—the dance embrace provided by local dancers—is in fact one reason for travelling to Buenos Aires.

Similar to the fact that I wanted to go to Buenos Aires, I wanted to dance with Argentine dancers, primarily because I have experienced that when I am dancing with Argentines I get to feel that real *abrazo* [tango dance embrace]. I haven't experienced that with just anyone, at least not anyone who is not trained in an Argentine way. I was out of words. On several occasions I have been out of words when I have entered into that embrace and positioned oneself before starting to dance. [. . .] You are pulled into an *abrazo* which is so comfortable and yet soft and musical. [. . .] I guess they have that from the childhood. [. . .] That's just the way it is. They have seen the embrace within a role model, a father or a grandmother. There is a straightening-up in that *abrazo*. Even if you're dancing with a really advanced European dancer it's not the same. I want to dance with the local men. I get really excited when they ask me up to dance. Because I am coming home in that kind of dancing. I felt it already the first time when I was there [Buenos Aires], when I could hardly dance. Like wow, this is how it is supposed to feel, like divine. [. . .] This is also what all people are talking about. It's actually a bit of a cliché. The embrace is the primary technical thing when you go to Buenos Aires to dance tango. (Daniella, 50-year-old, Sweden)

In Daniella's account, the Argentine dancers mark their particularity by their way of dancing, and particularly by their way of engaging in the tango embrace. Already as a beginning dancer, Daniella realized that "this is how it is supposed to feel": a reason for going back to Buenos Aires and search for those dancing encounters with local men which will possibly make her "feel that real *abrazo*". Implicit in the authenticity quest ascribed to the journeys is the stressing of a particular Argentine-ness, as in the accounts of an Argentine way of dancing, of embracing another dancer, of embodying the culture etc. Inscribing difference in places and people is an element in many streams of tourism, not least in dance voyages aiming for the origin of a particular art form. As in the salsa (Urquía 2004) and African dancing (Sawyer 2006), ethnic and racial assumptions help to shape what most dancers refer to as *Argentine* tango. The creation of Argentina and Buenos Aires as the origin and vibrant heart of tango involves stories of "blood", used as a metaphor by both visiting dancers and residents to impose cultural belonging and authenticity. Chicho Frumboli, a recognized Argentine tango performer and dance teacher known for having developed a characteristic dancing style in the tradition of *nuevo tango*, himself having moved to France, states the following when a journalist from one of Buenos Aires' tango magazines rhetorically asks him if "tango is the most Argentine thing one could do": "Absolutely. Tango puts you in relation with the Argentine history and culture. When I am dancing, I am transferred to places and times when I didn't live myself. I think it's in the blood" (*Tanguata, BsAs*, July 2007).

Although most practitioners believe that tango is primarily about the intimate dance communication and musicality—wherever in the world the dancing takes place—the same kind of cultural essentialism expressed by Frumboli is often present in tango tourists' objectives for undertaking a journey to Argentina. As Daniella suggests, one aim is to experience the tango through Argentine dancers, "the real stuff". Local dancers are often perceived as being born with the tango, meaning with the right mindset, bodily comportment, manner and emotionality, and are hence targeted by international guests who deem them capable of transmitting authenticity.

"Argentines dance with a natural passion, while Americans dance with a borrowed one", as one North-American dancer puts it (in Viladrich 2005: 541). At other times, the distinctiveness is described as a matter of cultural belonging and linguistic closeness to the poetry which opens up and deepens the impact of the tango. This is how Annie, a North-American woman in Buenos Aires on "tango vacation", describes her wish to experience the company of Argentine dancers.

> First of all it's the culture. They understand the music better because it's part of their lives. They understand the lyrics, that's the second thing. Sometimes the texts are really sad, someone broke up with someone or killed someone. They can interpret the music and put it in their steps. [. . .] I notice this when I dance with some Argentines and then some Americans, because they [Americans] have no "suck" [laughter]. I didn't get to dance a lot but with this Argentine guy he absolutely created a different atmosphere than people from here [San Francisco] would do it. I don't know how to tell you, it's all about the breathing, the connection (Annie, 54-year-old, U.S.)

Like Daniella, Annie frames her voyage to Buenos Aires in relation to the dancing experience with Argentine dancers. She speaks of American dancers as lacking that particular "suck", which creates an emotional intensity in the tango encounter. In Annie's account, part of the genuine touch originates in more vague factors, such as Argentine dancers' way of creating "an atmosphere", their "breathing" and way of "connecting". In fact, the magic "it" is "all about" these unexplainable embodied features, according to Annie. From the accounts in this section we might conclude that tango voyages are associated with authenticity, primarily relating to the historic and cultural framing of Buenos Aires as well as expectations linked to Argentine dancers as transmitters of deep tango knowledge.

EDUCATIONAL AND ARTISTIC EXPLORATION

The previous two chapters suggest that one aspect of the journeys is related to the *educational and artistic objectives* important in tango. For many dancers, the ideal of becoming a "fine" tango dancer involves rigorous dance training, cultural immersion and developing of artistic expression. Due to the belief structure of tango, with its imperative of constant progress, many dancers are keen to free up time to focus specifically on their dancing. The best holiday site for such educational aspirations is still believed to be Buenos Aires. The city is known for hosting the best tango dancers in the world and being the basis for some of the most influential tango schools and pedagogies. Moreover, there is an enormous selection and broad variety of schools and private dance teachers encompassing different dancing styles, levels and pedagogical devices. North-American Susanna, who went to Buenos Aires for a three-week stay, states that she was eager to develop her dancing. Although the Argentine *milongas* provided exciting experiences, she was mostly focused on "taking lessons" in order to "improve" her tango.

> It's very challenging, you always want to get better. Many times I just wanted to quit because I felt that there was no progress. There is always room to get better, to do more things. I had only been dancing for eight nine months when I got the opportunity to go there [Buenos Aires] and I just wanted to take as many classes as possible and experience what the tango was all about where people supposedly know how to do it well. Once I got there I started to do what I had to do. I was taking lessons, trying to improve my skill of dancing tango. Of course I wanted to experience the *milonga* but I primarily wanted to take lessons. (Susanna, 50-year-old, U.S.)

Tango dancers like Susanna travel to Argentina partly because of their deep investment in the tango and their aspiration to further deepen their *connaissance*. Dancers like Susanna wish to spend their days taking dance classes at various schools and with various dance teachers and spend their nights practicing the tango out in the Argentine *milongas*. In that sense dance journeys might be fused to a broader set of educational journeys with the aim of integrating learning processes within the recreational tourism experience. In the broader reach of education tourism—seemingly an expanding area of travel—we find examples such as language schools, ecotourism (Ritchie 2003) and journeys to battlefields or slave-castles to gain knowledge on certain aspects of history (Cohen 2011; Mowatt and Chancellor 2011). For some dancers, the educational element of the journey actually represents the promise of a voyage out of the ordinary. Accumulating a deeper knowledge of tango is conceived of as paving the way for a time-out-of-time existence. Refined dancing technique and deepened cultural connection are believed to take dancers to new levels of dance flow and tango bliss.

The non-formal character of tango knowledge, however, imposes certain conditions on the learning process. Dancing itself is mainly a bodily and sensual practice; moreover, tango is often spoken of in terms of a "sentiment". This suggests that the educational aspirations of a tango journey to Buenos Aires are not only associated with the high quality of dance teachers and tango schools, but target a variety of experiences. For instance, the city itself is believed to transmit knowledge and cultural connection. Some dancers perceive just being in Argentina, breathing the air and walking some of the famous avenues, as a means of realizing their educational aspirations. Others combine their tango classes with Spanish lessons and use their dance holiday to improve their language skills. Some dancers frame this within the tango context, suggesting that knowledge in the Spanish language is a means to connect with the culture (through poetry and everyday conversations with Argentines). In addition, many foreign dancers have developed an interest not only in Argentine tango culture but in Argentine history at large, including the country's past and contemporary history. This might be exemplified by a monthly German tango magazine, the *Tangodanza*, which offers not only a dance and events calendar for Germany and Europe, but also articles on Argentine politics and contemporary history. Visiting historical and political sites is perceived as a way of deepening the level of tango knowledge. As Lasse—who stresses his "solidarity" with the Argentine people—puts it, tango in Buenos Aires is fuelled with politics.

Lasse: In Argentina, politics and life is one with the tango. We don't find that here [Sweden]. That's why it becomes another kind of dancing. (Lasse, 58-year-old, Sweden)
Maria: Like what? What about it?
Lasse: Here [Sweden] it's a hobby, over there it's a lifestyle, a way of being. For them tango is an opportunity to express themselves artistically. To get it out, the economic hardships, the suffery. That's the big difference. The tango was formed during a time of misery. [. . .] Many [Swedish dancers] forget about the political aspects, they just see the dancing. But the political is in there, tango is political.

Lasse has been to Argentina three times and claims to have other motives besides dancing, in fact he tells that for everytime he travels to Buenos Aires he is less and less absorbed by the *milongas*. The educational prospects of his travelling stretches beyond "taking dance classes" and "visiting dance clubs", and partly targets the historical and political situation in the country. Still he frames this broader interest within a tango narrative, claiming a connection with "authentic tango" to involve a wider Argentine cultural and social context, "living tango the Argentine way".

EXISTENTIAL ADVENTURES

Tourism in general and tango tourism in particular are not only about accessing genuine cultures and particular sets of knowledge; they also aim towards subjective transformation and the accessing of more authentic selves (cp. Turner 1991). As Jonathan Skinner writes: "Tourism provides us with one of those 'fateful moments' (Giddens 1991: 112), a space and a time for both anxiety and opportunity, a point of transition during which reflexivity and attention to the self and focus upon self-actualization are heightened" (Skinner 2008: 339). Moreover, tango journeys might be conceptualized in terms of an existential endeavor, an aspiration to bring about subjective transformations and pave the way for new life trajectories. Let us start by returning to the conditions implied in the journeys. Voyages to Argentina are significant investments for many dancers, emotionally and economically. Most travelers stay for two weeks or more, some people for months. What inspires some of them to save money and take a month's leave from work is not only to make contact with the origin of tango, but also to connect with their "inner selves". One example of this is how Susanna makes sense of her travel to Buenos Aires and the fact that she "primarily wanted to take lessons". Dancing tango had taught her "things" about herself, aspects of her emotional life that she wished Argentine dancers would help her to work on.

> When you dance tango you start looking at yourself, the inside. I learnt things about me. One thing that I found out about me is that I am very insecure. I could not have anybody watch me. And because I was insecure I was tensing a lot, my right arm was always very rigid. I was falling off my axis, because the position of my body was totally wrong. So I took lessons [in Buenos Aires] not to learn patterns but basically to find out why I was tensing so much when I am dancing. (Susanna, 50-year-old, U.S.)

For other dancers the tango, and moreover tango life in Buenos Aires, represents a promise of a new life, or at least a radical break with their present life at home. For some, their passionate dancing interest is perceived as filling a gap in their lives, created by the end of a career or by children moving away from home. For still others, the bodily presence enabled through the tango is framed as a form of therapy which helps them process difficult feelings or a life crisis. For such dancers, a voyage to Buenos Aires represents a break from a gloomy or demanding everyday existence at home, a break from life itself. The tango, as a context for such a break, implies transformative promises, primarily through the intimate dancing experiences. Some tango travels take the form of ritualized journeys serving as symbolic passages to process a turn in life, be it the loss of a close relative or a failed marriage. For 63-year-old Ruth from San Francisco, the tango holiday came with a tragic backdrop. She states that she started dancing tango as an attempt to "get out of a dark place" in her life. She had just lost both her mother and her sister and had been laid off from work shortly before starting to dance tango. A therapeutic meaning was ascribed to the journey, which Ruth hoped would become an avenue for emotional recovery.

> I started dancing a year and a half ago and it was out of a very dark place that I was in my life. I had a few years before gone through a series of tragedies like my mother's death. I got laid off from my job ten days before my mother died and a year later my sister, my only sibling,

got killed in a car accident. [. . .] I needed something to take me out of myself and I started looking around what was out in town and I read about tango and I just showed up in my sneakers. [. . .] I'm in Buenos Aires, hoping to dance the darkness away. (Ruth, 63-year-old, U.S.)

For the Swedish dancer Magdalena, travelling to Buenos Aires became a symbolic journey ritualizing a transition in age. As she puts it herself, she wished to make the year she turned fifty "worth remembering". To my question of why she decided to go to Buenos Aires, she answered: "I wanted to travel to the Mecca of tango, to put my feet on that ground and find out what it is all about. [. . .] I had put up a goal. The year I turned fifty I would go to Buenos Aires. And this is what happened, it became my first trip. I wanted to do something that would really make this year worth remembering" (Magdalena, 50-year-old, Sweden). Swedish Linn explains the drawing power of Buenos Aires, an exotic faraway place, in relation to her hard years in a ballet school. "It was so different, so far from home. And I needed a break, I wanted to try out something new because I had been at this ballet school for long and it was really hard towards the end" (Linn, 21-year-old, Sweden/Argentina).

INTIMACY TOURISM

Other dancers emphasize that the intimate dimension in tango provides the transformative capacities of these journeys. As states Daniella and Annie in the previous quotes, the Argentine dancers transmit flow and presence ("the suck", according to Annie) and a sense of "coming home", with the words of Daniella. Drawing on such accounts, tango tourism might be approached as a kind of intimacy tourism, involving proximate body-to-body communication and at times romantic promises. Like other intimate voyagers, such as sex tourists and the coach surfers in Paula Bialski's study of so-called "intimate tourism" (2008; 2012)[2], travelers such as Daniella and Annie wish to experience intimate connections through close bodily tango encounters, preferably with Argentine dancers. In addition some dancers stress the playing with gender roles during their dance vacation. One example of this is provided in the documentary movie *Taxidancing* (2012) in which we encounter Susan, a British dancer in her late fifties. As the viewer encounters her for the first time she is sensually putting on a pair of tights and some make-up, explaining that: "A woman likes to feel that she is perfect when she goes to the dance-floor. The lipstick has to match of course." As we later on find her on the street, waving for a taxi, a man—possibly a local acquaintance—calls for her attention: "looking good, where are you going?", "to the *milonga*", she proudly responds. Dressed up in an elegant sleeveless dress and with her high heels in a shoe-bag, she tells: "For six years I've kept coming here [to Buenos Aires], four months every winter I come here. I come here to enjoy the warmth and to dance tango." The personal background to Susan's travelling is partly the lack of physical intimacy, particularly during her childhood. She recalls how her father and other family members kept a bodily distance towards her and each other. She explains this as possibly "British" and a reason for why Europeans chose to go to Buenos Aires. "When you get older the physical intimacy, to be held, is even more important. Maybe that's why people come to Argentina to dance tango. To experience this wonderful warm embrace that they might never have had in their lives."

As Susan and other dancers report, the particular destination of the travel—"hot" Argentina–enable them to live out ideals of femininity and temporarily "become a woman" they do not connect with at home. For some women this implies embracing a particular aesthetic which allows for "sexy" dresses and high-heeled shoes, whereas for others the dance holiday is believed to provide a rather safe space for engaging in flirty situations—with men as well as with women—without being "[held] responsible" for their actions (Törnqvist 2010a: 60–62). Other dancers believe that Argentine men are better at respecting female dancers' various ways of dancing. As Irene from the U.S. states, American men at home are very critical and will argue publicly about a dance error, whereas she has heard that Argentine men are gentlemen who let go of mistakes and put on their charms to cover up for a misadventure (Irene, 61-year-old, U.S.). In popular narratives of female dance travelers—tango dancers and others—such (hetero)sexual undertones, are quite frequent.[3] For instance, the autobiographical book *Tango—An Argentine Love Story* recounts the history of a San Francisco–based journalist and tango dancer who is going through the traumatic breakup of a fifteen-year relationship, and decides to go to Buenos Aires to repair her broken heart. What was supposed to be a two-and-a-half-month stay turns out to be an intensive tango year. The back cover reads: "Camille Cusumano has lived out many a mid-life woman's fantasy: packing her bags, slit skirts, and tango shoes and spending a year in Argentina. The result is a memoir that is like the dance itself: smooth, absorbing, and erotically charged.—Laura Fraser, author of *An Italian Affair*" (Cusumano 2008).

Such accounts call for a gender perspective on so-called existential adventures. Whereas many scholars have addressed the dilemmas emerging from tourists' processing of selves in so-called exotic places (Coleman and Crang 2002; MacCannell 1976; Urry 1990), few have actually approached these dilemmas through a gendered lens. However, voyages out of the ordinary are endeavors in a gendered terrain. Whereas journeys to foreign countries traditionally have offered avenues for men to engage in a masculinity project revolving around potency and liberty (Nilsson 2012; Strain 2003), a new stream of adventure journeys seem to attract mainly women. Dance trips to Argentina, Cuba and West Africa might in fact be approached as examples of this trend.[4] As is often the case in the male version of such voyages, freedom is manifested not only through erotic endeavors, but often with additional features of staged power and domination (Strain 2003). As some of the accounts in this chapter suggest, this seems to be partly true also in the framing of an existential dance voyage. Drawing on an observation made by Simone de Beauvoir, we might actually acknowledge these voyages as departing from women's everyday lives in male-dominated societies. Travels to faraway places might be used as means to break away, not only from quotidian routines, but also from gendered structures. For many women, the gender norms imply a life entangled with constant struggles to balance family responsibilities and professional careers. As de Beauvoir writes, women in their fifties and upwards, being an important group of tango travelers, are—due to their changed family situation—actually more "rebellious" than younger women. They are free from intimate family bonds, free to explore the pleasures of life. She writes:

> Her restlessness takes on eccentric expressions. [...] The woman might for instance start putting an effort into realizing dreams from her childhood and youth before it is too late: one starts playing the piano again, another one begins to sculpt, others start writing, travelling, learning how to ski or study a foreign language. Everything that the woman has earlier on denied herself, she now decides to do, before it is too late. (de Beauvoir 1949/1995: 680)

We should note, though, that holiday travelling away from normative structures sometimes creates new kinds of dependency relations. As the rich literature on women's so-called romance tourism—or sex tourism—in the Global South suggests, what represents an emancipatory journey for one person might actually involve subordination and new dependency bonds for another person, as when wealthy western women pay for sex and romance in Third World zones (Sanchez Taylor 2006). The relation between gendered and class-related structures within the existential dance journeys to Buenos Aires will be discussed in more detail in Chapter 8 and Chapter 10.

EMOTIONAL EDGEWORK

One aspect, not only of dance journeys but travelling at large, is the emotional experiences that travelers hope will result from spatial and bodily dislocation. In fact, average tourist consumption targets not so much artifacts and souvenirs but culinary discoveries, plunging into crystal-clear water and spectacular vista points—i.e. emotionally and sensually striking experiences. Many travel agencies use an emotionally charged vocabulary when advertising their trips, such as marketing holiday destinations with promises of happy and harmonious visitors. For many tango tourists the emotional objectives of their journey are partly due to the privileged position of feelings in tango.

As discussed in Chapter 2, dancers are even using techniques to intensify the feelings in tango (the *as-if* exercise). The context of a foreign country adds layers of emotional tension to the intimate situations in tango. Travelling across an unknown city by night in order to enter a dimly lit dance-hall without friends and familiar dance-partners creates fear as well as pleasures, liberty as well as limitations. In addition, the mythology surrounding Argentina and its capital conjures up an atmosphere of adventure. As Anna-Lena, a Swedish dancer in her late fifties, comments: "Buenos Aires sounds so exciting and alluring. The name in itself is exciting" (Anna-Lena, 58-year-old, Sweden). In addition, travel to a faraway destination is believed to affect one's relational presence with others. Some dancers hope that the level of emotionality and the kind of intimate encounters accessible on the other side of the world will be fuelled through heart-to-heart dancing with local dance partners, the mythological magnetism emerging from the old cafés and dance-halls, the crowded and sweaty dance-floors as well as the streets and smog of the Argentine metropolis. They believe that the faraway location takes the thrill of anonymous dancing intimacy to a higher level. A voyage out of the ordinary, taking them far away from their home milieu and the people they normally define as close, is thought to intensify the feelings stirred up by tango (see Palmer 2006; Winter 2008). In fact, the weak social bonds and the easy exits are by some believed to intensify the intimate connection.

In that sense tango dancing, and especially tango dancing in a faraway context, becomes an arena for emotional risk management. Drawing on the definition of so-called "edgework" provided by Stephen Lyng, one of the main researchers within the field of adventure sports, we might approach some of the dance tourists as embodying a "desire to experience the uncertainties of the edge" (Lyng 2005: 4). In line with the concept of tourism as a break from everyday life, the attraction of the emotional vulnerability in tango is by some perceived as an escape from or resistance towards mainstream culture, "the institutional routines of contemporary life" (Lyng 2005: 5), making possible a "time-out-of-time" existence. This can also be described as a means to create flow, what the dance researcher Helena Wulff describes as "a peak point when action and consciousness blend" and when a "transcendental state" is brought about (2008: 526). The more vulnerable the dancer is, i.e. the more values she or he puts at stake, the more intense she or he hopes the actual dance experience will become. In fact, some dancers explain that the uncertainty is part of what makes tango continually interesting. The emotional risk-taking enforces a strong idea of development, of discovering and challenging bodily and emotional limits. The interaction with risk in tango tourism is particularly linked to the Argentine dance-floors but shows similarities with the emotional thrills connected with other kinds of tourism. The Swedish dancer Ida, who in a previous chapter described her bodily reaction (stomach pain) to a "bad" tango experience (viewing her ex-boyfriend in the arms of another woman), speaks about the possible benefits coming from the vulnerability present in tango. In this quote she stresses the importance of leaving the familiar venues and to challenge herself with uncertainties of the unknown.

> I have actually noticed that the dancing often gets more intense and more interesting when I dance with strangers. That's why I try to go abroad to dance. The vulnerability that puts you in creates a tension that can be quite rewarding. The stakes are higher. I felt this in Buenos Aires. I was quite terrified at first, by the city and everything about the tango but that fear turned into a pleasure in the dancing. At home it's just dancing with the same men which can be fine but not very exciting. (Ida, 35-year-old, Sweden)[5]

The kind of risk-taking expressed by Ida, and the larger contours of tango voyages, might be put in dialogue with social class. According to Robert Fletcher, risk activities seem more attractive among the middle classes because "it is their privileged class position within this civilization that affords them the (psychological and economic) luxury to indulge in risk sport" (2008: 323). This implies a relation between economic safety and the willingness to expose oneself to risks in terms of a leisure-time hobby. Fletcher's claim suggests that it might not be a coincidence that tango travelers are mostly middle-class westerners, in most cases at least economically secure enough to embark on an edgy dance adventure. This might be contrasted to the economic risk management which large groups of people throughout the world—not least in Argentina—face in their daily lives (Whitson 2007). According to Ulrich Beck (1992), we might even talk of the contemporary world order in terms of a risk society, implying a shift from modernity to reflexive modernity and a greater sense of vulnerability among world citizens. Bringing in such perspectives adds layers of vulnerability and risk-taking to the study of tango tourism, of which the anonymous dance-floor intimacy is but one.[6]

CONCLUSION: THE TANGO ADVENTURE

According to some tourist researchers, all holiday journeys have an escapist element—although that element might be fused with their specific motives and expectations. Jeremy Boissevain, for instance, frames tourism as an avenue out of the ordinary. He states: "being a tourist represents time-out-of-time, a liminal period removed from the constraints of normal, everyday routine" (2002: x). This description is quite illustrative in relation to the framing of the tango voyages discussed above. Tango journeys, or at least the aspirations associated with them, are partly captured by Georg Simmel's description of adventure, characterized by its "dropping out of the continuity of life".

> The most general form of adventure is its dropping out of the continuity of life. "Wholeness of life," after all, refers to the fact that a consistent process runs through the individual components of life, however crassly and irreconcilably distinct they may be. What we call an adventure stands in contrast to that interlocking of life-links, to that feeling that those countercurrents, turnings, and knots still, after all, spin forth a continuous thread. An adventure is certainly a part of our existence, directly contiguous with other parts which precede and follow it; at the same time, however, in its deeper meaning, it occurs outside the usual continuity of this life. Nevertheless, it is distinct from all that is accidental and alien, merely touching life's outer shell. While it falls outside the context of life, it falls, with this same movement, as it were, back into that context again, as will become clear later; it is a foreign body in our existence which is yet somehow connected with the center; the outside, if only by a long and unfamiliar detour, is formally an aspect of the inside. (Simmel 1911/1971: 187–188)

Returning to the discussion in Chapter 2 regarding the reasons the dancers began engaging with the tango, we might in fact theorize the tango in terms of a Simmelian adventure, in the sense that tango dancing provides an avenue out of a divorce or a time of loss and grief, or simply a break from the tedious routines of everyday life. Doing so, we find several points of contact between tango dancing and the above descriptions of international travel. In fact, the kind of emotional, existential and bodily adventure associated with tango dancing creates a natural link with tourism, representing a "time-out-of-time" and a "liminal period" (Boissevain 2000: x). Certain dimensions of dancing and travelling simply seem to come together in tango tourism. The bodily nature of tango dancing, together with its perceived existential depth and intimate promises, actually seems to provide an answer to a rhetorical question posed by John Urry in one of his later works on mobility: "Given the significance of imaginative and virtual travel within contemporary societies, why is there an increasing amount of physical, corporeal travel? Why bother with the risks, uncertainties and frustrations of corporeal movement?" (2002: 256) Drawing on the discussions in this chapter, we might answer: because the bodily dislocation and risk-taking evoked by physical travel is part of a sensual, adventurous and existential pleasure. According to the dancers themselves, the tango journeys might be described as voyages out of the ordinary, providing avenues for breaking with everyday routines and making "the body come to life" (Urry 2002: 262).

To sum up, the travels discussed in this book harbor expectations of experiencing not only "genuine" tango, but also authentic versions of self. Some travelers hope the anonymous Argentine dance-floors will create an avenue out of a "dark place", or at least an arena for playing edgy games in the search for emotional thrills. Drawing on these discussions, we might conclude that tango voyages, just like most tourism, are inscribed with various sets of meaning. The tango travels harbor , *authenticity* and *cultural connection* (the travels aim for the Mecca of tango: the origin and the places that the tango poetry sings about), *educational goods* oriented towards dance training and cultural immersion, an avenue for processing *existential* questions as well as an *intimate journey* enabling *emotional edgework* in the "risky" Argentine tango environments (cp. Andriotis 2009). As will be discussed later on in the book, the quest for authenticity and the liberty claims inscribed in the existential tango narrative do not reflect the entire travel experience for most dancers; however, this chapter demonstrates that these are important values to negotiate and struggle over. In that sense the objectives and aspirations ascribed to the journeys—converted into everyday practices or not—are significant elements for understanding not only how tango dancing and tourism come together in the image of an adventure, but also the symbolic conflicts between the values associated with tango dancing and tourism, respectively. In fact, the values ascribed to dance voyages are crucial for approaching some of the clashes and dilemmas that we will highlight and explore in the next part of this book. Moreover, the expectations associated with travel to Buenos Aires do have something to tell us not only about the field of tango dancing but also about the transformative capacities ascribed to geographic movement, even in an era when spatial categories are under negotiation and sometimes claimed to have lost significance. We might in fact suggest that the somewhat "virtual" character of much daily social interaction makes the bodily promises involved in the crossing of geographic borders, as well as the crossing of wooden dance-floors, tempting. As Urry claims, in a rather exoticizing response to his own question, and along the line of some of the quotes in this chapter: "Those places where the body comes to life will typically be geographically distant—indeed 'other'—to sites of work and domestic routine. These are places of 'adventure', islands of life involving bodily arousal, from bodies that are in motion, natural and rejuvenated as people corporeally experience environments of adventure" (2002: 262).

5 Trading Tango

INTRODUCTION

Intimate dance voyagers are confronted not only with local dance partners and *milongas* characterized by their particular rules and manners, but with an entire marketplace of tango-dancing services and goods targeting them as tourists. Self-made flyers and home pages in English try to attract foreign dancers to various dance schools, private teachers, tango clubs, shoe and clothing shops and tango-profiled guest houses, bars and restaurants. Some tourist companies also offer special packages for tango dancers on a short-term vacation, which include classes, historical tours of the tango capital and guaranteed dancing company in the form of a taxi dancer. To get a first glimpse of the content and diversity of this market one can page through the generous publicity section in tango magazines such as *El Tanguata* and *B.A. Tango,* containing articles in both Spanish and English and distributed for free in most tango schools and clubs in Buenos Aires. The pages are covered with colorful advertisements attempting to attract the reader's eyes to a particular tango school, shoe brand or "beauty coach". In addition the pages contain the ads of tango-profiled photographers, orchestras, party organizers, Spanish-language teachers, airport transfers and city guides. The advertisements often contain photos and names of the people behind a particular attraction or service. The *milonga* organizers, dance teachers and DJs are all trying to make a personal connection with the presumed client. We should note that some of these services and items do not address tango dancers exclusively. However, the use of tango—its aura and already existing clientele—provides a particular market framing. This applies to the example of a so-called thermal massager couch, advertised in the tango magazines as "recommended by dancers and athletes" together with the language classes and airport transfers, reaching for a larger client group than dancers. Being advertised in a tango environment, with the help of the symbolic capital attached to tango, transmits belonging and trust.[1]

In this chapter we will look into the market of actors and services offered to tango dancers in Buenos Aires, particularly dance tourists. We will explore the content, structuring and function of this market and inquire into the conditions necessary for the success of actors. One underlying assumption is that the trading must be understood not only in relation to economic market logics and the demands of particular client groups, but also in relation to cultural embeddedness. In order to understand this market space, we must take into account the field of tango dancing, the context of international tourism and how values related to tango dancing and tourism, respectively, are negotiated among the providers as well as among the presumed purchasers. In order to explore these dimensions, this chapter looks into a number of services and actors. These are dance schools, private teachers (some of them so-called star dancers), taxi dancers, *milonga* organizers, tango-clothing vendors (including purchasers of tango shoes) and tourist agencies targeting tango dancers. Some of these profiled services, particularly those offered by the *milonga* organizers and tango teachers, have been selected because of their central role within the market. Others have been chosen because they diverge from the general features of the market; these include the taxi-dancing services which, as we will discuss in more detail in Chapter 7, make up a rather provocative element in tango tourism. However, this chapter does not primarily inquire into the variety of actors and services and their various modes of operating in the market, but rather aims at exploring the main *values*. What are the main values traded on the Argentine tango market and how can these values, mostly of a symbolic nature, be integrated within a market logic? Which tango values, if any, is it possible to convert into commercial values? What is required of those actors who are successful in meeting dance clients' demands? And what are the legitimate reasons for converting tango values into commercial items?

Rather than organizing this chapter according to the diversity of actors and their services, we will proceed according to the core values. One reason behind this choice is that the values fuse together in the dance services and goods for sale, implying that most actors provide several values at a time. To mention one example, many Argentine private dance teachers offer not only dancing knowledge and pedagogical skills, but also a certain degree of recognition within the field of tango, social networks, Argentine heritage as well as "charms" and a service approach. Throughout the chapter we will discuss *educational* values such as dancing skills and cultural knowledge, *accessibility* as a value particularly significant in relation to tourism, values associated with the *intimate emotionality* of tango as well as *authenticity* and the trading of *beauty* and a *tango aesthetic* (in the form of clothing, shoes, makeup classes and other products serving to improve the dancers' "looks"). We will also discuss tango status and *recognition* and how this is used in the advertising of dance schools and *milongas*. In addition this chapter wishes to raise some questions regarding the actual work implied in the trading of those tango values related to dancing in particular. Tango tourism involves various forms of body work and emotional labor through which dancing skills, cultural heritage and "charms" are transmitted and hence commercialized.

The delimited focus of this study requires a methodological remark regarding the three types of material being used. Exploring primarily the values traded by market actors has enabled me to use *embodied ethnography* as a starting point for the investigation. Being a tango tourist myself, and hence approached by market actors as a possible purchaser, has provided me with a methodologically valuable position. The fieldwork primarily covers ethnographic work in a number of Argentine tango schools, shoe stores, *milongas*, different tango hostels, special shopping events and a trainee day for future employees of a taxi-dancing firm. This part of the study has allowed me to collect examples of how the transmittance of feelings is used by tango workers in the framing of a dance class, how freelance taxi dancers approach their clients out in the *milongas* as well as how a shopping event promising a "fabulous night in the capital of tango" is advertised and brought to life. This chapter, however, is also based on a number of *interviews* with dance teachers, taxi dancers, the managers of a tango-tourist agency and a *milonga* organizer. Most of the informants work individually, as for instance the clothing vendor Mariano and the taxi dancer Miguel. Two of the informants, however, work within larger organizations: Linn, a Swedish dancer employed as a tango teacher by a well-known tango school, and Ezequiel, who manages his own taxi-dancing firm with around 25 employees. These two informants are important in terms of their position within tango organizations.[2] Thirdly, the material consists of *market advertising* conveyed by all sorts of actors in tango: dance teachers, *milonga* organizers, tango tourist agencies etc. This material revolves around the values at stake, attempting to capture dancers' interest through a seductive framing of emotionality, authenticity, skills and recognition. This material stems primarily from the Argentine tango magazines, a number of carefully chosen home pages and flyers and advertising brochures distributed in the Argentine *milongas*. Before moving on to the values traded on the tango market, however, I will sketch a brief historical background in order to situate the Argentine market space of tango within a larger economic and social context. Crucial for understanding the emergence of this market, targeting tourists in particular, is the economic crisis which has resulted both in a boost for international tourism and the kind of informal work which is common in tango.

TOURISM AND INFORMAL WORK AFTER THE ARGENTINE CRISIS

According to an Argentine survey from 2001, from ten to fifteen thousand people travel to Buenos Aires to dance tango every year. During the year 2000 the number of Argentine clubs in which people dance and consume tango doubled from 27 to over 50. Tango is a promising, expanding industry with yearly profits of U.S.$297 million. This survey indicates that ninety percent of the money that goes into the tango scene in Buenos Aires comes from abroad, that is to say primarily from European, North-American, Australian and Japanese tourists (Soomägi et al. 2002: 158). It is highly probable that these numbers have increased over the last ten years. Significantly, the number of tourists has increased since the economic crisis in 2001. One reason is that the falling peso has made Argentina a cheap country to visit. Another reason is that Argentina has made efforts to promote tourism, one of them being the creation of a Ministry of Tourism. In the following plea on their official home page, addressing both potential visitors and the internal political debate, the Minister of Tourism himself, Enrique Meyer, stresses the national importance of international visitors and foreign capital.

> Tourism is destined to continue to play a key role within this ambitious, promising work scheme adopted by the Government. Tourist development has been conceived as a Government policy, a common cause that we are all required to foster and protect from any changes in political leadership that may flow naturally from life in a democracy. We are convinced that Tourism is the best tool to generate real income and create the new jobs so urgently needed in Argentina. Tourism will significantly contribute in overcoming, once and for all, the extreme crisis bearing down on the Argentine society as a whole.[3]

According to various sources Argentina has been rather successful in its attempt to attract international tourism. In a 2011 report from the World Tourism Organization, Argentina was 2010 top South American tourism destination, with 5.28 million international visitors.[4] According to a report from the World Travel and Tourism Council in 2008, Buenos Aires and Argentina were showing strong growth for tourism. In terms of capital flow, international tourism brought U.S.$4.93 billion to the national economy in 2010, an increase of almost one billion from 2009 (U.S.$3.96 billion).[5] In addition, Buenos Aires is being highly ranked in lists of the most popular holiday cities. For instance *Travel + Leisure Magazine*, an internationally leading publication in tourism, ranked the city as number two on a list of the most desirable cities to visit in the world (after Florence) in 2007.[6] Moreover, Argentina and Buenos Aires are covered in a growing number of articles in tourist magazines and, in daily newspapers, almost as frequently in the tourism section as in the economy or politics section.

The promise of tourism as a prosperous way out of economic hardship is a promise also for Argentine tango dancers. For those who have been working as dance teachers over the years and those who have just started dancing, the growing number of dance tourists makes tango a way of earning an extra income in times when the job market provides few opportunities and the few jobs available come with low wages (Whitson 2007). In that sense, tango is not solely an intimate economy lived by the dancers out in the clubs, but also a possible job market. Tango has in fact become a diffuse market space that includes both well-established agencies with their own home pages and registered labels and informal transactions of services and goods taking place in the *milongas* or in the streets. In this section I will focus primarily on the informal character of the market, which is a significant consequence of the financial crisis. During economic hardship we are likely to find the expansion of informal markets in which people make a living on the hazy border between private and public as well as leisure time and work (González 2000). In fact, studies have shown that the particular history of Argentina has given informal work a permanent home after the economic crisis. Although the level of informal work is difficult to measure, investigations claim that it involved over sixty percent of all workers in 2002 (Whitson 2007: 125).[7] Many Argentines report that they are forced to take more than one job to be able to pay for housing and food. This results in hardship but also enforced creativity when it comes to finding job opportunities outside of the regular job market.

This is particularly true at times when vulnerable economies become tourist magnets. In tango we find many local dancers who are trying to make an extra income out of their hobby. As one so-called star dancer, Natalia Games, puts it in an interview in the magazine *El Tangauta*, the market space of tango has become vast and diversified since she started dancing in the nineties, each and every one is a teacher today. "There were no networks of teachers, there were just a few, and they were the great maestros. Not just anyone could start giving classes" (*El Tangauta*, February 2012: 32). The contemporary market space of tango is a diffuse terrain, blurring the boundaries between leisure and work. Many actors within the market space are dedicated tango dancers themselves and spend not only their work hours but also their free time in tango-related events. In addition, for many workers the tango is one profession out of many: a majority of private dance teachers, city guides and clothing vendors do not run a full-time formal business in tango but rather take small jobs when the opportunity arises. At times they meet their clients out in the clubs. Some of them visit the "touristy" venues, known for hosting a large international crowd, and approach promising customers with business cards and up-front invitations. Others are more discreet, trying to make sure that a "real" connection is established before they offer their dancing skills in the form of a private dance class. The tango market also involves people who make a living out of the side effects of dancing. One example is those people who stand outside the fancier clubs to wave in taxis for tired dancers, mostly tourists, who wish to go home. For every car they manage to hold, they are normally paid twenty-five centavos—or a dollar if lucky.[8]

The scale of tango in Buenos Aires requires the actors to profile their activities. When it comes to one of the main attractions, the tango clubs, we might notice that the tango scene contains milongas attracting senior dancers, gay milongas, large and luxury venues and small, local neighborhood clubs. We should also notice that one and the same venue—such as Salon Canning—can be the site for different tango clubs. This implies that several milonga organizers, with their specific profile and crowd, lease one and the same venue. However, the clubs inhabiting one and the same venue do not normally differ that much. This is partly in order for a location to keep more or less the same image and crowd over the course of the week. For some of these milonga organizers, one way of stressing exclusivity is by attracting a certain clientele—and raising the prices. As Elin, a Swedish dancer in her mid-thirties, comments: "In some places the clothing code was very strict, at the Niño Bien for example. A finer outfit, a nice dress for example, made you get a better seat [closer to the dance-floor] and better dances." To provide context for this statement we might note that this particular milonga is held in an exclusive two-floor building with well-dressed waitresses serving drinks and food at quite expensive rates. In addition, the hallway and bathroom make up a marketplace for shoe and clothing vendors. The audience features a mix of well dressed up Argentine and foreign dancers. In this context we should mention that rather simple dance venues exist side by side with the luxury sites. Among them are those *milongas* and dance schools which primarily target local dancers and which are not run primarily to make economic profit. For instance, there are certain *centros culturales* offering free dance classes and smaller clubs throughout the city which charge low—or no—entrance fees. These places are partly run to make the tango available to local dancers with low incomes, at times through the help of governmental support. Some organizers claim that these are the spots for "real tango", because few tourists find their way to them and the dancing and ways of socializing are reminiscent of the "old-time" tango. Hence these venues are less commercialized than the larger and better-known clubs.

One additional feature significant for the Argentine tango market is that foreign tango dancers, mostly dancers who once came to Buenos Aires as tango tourists, trade services and goods in various sectors. Swedish, Icelandic, North-American, German, Dutch and other nationalities are represented within the group of foreigners who live full-time or part-time in Buenos Aires to manage their own tango hostel, provide their own tango-tourist agency, trade dance classes, design tango shoes and give dancing performances. These actors have a rather low degree of legitimacy as traders of authenticity but are, on the other hand, acknowledged for their intermediary capacities as bridges between two cultures, as well as translators between two languages. Their language abilities, in English and at times another tourist language, their social networks in tourists' home countries and the fact that they transmit notions of safety and comfort through cultural familiarity (passing on advice such as "in our country we might do this, in Argentina however, this is not a common manner . . . ") make some of them rather successful. Some of these actors, primarily those organizing and "facilitating" dance travels to Buenos Aires, have created a niche for themselves, attracting primarily first-time tourists and beginning dancers. Throughout this chapter, we will encounter a number of these foreign actors.

TRADING KNOWLEDGE IN TANGO DANCING

Starting with educational values, a majority of the market actors offer some sort of dance-related knowledge for use in tango: be it dancing-technique skills or musicality training. In fact, the market at large comes across as targeting primarily the educational and artistic objectives of tango journeys. In the following we will focus particularly on the educational values related to dancing knowledge. Although tango voyagers are dancers at various levels, and some are professionally engaged tango teachers in their home countries, an absolute majority aspire to take dance classes with some of the internationally recognized Argentine dancers. Some go for group classes at well-known tango schools, whereas others take private lessons with acknowledged dancers. Devoted dancers with only a few months of practice tend to spend most of their days in dance schools and *practicas*, whereas more advanced dancers select a few private teachers to take classes with. In other words, there is a demand for skilled dancers and tango *connoisseurs* to transmit their knowledge on the market.

When looking into the educational values in tango we find that the teaching form has an impact on the values transmitted. What makes private classes distinctive in this regard is that they offer an intimate and rather personal setting for the learning process. This framing requires the teacher to involve several aspects of himself or herself. Not only do private dance teachers trade advice and critical judgments stemming from their own dancing skills and pedagogical training; they are also required to transmit recommendations and technique body-to-body. When taking a private class, the client gets to *feel*—and embody—the corrections and adjustments provided physically by the dance teacher. This is what many dancers appreciate about this learning situation in contrast to group classes, in which instructions are transferred primarily through verbal explications. The teachers rarely have time to dance with each and every student, making sure that they have correctly incorporated the dancing devices. Consequently, group classes are often available for a tenth of the price of a private class with a recognized dancer.

Transmitting the kind of knowledge required in tango, which is partly an embodied and sensual knowledge, at times demands a rather intimate body labor on the side of the service providers. For private dance teachers, as well as so-called taxi dancers trading their dancing company at the *milongas*, this means that the primary working tool is the body. The very nature of dancing entails that workers in various kinds of dance cultures are involved in a particular type of labor that we might label *body work*. According to Carol Wolkowitz, this refers to paid work that involves "the care, pleasure, adornment, discipline and cure of others' bodies", and more precisely, "employment that takes the body as its immediate site of labor, involving intimate, messy contact with the body, its orifices or products through touch or close proximity" (2006: 147). The physically intimate relation created between service provider and client in tango proves to have points of resemblance with the work of nurses and masseurs, in which the body is the site of labor, or rather in which a physically intimate relation between provider and client is created through touch. However, body work in tango is also conditioned and framed by the nature of the dancing. The fact that the tango is an improvised couple dance means that all movements are communicated corporeally, body-to-body and without choreographic figures. This, together with the intimate lead-follow dynamic in tango, entails that private dance teachers and taxi dancers are enforced to engage with their clients through touch and close bodily proximity. For these groups of tango workers, the work task involves not only dancing skills and the mastery of pedagogical explanations, but also knowledge in how to manage the intimate teaching situation. This implies adjusting the teacher's and the client's bodily comportment through careful placement of chest and hands; identifying the degree of physical closeness with which client and teacher are comfortable; and judging how to use the body to guide the customer across the dance-floor.

This indicates that possessing dancing skills—related to technical, musical and communicational matters—is just one condition for teaching tango. As stated when the Stockholm-based tango association *Tango Norte* advertises workshops by a star Argentine dancing couple—Jenny Gil and Frank Obrégon—they offer a "combination of two passions: dancing and teaching".[9] The Swedish dancer Linn provides further accounts of the combined work task. She was trained in ballet at the Royal Swedish Ballet School and is currently working as a tango teacher with a well-established tango school in Buenos Aires. She has signed a job contract for two years with the artistic manager and has, as a consequence, been trained according to the special features of the school. The two-year contract serves primarily to guarantee loyalty and confidence, on the side of the artistic director, as well as to keep professional secrets within the school. Linn explains that her dancing work in tango involves several duties and capacities, of which pedagogical devices are decisive. Providing compliments and appealing to the tango imperative of constant dance development in order to challenge the students to become "better" dancers are necessary parts of her educational task. When describing the specific teaching style at the school where she is working, Linn speaks about being good at explaining as well as encouraging students to practice harder—and come back to the school for more classes.

> The teaching style is very selling, so to speak, we give compliments and tell the students how good they are, that they will get better and

that they should come back for another class because "they have the potential of getting good". We must always explain why the student should do this or that, why, why, why, so that they really understand and think of this as a good way of learning tango. (Linn, 21-year-old, Sweden/Argentina)

The importance of being good at "teaching", which includes implementing strategies to keep clients, must be referred back to the vast market of tango services and the competitive Argentine job market. Typical for this kind of labor is that the workers are paid by piece wage. On a regular working day, during the tourist season, Linn is required to offer a minimum of four private classes, one hour each, for which she receives a forty percent proportion of the fee (150 Argentine pesos, around US$30), and additionally one group lesson for which she receives a proportion based on the number of students (25 percent of the total student fee). This system makes dance teachers, even those who are working as employees with profitable and well-known schools, keen to attract as many students as possible as well as to encourage them to come back to take classes, not with just any of the teachers in the school, but with her or him in particular. As Linn states, the teachers' degree of skill, recognition and loyalty towards the school shapes the conditions and economic terms of the body labor. For instance, for a private class she charges half the price charged by the more recognized dancers working at the school, whereas the artistic director—the star— charges a fee over four times as much as Linn's. As Linn and other service providers in tango declare, this makes it hard for her to make a living out of the job. Although the tasks—both formal and informal—take up most of her week (she is working six days a week, normally from ten a.m. to seven p.m.), she is not able to pay her housing and food with the revenue. (As in the case of Linn, she is lucky to partly live out of saved money from Sweden.) Still, the lower-ranked teachers know and accept that they are being paid less money for the same work that more recognized dancers perform. They accept it partly because they know that without the legitimacy and magnetism transmitted by the star dancers—the name behind a tango school—they would probably be paid much less. Some teachers also hope to gain valuable experience and credentials, as well as access to international networks, from working in the house of a recognized dancer. In that sense the symbolic capital transmitted by the artistic director might be used as a stepping-stone in a tango career. The fact that the managers and employers can provide rather poor working conditions for the intimate laborer in tango must be related not only to the "tough" competition within the Argentine job market at large, but also to the star qualities associated with teaching jobs in recognized tango schools. As Linn puts it: "This [job] is a dream for anyone who is dancing tango, particularly at my age". Although tourists who come to Argentina for dance classes are economically superior to their tango teachers, the symbolic capital associated with some of these teachers is part of the (re)shaping of relations between intimate service providers and their clients. Rather than being formed solely on the basis of economic status, they involve an exchange relation encompassing also symbolic values such as knowledge and status.

TRADING ACCESSIBILITY[10]

For beginners coming to Buenos Aires at an early stage of their dancing career, values having to do with dancing availability and access to the culture are significant. An example of how such values are converted into market goods is provided by the services of so-called *tango taxi dancers*. This is a group of market actors, for the most part male Argentine dancers, who sell their company as temporary dance partners in *milongas* and dance classes, primarily to female tourists. Like tango teachers, taxi dancers partly offer an educational service: they allow for their clients to practice steps, posture and communication and sometimes also trade their dancing company during workshops and tango classes. What makes this group of tango workers unique, however, is that they primarily provide accessibility to the dance-floor, particularly for those who do not wish—or do not have sufficient tango credentials—to engage in the process of selecting partners. In addition the taxi dancers offer comfort and emotional safety. During the paid-for hours, the clients might try out new steps on the dance-floor without being afraid that a "mistake" will scare the dance partner away.[11]

To understand how this can be a business at all, we need to take into account that the tango scene, with its many venues spread across the large city, is often experienced as difficult to grasp. In addition, many short-term tourists regard the dance scene as tough to manage due to its strict rules of conduct and rigid hierarchies, especially for beginning and intermediate-level dancers. For female dancers this is even more noticeable because most Argentine tango clubs convey a majority of female dancers and stick to the tradition of men asking women up in the play of *el cabeceo*. Taxi dancers are therefore mostly described, both by taxi dancers themselves and their clients, as an option for those who find it frustrating to play along with the game but still wish to throw themselves out on the dance-floor. For foreigners on a two- or three-week stay, taxi dancers can also act as invaluable companions off the dance-floor, offering local knowledge about the tango scene and the city.

As most taxi dancers are "freelancers", working outside of tax regulations and the formalities of a registered company, it is difficult to estimate the volume and size of this service group. Moreover, the fact that many of them dance for leisure as well as for business suggests that it is not always easy to discern who is working and who is not. Being an insider embodying the intimate economy of tango, though, helps one to distinguish the purchased dance relations in a *milonga*. My own first encounter with a taxi dancer was out at the club *Salon Canning*, and it was actually a recent Argentine dance acquaintance who pointed him out to me. "Are you sure?" I asked, when he nodded towards a couple at the dance-floor. To me they looked just like any of the dancers out on the floor. "Of course", he answered. "Do you think a guy like that would go out with a woman who cannot dance and is old enough to be his mother?" In fact, he was right. The man with the ponytail in his late forties was Miguel, a taxi dancer whom I got a chance to "chat" with in the bar later that evening. Miguel was outspoken and proudly told me that he was one of the "freelance" taxi dancers in Buenos Aires and that he charged eight dollars an hour for his dancing company. He spoke warmly about the evenings at work, cheerfully describing his clients as *pasajeros*, passengers, which he "took for a ride". From his perspective he was helping foreign female dancers who did not get asked up to dance or who needed some guiding around the clubs, at the same time that he was making a bit of money out of his passion for tango. Moreover, the customers often paid for his entrance ticket (normally around three dollars), a drink in the bar and on occasion a taxi ride home. He could not make a living out of tango, but this did not bother him. He had a job as a vendor in a telephone store and made a decent salary. The taxi dancing was mostly for fun, although it had become an important extra income during hard times.

Although Miguel represents the more common tendency for taxi dancers to work independently in the informal economy, using the *milongas* for promoting business and finding new customers, more organized businesses have emerged in response to the increasing number of international dance tourists. One such example is the small-scale business *Taxi Tango*. Although this business is a fairly recent addition to the scene, the manager, Ezequiel, has considerable experience in the market. With his clothing, trendy hairstyle and polished English, he is quite the representative of modern entrepreneurship, eager to discover and explore new markets. In contrast to Miguel's emphasis on pleasure and enjoyment, Ezequiel states unequivocally that taxi dancing is strictly business. In fact, it proves to be good business. Ezequiel has plans to expand, making the agency international and "cleaning up" what he considers to be its "poor reputation". As he puts it: "I have a twenty-year perspective. This is going to become an international business. We will send out employees to tango festivals in the U.S. and Europe and make the tango accessible to even more people" (Ezequiel, 48-year-old, Argentina).

Being a successful taxi dancer has the same requirements as being a private dance teacher, i.e. dancing skills and intimate body work. However, more important for the taxi dancer than the tango teacher is a friendly and accepting attitude. When the *milonga* is cold and picky, the taxi dancers offer their embraces without evaluations of dancing level, status, looks or social networks. In fact, Ezequiel, the manager of *Taxi Tango*, emphasizes the importance of being not an excellent dancer but an excellent service worker, and the importance of learning the English language well rather than being a "maestro" on the dance-floor. Furthermore, he clarifies that the people who wish to work for him need a high level of social competence and a particular talent for managing foreigners from different parts of the world. Dancers who want to "show off" in the clubs should look for work elsewhere. Indeed, Sebastian, a participant in a trainee day at the *Taxi Tango* agency, was "headhunted" for his ability to easily make contact with new people—and his good level of English. Yet the fact that the agency partly asks its workers to overlook and even disregard the function of the intimate dance economy makes him unsure if he will take the job. "There is something weird about a dancing job where you're not employed for your actual dancing", he declares during one of the breaks.

At the time of my fieldwork, *Taxi Tango* had approximately 25 employees, among them a couple of female dancers. The working hours they received varied, depending on season and demand, but most of them worked no more than one or two nights a week. Paying approximately ten dollars per hour and with a minimum booking fee of three hours dancing, the agency offered a financially rewarding form of employment. Most of the employees had other sources of income as well, such as work in bars and restaurants. Some of them saw taxi dancing as part of a longer career track in tango. Some hoped to become performers or teachers and viewed making the money and the experience of working with tourists as useful skills to pick up along the way. Others perceived the contact with foreign dancers as offering potential contacts for future dance-teaching jobs in Europe and North-America.

An additional example of what accessibility values might look like is provided by tango-tourist agencies, which are presumably expanding in number and volume. One example of this is an Argentine-based agency, offering "tango trips" advertised on their home page as "ten days in the birthplace of tango".[12] For between 1100 and 1350 euros, it offers a ten-day program including accommodation, city tours, visits at *milongas* (with a guaranteed dance partner), tango shows and shoe shopping. This does not, however, include airfare, transfers in the city, meals, *milonga* entrances or private lessons. In fact, tourists pay primarily for an accommodating service, offering accessibility to the tango venues. A similar tourist agency offering travel packages for tourists is managed by Monique and Steve, a North-American couple in their late fifties who spend part of the year in Buenos Aires working to offer comfort to tango tourists primarily from North-America. They offer tango-travel packages including hostel accommodation, guided tours in town, dance lessons and guaranteed dancing in the clubs. As Monique describes it, the tourists who join their agency go to the *milongas* together with them and thereby get introduced to "the right people". This means that they are asked to dance by local dancers. Some of these dancers do it out of social obligation to Monique and Steve, others are taxi dancers and are being paid to offer their dancing company to Monique and Steve's "guests" and others still see it as part of a fun night out to make dancing acquaintances with dancers from foreign countries. For Monique and Steve, the core of their business is not to provide connections with taxi dancers, but rather to offer a full package of comforting services, ranging from friendly company during shopping tours in town to a friendly atmosphere at the *milongas* provided by their social networks.

To sum up, we might understand taxi dancers as well as tango agencies as aiming at accommodating dance tourists and trading a shortcut to the dance-floor and tango culture. The main goods being marketed are accessibility, comfort and safety. They offer an avenue out of the intimate dance economy and the uncertainty and vulnerability associated with the social play at the *milonga*. They are not the most well-recognized dancers, nor are they trained in teaching tango; their work is specifically to be service providers in tango, offering those values which the culture harbors but which are scarce resources and hence difficult to access for dance tourists, particularly tango beginners.

TRADING EMOTIONALITY

The tango market mirrors the emotional imperative in tango dancing. In fact, emotions make up an important market value not only for tango teachers and taxi dancers, but also for those actors who trade tango items such as dance shoes and clothing. The Argentine clubs, for instance, are all about transmitting the "right feeling", defined in terms of their ambiance, music, décor, lighting and crowd. Those venues known for creating that particular "feeling" are greater successes in town than others. In fact, the transmittance of feelings is a key task for anyone who wishes to run a prosperous tango business. As already illustrated, most market actors frame their services in an emotionally loaded vocabulary—at times with visual images and slogans alluding to the "passion" and "sentimentality" of tango. However, these actors are required not only to frame their business in an emotionalized language, but also to fulfill the promises of a "tango night in tango city".

One example of how emotional experiences are traded on the tango market is conveyed in the following story of a clothing vendor who organizes shopping events in the form of a "tango happening", primarily for tourists. I got to know about this as I, without my knowledge, danced a *tanda* with Mariano in an afternoon *milonga* at La Confitería Ideal, one of the oldest and today most tourist-dense venues in Buenos Aires. After a set of three dances I received a flyer with an invitation to a party the following Saturday. From his careful way of handing over the invite I understood that I was supposed to feel part of a carefully selected few. Soon after, though, I realized that I was not the only one. Looking around the room, dominated by foreign dancers in their fifties, I glimpsed the characteristic pink-and-red flyer in the hands of many, particularly European and North-American, women.

Once I was at the party it struck me that American English was the dominant language, even though the venue was located in the heart of Buenos Aires. Chatting with some female guests out on the balcony, which offered a spectacular view of the entire city, I discovered that Mariano's business had been recommended to them by dancers at home. He had been described as charming, fun and "very much of gentleman", they added, smiling. Later on in the evening as I left the venue, I met a group of friends from the North-American East Coast in the elevator. They were tipsy from the wine and happy to have experienced a "wonderful tango evening". Not only had they gotten to dance with Mariano on the balcony, they had also found themselves "some real Argentine tango dresses" with high slits and black strass on the neck-bond. Although the dresses were much more expensive than those in a regular street store, they were cheaper than clothes at home, they reasoned. "And", one of them added, "it is much more fun shopping while sipping on a good glass of wine and watching the tango skyline of Buenos Aires!" This example is significant for the emotional values traded on the tango market. Like Tupperware parties, blending the coziness of an authentic home with a product market, Mariano's business concept is to integrate the private and the public, guaranteeing professionalism yet with a unique personal touch and an adventurous shimmer. He seems to be successful in situating the intimate and emotionalized tango experience within the context of a shopping situation.

Transmitting Intimacy

Returning to private teachers and taxi dancers, we find that they, besides offering dance advice and dance-floor accessibility, also trade emotional experiences. In fact, some tourists take private classes just to enjoy and be breathtaken by the company of a really good dancer. In that respect, many workers within the market space of tango are engaged in *emotional labor*, serving both to create and manage feelings. The term "emotional labor" is developed by Arlie Hochschild and implies that "the emotional style of offering the service is part of the service itself" (1983/2003: 5). Moreover, the aim of Hochschild's work is to explore the processes of commercializing the private sphere. She writes: "what was once a private act of emotion management is now sold as labor in public-contact jobs" (1983/2003: 186).[13] Like workers in various service sectors such as hotel receptionists and hairdressers, most people involved in the formal and informal market of tango sell their products with the help of emotions. This is most significant for those tango workers who "take the body as its immediate site of labour" (Wolkowitz 2006: 147). Dance teachers and taxi dancers are asked to perform not only bodily and mental tasks but also a particular emotionality. In order to make a client feel confident in her or his dancing and hence more responsive to the music and the lead-follow-dynamic, these service providers are supposed to recognize the emotional needs of the customer and assure the transmittance of confidence, joy and the particular tango feeling. This involves, for instance, creating a bodily and musical "flow" in the dancing that allows the client to loosen up and be carried away by the dancing experience and the atmosphere.

In tango, a dancing encounter also embraces expectations of intimacy through the transmittance of personality. Being a successful tango escort—and tango teacher—requires a mastery of identity representation and, moreover, a well-managed play of personality. Santi, a taxi dancer working on a freelance basis, explains that anyone who wishes to retain a client for an entire week cannot depend on dancing skills alone, but must also establish a personal connection and make the client "feel good". Tango workers need to make clients feel comfortable not only on the dance-floor, but also during dance breaks and in those situations where economic trading is taking place. However, balancing between professionalism and intimacy is a delicate task. Some private teachers and taxi dancers explain that every new meeting with a client forces them to draw a difficult line between *too* much distance and *too* intimate an encounter. The "tango feeling" demands close bodily proximity and emotional engagement—although an overly intimate embrace might evoke feelings of intimidation, both for the client and the service provider. Some taxi dancers describe how they manage the level of intimacy step-by-step, through a careful process of finding out how close to get. Some also use the *cortina*, the break between dance sets, as a means to reestablish both physical and emotional distance with a client.

The tango teacher Linn provides additional accounts of the significance of emotions and intimacy in tango labor. Her work tasks include not only teaching group and private tango lessons and performing at tango shows, but also becoming a "friend" to the students at the school, mostly tourists. In her estimation, 95 percent of the dance students at her school are tourists during the summer season, whereas the Argentine winter is off-peak season and results in fairly equal numbers of Argentine and foreign dancers. The employees are expected to make the dance students appreciate the school as their "holiday living room". This implies that Linn and the other teachers are expected to show new students around the school, sit down and have a cup of coffee with them, share stories from their personal life, take them to the closest cashier and help them out with all the questions they might have. In addition, the teachers are required to transmit the particular "energy" associated with the school and make the students "feel special". The fact that Linn herself is a foreigner might make this an even more important job task for her. This leads her to describe her work life as a balancing act between being caught up by the "positive" consequences following from being a public person in tango—i.e., becoming recognizable to local and tourist dancers out in the *milongas*—and protecting her private life. As she puts it, the managing of work time and private time also takes place in various dancing situations. Included in her job contract is dancing and taking turns with students in the *practicas* organized by the school. Inside the school she would not reject a student's invitation—to dance or to have a coffee. Out in the public *milongas*, however, she might turn an invite from a student down. However, she, as well as other teachers, acknowledges that "private" dancing with students off work generates job opportunities and income revenues. Therefore it happens that teachers agree when students suggest that they go to a *milonga* together. Linn, however, tries to leave her job the minute she walks out the doors of the school and no longer feels obligated to dance with students when she sees them out in the clubs. Still, she describes how the piece wage, based on the number of students she attracts to the school, functions as an incitement to extend her personal borders. She explains that she has actually become a much more "open person" since she started working at the school, as this "emotional style of offering the service" (Hochschild 1983/2003: 5) is part of the expected work task.

The nature of service work in tango, which at times has the main aim of making the client feel good about her or his dancing, highlights the importance of emotional management. The work implies not that taxi dancers and tango teachers transmit their own feelings onto their clients, but often quite the opposite. In the *Taxi Tango* agency's trainee day for future employees, the advice provided illustrates that the degree of personality and emotionality actually put into the work should be restricted. The manager, Ezequiel, asks the workers to think of ways to disguise unwanted feelings such as irritation and frustration towards their clients. Many tourists, he states, will be beginning dancers who will probably make mistakes and possibly make the taxi dancers "look bad" on the dance-floor. Working for the agency, he stresses, requires the management of personal concerns. Thus, the emotion work of taxi dancers—and tango teachers—is not only about producing feelings in their clients (reliance, intimacy, sensuality), but perhaps more importantly, also about managing the service provider's own feelings in order to produce a comfortable dancing experience for the client. This might be contrasted to the honor codex in tango. According to Ezequiel, this is actually a hindrance to the job tasks of taxi dancers and a challenge for his agency. In an interview he states: "The problem in finding workers in tango is that all dancers wish to be famous. If I make a job announcement calling for dancers who are willing to dance with beginners no one will come. They think that if they dance with a beginner dancer they will lower their degree of reputation" (Ezequiel, 48-year-old, Argentina).

The working conditions ascribed to taxi-dancing might be contrasted, not only to the honor codes but also to the emotional imperative in tango. This is striking in the documentary movie *Taxidancing* from 2012 portraying Susan, a British woman in her sixties on tango vacation in Buenos Aires, and "her" taxi dancer Juan Carlos, an Argentine man in his late fifties. The first time we get to meet them together, the camera eye captures the couple at the tango-club *Confitería Ideal*. Dressed in a black shirt and black trousers, Juan Carlos welcomes Susan at the entrance of the *milonga* and leads her up the stairs. Once at the dance floor he performs a comforting dance embrace together with the social small-talking and friendly charms which, in return, seem to make Susan experience a meditative pleasure. In his account, however, his job is not "pleasurable". In the following sequence, filmed at his apartment, he describes the dancing he performs at work to be radically different from the dance he once fell in love with.

> My way of dancing is something very sensual. Without enforcing you, with soft movements I lead you. One hour with a fine dancer is like the pleasure of travelling. [But] these women [his clients] are not graceful in their movements. Their bodies are stiff and they don't communicate. So I can't enjoy [dancing with] them. I enjoy dancing when the other person is communicating, when she transmits and response to the signals in the dance. [...] I never thought I would end up like this [as a taxi dancer]. I started dancing tango to meet young and beautiful women, the dance itself was beautiful and I was young. You can see it in the face, when someone is suffering. Like me, when I am suffering. Ok, it's my work but I cannot at all enjoy dancing [with these women]. There is no pleasure, I suffer.

Whereas "free" dancing is associated with pleasure, sensuality and beauty, Juan Carlos describes the taxi-dancing he does for a living as nights of "suffering". However, he is aware that he must hide his "real" feelings towards a client if he wishes to keep his work. The fact that visiting dancers return to him year after year indicates that he is rather successful, not only interpreting the emotional needs of his clients, but also managing his own feelings.

Sexualizing Tango Work

At times the transmittance—and management—of tango-tuned feelings contains romanticized or sexualized elements. In addition, the gendered and partly (hetero)sexualized world of tango dancing suggests that sexual charisma and charms are symbolic goods valuable both to hobby dancers and market actors. As an example of this, Linn explains that romantic charms—particularly on the side of the male Argentine dance teachers— are part of a successful "business concept" within her tango school.

> It's a business strategy, I was about to say. It is like that, blond girls, or at least European girls think it is really exciting with an Argentine guy. Of course, if they take a private class with a really sweet guy who tells them how good a dancer they are and how nice *boleos* [a dancing movement in tango] they can make, of course they will come back and take more classes with him. [...] Argentine guys are very charming

and nice and open and talkative which makes it easy to love them. And of course this is selling a lot. (Linn, 21-year-old, Sweden/Argentina)

An additional example is provided by the Swedish dancer Daniella, who describes how a famous teaching couple uses "handsome" young Argentine men to attract foreign women to their tango school and how a close friend of hers is under the spell of these "good looking guys".

> I was at this tango school which is pretty famous abroad. But the famous teaching couple was not there, instead there were a bunch of young good-looking guys who took care of all those girls who came there to take classes. And the only thing these guys did was to smile and bat their long eyelashes. They embraced me to the point that it hurt and these guys tried to put you on some pedestal with their seduction technique, like "oh you're so special". But I saw through this really fast. [. . .] I got so tired of it all but my Russian friend, she was just like "oh this is amazing". She was in love with each and every one of them. (Daniella, 50-year-old, Sweden)

The accounts given by Linn and Daniella suggest that sex is present in tango work, not through the presence of naked bodies, kissing or sexual acts, but through the use of certain manners (charms, flirtations, sexual aesthetics). If the teacher is a man and the client a woman the heterosexualized framing of tango might call for a certain degree of gallantry, not as a means to undertake a sexual transaction, but rather as a way to socialize in a "tango manner" and as a way to conform to representations of Argentinean masculinity. Certain service work in tango is also affected by an overall associative link between tango dancing, romance and sex. Returning to the example of taxi dancers, we find that the name as well as the service borders closely on sex. Male Argentine sex workers are often referred to by the term "taxi boys", and the myths and legends of tango itself claim that the dancing emerged from the brothels of Buenos Aires. Newspaper documentation from the early nineteenth century describes the new music halls, cafés and night clubs of Buenos Aires as venues where female dancers excited male clients in order to initiate sexual transactions through bought dances. As Dona Gay states in her book on the history of the gendered formation of the Argentine nation-state: "the tango often served as a prelude to commercial sex" (Guy 1995: 142; cp. Denniston 2007).[14] When taxi-dancing is approached through such points of resemblance, it seems that association and metonymy allow tourists to perceive the service as a potentially exotic and curious attraction.

However, the associations between tango and sex also generate a particular kind of risk, referred to especially by female taxi dancers. Although none of the taxi dancers I interviewed had experienced clients with outspoken expectations of a sexual continuation of the dancing, the intimate nature of the work made some of them—particularly women—cautious. For instance they took measures to avoid unsafe situations, such as meeting customers inside the tango clubs and bringing friends along. A group of female taxi dancers I talked with also explained that they had developed some means for dealing with potentially "sleazy" or "pushy" clients. They would "stop going" with a client who was acting too intimately and made sure that one or several friends were out dancing in the same club. Even if nothing normally happened, meeting a stranger in a night club made some taxi dancers, especially new ones, anxious. Gabi, a 25-year-old dancer, described her first meetings with clients as "weird dates". She said that the arrangement was similar to that of a romantic blind date in that you are given a name, some physical attributes and a time and a place, with the difference being that a money transaction is part of the deal. Though her experiences with customers had been entirely positive, she still felt that she was subject to a different kind of vulnerability than male dancers. She was willing to sacrifice the independence that "freelancing" provides for the safety that an agency offers. Loss of freedom over choice of clients, behavior and work hours was balanced for agency workers by the extra security, both personal and financial.

However, it is necessary to make a comment regarding the associative ties between the work provided by taxi dancers, tango teachers and sex workers. First and foremost, tango workers do not offer regular sexual services (sexual intercourse, oral services etc.). Moreover, the emotional labor and intimate body work they deploy is actually designed to manage the very associations with sex, at times framing their services in a negative way. Tango workers must walk a tightrope between embracing the positively connoted associations with sex work (a public curiosity) and distinguishing their services from those of intimate escorts who sell sex more directly. Responding to the sexualized nature of tango, Ezequiel, for instance, emphasizes that *Taxi Tango* is not an agency for "Latin lovers". He stipulates that no flirting with clients is allowed and that romantic or sexual invitations are not to be accepted. Even though he admits that he has received a lot of international press attention from the associations with sex and that it has "boosted business", he wishes to disassociate his agency from sex work. This relate not only to the reputation of the company but also to clients' desires for non-overtly sexualized dance partners. As discussed in a previous chapter, many female tourists state that they feel more comfortable with partners, both teachers and taxi dancers, who separate dancing from sex. In addition, Ezequiel believes that developing intimate relations might conflict with business logic. He speaks of the importance of guaranteeing a professional distance that keeps dancers from getting too emotionally or physically involved with a client, as an overly emotional and personal involvement would corrupt the attempted professionalism. An additional example of this is provided by the dance teacher Linn. In her description of "charming" Argentine teachers who attract clients through their romanticized acts of performance, Linn explains that the dance school actually takes measures when the teachers "go too far". Linn explains that some male teachers have sexual affairs with their students "all the time" and that this has made the manager of her school implement restrictions. At times the school has even attempted to forbid sexual relations with dance students as this "causes us problems. The student will be really upset once the relation is over, she will tell all her friends that the teachers in this school are really bad, that they are doing this and that to their students" (Linn, 21-year-old, Sweden/Argentina).

In line with Hochschild's claim that service providers are asked to manage their feelings—rather than unleash them—the conditions for tango workers in tourist-dense tango schools and taxi-dancing firms revolve around this balancing act. The emphasis from the perspective of the managers in tango seems to be on the creation of a service-minded and business-adapted charm, friendly and intimate—due to the nature of the work—but not sexual. The tango workers are supposed to make use of their emotionality to attract clients—but are prohibited to actually "feel" for their clients, as feelings and intimacy outside the restricted working situation are believed to create "problems". This, we might claim, partly has to do with the tourist framing of the Argentine dance market, requiring tango to be offered in safe and comforting spaces and manners—as opposed to "real" feelings and intimacy connected with uncertainty and, as a consequence, potentially broken hearts and broken economic contracts. Hence, teachers and taxi dancers are asked to trade a kind of manufactured and controlled intimacy, through which both clients and employer are partly in charge of the tango worker's emotional life.

TRADING TANGO AUTHENTICITY

In those parts of the market which target tourists, authenticity is an important value. As discussed in a previous chapter, this value is related primarily to Argentine culture and the significance of the tango spaces of Buenos Aires. Hence, part of what tango teachers and club organizers in Buenos Aires are attempting to offer to tourists is a flavor of "real tango". This implies that the production of cultural difference is further reproduced when dance schools and teachers promote their services. In order to maintain Buenos Aires' identity as the city of tango, and hence create tourist value, dancing in the Argentine capital is often advertised as something essentially different from tango dancing in other parts of the world. This is exemplified by a tango tourist agency which offers personal accommodation and tours around the city. When opening their webpage, the reader is addressed by a personally framed invitation from the "local" guide, Carlos.

> Buenos Aires is the City of my love, the Tango, the city where I was born and grew up, in the barrio Florida. Buenos Aires means

to me pulsating life, movement and a tango-culture that weighs tons but keeps inventing itself every time again and keeps growing. I love to show you around all the secret places where Tango & life are pulsating nonstop, introduce you to the authentic culture of contemporary Tango in Buenos Aires and bring you even closer to the roots of your passion. Immerse yourself in 10 days of pure Tango! I am looking forward to travelling with you! Carlos[15]

In this invitation, the travel agency appeals to visitors' desire to experience "the authentic culture of contemporary Tango". The fact that the "tango trip" is offered and guided by an Argentine tango aficionado, who "was born" and "grew up" in the city of his "love, the Tango", transmits authenticity values. In addition, Carlos promises to share tango confidences with travelers and show them the "secret places where Tango & life are pulsating nonstop". At other times, the references to authenticity made in order to trade tango services and items comes with a racialized and (hetero) sexualized framing. Magazine advertisements and flyers are often covered with photographs portraying brown-eyed men and women in "sexy" dancing postures. One example of this is a one-page advertisement found in several of the freely distributed tango magazines around the year of 2007. Under the heading "Elegance and sensuality", a clothing store promotes its goods with the help of a woman sensually posing on a chair, her legs spread to expose parts of her inner thighs dressed in fishnet stockings. The only part of her face that we get to see are her blood-red lips; her eyes and nose are covered by a black hat. Behind her hangs a red velvet curtain.[16] This ad plays with various symbols of tango and Argentine history. The most striking example is the placement of a bandoneon (the Argentine accordion which gives tango its specific sound) in the woman's lap. Another example is the implicit references to the brothel, through the use of red curtains and a "sexy" pose. The market values linked to authenticity are, however, also expressed in more modest ways. One example of this appears in a conversation with North-American Steve and Monique who, shortly after having said that "tourism is what we do for a living", add that they also teach Argentines how to dance tango. "We also have students from here. We do have Argentine students" (Monique, 56-year-old, U.S./Argentina). In other words, an agency that rather overtly targets tourists is urgent to stress that they also have Argentine dancers as clients. This, we might claim, indicates that the purchasers on the market, in this case dance students, transmit values onto the dance schools and tango agencies, in this case authenticity. Furthermore, Monique's additional comment might be interpreted as a way of marking anchorage within the Argentine dancing community. Their attraction power over Argentine students constitutes a symbolic tango credential which presumably will also attract foreign dance students. Like Steve and Monique, other dance teachers, *milonga* organizers and clothing vendors acknowledge the importance of "being around" as a way of keeping themselves updated, gaining knowledge of the latest trends around, meeting potential customers and maintaining their social networks. However, more than anything, their active participation within the tango world is a marker of authenticity. Credibility credentials in relation to values linked to authenticity depend heavily on market actors' participation in the everyday tango milieu, i.e. their degree of connectedness with everyday cultural practices and routines.

This implies that there are two interrelated elements in the authenticity value traded in tango. One is strictly bound up with the Argentine culture—represented through cultural heritage and markers of cultural belonging (at times racialized). The other is related to market actors' investments in tango culture, their personal tango dedication and level of cultural embeddedness. In this framing, authenticity is linked to values such as engagement and sincerity in relation to the local community. Whereas the first authenticity notion requires "Argentine" workers, the second one paves the way for "non-Argentine" dancers and tango aficionados to trade authenticity. However, the fairly blond and blue-eyed Swedish teacher Linn, who was trained in an Argentine tango school, states that she will "never be paid as much as an Argentine teacher", especially not when going on tour to Europe or North-America. According to her, tango dancers outside of Argentina worship Argentine dancers and will never treat her with the same kind of respect and payment—although she "might be as good a dancer as some of them". Her account suggests that the rather essentialized framing of authenticity trumps the notion of authenticity as a value accessible for anyone invested deeply enough in the tango.

TRADING BEAUTY AND TANGO AESTHETICS

As noted in Chapter 3 and the discussion of sexual capital, "looks" as well as interactive skills in charms and flirting are important in tango. This is how we can understand the rich offering of services and goods aimed at improving the body—making it "more beautiful"—and the fact that many tango dancers are buying into these products and services. Exploring the sexualized and racialized advertisement from the clothing store discussed above, the trading of authenticity values is at times intertwined with a tango aesthetic, possible for all kinds of dancers—Argentines and others—to embrace and, moreover, to purchase. The market of tango goods involves clothing, tango shoes, accessories and makeup classes offering a tango-tuned aesthetic which allows for clients to transform their bodies and appearances to suit the Argentine dance environments. In one sense we could also include dance classes within this category, because they trade the adaption of the dancing body not only to be better suited for dancing, but also to harbor and represent beauty values acknowledged in tango, such as a straight posture, extended legs and flirtatious adornments.

One example which targets values associated with beauty and tango aesthetics is the market for Argentine tango shoes. The role of tango shoes, especially those designed for women, deserves a chapter in itself because it attracts an interest bordering on a fetish for many dancers. Let us begin by stating that dancing shoes are far more than functional objects serving to facilitate the dancing. Rather, they aim at creating a sense of beauty. The high heels are valued as desirable items in themselves, transmitting not only sensuality in the dancing (extending dancers' legs and straightening their postures) but also tango aesthetics. Tango shoes come in all colors and models, from silver stilettos to those made with green imitation snakeskin, and are often advertised and perceived as an "arte para bailar", an art for dancing, as the brand Neo Tango puts it. The role of the shoe market is indicated by the many advertisements in tango magazines as well as by the recommendations provided by former tango tourists on where to go and what the differences are between different brands.[17] Many female tourists describe how they get hypnotized by the "shopping devil", returning to their home countries with way too many pairs of shoes. For instance, the Swedish dancer Anna-Lena explains that she had decided not to consume tango goods on her second trip to Buenos Aires but still ended up with five pairs of new shoes and two "real tango dresses". Most tourists are motivated to engage in their exaggerated shopping by the relatively low prices; a pair of tango shoes costs around U.S.$100–200 in Buenos Aires, whereas in Europe and North-America the normal prices for imported Argentine brands are twice as much or more. However, shoe shopping in Argentina is not only an economically motivated enterprise. In fact, it is often described as a sensual joy. Some dancers describe the pleasures of walking some of the inner-city blocks which provide a location for most of the tango shoe and clothing stores, wallowing in the endless colors, shapes, heels and details of the shoes, together with the smelling and touching of fine leather and the visual pleasure of a seemingly endless creativity. In that sense, tango shoes can be described as *magic objects*—first and foremost, because they participate in ritualized identity work among the dancers, particularly women, reflecting level of dancing and aesthetic preferences. For some dancers the transition to a higher heel reflects a dancing advancement and an intensified identity as a tango dancer. Tango heels, often measuring around ten centimeters in the shape of a stiletto, transmit a mixture of fear and desire among beginning dancers who aspire to achieve a level of dancing in which the use of such heels will be fully mastered.

An additional example of what the beauty market in tango has to offer are the comforting travel packages combining tango dancing with plastic surgery. In fact Argentina is said to be a world leader in beauty operations, and some tourist agencies actually promote themselves for their expertise in this area. Some agencies are using the sensual and romantic language of tango to sell their knowledge of Argentine cosmetic surgery, particularly to temporary dance tourists. One example of this is a North-American tango teacher and tourist organizer who offers her services to (tango) tourists who wish to have plastic surgery. On a webpage used previously by the same agency, at that time with the heading "Nip Tuck Travel Buenos Aires", a front-page photograph featured a "perfect" female bum in a bikini bottom. The text following the photo offered a visit to Buenos Aires, a city of "tango, romance and excitement".[18] The fact that the webpage has changed its name and that the photograph has been removed might tell us something about the implicit rules for how to advertise somewhat questionable services and products. The edited page now provides a more professional and expertise-focused role. Under the heading "Cosmetic surgery travel to Buenos Aires", they claim to offer the knowledge and arrangements necessary for tango tourists to prepare for and go through surgery. As on the previous webpage, however, tango and plastic surgery are still offered as a combined holiday experience. As stated: "Tango lessons? Buenos Aires is home of the Argentine Tango. Start your lessons before the surgery and then resume as you feel up to it during your recovery."[19] Not only is this marketing noticeable because of its approach to the recovery process; it also provides an example of how the tango transmits value to a market outside of tango dancing. By associating the surgery with tango, and through advertising the service in tango-related spots (as a link on a tango webpage), new groups of clients are addressed.

TRADING TANGO RECOGNITION

The values traded in dance schools, clothing stores and milongas are not only dancing skills, pedagogical excellence and intimate body labor, but also recognition or what we might actually conceptualize as a form of symbolic capital. Tango, like other symbolic markets, is all about cultural distinctions and the making of a name magnetic enough to stand out and attract clients in the swarm of offers. Not only tango dancers but also milonga organizers, dance schools and shoe shops are evaluated and structured according to a competitive narrative reflecting status within the world of tango. Turning to Bourdieu's work on the fields of art and literature, we find that recognition is absolutely everything in a market which depends heavily on a symbolic economy. As Bourdieu writes: "For the author, the critic, the art dealer, the publisher or the theatre manager, the only legitimate accumulation consists in making a name for oneself, a known, recognized name, a capital of consecration implying a power to consecrate objects (with a trademark or signature) or persons (through publications, exhibition, etc.) and therefore to give value, and to appropriate the profits from this operation" (1980: 262). The trademarks in tango often revolve around the names of particular dancers or dancing couples. Just as in the intimate dance economy, dancing skills, together with charisma, authenticity credentials and the right social networks, are what attracts attention to certain shoe labels, tango schools and dance clubs. In the advertisements for tango schools and private teachers, the names and photos of famous dancers are used to attract students—although the "name" transmitting recognition to a particular school might actually not be a frequent teacher. Taking the example of the well-known *Tango-Escuela Carlos Copello*, the dancer behind the school—Carlos Copello—is promoted as "el rey del Tango" (the king of tango) and appears on the front of a two-page tango magazine ad in the form of a nostalgically glamorous black-and-white photograph. In order to further stress the importance of the "name", Carlos Copello's son Maxi Copello—a carrier of the name—is promoted as one of the important teachers and performers at the school, and appears in an additional full-page photo. When going over the schedule, however, one finds that most classes are given by teachers other than the Copellos. Those teachers, however, lack credentials and are not believed to attract students in their own names.

One way to approach the important, yet elusive, credentials linked to status and recognition is that they bring all the values previously discussed together into one. This might be exemplified by a closer look at the so-called *star dancers* who have become names powerful enough to consecrate other dancers and objects. This is a select group that embodies several, if not all, of the tango credentials discussed in Chapter 3. Most often, they are not only excellent dancers technically, musically and communicatively (some of them have won prizes in tango competitions such as *El Campeón Mundial de Tango* and *El Campeonato Metropolitano*), but also display authenticity values in regard to their often long-term commitment to the tango (some of them having been born into famous tango families) and their strong social networks with other recognized Argentine dancers, musicians and artists. In addition, the star dancers seem to develop entrepreneurial skills over time. Some of these dancers run their own tango schools in Buenos Aires and have developed their own dancing style, whereas others are recognized for their classic style or their pedagogical excellence. They are invited to perform dance exhibitions in the popular *milongas*, they go on tour all over the world and they take turns appearing on the covers of the Argentine tango magazines, with glossy and often "sexy" photographs. Being covered by the tango press is one of the most prestigious forms of official publicity dancers can get, as the magazines reach a large audience and are ascribed legitimacy in their coverage and identification of the latest trends and internal relations in tango.

As a consequence of their recognition and privileged position within the field of tango dancers, the "stars" are in the position of wielding symbolic power. This implies that they are able to consecrate—or discredit—other dancers, as well as to evaluate and rank *milongas*, other dance schools, dancing styles, choices of music (tango DJs and orchestras), aesthetics, body styles, manners and language. In fact these dancers are in the position of defining tango itself, and are given the space to do so in interviews and chronicles in tango magazines and other public forums.[20] One tradable market value in relation to the star performers is actually their presumed transformative magnetism. Some tourists choose to take classes with star dancers at the well-known tango schools partly in order to access the status these dancers and their trademarks transmit onto their students. In addition, the capabilities and values associated with symbolic power respond to the existential objectives ascribed to Buenos Aires and the tango by some of the tango voyagers.

These dancers are treated as stars in the Argentine tango venues. This is noticeable also when they go on tour with dance exhibitions and workshops: in the local dancing communities they visit, they are worshiped and given high praise for their expert knowledge and cultural heritage. In addition, the position of these dancers comes with advantages also in relation to the romantic aspects of social tango life. Male star performers in particular are often surrounded by female dancers of all ages and nationalities who court them in hopes of becoming their dance partners, friends or girlfriends. To use the vocabulary of Bourdieu, this might be described as an effect of a charisma ideology, strong enough to evoke feelings and create affective relations between people (Bourdieu 1980: 263). In addition, the magnetism and symbolic power of this group adds value to tango at large, not least in a global context in which so-called Argentine star dancers export the tango to other countries, in the form of performances in acknowledged theatres and workshops in foreign dance institutions. This group of dancers is also important to the field at large because they reinforce the development imperative in tango, the driving force to become a better dancer, which is one of the engines behind the market of dance schools and private teachers. Moreover, they mirror and legitimize the meritocratic order in tango, as their dance trajectories are sometimes framed to transmit a sense of justice. In public interviews this group of dancers often declares that it is their passionate love affair with the tango and their committed, long-term and rigorous dance training which have brought them admirers. In addition, the fact that these dancers are Argentine, with some few exceptions, is an important driving force for tango tourism. Although these dancers are often abroad, touring and performing, the fact that they have their artistic base in Buenos Aires ascribes symbolic capital to the city and makes it attractive for local as well as foreign dancers. In addition, the star dancers transmit symbolic capital to the venues they visit and the social networks they engage in. This shows not least in the photo gallery section of the *B.A. Tango* magazine. In the coverage of recognized dancers' birthday parties and other festivities, the social relations in tango—revolving around the famous names—are mapped out and visualized. This also occurs in certain publicity campaigns using the names and faces of famous tango dancers and musicians to "boost business" (see for instance the shoe brand *Fabio Shoes*, which has created a campaign in which famous tango singers pose with brand shoes). This implies that clients within the market do not necessarily purchase the values transmitted by these dancers from the dancers in person, for instance in the form of a private dance class. The symbolic capital linked to the star dancers can actually be used (purchased) and traded by other actors, such as *Fabio Shoes*. In the example of the *milonga*, star performers and dancers with long-term *connaissance* of tango transmit status credentials to a club and make it attractive simply by hanging out in the bar. Their choice of one or the other *milonga* might be made on the basis of the dancing level at the club, a long-term friendship with the club organizer, offers of free drinks in the bar or simply the club's proximity to their home. Whatever the reasons, their presence transmits symbolic capital to the club and attracts other dancers, recognized as well as beginning dancers, to that *milonga*.

As follows from the logic of exclusivity in tango, not all dancers can become stars—even though they might be dancers as excellent as those "on top". An inflation of the label would in fact lower the values connected with fame. In that sense, the star dancers are under constant challenge from up-and-coming dancers who wish to win their job chances and glory. What makes this a delicate relation is that this group of tango professionals leans on the credibility provided by other dancers—professionals as well as hobby dancers, locals as well as tourists. In that sense, the star dancers depend on their broad networks, at the same time that they must distinguish themselves as tango nobility in regard to the conflicting relations of rivals and possible inheritors.

Tango Trademarks

In the following section we will explore the significance and function of star performers through an example of a tango school that has made itself a successful name: *DNI Tango*. As stated on their official home page, accessible in both Spanish and English, *DNI Tango* is a "tango school, dance company and store—with its proper identity".[21] This school has been successful in advertising a young, creative and relaxed venue for exploring tango. This approach has particularly attracted a younger crowd of foreign dancers and has led to invitations to countries throughout the world. The school was founded by the tango dancer and choreographer Dana Frigoli (together with Pablo Villarraza) in 2005 and is currently directed by her. Part of the success story is bound up with her—and Pablo Villarraza's—artistic legitimacy. Dana Frigoli won, for instance, the Argentores prize for best contemporary Argentine choreography in 2012. In addition, *DNI Tango* is a dance company which has won prizes and which is invited to perform their shows throughout the world. This kind of official cultural acknowledgement creates symbolic value regarding the level of artistic performance, creativity and dancing skills which are transmitted to the school as a whole. Dana Frigoli has also made herself and the school a name through her pedagogical method, a technique for deepening the dancing through incorporating yoga, contact improvisation and theatre into the tango. To further differentiate the dancing and teaching style from others it has been conceptualized with a term, presented on their home page as the *Tango Tecnología Conceptual*.

The recognition linked to the star dancer—in this case Dana Frigoli—together with the school's success in forming an attractive concept targeting primarily young foreign dancers, has allowed *DNI* to expand its business. In addition to teaching and performing tango shows, *DNI* runs a shoe store providing various models and sizes of traditional men's, women's and training shoes. The school has also launched a web store offering shoes as well as various kinds of tango clothing and has opened a restaurant and bar serving "healthy dishes" (*Comer bien—Comida sana*). During the spring of 2012, the school provided fifteen dance teachers, according to the *DNI* official home page, but intends to recruit more employees (in the fall of 2012 they invite dancers to a work audition through their Facebook account). The teachers—in their twenties and early thirties—are all presented on the home page with black-and-white studio photos together with short bios styled to create an intimate and personal invitation. The presentations of the "crew" transmit charisma: the teachers appear as strikingly attractive, both in terms of physical appearance and in relation to their various and exciting artistic backgrounds. Although these teachers are advertised in terms of their particularities and their training in various art fields, the home page stresses that they have all "been formed by her", Dana Frigoli. In that sense the recognized name behind the school consecrates and ultimately assigns a quality credential to other dancers in the crew.

One additional area in which the significance of a name is striking is the market for tango accessories, particularly dancing shoes. The trade in tango shoes provides an additional example of the consecrating power of the names of recognized star dancers. In fact more and more so-called star dancers, dance schools and tango companies are launching their own shoe brands, partly as a way of expanding the areas of profit from a strong trademark. Some brands make a name for themselves through the use of famous dancers and recognized tango schools, such as *DNI Tango*, mentioned above. A brand like *La Vikinga* is based on the nickname of an Icelandic dancer who also runs her own dance school, tango hostel and *milonga* (known not least for its queer-friendly approach). "Her" low-heeled shoes are advertised by stressing the importance of comfort with an "advanced design". We might also mention the exclusive brand *Comme il faut*, advertised as "los mejores zapatos para bailar tango"—the best shoes for dancing tango—with its boutique in the wealthy neighborhoods of Recoletta. This brand stages exclusivity in several ways, not least through its geographic location and the ritual of entrance: in order to enter the store one has to knock on the door and undergo scrutiny from one of the assistants before being let in. Although we might assume that few clients are actually being rejected at the door, the entrance process transmits a feeling of selectivity and uniqueness.

In most cases it is not the actual dancer behind a name who designs the shoes; rather, they provide a general concept which is handed over to a number of shoe designers and shoe makers to realize. This is to say that the symbolic and economic value of these shoes lies not primarily within the craft or the quality of the leather (although choice of material is important), but in the magnetism of a name. The recognition is carved into the leather and provides a mark of quality in itself. In return, the surplus value generated by the "name" adds credentials to the trademark and the star dancer or tango school behind a name. In that sense, creating a successful label within the market of tango shoes and clothing does not always require general design skills and recognition within the world of fashion, but more importantly a name within the field of tango dancing. One important value being traded within the market of tango artifacts is, hence, the recognition it promises to transmit to the purchaser.[22]

Globalized Gift Exchange

Tango not only takes the form of North-to-South travelling, but also influences and helps to realize an opposite kind of journey for Argentine dancers.[23] The so-called star dancers make a large proportion of their income from international touring, giving dance performances and tango classes in Europe, North-America, Australia and Asia, where the fees are dramatically higher and the revenue-generating work intensified. Workshops and private classes are quickly booked, even though the teachers might charge twice what they earn teaching in Argentina. Some clients still perceive this as a fairly "inexpensive" way to take classes with some of the world's best-known tango dancers, compared to the costs involved in a journey to Argentina. Some star dancers spend most of the year abroad, travelling between various festivals and dancing communities, often through contacts made with temporary dance visitors in Buenos Aires. Some of these dancers even settle down and carry out cultural translation while exposing the tango to new milieus (Viladrich 2005). For those dancers who are based in Argentina, the touring is not only a job market in itself but also an advertisement strategy to find new groups of clients who will attend their classes once they visit Buenos Aires. In addition, tango tours throughout the world is a marker of success and generates—in itself—symbolic capital. This is one key to understanding that advertisements for tango lessons with well-known dancers often convey information about their touring schedule. One example of this is a page-two advertisement for the well-known tango couple Gustavo Naviera and Giselle Anne in the February/March 2012 issue of *Tango Map Guide*. Half of the full-page commercial provides information about their 2012 world tour, including jobs in Italy, Switzerland, Taiwan and Canada. Besides making up practical information for presumed clients, such announcement transmits international recognition and fame. Also dance tourists take active part in this exchange. Certain foreign visitors undertake their journeys to Buenos Aires as part of a market strategy. They come to Argentina partly to make contact with high ranked dancers for future collaborations. For the group of semi-professional visitors, who often run their own dance school or *milonga* at home, a friendship relation with and visits from well-known Argentine dancers strengthen their trademark and fuel it with authenticity credentials. This creates global exchange relations between Argentine star dancers and a particular group of semi-professional tourists, which both groups hope will generate job opportunities and, moreover, recognition.

The international job offers are characterized by the uncertainty characteristic of gift exchanges. On the one hand, the Argentine dance schools and private teachers depend on their relations with international tourists. Tourists make up a large part of the clientele of many dance schools and *milongas* and thereby provide a significant revenue. For certain groups of workers within tango, the tourists also represent a specific promise as they are gatekeepers for job travels to Europe and North-America. Moreover, dance teachers and club organizers depend on the informal publicity emerging out of global social networks. Stories of "marvelous dancing"—and devastating criticisms of "mediocrity" or "snobby" teachers—are transmitted through small talk and rumors in Buenos Aires and in international tourists' home countries, and lay the ground for the selection processes carried out by tango communities throughout the world when they choose which Argentine dancers to invite to next year's festivals and workshops. On the other hand, there are obvious advantages for those tourists who engage in relations with recognized Argentine dancers. Frequenting a well-known school and taking private classes with a recognized dance couple, instead of moving between different schools, helps to create beneficial social relations which might be used out in the *milonga*. Just sitting at the same table as a well-recognized dancer, or perhaps even getting to dance with an acknowledged teacher, drastically increases the chances of getting to dance also with other "fine" dancers. In addition, the purchasing of goods such as tango shoes and particular clothing from a dance school where one has actually taken classes and made friends with teachers and staff might be a way of trading money for prolonged friendship, as the transactions make the client a dancing advertisement out in the clubs. Furthermore, face-to-face shopping at times involves "friends' prices" depending on the client's degree of loyalty to the school.

CONCLUSION: MARKETIZING SYMBOLIC VALUES

Following Partik Aspers and Jens Beckert, markets can be defined as "arenas of social interaction in which rights for goods and services are exchanged for money under conditions of competition" (2011: 4). From the discussions in this chapter, we might come to the conclusion that the "conditions of competition" within the tango market are intimately intertwined with the symbolic dance economy. This implies that the values acknowledged by the dancers in their engagement with temporary partners out in the dance clubs are to a large degree the same values that are being traded for money in the market space of tango. One of the most important values being commercialized is qualified dancing skills together with tango recognition, in the form of an acknowledged name. As shown in this brief exposé, other values are also traded. Just as in the intimate dance economy, social networks, intimacy, authenticity, emotions, sexual charisma and charms are converted into market values. We might also conclude that the actual pricing of different services and goods is based on the intimate dance economy. This implies that the most recognized star dancers are the most expensive teachers whereas newcomers on the market are required to offer bargains and reduced prices in order to compete over clients. This implies that the tango represents an internal market space, practically reasonable for insiders, i.e. those dancers who embody the belief system and incorporate a "feel for the game". To the uninitiated the different pricing of shoe brands and dance teachers, at times differing by a hundred percent or more, often appears as a mystery. To the in-group, however, the prices mirror the structuring of the field and the evaluation of different actors' dancing skills and status. In cases where the price is not equivalent to the values being traded, the market normally regulates itself: few dancers will pay an unknown teacher with intermediate tango skills the same amount of money as an experienced teacher with international recognition.

As important as it is to know one's value in economic terms, one requirement for actors who wish to be long-lived on the market is to downplay economic interest. Drawing from studies by Bourdieu (1980: 262; 1998) and others (Zelizer 2005), it is plausible to believe that the disavowal of market values partly functions as a predisposition for accumulation of symbolic capital in tango and hence, as a result, economic growth. Providing an example of how this is expressed among the market actors themselves, Ezequiel, the manager of *Taxi Tango* and himself an active taxi dancer, describes the "deeper aim" of his business concept as "develop[ing] tango", and not primarily "mak[ing] money".

> To me tango is very deep, from all its angles: socially, emotionally and culturally. I can't imagine living without tango. [...] I am a person with a hobby who is paid to take it further ahead. What I mean is that the main goal is not to make money, the deeper aim is tango, not the money. The money comes as a result of developing this hobby. (Ezequiel, 48-year-old, Argentina)

An additional example is how Linn describes the expanding market of tango dancers who wish to work as teachers. Many of them are attracted by the values from within the world of tango, rather than by economic motives. "Lately there are countless numbers of tango teachers of whom most offer no quality whatsoever. All people want to become teachers—or well, the tango people, those who go to the *milongas*—they give up their careers and work to teach tango but they don't understand how much work this requires" (Linn, 21-year-old, Sweden). According to her experiences, for most dancers becoming a professional in the world of tango actually requires economic investment. At the school where she is working, many students wish to work as teachers and turn to the manager with requests for jobs. The manager responds by encouraging them to keep coming to the school, taking group lessons and private classes. For many average Argentines, this implies not only time investments but also a significant economic sacrifice which might not be rendered back, at least not in economic terms. This example suggests that the misrecognition of money is not only discursive but also implied in practice. At times to such a degree that what is supposed to be a job path generating rewarding wages, challenges the dancers' economic safety.

These examples suggest that the kind of rationality at stake must be related to the functioning of the embodied logic of the field, discussed in Chapters 2 and 3, rather than being seen as a function of a pure market logic, aiming for to maximize economic profit. The same goes for the rationality structuring the intimate economy. Let us start by saying that not all tango tourists strive to dance with the "finest" and most recognized dancers; equally, not all market actors aim for symbolic recognition and economic success. As discussed, the Argentine tango scene also contains dance schools and tango clubs with low recognition within the world of dancers, most of them hardly known of by tango tourists, and with low—or no-fees for their services. Secondly, we should be careful about how we conceptualize those dancers who quite clearly strive for certain goals, symbolic and economic. Using the terminology in previous chapters, we might in fact suggest that they act according to a tango *illusio*, an embodied conviction, shaped by the logic of the field. These dancers' actions, we might argue, are examples of a practical reason adapted to the belief system and honor code of tango which, at least partly, encourages dancers to develop their dancing and strive for recognition by other dancers. Rather than being individualists, egoistically endeavoring to fulfill their needs (and to make money), they might in fact be approached as collectivists, acting according to the logic of a social field. In one sense, however, the logic of the field and the conditions linked to market spaces seem to match. Striving for recognition creates both symbolic and economic surplus value. The symbolic tango values are converted into economic values, and are hence accessible through the trading of economic capital. This is what happens when advanced dancers make use of their skills and their recognition within the field to get paid for their actual dancing or the capacities linked to their "names". Such conversions are, however, at times a source of provocation and protest, among local dancers as well as tourists. Once tango dancing is made a commodity tradable on terms equal to those of grocery products, the intimate dance economy is mixed up with credentials which are not fully recognized, such as money.

As will be discussed in the following part of this book, it is not in any way given what the consequences of this kind of commercialization of symbolic values might be. Although the market actors themselves possess both tango credentials and entrepreneurial skills, the conversion of values from a dance-floor setting to commercialized trading, through the translating means of money, is not always a straightforward process. In addition there are values traded on the market that lack legitimacy in the dance economy, such as service-mindedness and dance-floor accessibility. We might also notice that some of the values ascribed to both tango dancing and dance journeys cannot be countenanced by market actors, partly because of the nature of these anticipated values. It is, for instance, easier to serve educational objectives than the existential concerns and adventurous objectives of certain dancers. In fact, such qualities are actually often made sense of in opposition to market logic. That is to say that these values face devaluation if they are subordinated to market adjustments and price-setting practices. This, we might suggest, is one example of how the field of tango at times blocks the market. In order to approach such matters we are required to leave the market actors and move on to the presumed customers—in the case of this study, primarily the tango tourists. In the next part of this book, the implications of a market trading symbolic tango values will be explored from various angles. One theme that emerges involves the negotiations of economic and affective relations. In the following four chapters we will inquire into the aspirations, discourses and actual practices bound up with dance journeys and how the market space of tango is negotiated along with them.

Part III
Negotiating Tango Tourism

6 Tourists and Other Tourists

INTRODUCTION

Cutting across national borders for the sake of recreation and holiday excitement is activating new sets of temporary identities. As discussed in Chapter 4, putting feet on foreign land, together with a range of everyday practices such as dining at particular restaurants and visiting historic sites, is sometimes described as part of a liberation process, freeing the subject from everyday routines and demands (Beedie and Hudsom 2003; Boissevain 2002; MacCannel 1976). However, while freeing the subject from certain demands, the holiday activates identities bound up with new requirements and limitations, at times seemingly hindering the quest for so called "real" experiences (Maoz 2007). Characteristic of tourism in general, and more specialized travelling in particular, is that tourism and (other) tourists are sometimes regarded as contaminators of authenticity. This can be spotted in a somewhat paradoxical comment often heard among travelers in holiday sites: "We won't go there again—too many tourists". This normally implies that a place has lost its connection with local customs and hence its ability to perform and offer the flavor of "genuine" Greece, Peru or Jamaica. Although this might be of less concern within certain forms of holiday travel, for instance recreation journeys to beach resorts appreciated primarily for their enjoyable climate and cheap services (Dielemans 2008), the ongoing symbolic struggle over the production of authenticity is significant in many areas of international tourism (Andriotis 2009; Cohen 2008, 2011; Coleman and Crang 2002; Crick 2005; Strain 2003; Urry 1990). In fact, this prime value in tourism is often made sense of as threatened by tourism. This dilemma is the point of departure and focus in the present chapter.

Just like budget travelers, many tango dancers seem to be rather unwilling tourists. As one female dancer asks rhetorically on Tangoportalen, the Swedish webpage for tango dancers: "I have been to Buenos Aires, does that make me a tango tourist?" Her question highlights the negative framing of a tourist identity common among tourists aiming for the discovery of a cultural art form. In fact, this rhetorical question captures one of the conflicts implicit in the notion of tango tourism. In short, tango dancing and tourism, respectively, are associated with somewhat different meanings. The dance voyagers—on the one hand—aspire to be full members of the tango community they are visiting. They aspire to access authentic experiences with deep emotional impact by means of their bodily investments. The tourist market, on the other hand, addresses the dancers as clients within a market of economic transactions. Such an address mirrors the foreign dancer's status as a temporary visitor, not an equal member in a cultural community. As Birgitta Holm puts it in her autobiographical book on tango and other couple dances: "In the world of [Argentine] *milongas* I did not want to be a 'client'" (Holm 2004: 112, my translation).

The identity work in tango tourism must be related to a more general set of class-related distinctions. In fact, tourism in general makes up a social space in which people engage in the editing of self, through (re)producing distinctions regarding consumption and taste (cp. Crick 2005). Studies show that negative values are at times inscribed into tourism, not least in the context of cultural middle-class travelers (Urry 1990). "The term 'tourist' is increasingly used as a derisive label for someone who seems content with his obviously inauthentic experiences", writes MacCannell in the mid-seventies (1976: 94), an account to which Coleman and Crang assent nearly thirty years later: "Tourism is thus associated with the McDonaldisation of travel" (2002: 2). Particular streams of tourism—such as travels to connect with a dance form's cultural origin—convey their own play of distinctions and create their own hierarchical structure. Given the focus of this book, we will explore dance tourists' relative unwillingness to be tourists not only in regard to a play surrounding class and taste in general but mainly in relation to the field of tango dancing and the intimate dance economy. Similar to other tourists, tango travelers shape a value system of "do's and don'ts" (Elsrud 2011: 613), indicating which clubs to visit, which dancers to engage with and which services and items to purchase.

To sum up, this chapter aims at exploring the cultural production of tourism in the intersection of tourism and tango dancing. This will involve an investigation of the framing of tourism as a set of practices and a form of identity work bound up primarily with tango dancing. Returning to the discussion in Chapter 4, we will partly approach these negotiations as aspects of a narrating practice which reproduces implicit conventions for how to speak about and make sense of travels to Buenos Aires. Central to these negotiations are the dividing lines—and possible conversions—between legitimate and illegitimate practices in the crosscutting areas of tourism and tango. Such boundary work targets the area of consumption, through evaluating practices distinguishing between various dance clubs and dancing services, and the managing of relative economic wealth. Throughout this chapter we will explore how the aspiration to experience authentic tango life—and moreover, to develop authentic selves through Argentine tango—is manifested and managed in a world of commercialized tango and economic stratification.

This chapter is divided into two parts, each of which takes on the authenticity quest from a distinct angle. In the first part, we will return to the discussions in Chapter 4 and explore some aspects of everyday holiday life in Buenos Aires. This exploration indicates that tango tourism creates restricted physical and social geographies. Many tango tourists spend most of their time in Argentina with other tourists, frequent clubs with a high proportion of foreign dancers, and invest in safety and comfort. In that sense they come across as engaging in practices similar to those of many groups of tourists throughout the world and actually seem to be quite happy doing so. However, as discussed in the second part of the chapter, many tango tourists also engage in a form of identity work partly serving to distance them from tourism and tourist practices. Describing how such distinctions are created and managed, we will discuss a number of dichotomies to which both local dancers and tourists relate in their sense-making of tango tourism. In short, these binaries revolve around the presumed clash between cultural values, such as authenticity, and tourist adjustments; money and honor; individuality and conformity to conventions of tourism; and deep tango in contrast to the image of a shallow holiday.

VOYAGE INTO THE ORDINARY

In Chapter 4 we concluded that the tango holiday, for mandy dancers, was bound up with an aspiration to have out-of-the-ordinary experiences. For some dancers the tango voyage is wished to contain an existential dimension, as it promises to offer new identities and life tracks, emotional thrills, a particular kind of intimacy together with a distinct cultural knowledge, believed to be accessible only in the capital of tango. In short, the tango journey to Argentina is not anticipated as yet another vacation week in a sunny tourist resort but rather as a time-out-of-time experience. However, the quest for authenticity and the wish to "get emotional" is not necessarily reflected in the same ways in everyday holiday life. As shown in various studies, peoples' actions on holiday often seem to contradict the framing of a journey, as it appears in narratives for public display (cp. Bruner 1991; Larsen et al. 2011). In the following sections we will explore tango tourism from such an angle. Although many tango travelers identify themselves as dancers rather than tourists, and attempt to stage themselves primarily as dancers, most of them are involved with other foreign visitors and with numerous tourist practices. Many visiting dancers live in tourist dense areas, in tango hostels with other tourists, they spend nights out in well-known tango clubs, with a large proportion of foreign dancers, what some would call "touristy" venues, and they spend part of the vacation purchasing tango related "souvenirs" for use back home (dance shoes, music collections, clothing). In fact, the everyday life of many visiting dancers seems to enforce limitations when it comes to risk-taking and social networking. Hence the everyday practices of tango tourism often seem to be directed towards familiarity and safety rather than "non-touristy" out-of-the-ordinary experiences.

Social Familiarity

Tourist spaces are often constituted as enclaves centered on certain neighborhoods which serve the needs of safety and amusement, through the offering of restaurants, shopping and entertainment (Dielemans 2008). When it comes to Buenos Aires a somewhat similar geography is discernible. The tourist clustering is visualized in the so-called *Tango Map Guide* provided for free in most guest houses and clubs. The map, continuously updated to provide the latest information, covers a limited area of Buenos Aires and points out a restricted number of tango-related spots such as the most well-known *milongas* (listed Monday through Sunday), the larger shoe and clothing stores, certain tango hostels and some additional locations for purchasing tango commodities. The safe areas of picturesque San Telmo, parts of the city center and the centrally located Avenida Corrientes are indicated with red and black dots, whereas the outskirts of the map appear as tango-free zones, or at least tourist-free zones. When studying the map more closely we find that certain parts of the city center are "shoe blocks", where the stores line up one after the other on the centrally located street Riobamba. We also find that an additional tango neighborhood is located in the "hip" Palermo Soho. This neighborhood allows dancers to walk between large well known *milongas, practicas,* dance schools and tango hostels—together with a generous selection of wine-bars, boutiques and trendy cafés which makes this an attractive area also for other tourists visiting Buenos Aires.

As most tourists are in Buenos Aires to experience tango on a rather short timetable, normally two to three weeks, they tend to spend most of their time in the "tango neighborhoods". Many visitors also choose the location of their stay in relation to the placement of the tango clubs and dance schools they wish to frequent. Mostly they stay in so-called tango hostels with other tourists, at times equipped with a dance studio and private teachers, or they rent an apartment in these areas through the help of a tango agency. The clustering of venues in particular neighborhoods facilitates everyday navigation. Many visiting tango dancers spend the majority of their stay within these areas; the limited time, some of them say, makes larger expeditions throughout the gigantic city difficult to manage. This has consequences for the organizing and content of most tourists' social life in Buenos Aires. The clustering of venues tends to restrict not only the physical space of the holiday but also its social geography. In that sense, this selection of tourists seems to follow a trend in leisure travelling. Rather than exploring new relationships with people in the holiday sites, most tourists from around the world use their vacation abroad for developing already existing relations such as family and friendship bonds. Also, among tango voyagers the relationships which tend to develop during the dance holiday involve people who already know each other or meet through common friends in the Argentine tango areas. Many dancers actually travel together with a friend or in a group of dancers from their home community. Also those who travel alone tend to end up spending a great deal of time with people from their home country or with other tourists they meet in their hostel. One reason many tourists leave Buenos Aires without having made friends with Argentine dancers, despite the fact that most of them have probably experienced their dancing company, has to do with language difficulties. For visitors without knowledge of Spanish, engaging in deeper conversations as well as everyday interaction with local dancers is at times difficult. Although many Argentine dancers manage a certain degree of English, the social world surrounding the tango—the chitchatting around tables, the light and the heated discussions in late-night bars—is exclusive to those who can converse in Spanish. In that sense a holiday in Buenos Aires does not necessarily provide a geography for transnational encounters, but rather seems to create new meeting-spots primarily for dancers from the same dancing community, country or continent.

This must be related to the somewhat hierarchically structured tango communities in the dancers' home countries. For some visiting dancers, Buenos Aires becomes an important experience as for enlarging social networks at home as well as to find new dance partners when visiting European tango festivals. Some foreign dancers stress that it is "easier to get to know people from home when meeting them abroad" (Stephan, 32-year-old, Belgium) and describe the new friends from their local dancing community as a rewarding consequence of the trip. The shared sense of being an outsider creates bonds between former strangers who, at times, keep dancing together in tango venues outside of Argentina. The fact that it is easier to dance "beyond" ones level in Buenos Aires partly has to do with the vacation context. Social holiday life together with other tourists, in restaurants and tango hostels, activates the gift economy and comes with dancing obligations, meaning that those who would not normally dance at home might do it out of growing friendship bonds or politeness. We should also notice, however, that some dancers use the Argentine holiday as a context that allows them to act out of the tango economy. Consenting to risk losing face on the dance-floor and dancing "below" their level, is explained in relation to the limited stay. As Belgian Stephan puts it: "what is happening in Buenos Aires stays in Buenos Aires." For him the city functions as a geographic bracket; hence dancing experiences and dance constellations formed in Argentina are limited to the end of the tango holiday.

Safe Spaces

The creation of tourist enclaves is not only a matter of efficiency and time-saving, but also has to do with risk-management. Staying among friends from home or together with other foreign dancers is a way of creating safety when visiting a country far from home. The emotional spectrum of tango tourism, like that of most international travel, involves a certain degree of fear: the fear of being a victim of physical violence, of being robbed, of being hit by a car, of suffering food poisoning or rare diseases. It might not be a coincidence that the freely distributed Tango Map Guide, primarily addressing tango tourists, offers the location and telephone number of the Tourist Police as well as the number of a free Tourist Assistance Line. Buenos Aires is for many visitors an exciting but also a rather frightening city to visit. Many travelers report on being in shock during their first days. This is a huge city, inhabiting aro und thirteen million people, with loud and lively traffic running all day and night, crowded streets and striking signs of poverty. Some speak of the difficulties just of locating themselves in the enormous city and finding the correct route to a particular address.One example of how this affects the social spaces might be drawn from the fact that many tourists use taxis—together with other tourists—rather than public transportation. This is explained as a matter of "saving time", not least because the city's bus network is structured in a rather complex way, and a way of avoiding risky situations, for instance being pickpocketed in the crowded subway. The choice of transportation as a risk-management practice is an additional example of how the geography of many dancers is restricted to certain areas and certain people.

The creation of risk is particularly bound up with the economic hardship of Argentine people, but also with what is described by some as a mental untrustworthiness. As discussed in Chapter 3, cultural essentializing not only occurs in positive ways, glorifying the "authentic" presence of Argentine dancers, but also brings about negative evaluations. This is emphasized in a comment on the Swedish webpage Tangoportalen, in which a female dancer remarks on Argentine unreliability. "Of course I feel pity for the people over there [in Argentina] but it is not helping them to learn how to fool 'gringos'. Take for instance these 'beggar children' who enter the restaurants, with newly washed clothes without marks and clean hair. I believe it's great fun for these kids but there are also real poor people who need help and we don't find them at the *milongas*" (Patricia, Tangoportalen). First-time tourists in particular are often told that the dancefloors are minefields. Colorful anecdotes describe *porteño* men who wish to sexually conquer as many tourist women as possible, some with the goal of finding a rich mistress to buy them a flight ticket to Europe. In these stories the assumption that Argentine men are "untrustworthy" blends a sexualized and racialized narrative with the presumed consequences of economic hardship. In addition, such stories often advise tourists to look out for "sketchy people" in the dance venues. This involves risk-management in relation to gender (men), racial regimes (Latin-American looking people) and class (particularly those local men embodying signs of poverty). Following from this framing, frequent in many holiday sites, local people are targeted as a potential problem and hence supervised by tourist agencies or, in the case of tango, by club owners and tango stores. This might be even truer in times of prosperous tourism—and economic decline. The Argentine dancer Martin tells a story of local dancers who are prohibited from certain *milongas* because of an underlying economic interest in creating "safe" spaces for tourists. "I have heard of Argentines who go to the *milongas* with foreigners and steal everything, their earrings, necklaces, wallets. There are warnings out there: 'don't go home with that guy, he will take everything, even your panties'. That is what I heard, perhaps it's true, perhaps not. These people are being prohibited from entering many *milongas*. For the notoriety. [. . .] Today this is an economic matter, the owners wish to keep their clients, the tourists" (Martin, 58-year-old, Argentina).

Corresponding with a lived experience of risk or not, the many stories of dangers in Buenos Aires and the low motives of "tango tricksters" are present in shaping a restricted social geography. No matter how few in number the incidents are, the (re)produced worries play an important role in the visitors' navigation throughout the city. In addition, the warnings seem to take on a life of their own, circulating as rumors without obvious addressees. At times they prove to be more dramatic than the actual situations, places and people they warn about. According to Elin, both local and foreign dancers warned her of certain areas. "It is rather shabby around that place [Niño Bien] and everyone made a big affair of the risks. Like: 'watch out, grab a taxi at once, take care'" (Elin, 35-year-old, Sweden). Once Elin got to the club, however, she did not feel at risk at all; the imagined neighborhood was far scarier than the experienced one. Moreover, the reports of a dangerous city crowded with thieves and illegal tango businesses trying to make money out of naïve foreigners do serve the purpose of certain actors within the market space of tango. In this context non-Argentine actors seem to be given a comparative advantage. Although most tourists wish to encounter "real" Argentina and "real" Argentines as dance partners and mediators of the culture, some consider it safer to embark on these encounters with the helping hand of another foreigner. One example of how perceptions of risk create a restricted social geography is the choice to travel in semi-organized ways, using the services of tourist agencies or arrangements made among friends. This is what makes up the business idea of North-American Monique and Steve's tango agency, which offers tourist packages to the "tango capital". From their perspective they are non-Argentine experts on Argentine culture—on its delights, but also its "mentality" and the associated traps for European and North-American visitors. The business idea is to make foreigners feel secure and offer a "quality mark" that helps to protect visitors from the "tricksters". Hence, adding to the narrative of dishonest Argentines—as they do in the following quote—is boosting business. However, the following conversation suggests that part of their strategy is to offer what they state to be protecting their clients from: "lies" that will "allow them [tourists] their dreams".

Steve: We've been here four and a half years and we're still learning things, we're still learning about the lies we've been told. Because everyone here lies, because they want to be nice or they want to be comfortable or they want to tell you nice things so they are not going to tell you the underbelly, they are not going to tell you about the pain. They will tell you how great everything is. It takes years to learn that it's not like that. [. . .] You can't tell this to people [tourists] because it will burst their bubble. You can't tell them that these guys are going to hassle you, that they are after either it is just sex, or it's money or it's a ticket back to the States or it's sponsorship in tango, with your help they will get to the States to teach, or it's to get students to teach. You can't tell people that, you have to allow them their dreams. Because what they do, instead of just accepting it, they turn on you. "I don't like him, he is so rude. I don't like him . . .". And you lose clients, like this [Steve snaps his fingers]. (Steve, 58-year-old, U.S./Argentina)

Monique: It is obvious. Some people who come here for the first time dance with people who they will tell "it's beautiful dancing with you" and a guy will answer "it's free this time but I charge, I'm a taxi dancer. So if you want to dance again here is my card. This is how much I charge." Or "I'm a teacher". (Monique, 56-year-old, U.S./Argentina)

In relation to tango tourism it is important to add one dimension to the perceived risks. Tango voyagers not only mange the fear of being robbed in the streets, but also take measures to handle the emotional risks in tango—particularly in Buenos Aires where the stakes are, if not higher, very different. As Elin explains, "coming to Argentina, if you dance tango, is like getting to the base line. So it was very emotional getting there and dancing in all those places where it happens. I was actually quite nervous the first nights so it was good having friends from home around [Elin was out with her co-voyager, a male Swedish tango dancer]. The first night out there were actually two more Swedes in the same milonga as us" (Elin, 35-year-old, Sweden). Like Elin, many dancers report that their first nights in town differed from the expectations they had of anonymous dimly lit dance-floors where strangers fall into each other's arms. Rather than putting themselves in edgy situations, most dancers I met actually tried to reduce the emotional risk-taking by securing their first nights with friends and well-known dance-partners. In other words, tourists are trying to avoid not only physical risks but also emotional ones related to the world of tango. Often the two interrelate, however, as in an account from San Francisco-based Pam, who is in her mid-fifties. Pam regards herself as a frequent solo traveler but claims that she would not consider going to Buenos Aires on her own; she prefers travelling there in the form of a group voyage organized by "people from here [the US]". This, she says, is partly because she is new to tango; she needs the reassuring company of other and hopefully more advanced dancers. But it also has to do with what she has heard about the city. Argentina, she says, is "too much, too big of a city with actual dangers for a gringo like me" (Pam, 52-year-old, U.S.). This account, together with the business strategy of Steve and Monique, indicates that being a European or North-American lends (safety) credentials to those working in the tourist market of Argentine tango.[1] In this way, the case of tango tourism illustrates how the cultural production of emotions, in this case feelings of risk, fear and uncertainty, fuses with the creation of a limited tourist geography bound up with commercialized tourist spaces. In addition, this example illustrates how tourist fear paves way for the creation of new job opportunities. The taxi firms and the semi-gated tango hostels benefit from this, as do businesses which offer *protection from*—rather than access to- "real" Argentine tango life.

DEEP TANGO, SHALLOW TOURISM

These general patterns lead some dancers—among them many tourists—to express concern over the streams of foreign dancers coming to Buenos Aires. These concerns are formulated most commonly by more experienced dancers and those foreigners who have visited Argentina on several occasions. This is to say that those tango dancers invested with symbolic capital and dance credentials seem more likely to reject those tourist trajectories that are restricted to certain areas and the comfort of a travel agency. Some dancers, Argentines and foreigners, take these concerns one step further and argue that the increasing streams of foreign dancers in Buenos Aires are devastating to tango culture. Some dancers identify the problem with tourism as the ongoing adaptions of the *milongas* and tango schools. As one female *milonga* organizer and tango teacher puts it, the problem with tango tourism is that the expanding number of foreigners—particularly beginning dancers—leads the professionals in tango to adapt their services to suit the tourists' demands. If European dancers have a hard time figuring out how to make *el cabeceo* work, some *milongas* try to organize the dance evenings in other ways, so that temporary tourists can participate on their own terms, she claims (Natalia, 52-year-old, Argentina). Some dancers argue that this development has to do with Argentine hardship and conceive of the problem with tourism as the commodification of tango. As one female dancer writes on the interactive Swedish webpage Tangoportalen: "As long as there are tourists who want to dance and as long as there is a large population living under economic hardship there will be people who are willing to dance for money. [. . .] It is not only the tourists who find this to be a sad development. How do you think it feels for a serious local dancer to see the entire soul of the tango distorted into something that it isn't, something commercial. The tango is their pride and now they see a distorted image being shown off for tourists" (Jannike, Tangoportalen).

There are also those dancers, among them foreigners working within the market space of tango, who claim that the deprivation of tango culture is a function of the "Argentine mentality". Rather ironically, Steve, the North-American manager of a tango-tourist agency, criticizes not primarily the tourists but the Argentines for "selling their culture". "Argentines want so much to be liked. They want you to be happy and they want to be liked that they will give away their culture, they will sell their culture. They need money, an income, they will sell their culture. It is very very, I think, bad for tango" (Steve, 58-year-old, U.S./Argentina). According to Steve, tourists come to Buenos Aires for the dancing experiences, but tango—according to him—is more than the actual dancing: it is a culture, a lifestyle, a philosophy and a sentiment. These other elements, however, are vanishing as a consequence of tourist adaptions, he claims. This, he continues, is because foreign dancers lack knowledge; they lack a deeper sense of tango: "no one in the United States knows what tango is about. They don't come here for tango. They don't even like the tango. They come here for other reasons. They come here for . . . for some sort of dream. [. . .] They romanticize it. North-Americans don't like tango. What they like is dancing, music and art. [. . .] but the tango is far more than a dance." For Steve, tango outside the borders of Argentina—or even outside Buenos Aires—is an utter impossibility. In his view, the soul and the sentiment of the culture is bound to the Argentine capital.

Still others claim, quite to the contrary, that it is in the pure dancing venues, the *practicas*, that "real" tango can be found. One Swedish dancer, himself a tango teacher in Sweden running his own dance studio, suggests that the *milongas* are in fact "tourist traps". In his view, searching for the values acknowledged by Steve—the culture, history and philosophy of tango–lead tourists to venues and dance schools characterized by stereotypical and old-fashioned tango representations, frequented primarily by tourists (Marcus, 30-year-old, Sweden). There are also those dancers who claim that the constant stream of tourists is what keeps the tango in Buenos Aires alive. Without the impact of dancers from all over the world, tango in Argentina would become a museal and rather one-dimensional art form, they claim. In their view, the clashes of various—and at times rather unorthodox—dancing communities and dancing styles obstruct any attempt to essentialize the dancing.[2] In addition, some dancers—local and foreign—suggest that the many professional foreign dancers actually elevate the status and credentials of the Argentine *milongas* and dance schools.[3] The Swedish dancer Daniella formulates this argument rather dramatically. She claims that "Buenos Aires is nothing without us, the tourists", and continues:

> We are everywhere these days. When you are out in the larger well known places sixty percent are tourists, I would say. Flourishing tango tourism is what makes these places go around. Most people don't think about this. That it is only a few local people who actually dance tango. If you take away all the dance tourists there wouldn't be much left. You would have the young dance teachers, the ones who have made themselves a name, their followers, their footmen, and their schools. The rest is tourism. (Daniella, 50-year-old, Sweden)

Although Daniella states that Buenos Aires is nothing without the tourists, she herself wishes to distance her journey from the patterns of many foreign tango dancers. She perceives herself as "more of a dedicated dancer" than a tourist and makes a clear distinction between her own "deep" interest in tango and those dance tourists who only get to "scratch the surface". This is expressed in the following statement whereby she engages in identity work aimed at creating a divide between tourists and *tangueras*.

> We [Daniella and a friend, also he a Swedish tango dancer] lived in this tango hostel with some pensioners. One couple who had been married for twenty years and went to Buenos Aires to fulfill a dream they had for long time. They will scratch the surface of something they will never get at. I am down on a level where I have learned the names of the stars who travel throughout Europe. I am so much into tango, so extremely interested that I find out everything. They [the "pensioners"] might go to these tango-shows, you know, where I could not put my feet. I am absolutely not interested. [. . .] Of course I am a tourist but I think I am more of a dedicated dancer. I am actually a collector. I collect dance experiences and I collect music. It is the dancing experiences that stick with me. Twelve minutes of commitment. Then we have all those places outside town which look like nothing where the seventy old Argentines drink *mate*, the genuine places. This is what I want to experience. We were at one of those places, a really traditional one, *Sin Rumbo*, outside town. There were no tango tourists, no nervous tourists sitting in a corner waiting to be asked up to dance. There were only Argentines around a long table, drinking and gaggling. (Daniella, 50-year-old, Sweden)

Although Daniella herself engages in some "typical" tourist practices, such as her choice of housing, she distinguishes herself from other tourists by stating that she "is down" with the tango. Daniella makes a point out of her "extreme interest", exemplified by her specialized and deep *knowledge level* (having "learned the names of the stars who travel throughout Europe"). Furthermore, she frames her quest for authenticity in relation to "genuine *places*" and *people*,, such as the traditional *milonga Sin Rumbo*, frequented by "Argentines" ("no nervous tourists sitting in the corners"),. The distinction between herself, a dedicated tango dancer ("so much into tango, so extremely interested"), and other tango tourists is also reflected by her emotional investment in tango and the economic and social sacrifices she has made in order to realize her journeys to Buenos Aires (during the interview she speaks about how she has struggled to find money for the travels). The fact that she is so deeply invested in the tango actually removes the potentially "shallow" connotations linked to certain "touristy" practices. The fact that Daniella was staying at a typical tango hostel, recognized as such not least from the appearance of the other guests ("pensioners" who "will never get at" the tango), is in her own statement compensated for by her long-term commitment. She actually laughs when she speaks about the hostel, declaring that it was rather amusing to stay in a place full of "tango kitsch". She has tango credentials and confidence enough to know that her stay in a typical tourist venue is not a threat to her dancer identity.

Similar to Daniella, also other tourists engage in evaluating places, people and practices according to their degree of authenticity. Rather than making grand claims about tourism in general, local dancers as well as tourists often take part in much more specialized boundary work. One aspect of this is the ongoing play with identities in the nexus of tango and tourism. A similar example of how dance tourists in Buenos Aires negotiate meaning with respect to their tango holiday is found on the blog post of a Canadian woman, Emma, who reports from one of her yearly visits to Buenos Aires. She summarizes the motivations for her preferences for certain *milongas* as follows: "high quality of dancers, less tourists". Besides the distinction between "tourists" and "good dancers", she stresses her own local anchorage through stories about her friendship with Argentine dancers. Later on in the same blog post, Emma describes how she is getting further behind the "décor" of the tourist-friendly *milongas* and dance schools through ameliorated dancing and the acquaintance with a local "*tanguero*".

> I feel that for the first time in all my trips to BA, I am finally penetrating the real city. Last night we were invited by a dancer called Enrique (butter boy) to an *Asado* (a barbeque) at his house. [. . .] This experience was another foray into the real BsAs, one that most tourists who come, dance at *milongas*, buy shoes, and visit touriosites don't get to see.[4]

Like Daniella, Emma distinguishes herself from those tourists who are trapped in various comforting tourist services. In her account Emma's experiences beyond the tourist map are portrayed as a way of accessing "real BsAs". In addition, Emma values the authenticity ascribed to local dancers. However, in this statement the local dancer Enrique—with the rather humiliating nick name "butter boy"—seems to be made sense of as a *means* to reach certain goals, i.e. a means to access "genuine" experiences and authenticity credentials, rather than being described in terms of his personality. With an erotically charged language, somewhat similar to that used by nineteenth-century male western colonizers (cp. Said 1995), Emma describes her "penetration" into the "real city" through the guidance of a male native inhabitant.

Consumption and Authenticity

Some tango voyagers link the problem with tourism to the commercialization of tango, suggesting that tango is something radically different than what can possibly be offered on a market space. As formulated on Tangoportalen, the problem with tango tourism is that the "soul of the tango is distorted into something that it isn't, something commercial". In the above statement by Canadian Emma, a similar distinction is made, this time between tourists who *buy* themselves experiences—"dance at *milongas*, buy shoes"—and those who *merit* them freely through dancing skills, cultural integration and personal relations. In Emma's account it is striking that she takes pride in being "invited" to, rather than paying for, a tango evening at a local dancer's home (through the arrangements of a tourist agency). This might also be contrasted to the act of paying for entrance to commercial venues, here framed as a practice which positions the visiting dancer as a client and a tourist. Accessing "real" Buenos Aires is in her account equivalent to a non-commercial "foray".

For many dancers, though, both locals and tourists, the line between commercialized and authentic tango is not that sharply defined. Most tourists do engage in various types of tango-related consumption. Rather than avoiding commercialization as such, the negotiations revolving around the tourist identity tend to be about making the right choice when selecting between "genuine" and "touristy" dance services, events and shopping situations. In fact, the consumption of tango makes up a constitutive arena for producing desirable identities as well as managing unwanted ones (cp. Bauman 2007; Featherstone 2010). Through engaging in various kinds of market activities—shopping or glancing through the commercial section in the tango magazines—people respond to a particular address, attempting to acknowledge potential customers as tango dancers, sensual and feminine women etc. When it comes to tango dancing there are various market-related situations which primarily address the clients as dancers. Entering a tango boutique with select tango items and receiving the personal service of a seller with a high status in the world of dancing (perhaps herself or himself a dancer), finally purchasing an item and being applauded by other dancers (clients) in the store reinforces the dancer identity and a tango membership. In fact, such situations indicate that engaging in consumption practices is not necessarily a challenge to the dancer identity, rather it seems to reinforce it. Instead, the potential problem of commercialization is bound up with finer distinctions, intimately intertwined with the negative framing of tourism. One example of this is the Argentine tango-shows performed in fancy restaurants visited primarily by tourists. These shows are often dismissed as *inauthentic* tango attractions "made for tourists, not for tango dancers" (Beth, 43-year-old, U.S.). Such commercialized tango is further associated with "unreliable" market actors with a low degree of anchorage and status in the world of tango dancers. This is how Swedish Anna-Lena links the tango-shows with a notion of an unwanted "tourist market".

> All teachers and schools where I have taken classes have been very reliable and professional. It hasn't been like a tourist market at all. Neither me nor Rolf [her Swedish travel partner and cohabitant in Buenos Aires, and also a tango dancer] have been to these tango-shows. There are just no reasons going for the tourist magnets. (Anna-Lena, 58-year-old, Sweden)

In her understanding tango-shows in kitschy restaurants are bound up with a market space primarily for tourists, not tango dancers. The market actors targeting tango dancers, on the other hand, are described as "professional" tango schools and recognized dance teachers. In that sense these market actors partly elude the negative associations of a *tourist* market. Moreover, in Anna-Lena's understanding the high educational level in the dance schools where she was taking classes partly reduced the associations of a market, in general ("it hasn't been like a tourist market"). In that sense, paying for dance classes and tango expertise is not primarily made sense of as consumption, but rather as a means to achieve important knowledge (dance classes) and valuable items impossible to purchase elsewhere (such as the Argentine shoe brands and particular music recordings).

The examples discussed in this section indicate how the commercialization of tango and the activation of a client—as well as a tourist—identity come into play. In some cases, entering a client role actually functions as a way of enforcing a dancer identity—as shown by the example of shopping for tango shoes in recognized stores. Other cases, such as the "touristy" tango-shows which are avoided by most dance tourists, demonstrate how a consumption situation is perceived as threatening to the dancer identity. One reason for this is that this kind of tango consumption risks "contaminating" the spectators or revealing them as "tourists" with a shallow relation to tango.

Money and Honor

A related area in which tango dancers negotiate the significance of a tourist identity is the managing of money. For the kind of travelling at stake in this book, with its intimate, emotional and existential dimensions, the relative economic wealth on the side of the tourists is in some cases understood as a signifier of an outsider. We might relate this to the myth of tango's origin, portrayed as a rough working-class culture far from the luxury tango venues found in today's Buenos Aires. One aspect of the potentially problematic relation between the relative wealth on the side of the tourists and the economically "deprived" tango culture is the misuse of money. Examples of illegitimate actions in relation to economic capital are often mentioned when both local and foreign dancers speak of the negative impact of tourism in Buenos Aires. In some accounts, money is spoken of as almost an artifact that one has to carefully interact with so as to not be identified as an "outsider"—and be robbed. One example of this is found on a North-American home page providing recommendations and advice for Americans travelling to Buenos Aires to dance tango. Under the heading "Money matters in Buenos Aires", a North-American tango teacher who has moved to Buenos Aires, states: "If you pay a taxi driver with a large bill, it is an opportunity for him to pass false money your way. He figures tourists don't know the difference. Don't open your purse to take out your wallet. It would be better to have small change ready in your pocket. Have money ready in hand when you enter a *milonga* and try to be as discreet as possible when paying the waiter".[5]

For certain visitors the importance of "blending in" and not revealing their economic status is bound up with the fear of being taken advantage of economically. In satire stereotypes, tourists are often made sense of as rather naïve or even cynical people who—due to their lack of connection with the places they are visiting—are easy "to fool". This is one key to the many pieces of advice about how to behave in the Argentine *milongas*. Although the fear of being robbed is overshadowed by the fear of not being accepted as a dancer, we might notice a kinship between the two. For first-time visitors there are several home pages and books in which more experienced foreign dancers share strategies for how to act and dress to better fit into the crowded Argentine tango venues, ideally being approached as "one of them". The underlying message in these books is that the "fool" is easier to "fool", meaning that the honor code of tango (not to act off script) serves to protect its members from emotional risks. Played out in the context of tourism and economic hardship, the importance of acting according to an honor code also involves physical and economic risk-management.[6]

In addition, the context of tango tourism evokes particular concerns when it comes to the fear of "paying too much"—i.e. paying more than others, implicitly local dancers—for dance classes and tango shoes. In recent years some tango tourists have actually complained about the increasing prices of shoes and private classes in Buenos Aires as a result of a more stable Argentine economy. The fact that the prices are dramatically lower and the quality of teachers and clubs generally higher than at home implies that these reactions are not linked to the actual prices but rather to the underlying meaning they communicate. The fear of "paying too much" might in fact be related to dancers' negotiation of a tourist identity and the potential tourist shame evoked by paying "tourist prices". In that sense, not only the selection of services but also the prices paid for these services and goods are identity shaping. Paying "too much" is a traditional marker for out-groups, in tango and elsewhere, whereas "reduced" prices characterize the relations between in-group members .

An additional example of the identity work connected with the "money matter" is found in a comment made by the Swedish dancer Lasse, providing an equality argument. Lasse has been to Buenos Aires three times and describes his relation with Argentina as "sincere and friendly". He feels at home in the city and always longs to go back. In the following conversation this self-understanding is further stressed as he points out American and Russian tourists who make "fools out of themselves" by trying to put themselves "on top" economically.

Lasse: You don't want to come up with moral advice [in relation to Argentine poverty] and you don't want to throw money all over the place and act like an American tourist. They are just horrible when they travel the world and behave like that. (Lasse, 58-year-old, Sweden)

Maria: Like what?

Lasse: Well they throw their money around, they make noises and they shout, they act as if they owned the world. Unfortunately it is often like that. I often saw this when I was there [in Buenos Aires]. Russians as well, they are like the Americans. As tourists in the street and when they try to buy all the national antiquities. [. . .]

Maria How did you manage it [Argentine poverty]?

Lasse: I tried to blend in as far as possible. You need to be a little discreet in your approach. For instance when you take a cab you shouldn't pull up fifty pesos as a tip, you shouldn't do that. I don't think they would like that. Instead you should try to be just like anyone. "Here is all my money", that is like stamping on them, putting yourself on top. Making a statement that I am rich and you are poor, you know.

"Showing off" with the help of money is interpreted as an offense to Argentine culture at large and the world of tango in particular. This might be put in dialogue with an Argentine commentator pointing to the risk involved when tourists play the game of honor the wrong way. "'Only a *gringo*', says Sábato, 'would make a clown of himself by taking advantage of a tango to chat or to amuse himself'" (Taylor 1976: 289). For Lasse, however, "not making a fool out of oneself", showing respect towards the place one is visiting, is also a political act.[7] The personal context of this quote is Lasse's political engagement. Downplaying his relative wealth is a way of not playing along with a political history in which the Global North, primarily the U.S., has tried to buy itself political legitimacy and military respect in Latin-America.

Tourism Conformity and Tango Individuality

In the negotiations tango is often constituted in relation to a notion of individuality, whereas tourism is linked to collective conformity. This is expressed, not least in the objectives of a voyage out of the ordinary, a travel allowing for a time-out-of-time. This might be put in dialogue with a more general trend regarding western middle-class tourism and a tendency to distinguish so-called "mass *tourism*" to cheap beach resorts from "knowledge *travelling*" to culturally refined sites, so-called genuine places (Larsen et al. 2011; Urry 1990). In such formulations, a fixed noun (tourism) is contrasted to the mobility, agency and individualism implicit in the verb "to travel". One example of such boundary work in tango is found on the Swedish webpage Tangoportalen, in which several dancers address their experiences from Buenos Aires. Many comments revolve around the temporary visitor (the writing subject), and her or his level of connectedness with the culture. As in the blog post by Canadian Emma, some of the Swedish dancers are proud to have found individual avenues off the collectively imposed tourist track. The following dialogue between two female dancers provides an account of how credibility is negotiated through a rejection or rather an escape from an imposed collective identity. One of the dancers, Jannike, argues that visitors who wish to experience the "real stuff", meaning tango dancing outside of the tourist market and the tourist places, need to search on their own. "If you want to get rid of taxi dancers and *milongueros* you need to find the other *milongas*, where those who were born and raised with tango go to dance and have a good time, not to pay or pick up some rich tourist". Patricia agrees with her. "If we go to BA the choice is free for anyone to [. . .] visit the tourist places—or not. I have my particular favorite place that no one will ever hear of because I want to be the only tourist there". Jannike again: "Great! Me to!! I have my own native tango guide and that is pretty good if you want to find the genuine places, but of course not everyone has the opportunity and privilege of having family and friends in BsAs".

In these statements tango authenticity is constituted in relation to individuality through the display of friendship bonds with "native guides" and through the discovery of dance venues off the tourist map. In addition, in all these accounts authenticity is constituted through a negation of tourist practices such as engaging in "touristy" consumption and frequenting "tourist places". These negotiations reflect a play with markers of social class. Although economic resources make possible a larger degree of individual agency and choices, the context of tango tourism frames such privileges as the basis for a collective category: in its most negative framing, the stereotypical *gringo*. Being acknowledged as a member of another collective, "the locals", by means of "blending in", is in this context actually a signifier of individuality—as a consequence of the escape from conformity. In this particular context, passing as an Argentine enables a break with—rather than an embrace of—an identity category bound up with class markers and nationality. The same seems to be true for the dancer identity in relation to the negotiations surrounding tourism. In this particular context, tango dancing also represents freedom, transcendence and individuality.

The quest for individuality and authenticity is, however, bound to a dilemma. When many tango tourists are striving for the same values—be it authenticity or individuality—the values strived for actually tend to become elusive. When all tourists wish to be individual, they are adapting to a collective ideal. This entails, though, that "new" forms of rejecting a tourist identity appear. Rather ironically, avoiding the practices and excitements associated with a voyage out of the ordinary might in fact enable an identity play with values such as individuality and authenticity. This is portrayed in the case of the Swedish dancer Anna-Lena, who has been to Buenos Aires twice. She tells a story of how the organizing of her holiday life followed her routines from home and how this actually resulted in something quite different from the sensation of living inside a tourist enclave. Early on in the interview Anna-Lena speaks of Buenos Aires as an exciting and alluring place ("the name as such is exciting"). Although the extraordinary magnetism seems to have attracted Anna-Lena to Buenos Aires in the first place, her actual stay in the city was characterized by ordinary routines. She explains that she and her co-voyager, he also a tango dancer, tended to stay at home at night rather than trying to catch all the *milonga* excitement. As she puts it, they were busy engaging in everyday life: they did "cook a lot at home, we made our daily tours to the grocery so it was almost as if we were living there. Our neighbors and the cashiers in the supermarket were greeting us in the street. Our work was to go to the nearest tango school and take tango classes". This holiday lifestyle appears to have opened ways for Anna-Lena to relate more closely to the local Argentine community. The fact that she was not seduced by the promises of an individual "voyage out of the ordinary" actually seemed to distance her from other tourists. As she describes it herself, her daily tango life—not aiming for late-night adventures—appeared to distinguish her from "most other Swedish tourists", as she puts it. In fact, not searching for extraordinary experiences and a "time-out-of-time" existence made her trip rather different from that of most tourists.

CONCLUSION: NEGOTIATING TOURISM

The cultural production of tourism involves negotiations of values and identities. In relation to tango, one of these negotiations revolves around the significance of authenticity and the fact that authenticity values are both aspired for in tourism and perceived as being threatened by tourism—through the presence of other tourists as well as the engagement with tourist practices, venues and market items. In relation to tango tourism, one of these concerns is related to the visitors' attempts to distance themselves from a tourist identity as a means of constructing themselves as dancers. One example of such identity play is the rejection of tango-shows in luxury hotel restaurants, with the claim that these are "touristy" tango attractions created for "tourists"—not dancers. However, parallel to such boundary work—serving to create distinctions between tango and tourism—dance visitors in Buenos Aires actually engage in rather ordinary tourist practices. Whereas the motives are framed within a sublime vocabulary (existential endeavor, transformation of self, authentic tango), the actual everyday practices in the destination site seem to be shaped by factors having to do with convenience, comfort and safety together with recreational aims. Just like other tourists throughout the world, many tango voyagers seem to be happy engaging in tourist activities such as dining at picturesque restaurants, visiting historical sites and consuming souvenir items in the form of tango-related goods. In everyday holiday life it actually seems as if the average dance tourist downplays the importance of avoiding "non-touristy" experiences for the sake of "having a good time". In addition, foreign tango dancers in Buenos Aires seem to avoid the risk-taking some of them mentioned as part of a tango adventure—in relation to both physical and emotional risks. Many dance tourists seem to appreciate the company of other tourists, primarily visitors from their home country, rather than striving for "time-out-of-time" adventures with strangers. In that sense, the adventure out of the ordinary seems rather restricted in scope and tends to imply a journey into the ordinary. In fact, when approached in terms of their actual routines and holiday practices—not the expectations and promises associated with the journeys—many visiting tango dancers seem to have more in common with other tourists in Argentina than with local Argentine tango dancers.

One way of understanding how tango tourism can involve both everyday tourist practices and strong rejections of a tourist identity is to identify differences between different groups of tourists. We might suggest that dancers like Daniella, Emma, Lasse and some of the commentators on Tangoportalen are defending a non-touristy way of touring Buenos Aires. For reasons having to with political commitment (Lasse) or simply an image of how to get as much out of the tango trip as possible (Jannike), these dancers celebrate avenues out of the tourist enclaves. The boundary work between tango and tourism takes on concrete aspects in this framing as tango tourists convey advice such as for other visiting dancers to get beyond the "tourist décor" through friendship relations with Argentine dancers (Emma) or visits at "traditional" clubs far out of town (Daniella). This is to say that the gap between what tango tourists claim to be aspiring for and what they actually seem to be doing represents different takes on the journeys. We should also recognize that, for some dancers, the divide between the *grand* expectations of existential and adventurous excitements and a rather ordinary holiday life has to do with the perceived risks. One possible explanation is that attempts to live an emotionally exposed life in Buenos Aires are experienced as too risky, especially among some groups of female dancers. Rather than putting themselves in emotionally and physically edgy situations, some of them choose to take safety measures such as the company of other tourists, the purchase of comforting dance services and the choice to travel via taxis rather than public transportation.

In order to make additional sense of this divide, however, we must provide a methodological remark regarding a general attempt, both among tourists and tourist researchers, to convey the specificities of a particular journey—be it ecotourism, sex tourism or tango tourism—within the rather ritualized interview situation, as well as when tourists are chatting with other tourists and in holiday narratives told upon the return. Following a media logic, the public displays in blogs, webpages and autobiographical travel novels also involve the exposure of extraordinary and remarkable details, rather than telling a commonplace story of daily routines. This implies that we might risk losing sight of the everyday holiday practices when exploring the specificities of a certain kind of tourism. Such a concern is important in relation not only to tango tourism but to all sorts of tourism investigated for their particularities, such as tourism to war zones and so-called knowledge expeditions into untouched nature/culture. Rather than *only* experiencing overwhelming dancing in late-night *milongas* (or *only* engaging in sexual purchase, as in the cases of so-called sex tourism), these groups of tourists are involved in various everyday tourist practices and routines. Just like most other tourists, tango tourists (and so-called sex tourists) travel by aircraft, pay their hotel bills with credit cards, collect souvenirs and enjoy the warm climate.[8]

The additional fact that those dancers who seem keen to avoid "touristy" Argentina are implicated in tourism must also be related back to the field of tango dancing. As for Daniella, who stays in a "kitschy" tango hostel and travels with another Swedish dancer with whom she spends much of her holiday, is still keen to state that she is more of a dancer than a tourist. In order to understand such duplicity, we might look into the production as well as the consequences of a cultural narrative of travel. In a study of backpackers, Torun Elsrud describes how tourists engage in narration practices and thereby make "investment in travelers' capital", specifically connected to the world of budget travelers. "By relating to a specific narrative—that of independent travelling as risky and adventurous—in individual ways, travelers can position themselves within a backpackers' hierarchy. Through symbolic expression, through the investment in travelers' 'capital' [. . .], a hierarchical value system is maintained in which the experienced, the *avant-garde* of tourism, define 'the do's and don'ts'" (Elsrud 2001: 613). The creation of risk, as a central framing of these travels, is bound up with a particular identity work with potentially rewarding effects. In fact, her informants believe that their accumulated "adventurous identities" will help them not only to connect with other budget travelers, but also throughout job application processes and in social networking in general (Elsrud 2011: 613). In relation to tango journeys, we might notice that no matter whether the dancers have improved their dancing or made connection with Argentine dancers and tango culture, the framing of the journeys in a tango-adequate language comes with certain rewards—on holiday as well as at home. In relation to the objectives discussed in Chapter 4, the framing of the dance journey might in fact be read as forming a privileged narrative reflecting normative discourses about tango which ascribe transformative powers to the dancer. This is to say that dancers' accounts of their journeys to Buenos Aires might be read not necessarily as accounts of what they spent their days in Argentina doing, but rather as examples of how to speak a tango language. Moreover, the grand narrative of tango voyages reflects general discourses of our time which might be gratifying also outside the dancing milieus. In fact, dance tourists speak the language of individualism, risk-taking and connection with self. This might function as a means to create an image of a self-confident, exciting and emotionally connected person well suited for demands also off the dance floor.

This is particularly true for public blog posts and autobiographical novels, but might also be framed within the interview situation. Accounts like those given by the dancers on Tangoportalen, for instance, might be read as notes which shape and edit the dancers' public image—in this case as more authentic and more dedicated tango dancers than those foreigners caught up in "touristy" venues and practices. This implies that the accounts of deep connection with the culture not only reflect a wish to discover tango outside of comforting tourist services but also make up constitutive accounts which must be related to the intimate dance economy. The identity conflict between being a tourist and being a dancer is intertwined with the investments—and sacrifices—presumably made in relation to tango. This is how we can understand the many stories of foreign dancers who face difficult situations in Buenos Aires, particularly those found in the expanding autobiographical literature on tango, which with the endnote that it was worth the trouble (see Cusumano 2008; Palmer 2005; Potter 1997; Winter 2008). Such stories constitute proof of dedication and deep connection with the culture and hence function as authenticity-accumulating anecdotes.

This suggests that tourists' home lives are present during their tango holidays. Once at home, tourists might stage their visits as a showcase of the latest dancing trends in Buenos Aires, new pairs of dancing shoes and the sharing of colorful anecdotes. In that sense, the holiday investment involves not only improved dancing skills but also symbolic city landmarks and the embodiment of Argentine culture through mastery of language (Spanish words with the particular Argentine accent), bodily expressions and aesthetics. In fact, although the shaping of holiday memories functions to prolong the holiday, it is also another way of adding to the semi-public

160 Tourism and the Globalization of Emotions

construction of self and addressing the evaluating gazes of others. In that framing the *tourist* holiday can be used to create *tango* credentials. Much like other tourist practices, the collecting and public sharing of holiday experiences are conducted with the help of cameras, blog posts, the consumption of typical "goods" and, in the case of a dance journey, a set of embodied practices and manners (new dance movements and dance steps, a refined body posture etc.).

The possible "staging" and editing of the vacation—stressing certain aspects but not others—should be approached from dancers' embodied worldview. This is to say that some elements are simply not perceived as relevant information from a tango-dancing point of view. In their quest for authenticity, many tango voyagers seem, for instance, to make a distinction between tango culture and the rest of Buenos Aires. Although most dancers wish to encounter "real" Argentina, few would rent apartments or rooms in the local *barrios* outside the city center; few would even recognize the point in melting too deeply into everyday Argentine life. Rather, the search for authenticity revolves around the dancing experience and the particular tango culture. In short, authentic experiences prove to be important in relation to certain practices and experiences (those related to tango)—but not others (those related to the means of travel and everyday tourist routines). Hence, going to "touristy" restaurants and participating in city attractions and shopping unrelated to tango—as well as the decision to stay at fancy hotels and hostels in tourist-dense neighborhoods—are not a concern as long as these practices are separated from life at the *milonga*. At the *milonga*, however, most dancers wish to be dancers—and viewed as such by other dancers.[9] From these accounts we might suggest that tango voyagers are elaborating on a divided notion of authenticity focusing on particular aspects of the Argentine culture. This implies that dancers like Daniella stress the significance of discovering the dance embrace with Argentine dancers ("this is what it should feel like") at the same time as she and many other dance voyagers are happy to live with other tourists in some of the wealthier neighborhoods, and actually spend most of their time in Argentina with other tourists.

To sum up, the intersection between tourism and tango appears to be messy. On the one hand, it seems as if many tango travelers do not wish to be acknowledged as tourists. On the other hand, they engage in tourist practices and try to avoid some of the risks involved in a tango journey. We might conclude, though, that authenticity is a crucial value to the dancers, important enough to be decisive in the selection processes regarding where to dance, what to consume, who to "hang out with"—and moreover the objective of endless reflexive and narrative practices. The accounts discussed in this chapter indicate that authenticity is a privileged theme in the sense-making of tango voyages to Buenos Aires—whether the dancers embody these narratives in their everyday holiday routines or not. This suggests that, instead of dismissing the narrated tango journeys as false, we should evaluate discursive identity work as an important aspect of tango tourism. For analytical reasons, however, there is a point in making a distinction between public narration and everyday practices. The fact that such gaps exist tells us something important about the logic of tango—revolving around individuality and a play with distinctions—as well as about tourism, yet another arena in which people negotiate class-related markers and edit selves.

7 Commercialized Intimacy

INTRODUCTION

The values at stake in the negotiations over commercialized tango and tourist adjustments are not only bound up with the quest for authenticity. In fact, intimacy is another delicate dimension which plays a role in the intersection of tango dancing and tourism. In this chapter we will inquire into the ways in which dancers negotiate the commodification of a culture praised for its intimacy and emotionality. What happens when a price tag is put on experiences that dancers wish to have in mutual agreement and out of spontaneous actions? And why, on the contrary, is that economic interest often seen as opposed to values such as intimacy and authenticity, at a time when most parts of modern life—including tango dancing and holiday travelling—are organized through monetary transactions? How are these conflicts made sense of, negotiated and emotionally lived by people, in this case tango dancers on a dance vacation in Buenos Aires?

Throughout this chapter we will explore the cultural imaginaries that structure dancers' perceptions of and actions in relation to a market of dance services and tango goods, with a particular focus on the economic trading of dance partners. In fact, the services offered by *taxi dancers* will be used as a methodological detector to address the concerns evoked by a commercialized dance intimacy. As discussed in Chapter 5, this is a group of predominantly Argentine men who sell their dancing company to female tourists in the tango venues. Although there are tourists ready to pay for this service, taxi dancers are often perceived with suspicion or distanced curiosity. Even though taxi dancers themselves assure their potential clients that their objective is to secure an intimate tango experience through the transmittance of deep embodied tango knowledge, many dancers fear the opposite. In short, some dance tourists see this service as incompatible with the values searched for during their dance voyage. This has to do with two factors. First, taxi dancers are believed to offer a paid-for *shortcut* to the dance-floor, transgressing the boundaries and hierarchies of the intimate economy as well as the many rules and rituals surrounding the *milonga*. Secondly, taxi dancers are believed to offer a paid-for *tango intimacy* which turns dancing into a manufactured commodity.

However, this chapter will not be limited to targeting the values at stake in these conflicts. In a third section we will also explore cases in which the commercialized dance intimacy offered by taxi dancers is actually being legitimized. We will discuss examples in which dance tourists manage to make sense of their paid-for tango with taxi dancers within a narrative of intimacy, romance and authenticity. One example will allow us to look closely into how a (heterosexual) romantic narrative is used to make the purchased tango experience "real" and hence distinct from what is rejected as a routine commercialized intimacy. Discussing instances in which taxi dancing is perceived as incompatible with the world of tango as well as instances in which the service is made sense of from within the world's own discourses and narratives, we are able to address questions of *when*, *how* and *why* a commercialized intimacy is framed in negative terms and hence explore certain aspects of the boundary work in tango tourism.

TAXI DANCING AS A SHORTCUT

As discussed in a previous chapter, the world of Argentine tango dancing can be described as an intimate economy structured by dancing skills, authenticity capital and sexual charisma—in terms of physical appearance and sexual accessibility—together with social networks and economic capital. Although these values all function as credentials, in the sense that they can be traded for dances, friendship, valuable knowledge and material goods, each enjoys a different status. Whereas economic capital is often linked to power and social status elsewhere, the world of tango proves to be one in which it is made sense of in rather opposite terms. On the dancefloors of Buenos Aires money is sometimes even interpreted not in terms of a possession, but as a *lack*—of dancing skills and the right tango embodiment. One example of this is found in the reactions towards extravagant, expensive shoes on beginners' feet, which, at times, are interpreted as an indication that money has been used to replace or compensate for a lack of dancing skills. The reactions towards expensive shoes on beginners' feet have to do with the use of money as a *shortcut* to access the values of tango, not least the intimate dance embrace, without corresponding with deep embodied knowledge required by the culture.

This is also partly what taxi dancers are accused of providing: a shortcut for beginning and mainstream dancers to participate beyond their level of dancing, as well as cultural integration in exchange for money instead of long-term practice and experience within the culture. The managing of market logics within the dance economy is beautifully expressed in the Swedish tango dancer Birgitta Holm's autobiographical book *Pardans (Couple Dancing)*. In the passage quoted below she describes how the identity of being a tourist and a presumed client within a market adds complexity to the already complicated economy played out on the Argentine dance-floors.

Different from most tango teachers in Buenos Aires, Angel is a *milonguero* who goes out for his own pleasure's sake and who almost got himself a bad reputation as a womanizer. But this increases his credibility as an instructor. [. . .] I came to the afternoon *milongas* with a plunging neckline, dressed to be part of the play. I was awake as an owl, not to let any chance of eye contact slip my attention. With an immense effort I tried to fixate the gaze of some of the men around the table. Every dance was a trial of strength and victory, even though it might be a blank, viewed as a dance. The reasons behind why they wanted to dance with me, I figured, were rarely pleasant: to have been paid or offered a free entrance in exchange for their dance accompany; to hope being able to attract you as a student; because they feel sorry for you. It was acceptable if they invited me because they conveyed curiosity or attraction. But it was only genuinely fun if I believed that it was because they thought they would enjoy dancing with me. (Holm 2004: 112, 117, my translation)

This quote provides an image of how the intimate dance economy is activated in intersection with a market space targeting tourists. Among the reasons local dancers might have for dancing with Holm, she rates taxi dancers' motivations the lowest. Those dancers who have "been paid" to invite her would hardly provide a pleasurable dance set. She goes on to state that romantic reasons or interest in her as a person would be "acceptable", but only those reasons having to do with her dancing qualities would allow her to really enjoy the dancing. Avoiding the comforting services offered by "paid" dancers—taxi dancers—is also made sense of as a matter of tango honor: "bought" dances simply lack the status of dances merited on the basis of dancing skills, or at least romantic or social charms.

In line with dancers' aspirations for tango recognition together with the discussion in the previous chapter, the problem of taxi dancers must be related to what their company signifies and how it reflects the customers' wishes. One reason some dancers did not want to hire a dance company was that it would identify them as tourists, and particularly beginning tourist dancers. One example of this is found among a group of female friends in their late fifties from the North-American east coast, visiting Buenos Aires for a two-week stay. Some of them were beginning dancers, whereas others had been practicing tango for a couple of years. In an interview they told me that they never thought of hiring a taxi dancer. After some days, however, I discovered that they had been paying for a similar service from an Argentine dancer named Pepe. They met him in *Club Gricel*, one of the mixed *milongas* in town targeting a middle-aged crowd, on one of the visit's first evenings and decided to take private classes with him in the apartment they rented. As the relation deepened they also paid him for taking them on tours throughout the city and for participating in private dance evenings in their temporary residence. Sometimes they paid him in cash; at other times they invited him to join them at a restaurant or to eat with them at home. Pepe quickly became more of a friend than a distant teacher and was awarded more enthusiasm for his charm and personality than his actual dancing skills. The women even complained about his ways of explaining steps and postures. Still, they all seemed happy with his company. When I asked them how this differed from hiring a taxi dancer, they first turned silent, and then Miranda said: "It just didn't feel right to pay for a taxi dancer, I mean, we are all asked to dance. And I wouldn't want to be seen with a *taxista*. Pepe isn't a fabulous teacher but that is what we pay him to do. And he actually gave me some good advice on how to loosen up my arms so that's different" (Miranda, 55-year-old, U.S.).

The fact that the women had no concerns hiring a private teacher who came to their apartment, often for longer hours than planned, indicates that their attitude towards taxi dancers was partly a matter of the negative associations of this service. Hence, the women's reaction primarily tells a story about the play of social status in tango. Being spotted with a taxi dancer suggests that a dancer does not hold credentials strong enough to dance on her or his own merits. Similar concerns were shared in a discussion thread on the Swedish webpage for tango dancers, Tangoportalen. In a blog thread titled "Taxi dancers and tourist dancers",[1] experiences and reflections regarding the commercialization of Argentine tango are shared, primarily by tango practitioners who have been to Buenos Aires and those attempting to go there. One particular focus is the services offered by taxi dancers. One dancer who had made a dance journey to Buenos Aires, Patricia, brought forward an argument similar to Miranda's for why she rejected offers from taxi dancers—or tourist dancers, as she calls them: "I see a 'risk' going to the *milongas* with those well-known *milongueros* who dance with women for money. It might happen that the other dancers will 'leave you alone' and then you will miss out on many fine dances with someone who really wants to dance with you in particular!"

The fear of being "fooled", touched upon in the previous chapter, is also present in the dancers reflecting on taxi dancers. By some tango tourists, the escort dancers are partly seen as a group of "tango tricksters" who have learned to take economic advantage of naïve foreigners, particularly "lovesick women". As Katrin writes on Tangoportalen:

> Tourist dancers: if I pull it to the extreme it is a *"sol och vårare"* (men who seduce women in order to rip them off), who during a period of their life live off of rich tourists. They go to bed with every new group of tourists. [. . .] The tourist dancers are also those dancers who are hired by the *milonga* organizers to dance with the women who will not be asked to dance. (Katrin, Tangoportalen)

This passage makes a connection between a loss of money and a loss of honor, both potentially a result of engaging with taxi dancers. It also points to the fact that the semi-private relationships between service provider and client are believed to create more harm than do fraud in relation to more distant market transactions. The degree of vulnerability—on the part of the tourist—is supposedly larger when emotional experiences are involved than in transactions of material goods. Paying a little bit too much for a pair of shoes causes less damage, emotionally and in relation to one's position within the dance-floor hierarchy, than paying (too much) for dancing company. Thus, it might be suggested that the fear of being fooled is not so much about the actual loss of money, but more about the potentially damaged prestige and self-image reflected by other dancers.

However, the reasons for not paying for a "shortcut" to the dance-floor have to do not only with tango recognition and a fear of being fooled, but also with some of the motives behind the dance journeys. For example, Magdalena and Elisabeth on a three-week stay in Buenos Aires, decided before leaving Sweden not to hire a taxi dancer. They perceived the services offered by taxi dancers as a comforting paid companion and a helping hand that would actually come in the way of their attempts to try out the dance scene on their own. Rather than securing an evening out in the *milongas*, establishing beforehand the company of a dance partner and avoiding the risk of exposing themselves to the emotionally difficult selection process, they conceived of the journey as a way of challenging themselves and getting to experience "the real thing", as Magdalena explains it:

> We didn't want to [hire a taxi dancer]. We had talked about it before leaving but we wanted to break in on our own. If it's not possible for us to dance we will get the experience that it was difficult. We didn't want to do anything else but the things that this world has to offer. We didn't want to do a tourist special. (Magdalena, 50-year-old, Sweden)

Along with some of the dancers quoted in Chapter 6, Magdalena wishes to avoid doing "a tourist special". In her view, taxi dancing is a service only targeting tourists and a commercialized "rescue" from "the things that this world has to offer". This suggests that dancing is only one of Magdalena's aspirations. In fact, if dancing is done at the expense of "real" experiences of tango in Buenos Aires (as being "difficult"), she prefers obtaining those experiences rather than dancing her evenings away in a paid-for-embrace.

TAXI DANCING AS MANUFACTURED INTIMACY

The quote from Birgitta Holm's autobiographical book also sheds light on the relation between the emotional imperative in tango, i.e. the cult of strong feelings and intimate dancing connections, and the supposedly cold logic of economic transactions. When the topic of taxi dancers came up in small talk and interviews with dance tourists, some of them insisted that feelings and more specifically the *tango feeling* could hardly be transmitted when both parties knew that a money-based transaction had taken place. In a word: feelings cannot be bought. Dancing should be based on mutual agreement and be free from interests other than those related to tango. This is one of the main arguments also in the discussions on the Swedish webpage Tangoportalen. Patricia, for instance, formulates her concerns as a matter of "believe[ing] in the dancing":

> I believe in the dancing as such . . . either dancing for free or not dancing at all. [. . .] The day I will not be able to dance at the *milongas* (not being invited or not having invitations accepted) also I will consider paying for the fun . . . if it would still feel like fun and if I would still travel to Buenos Aires. I wish to continue being naïve and believe that all women who can dance also will be able to dance in BA, without paying for it. [. . .] The travel expenses are payment enough and the fact that I change my dollars in place and spend every cent of it. (Patricia, Tangoportalen)

"Believe[ing] in the dancing", implies a belief in the tango economy. "All women who can dance" should be "able to dance in BA". For Patricia, taxi dancers symbolize the end of such belief and hence her enjoyment of tango. "Paying for the fun" equals no fun. Another dancer on Tangoportalen, calling herself Milonguera, agrees, stressing the importance of "mutual agreements" in tango dancing, here formulated from the perspective of the taxi dancer: "One thing is obvious to me, the dance has to be a 'mutual agreement'. I myself would not want to dance against my will, being forced up onto the dance-floor and brutally being thrown around like a ragdoll". Not hiring a taxi dancer is, according to the logic of this account, a matter of "not doing to others what you do not want others to do to you". The notion of "dancing against" one's will is here extended to imply various negative consequences related to a power imbalance. Taxi dancers are described as "being forced" to the dance-floor and being "thrown around like a ragdoll". This argument is underlined further as some dancers stress the similarities between taxi dancing and sex work.[2] One example of this is found in a comment made by Sahar on Tangoportalen:

> I think of this [taxi dancing] as a sad phenomenon. Although I find prostitution much worse I can't keep from seeing the similarities. Both customers buy into a human encounter on an intimate level and expect/demand that the other party will offer himself/herself physically but also emotionally (at least in tango . . .) Isn't the idea that someone wants to dance with you *out of free will* fundamental for a pleasant dancing experience? [. . .] We always have the opportunity to express our gratitude. If money is involved and a contract signed the taxi dancer has to suffer a difficult dancing experience. (Sahar, Tangoportalen)

Sahar expresses a general criticism of the commercialization of "human encounters". By comparing taxi dancing with prostitution she stresses the lack of free will on the part of the service provider and the hardship to which this might subject them, here expressed as an economic "contract" which forces the taxi dancers to "suffer a difficult dancing experience". In addition, Sahar points out the level of emotionality in tango and implicitly suggests that the experience for the client can hardly be enjoyable because both parties know that one of them is not dancing according to her or his emotional will. These considerations illustrate not only how the services of taxi dancers are associated with illegitimate sex work, but also how taxi-dancing challenges some important elements in the belief system of tango. As discussed in previous chapters, the tango is in fact a strongly individualistic culture revolving around notions of subjective emotionality, freedom and choice. This is manifested not least in the code of conduct surrounding the asking-up procedure. In fact, every *milonga* is made up of a constant stream of negotiated individual wills and choices, a logic which taxi-dancing services disregards when offering their dance company for money. The embracing of the spontaneously emerging dance-floor intimacy in tango actually conforms to Anthony Giddens' idea of pure relationships and plastic sexuality. He describes these relations as typical of the individualism and flexibility of late-modern societies. The relations are based on equality and sustained only by mutual satisfaction. In Giddens' own words: "it refers to a situation where a social relation is entered into for its own sake, for what can be derived by each person from a sustained association with another; and which is continued only in so far as it is thought by two parties to deliver enough satisfaction for each individual to stay within it" (Giddens 1992: 58; cp. Bauman 2007).

An individualist discourse on authentic emotionality, together with the significance of a free will and mutual agreements, is crucial for understanding the boundary work negotiating the intersection between tango and tourism. In order to visualize this we might look into the dividing line made between what is perceived of as a problematic paid-for tango with a taxi dancer and the legitimate paid-for tango with a dance teacher, reflected on in an earlier quote by North-American Miranda. Although both taxi dancers and (private) tango teachers provide a bodily and emotional dance intimacy in exchange for money, the two services are believed to differ in one important respect. The practicing of steps in studios is perceived to be part of an educational agenda and hence to be a rather technical matter (together with the accessing of social networks and information), whereas the task of taxi dancers is often framed as dancing for the pleasure of dancing, and hence as a service aspiring to offer intimacy and emotional experiences. The emotional aspects of taxi dancing are what rhyme poorly with the commercial framing. As suggested in the comments made on Tangoportalen, the *act* of dancing tango, its bodily and musical movements, can potentially be disengaged from feelings and hence be bought as a strict teaching service (private teachers), whereas the *feeling* of mutual communication and intimacy disappears when economic transactions are involved (taxi dancers).

LEGITIMATING TAXI-DANCING

However, there are ways to negotiate the potentially problematic associations implicit in the services offered by taxi dancers. In fact, these services would not exist if there were no dancers happy to pay for intimate dance company. Jenny, for instance, writes on Tangoportalen that she has not yet been to Buenos Aires but if she goes there she might actually hire a taxi dancer: "If it would drastically change my possibilities of getting to dance, if I would learn something from the experience and if it would not feel too weird or humiliating, which I cannot know before I have been in the situation. And if I would be judged as an easily fooled *gringo* I can take that—I have never believed that one can integrate into a new country in a couple of weeks or months." (Jenny, Tangoportalen) British Susan, in the documentary movie *Taxidancing* (2012), frames the purchasing of Juan Carlos' taxi-dancing services from the view of the vulnerability in tango, striking harder on women than on men. As she recalls memories of being rejected at the *milonga*, the camera eye sweeps over the many women at *Confitería Ideal* sitting alone waiting for a dance. Some of the women are smilingly glancing through the hall, as to make contact with possible partners, whereas others seem to have given up. "For a woman it's a feeling of impotence and powerlessness. You are powerless and there is nothing you can do about it. No matter how well you dance there is nothing you can do. And the men, on their hand, are dancing one dance after the other. It's not a very nice feeling." Other women who did hire the company of a taxi dancer described the hours with arranged partners not so much as an emotional experience but as a way to gain dance experience and to practice dance figures with a more advanced dancer. A "taxi-dancer-as-means" account is, for instance, found in a blog entry on Tangoportalen made by Selma, a Swedish dancer who hired a taxi dancer when she visited Buenos Aires. She writes rather unsentimentally about the up-front economic transaction and underscores that the taxi dancer's task was mostly to act as a "support-dancer", helping her to improve her dancing during classes and *milongas*.

> It never came to my mind thinking that I had paid for an equal encounter, but rather for a non-equal encounter between "mutually agreeing parties". I never fooled myself into believing that I would get an emotional kick out of this. What I wanted to get from my money was knowledge and practice in tango as a dance, thanks to the fact that those I hired were more experienced than I am. [. . .] The female American dancer, however, who introduced me to the idea thought that there was more in it than there actually was. (Selma, Tangoportalen)

In this account the *purchased* dances with a taxi dancer are made sense of as a means to improve the chances of getting to experience *real* dances. In this configuration, the taxi-dancing service is equated with the job of a dance teacher, as the *taxistas* are described as "more experienced" dancers who can offer "practice in tango". Selma clearly stresses that she is not looking for "emotional kicks" or an intimate "equal encounter". This point is further stressed by the counter-case, the "female American dancer" who hoped the service would include more than actual dancing, presumably romance and sex. Distancing herself from such aspirations, Selma positions her own purchase as removed from the associations with sex work and the negative framing following from such associations.

There are also those dancers who point to the beneficial consequences for the local tango economy. Some women who actually did hire taxi dancers described this as a way of supporting the local economy, in decline after the financial crisis. Similarly, some dancers stress that the entrepreneurship surrounding tango is important for local dancers and the recovery of the Argentine capital. As one dancer on Tangoportalen asks rhetorically: "Free dancing? The economic conditions are different for them. They are eating with the money that we waste when we are having a good time. Then why should it be free?" (Isabel, Tangoportalen). Another dancer, Jenny, asks why people get so upset over the fact that good dancers take on dancing jobs to support themselves. "If I got this right the t-o-t dancers [taxi and tourist dancers] are professionals and semi-professionals in this area who make money out of something that they at least partly like doing. Like writers, musicians and artists who take jobs which are not what they primarily want to do but still are ok. [. . .] Why get so upset over this phenomenon?" (Jenny, Tangoportalen). Also the discourse of authentic feelings has given rise to critical comments, questioning the notion of "free dancing". Mats, who has not been to Buenos Aires and disassociates himself from "glorified travel" to Argentina, writes: "The politically correct opinion is that all dancing that doesn't take place between 'equal and mutually agreeing parties' is reprehensible. And that money makes equality impossible. But is equality really necessary for both parties to get something out of the dancing, and what are the actual criteria for equality that we wish to create? Do we want to define 'sound dancing', danced by 'good people', and distinguish it from 'unsound' and 'destructive' dancing?" (Mats, Tangoportalen)

However, there are also those customers who make sense of the taxi-dancing service in a somewhat opposite way. Some of them use a discourse of emotionality and authenticity—bound up with Argentine dancers—when ascribing meaning to the commercialized dance relation. As Annie, in her fifties, declares candidly: "I was very lucky and very smart because [. . .] I was afraid that I was not going to be chosen. I hired a taxi dancer so that will guarantee a dance with an Argentine" (Annie, 54-year-old, U.S.). The dancing service provided by Argentine taxi dancers is made sense of as a way of securing an authentic tango experience, transmitted by the dancers' cultural heritage, instead of "dancing with American guys from home". Additional examples show how a (hetero)romantic script is used in customers' attempts to place the taxi-dancing experience within a narrative of free will and emotionality. The account of Susanna, a North-American tango dancer, originally from Mexico, illustrates the ambiguous significance of romantic desires in transactions of intimate dancing for money. When she tells the story of how she got into an increasingly tighter embrace with her taxi dancer Osvaldo, the potentially problematic impact of money fades away as the level of intimacy intensifies.

Susanna states that she looked not only for a dance partner, but also for the company and the knowledge possessed by local dancers. Some more advanced dancers at home had recommended that she hire a taxi dancer and had given her a couple of names, of which Osvaldo's was one. On her arrival Susanna called him up and they ended up dancing almost every day during her two-week stay. She took private classes for forty dollars an hour and hired his company as a taxi dancer out in the nightly *milongas*. For his services as a taxi dancer he normally charged ten dollars an hour but, as she said, he gave her a reduced "friends' prize". Moreover, he shared plenty of stories and colorful anecdotes with her that she would later on tell her friends back home. He also trained her in how to proceed with a successful *cabeceo* and how to maintain a posture and face that would trigger the interest of other dancers. In addition, Susanna told me, Osvaldo became more than just a "dance escort". The very last evening of her stay they were out dancing at the *Niño Bien*, one of the larger clubs with a mixed crowd of Argentines and foreigners of all ages. They had made an agreement to dance for two hours, but time flew and, before they knew it, the evening got late and Susanna had to head back to the hotel to pack her last bags and get a few hours sleep before the early flight. Out on the street, Osvaldo suddenly pulled her towards the wall and kissed her—passionately, she added when recounting the event to me. Although she had not seen it coming she was not surprised. She had felt an increasing intensity over the weeks, she said: the embrace got tighter every evening and she could feel the "tango sparks". Yet, the moment was soon to be over. Some minutes later a taxi pulled up next to the sidewalk. While kissing her good-bye one last time, Osvaldo whispered that he was married but that he had "enjoyed every moment of her stay". Susanna was thrilled over the *finale* of her visit. With or without a ring on his finger, Osvaldo was a real *porteño*, she explained, "a real man of tango". "And that kiss, what a perfect ending to my trip! Isn't that *so* Buenos Aires?" (Susanna, 50-year-old, U.S.).

Yes, what about the kiss? Was it a spontaneous expression of suppressed attraction, vivid proof that real desire can appear in relations initiated on the basis of an economic transaction? Was it an extension of the intimate embrace, of the training device that "you should dance the tango *as if* you could go to bed with the person in your arms"? Or was it part of the tourist deal—as Susanna puts it, the perfect ending to her holiday and, moreover, to her investment in an intimate service?[3] And what about Osvaldo? Did he perceive the kiss as part of his job or rather as the more enjoyable side of the tedious work of teaching foreigners how to dance tango? Was the kiss an attempt to save his male honor, as though by conquering Susanna sexually the potentially shameful act of having *been bought* could possibly be mitigated? Could the manifestation of an active potent masculinity initiating sexual activity even switch the roles from "service provider" and "client" to "man" and "woman" and hence also change the power relation between Latin America and the U.S.? Using flirtatious behavior and engaging in heterosexual romantic play could actually be interpreted as a way of reinstalling oneself as an active subject, in place of the passive worker submitting to the desires of tourist clients and management.

We will not get any definite answers to these questions. What we can say something about, though, is how Susanna made sense of the situation. When she told me about Osvaldo and her last evening in town she explained that she never dwelled on the reasons behind the kiss. She was happy to return home with an experience that lived up to her expectations of tango life in Buenos Aires. She had discovered the city and the dance clubs with a local dancer and been able to sense the force of the intimate play, yet without being emotionally wounded. She got on the flight back home with butterflies in her stomach but no heartbreak, she said. Neither did she see the kiss as an act of infidelity towards her boyfriend back home. Rather, it was part of the *tango feeling*, she explained. "What we did out there was no different from what we did on the dance-floor. Actually the embrace was hotter on the dance-floor than when we kissed on the street." Yet, the kiss played an important role when she told her close girlfriends at home about the trip. It was proof that she had transcended the category of a greedy *gringa* to become a true *tanguera*, a tango-dancing woman capable of creating the distinctive dance-floor magic with a partner. In her understanding, the kiss demonstrated that the connection was "real" although the relation was framed by a financial agreement. In sum, transforming Osvaldo from a service provider to a passionate lover made her tango vacation one of genuine affect instead of purchased dances. In that sense, some elements of Susanna's account are similar to the reasoning implicit in the previous quote from Birgitta Holm's book on tango. In Holm's ranking of the different motives local dancers might have for dancing with her, romantic aspirations clearly trump economic ones, even if she prefers being selected for her dancing qualities.

Although the use of a romantic language of "magic" and "tango sparks" helped Susanna make sense of the economic transaction within a narrative of authentic feelings and free will, the story also provides an account of how money is used to buy oneself freedom from emotional bonds and vulnerability. As Susanna declares, she left Buenos Aires without being heartbroken and without feeling bad and shameful in relation to her boyfriend at home. The frames of the economic transaction actually created a limit to her feelings for Osvaldo. This reinforces an argument made by Georg Simmel. The conflict between economic transactions and intimacy discussed in his essay on prostitution (1907/1971) might be expressed as a matter of inconsistency. He argues that money creates social and emotional distance whereas intimacy asks for people to create durable bonds. In his understanding money is the most impersonal objectified value and, in that sense, is in sharp contrast to the nature of people's need for close relations.[4] In relation to Susanna and Osvaldo, money might have functioned as a mediator to create personal distance which in fact made it easier to relate to the various roles and expectations in the dancing; in Susanna's example, these included the shifting romantic feelings for her paid-for dance partner. In fact, the economic trading seemed to create both emotional closeness and distance. The delimitation in time and space—enforced by the economic transaction—made it easier for Susanna to enjoy the dance intimacy. However, and rather paradoxically, the writing off of feelings also made it easier to feel.

Like Susanna, other tourists declared that they were happy to exchange money for dance sessions as long as a rewarding dance experience was achieved. However, it was important to them that the contracted dancing satisfied the criteria of "real" tango, meaning a sincerely established dance connection through bodily communication. This is consistent with some evidence from Elizabeth Bernstein's studies of sex workers and their clients. The male clients in her investigation searched for "real" sexual experiences provided by engaged, personal and sincere paid-for sex partners, within a restricted social frame. Some of them spoke of their sex consumption in terms of a limited adventure outside their normal life with a wife and family—and not as a substitute for an absent sex life (Bernstein 2007: 119–125). Like those men, dance voyagers like Susanna and the previously discussed North-American women who hired a private dance teacher spoke of the paid-for bodily encounters in dance studios and *milongas* as a sensual dance experience, most of the time as "real" and authentic as non-purchased dances. They paid for the teachers' and taxi dancers' particular dancing skills (that is what made these dances so pleasurable, some women said), not just for the arms of any Argentine man out in town.

Returning to Susanna, the negotiation of money and intimacy also seems to involve an idea of equality. This is manifested in a situation whereby some non-tango dancing friends paid Susanna for a taxi dancer out in a fancy show-restaurant. As the stage performance ended, some people from the audience went to a small wooden floor in the middle of the room to dance, she told me. The music had been playing for some twenty minutes when a young man appeared before Susanna. Confused by the unfamiliar face, she turned to her friends. Their eager smiles encouraged her to get up on the dance-floor. Twenty-year-old Miguel proved to be a taxi dancer and her friend's farewell present. When she told me the story she explained that he was a good dancer and—she added—very cute, but she did not feel comfortable. "Dancing with someone that young and for money was all new to me. With Osvaldo it was different. He is an old guy, ten years older than me [. . .] there is something in it for him. I might not be an excellent dancer but I am still a hot *tanguera*", she said laughing.

Another way of describing the different experiences is that in Susanna's relation with Osvaldo the involvement of money could partly be hidden. He was, as she claimed, "getting something out of" dancing with her besides money, whereas it was possible that a "cute twenty-year-old" could have no other reason besides extra income for asking up an intermediate dancer like her. In that sense "real" affection, or at least the prospect of genuine feelings, ironically became a condition for legitimating the service. In other words, Susanna did not worry over the simultaneous existence of money and intimacy. On the contrary, in her understanding the kiss constituted a means to reduce the negative impact of a commercialized transaction.

CONCLUSION: NEGOTIATING COMMERCIALIZED INTIMACY

The aim of this chapter has been to use taxi-dancing as a detector to make visible some of the conflicts bound up with a commercialization of tango and the implicit tourist adjustments. Throughout this chapter we have discussed how the services of taxi dancers challenge the belief system of tango in two important ways: *first*, by offering accessibility to the dance-floor through the use of economic capital—rather than through merit based on commitment and rigorous dance training—and *secondly* by offering tango intimacy for money—rather than by means of mutual free will based on authentic feelings. As some dancers quoted in this chapter put it: the particularity of tango, its intimate embrace and emotional pleasures, should not be for sale; rather, tango dancing should offer an intimate avenue out of commercialization.

These reactions suggest that three main discourses are relevant when negotiating commercialized intimacy in tango. The first one targets a particular form of *emotionality*, implying that tango is all about the intimate communication and momentary magic experienced through the dancing. In addition, this discourse contains a notion of individualism and pure relations, suggesting that the tango constitutes a form of intimacy which people should enter by means of free will. The second discourse has to do with *authenticity* and relates to the field of tourism and the cultural production of taste as a mode of distinction. Drawing on the discussions in the previous chapter, this notion is associated with a distinction between those travelers who are believed to connect with the culture and the "cheap" and "touristy" ones who resort to a paid-for shortcut. Such a shortcut is believed to be offered by taxi dancers. Implicit in this notion of authenticity is a discourse of *honor*. The (mis)use of money, exemplified by what is perceived as an exaggerated tango consumption or the purchasing of illegitimate items and services (such as taxi dancers), is made sense of as an offense towards the tango culture.

We should be cautious to note, though, that the service of taxi dancers does not challenge the institutional regulation surrounding intimacy in tango. In fact, the taxi-dancing service respects the *milonga* rules in regard to the level of physical intimacy and the social managing of intimate relations. As Ezequiel, the manager of *Taxi Tango*, puts it, it is important for his employees not to "take advantage" of the situation and extend the dance intimacy into a sexual affair. In his words, this is not a firm for "Latin Lovers". The fact that most taxi dancers work with several clients at a time also follows the *milonga* custom of changing dance partners to avoid becoming "over-intimate" with one particular partner (although many taxi dancers stay with one dance partner throughout an evening). Rather, it is the economy of tango which seems to be challenged by this service, offering shortcuts to values which should be merited through legitimate tango credentials. However, as discussed throughout this chapter, this is believed to threaten also the experienced level of intimacy in the dancing. The commercialization of feelings, in the form of a price tag put on emotional experiences, and hence the blocking of spontaneity, are believed to have a negative impact on the connection in the dancing. This suggests that rather than challenging the *milonga* regulations surrounding intimacy, the taxi-dancing service challenges an emotionally charged discourse of intimacy. This case thereby highlights that the negotiations over various aspects of intimacy and authenticity are difficult to separate. In fact, we might claim that most negotiations in tango, including those related to values such as authenticity, tend to return to the distinctive intimacy in tango, which is perceived as the heart of the dancing.

This chapter also suggests that the taxi-dancing service, tather than being fixed as an illegitimate element in Argentine tango life, is made the object of discursive struggles and hence undergoes symbolic shifts in meaning. The reflections of Susanna, Jenny and Miranda, among others, imply that the potential conflict between a commercialized dance intimacy and values such as emotionality, authenticity and tango honor is under negotiation; in fact, the question is not so much *what* to consume but rather *how* to consume and how to *make sense* of the purchase. In transactions through which money is believed to function as a mediator to access not the intimacy and emotional thrills as such, but rather the means to undergo such experiences, the use of economic capital in exchange for intimate bodily work of private dance teachers is not perceived as a problem. As shown in the advertisements of dance schools, shoe brands and beauty salons, the services and goods are sold with promises of *allowing for* excellent and emotionally stimulating dancing. When it comes to the services offered by taxi dancers, however, many dancers declare that they do not wish to pay for the dancing experience *as such*, meaning the presumed "tango magic", the emotional and intimate components of the dancing. In that sense, the attempts to legitimate the purchasing of taxi dancers engage with the same kinds of discourses that are used to discredit the service. The clients make sense of the taxi-dancing services within an educational framing of tango tourism as well in accordance with a discourse of authenticity, romanticized feelings and mutual agreement.

8 Sex, Romance and Tango

INTRODUCTION

One area in which the impact of a tourist market and a client identity is linked to a specific set of dilemmas is that of romance and sexual affairs. The "sexy" aura of the tango together with the stereotypical representation of Argentine (men) as "Latin Lovers" suggests that tango journeys are infused with romance. Some dancers also acknowledged that they had experienced "sexy" dancing in Buenos Aires; some of them even ended up dating local dance partners and had several sexual affairs during their holiday. For certain travelers, romance is believed to make up a "natural" comportment in tango just as in other hobbies. This is what North-American Susanna believes. As discussed in the previous chapter, she actually did experience an arousing attraction to the taxi dancer she hired during her stay in Buenos Aires and had a short intimate moment with him off the dance-floor. She admits that the intimate dance form and the dramatic emotionality expressed through the music make it easier to fall in love, but she also believes that romantic feelings appear "everywhere". As Susanna points out, people end up in each other's arms in book circles as well as on the dance-floor, with the noticeable difference that few people would claim that book circles—for that reason—are "all about sex".[1] For obvious reasons tango dancers, just like choir singers and co-workers, fall in love with each other and engage in sexual affairs. This, however, is not the main promise and motive behind most tango trips to Argentina, at least not when dancers are asked about their travel. And although this is true for certain voyages, something quite different also seems to be at stake in tango tourism. For some dancers the sexual representations of tango actually conjure up a problem which leads them to actively avoid romantic or sexual situations in tango. Still, all tango tourists are—for various reasons—forced to reflect on and practically manage the associations between tango and sex.

In order to address the provocative and yet unsettled rapport between sex and tango, this chapter aims at examining the ways in which dance voyagers make sense of and negotiate this relation. As in the discussion of commercialized tango, the matter of romance and sex is not so much a question of whether tango tourists engage romantically with local dance partners or not. Rather tango tourism entails a delicate play of distinctions in regard to the affective and intimate relations in tango, the "do's and don'ts". This is to say that dancers negotiate meaning, including the practical managing of *how* to do intimacy and romance—on and off the dance-floor—with *whom* to be intimate and how to *make sense* of intimate experiences in tango. The main key to understanding these negotiations is tango culture itself, and not least the *milonga* regulations surrounding intimacy. However, the loosely formed continuum between intimacy, romance and sex in tango changes shape and character when infused with racial and class-related aspects. The context of global tourism, involving economic inequality and the attractiveness of foreign capital together with exoticized representations of Argentine dancers, is one such decisive component in the sense-making of transnational sexual affairs—not least because of the associative ties with sex tourism. This implies that romantic relations between two foreign dancers, or between two Argentine tango dancers, are not made sense of in the same way and with the same tension as the cross-cultural—and moreover cross-class-relational— affairs between tango tourists and local dancers.

In this chapter we will discuss cases of dance tourists who have taken the tango embrace outside the *milonga* and gone on dates with local dancers.[2] We will also explore the sexual, moral and racialized gender regimes present in the critique of affairs between tourists and locals. By doing so, this chapter wishes to unfold the ways in which class and race, fused together in a Global South–Global North relation characterized by inequality as well as by attempts to overcome difference inscribe meaning and significance to heterosexual romance in tango. Not least, we will ask why the relation between sex and tango is seemingly so provocative to dancers, especially when visiting Argentina, and why some of them are keen to draw a sharp line between sex and tango. What are the reasons and consequences of such a divide?

This chapter takes off from a discussion of a number of historical accounts regarding the tango-sex relation. In addition, we will inquire into the distinctions between sex and tango in relation to a contemporary tango *illusio* and the defense of an autonomous cultural field. In the following sections we will interrogate the tango-sex rapport from various angles, one of which is the relation between class and heterosexual romance. This discussion highlights the critical nexus of heterosexual romance and social class in the context of tourism in an economically vulnerable—as well as sexualized and racialized—part of the world. However, tango tourism involves a dynamic that is quite the opposite of that of various cases of sex tourism. Rather than allowing for an engagement in sexual holiday affairs, the economic inequality between the intimate counterparts in tango seems to undermine the interest in such affairs, at least for some female tango tourists. In the final section we will explore dancers' perceptions of authentic romance. It is suggested that dancers elaborate on a notion of equality and sameness, particularly in regard to class differences. This entails that dance journeys, at least for some dancers, entail an enforcement of romantic boundaries, rather than creating avenues for sexual excitements in faraway tango-land.

TANGO AND SEX: THE SACRED AND THE PROFANE

As discussed in Chapter 2, the fluid tango intimacy both facilitates romantic engagement, along with what some dancers describe as the potential to "fall in love with anyone", *and* enforces limitations. Although the boundaries between dancing, intimacy, romance and sex often blur in the dancers' sense-making of their own tango experiences, efforts are at times made to hold these categories apart. Such attempts can be traced back to early twentieth-century Buenos Aires. In her fascinating book on tango history, Marta Savigliano exposes a number of books and essays written by male *tangueros* primarily in the 1920s and 1930s, showing that (heterosexual) romance and sex were partly made sense of as a threat towards the macho cult of tango. The investments in sexual desires—and implicitly women—were believed to turn men into passive servants, far from the brute and wild-hearted men thought to represent the tango. Interest in women sometimes even imposed the label "queer" on men, suggesting that they were less manly than those men who put their male friendships center stage. Savigliano explains the problem with heterosexual desires in tango to be associated with the importance of male relations in a male-centered society, "a cult of 'authentic virility'" (1995a: 43).

At that time, the problem with sex in tango was also bound up with the symbolic configuration of tango as a sacred and refined culture in opposition to sex as a casual act stemming from bodily needs. In this way the erotic potential of tango—being a symbol of force—is actually distinguished from sexual and feminized needs. In a 1933 essay Martínez Estrada describes tango as the sexual act itself "without neurosis" and claims that the sensual relations with women "exhaust the potential eroticism of the dance" (in Savigliano 1995a: 43). As Ernesto Sábato writes in an effort to explain this, tango culture wished to elevate its aficionados above the relative coarseness of everyday life, which involved sex as a commodity in the brothel: "It was not [sex] that the lonely man of Buenos Aires was worried about; not what his nostalgic and even frequently cruel songs evoked. It was precisely the contrary: nostalgia for love and communion, the longing for a woman, and not the presence of an instrument of his lust" (in Savigliano 1995a: 45). Although tango is said to have emerged in the brothel, the refined culture surrounding the music, poetry and dancing expressed a wish to get away from this origin, associated with instrumental bodily needs.

As discussed in a previous chapter, the limitations and restrictions in regard to tango intimacy can in fact be related to these historical accounts.

As discussed in Chapter 2, some dancers argue that the high level of dance intimacy in tango should not be mixed up with feelings of sexual attraction. Rather, tango dancers should learn to manage the feelings evoked by the high level of bodily closeness and convert them into an artistic expression. As Betty from the U.S. states, dancers with many years of tango *connaissance* are not struck by the sexiness of the tango but rather by the sensual communication and the particular degree of intimacy which is difficult for "outsiders" and beginners to fully grasp and understand.

> When I first started dancing I just thought "this is so incredibly sexy, how can people not just go have sex in the bathroom during the *cortina* [the break between two dance sets]?" But it's different now. I have been dancing for about two and a half years. The level of intimacy that I feel that I'm connecting with now is actually different and better and more intimate than the sexual aspect of it. [. . .] It's incredibly sensual but not necessarily sexual. (Betty, 46-year-old, U.S.)

As in the historical accounts, the contemporary separation of tango and sex, and the critique of those dancers who fail to maintain the distinction, can be understood as a way of protecting the culture from external influences. Using Mary Douglas' (1966) terms, sex might be approached as a "dirty" ingredient which risks degrading the entire culture as it takes focus away from the sublime dance communication and allows other values and needs to overshadow the refined tango. We might even approach the distinction between sex and tango along a Cartesian body/mind dichotomy. Achieving and managing the full spectrum of sensual tango dancing involves both body *and* mind in a way that sexualized bodily needs do not admit ("the presence of an instrument of his lust", as Sábato puts it). In that sense the tango-sex relation includes a distinction between the low and the sophisticated, the sacred and the profane. Engaging with and reproducing such a distinction seem important for some dancers, not least as a way of staging themselves as "serious" dancers and further along in their tango development than beginners, as Betty in above quote. This is apparent also in the many accounts which express ambiguous and multiple sensations. One such example is found in an interview with Anna-Lena in which she corrects herself when speaking of an Argentine dance partner much younger than herself. She starts by declaring that she "loved dancing with [him]", that she would "like to take him home" and that it was "kind of passionate", but then she restrains herself and continues: "well not passionate in that way, but dancing passion. It's because he is dancing with a lot of feelings, very seriously, like he is giving 120 percent every time he is dancing" (Anna-Lena, 58-year-old, Sweden). Clearly, the immediate sensation of this dancing experience is fuelled by sensual and erotic sensations. However, when reflecting on it more carefully in an interview situation, Anna-Lena relates the strong feelings only to the dancing.

As mentioned in Chapter 2, there are sometimes practical, dance-related reasons for maintaining a clear boundary between sex and tango.

Some women describe the problematic influence of sex on tango in terms of sexually flirtatious behavior which hinders them from fully engaging with the dancing. Overly intimate invitations were thought by some dancers to disrupt the physical and mental dance presence as well as the confidence in a dance partner. Others declared that they did not know how to play along with the flirty games in a relaxed way, especially not according to Argentine rules of conduct, and in the Spanish language. Figuring out how to behave in these situations made some of them "drop focus and dance axes" (Karin, 46-years old, Sweden). Others spoke of awkward situations in which a temporary partner tried to "take advantage" of a shared intimate moment. Some even reported up-front sexual harassment on the dance-floor. In that sense the distinction between tango and sex might also be interpreted as a way of protecting the dance-halls from people who use the tango as a shortcut for accessing sexual pleasure or who conceive of tango as a "romantic market", without subjecting themselves to the complex structure of the dance movements and without being prepared to make bodily and emotional sacrifices.[3]

Following from this discussion, the relation between sex and tango might be approached as an intriguing example of how the logics of other value spheres are partly subjected to conformity once they are confronted with the tango. The cross-sections of tango, sex and love make up one example of how norms and practices linked to other value spheres adapt to the logic and rules of the *milonga*. In this and other chapters, we have discussed various examples of dancers who limit the romantic moments emerging in tango to the world of the dance-floor. By restricting sexualized feelings instead of "taking them home", some dancers claim that they are able to intensify the dancing—and hence sublimate the cultural consumption and raise the tango to a higher level. Another example of this adaption is how the norm of exclusivity and twosome-ness in discourses of sex and romance is modified and actually abandoned when it comes to dance-floor "romances". In order to prevent the logic, practices and discourses of sexual relations from trumping the dance relations, the intimate and potentially romantic relations in tango are stretched out to cover several relations at a time. This might be interpreted as a rule which encourages loyalty to tango culture at large and particular dancing communities rather than to a single interpersonal relationship—and implicitly, to a value system different from that of tango.

An additional factor has to do with the fact that the representations of tango as equal to sex have been annexed by other cultural pursuits. The sexualized metaphor of tango and the fact that it is represented and used elsewhere—in publicity, fashion and pop lyrics—might actually be a reason dedicated dancers react to a sexualization of the tango. The fact that the sexualized metaphor is created for use elsewhere, outside of tango, makes some dancers despise sex in tango as a media stereotype, far from "real" tango. As in the debates occurring in early twentieth-century Buenos Aires, it may be that sex today is constructed as an inauthentic way of doing the tango. In contemporary tango (tourism), as a result of the stereotypical representations of tango as sexy and passionate, sex associated with exoticized and touristy representations—"tango kitsch"—is understood in contrast to deep tango *connaissance*.

HETEROSEXUAL ROMANCE AND SOCIAL CLASS[4]

The context of tourism and tango voyages involves further lines of distinction between sex and tango which bear both similarities to and differences from those proposed by tango advocates in the 1920s and 1930s. Returning to the discussion in Chapter 4 of the objectives ascribed to the voyages, hardly any of the dancers I interviewed openly described the aim of their trip as a search for love or sexual adventure. Instead, most of them said that they had strict dancing in mind. They were all there to take classes with the best teachers, watch exhibitions with world champions, experience the dance venues "where it all once started", as well as impress friends at home with a touch of "real tango". In order to understand dancers' ambiguous relation to romantic and sexual adventures in the holiday context, we must take broader discourses on (heterosexual) romance into account together with the impact of international tourism in fairly vulnerable economies. In the following sections the nexus between class, ethnicity and sexuality appears center stage. We will explore how the production of heterosexual romance engages with ambiguous racialized gender regimes as well as a class imperative requiring romantic subjects to be equal in terms of living conditions and financial status.

As various dancers in this study report, travels to Buenos Aires create a particular circumstance in which the blurred boundaries between dancing intimacy, romance and sex evoke both pleasures and precautionary actions. As in several pop-cultural narratives, economic and social differences are made sense of both as creating attraction and as putting an end to heterosexual romance. As in most passionate adventures on foreign ground one source of excitement is that the visitors believe they are meeting people they would not have met elsewhere. The temporary status of the affairs makes accessible those desires and practices unattainable in places "at home". Like the tango itself, the liaisons are sometimes described as illusions. As in the tango songs lamenting over lost lovers, however, the romantic mythology inscribed in temporary adventures far from home often also entails complications. As in many Hollywood movies, romance is produced along a narrative of difference in which diversity is believed to create obstacles as well as bring out stronger feelings and commitment as the dramatic tension dissolves.[5] However, there are situations in which the dividing lines make not only love relations but also romantic feelings impossible. When difference involves the "wrong" dimensions or is perceived of as too great, the potential romantic trigger is turned into a brake pad. This is particularly true in relation to class divides. In several of the stories in which the presence of tango tourists in the arms of local dance partners is understood as "questionable", the dimension of class is a circumstance which is interpreted as "falsifying" the romantic affair.

One example of how class differences are negotiated by tango tourists is found in the following story about Rebecca, a 43-year-old Australian tango dancer on a four-month-long tango visit to Buenos Aires. Rebecca engaged romantically with several local men during her stay, most of them tango dancers whom she encountered in the *milongas*. Although the adventures were all "amazing", as she puts it, she keeps returning to the economic divide between herself and the local lovers. In some cases, the financial status of her Argentine dates actually became an authenticity problem in relation to a discourse of pure (heterosexual) romance. At times Rebecca feared that some of them were out for something other than her love. For instance she recalled a man who made her pay for the coffee on their first date. They had met on the dance-floor at club *Niño Bien*, danced well together and had a fun time making light conversation in the breaks between dance sets. Before leaving the club they decided to meet up for a coffee in town a couple of days later and exchanged telephone numbers. The date went well. They had a good time walking around the old neighborhoods of San Telmo and finally ended up in a small bar. However, when the bill arrived the man went to the bathroom, leaving her to pay. This put Rebecca in such a bad mood that she decided never to see him again. She explained that her disappointment was due to the revelation of *his* real nature. What first appeared to be a "nice and cute guy" turned out to be a "trickster sneaking out the backdoor". But more importantly the reaction was identity-shaping in relation to *them* and *her*. When it comes to the construction of *them*, a potential romantic couple, the act involved money in a situation where it did not belong, at least according to Rebecca. Rather than being based on attraction and sincere interest in her as a person, it occurred to her that the motivation (for him) might have been financial. "Maybe", she reasoned, "paying for coffee and later on dinners, tango classes and flight tickets, was part of a larger economic deal." In relation to the specific context of being in a much poorer Latin-American country, Rebecca feared this risked making her "another fooled foreigner".

Additionally, her reaction had to do not only with a wish to experience authentic romantic adventures outside the frame of economic interest, although restricted in time and place, but also with the production of gender. Although many dancers object to the descriptions of tango as reproducing stereotypical gender imaginaries, the rituals of several dance-floors and the representations of Buenos Aires are often invested with a traditional notion of femininity and masculinity (cp. Archetti 1999; Guy 1995). Some women also declare that they came to Argentina wishing to explore a femininity characterized by traditional gender roles. For some this involves aesthetic ideals of femininity, conveyed by slit skirts and high-heeled shoes, as well as the engagement in restricted role-play far from their everyday lives. This partly involves an idea that men are in charge of heterosexual flirting. Dancers like Rebecca declare that they want to be treated like "real women" and hope that Argentine tango life—and moreover Argentine men—would offer charms and recognition. Part of such a heterosexual imaginary is the performance of economic agency. Informants from the U.S. are particularly prone to declare that their "ideal man" would not only deliver flirtation, flattery and compliments, but also dinners and drinks along with material gifts. In effect, some informants express a romantic idea in which the woman performs (economic) passivity and subordination. Such ideals are part of Rebecca's strong reaction to her date. The exposed economic inequality between them made it difficult for her to engage romantically. Rebecca explains the rationale for not "engaging seriously" with a man she has to support, which is partly a consequence of being brought up "as a woman".

Rebecca: I'm not so sure that I'm prepared to support a male, I mean financially. If I would engage with someone from here seriously, it would basically be me supporting them, and I'm not ready to support a man. [. . .] I want someone who is my financial equal and unfortunately these *porteño* men . . . although they have other things to offer, I suppose, they have the dance and a culture that is more exciting and passionate. I suppose that might balance it out. [. . .] But still, I'm forty-three. I was raised with the idea that one day I will find a man who will support me and that hasn't happened and now I'm financially secure so at least what I'm expecting is that the man I find will be my financial equal. I'm not talking about numbers in the bank just the ability to do the things you want to do. (Rebecca, 43-year-old, Australia)

Maria: So it would be difficult for you to be in a relationship with someone who depends on you financially? [. . .]

Rebecca: It would be a horrible position to be in, to start to think that maybe he is only with me because of my money. It would be horrible.

In other words, heterosexual romance is here produced as a power relation in which femininity, masculinity and attraction interrelate with a material dimension. We find a counter-case addressing this relation in women's sex tourism in the Caribbean and West Africa, where women are in charge sexually by virtue of their economic dominance (O'Connell Davidson and Sanchez Taylor 2005; Sanchez Taylor 2006). In contrast to such examples, the context of tango tourism seems to turn the significance of unequal economic living conditions upside down. Rather than opening up sex-for-cash transactions between westerners on holiday and locals in the Global South, the (romantic) framework of tango seems to turn the lack of financial power and economic potency on the part of the men into an obstacle. Hence, the hardship within Argentine society seems to block, instead of fuel, a wish to live out a dream based on hetero-romantic ideals of femininity.

RESPECTABILITY POLITICS

A further reason Rebecca reacted strongly to her date's behavior is that it risked putting her in bad company. An ill-reputed character which appears in tango rumors spread among tourists and local dancers in Buenos Aires is that of a foreign woman naïvely—or cynically—searching for affect and love in exchange for money. One example is given by Martin, an Argentine dancer in his late fifties. He retells a story which according to him circulates in the *milongas*.

> I heard of these dance tourists, these women in their seventies with a lot, lot, lot of money who were together with these Argentines who took their money, who said: "I have to fix my car", and the woman with a lot of money pays him to fix his car, and so on. In those cases the woman is clearly conscious about it, like "I will allow this, I will pay for this". Because she knows what she gets. (Martin, 58-year-old, Argentina)

In Martin's understanding, the affairs between (old) wealthy westerners and Argentines short of money come across as cynical economic transactions in which the women "know what they get". Like the sense-making behind the consumption of taxi dancers, the purchase of a boyfriend indicates not potency but rather lack, on the side of the women: a lack of sexual charisma, looks and youth. When bringing up these kinds of stories, true or not, in interviews with dance tourists, some of them respond by speaking of the shameful personal defeat of being someone who has to pay for things you are supposed to receive by virtue of personality or rigorous dance training—such as affection and intimacy. Money attracts sex, many reason, but not romance and love. Some even claim that it is better not to get involved in any kind of romantic affair if there is a risk that an economic interest might be involved. "If I started sleeping with my private teacher I would eventually ask myself if he flattered me romantically in order to keep me as a client", says Maj (52-year-old, Sweden). As in the reflections on taxi dancing, the involvement of money is also in this sense believed to undermine the chances of discovering *real* romance in tango. Other dancers frame their concerns within a political analysis. Some dance tourists actually react strongly against what they perceive of as examples of western exploitation through which the economic and political situation in Argentina is taken advantage of by certain groups of tourists.

However, the image of the deviant female sex tourist and the dichotomies between sex and tango as well as economic and romantic relationships also need to be read through the broader cultural discourses of tourism and female sexuality and the cultural significance of social class. Most women who embark on a journey to Buenos Aires belong to an economic and more importantly *cultural* middle or upper middle class. Maintaining one's image as a member of this group involves a notion of respectability, in Beverley Skeggs' use of the word (1997; 2005). In one of her studies of reality television shows, Skeggs explores how a group of British working-class women are constituted as cheap "white trash" through their embodiment of a vulgar and loud sexuality (Skeggs 2005: 968–969). This has similarities with some frequent representations of female sex tourism. Even though the women in search of love and affection in foreign countries possess the economic means to travel far into the Global South and pay for temporary boyfriends, they are often described as culturally and morally cheap. In one media representation of Canadian women's so-called romance tourism to the Caribbean islands, the moral features are additionally manifested through the description of their aging (and hence unlovable) bodies: "You go to a party and see couple after couple of older, quite substantial—I mean overweight—white women with very young, very lithe black men. [. . .] It's quite a curious thing" (in the *Ottowa Citizen,* 27 January 2007).

Such respectability politics is partly what tango-dancing women respond to when positioning themselves and their holiday in Buenos Aires as distinct from sex tourism. Most of my informants conceive of their intimate voyage as a culturally refined way of discovering the world—a genuine exploration of an art expression and its culture, in contrast to the culturally vulgar sex travels to Jamaica and Ghana. In that sense, the women reproduce a set of cultural hierarchies between ways of travelling and engaging romantically with the world. One example of how this is done is found in Birgitta Holm's autobiographical book on tango and other couple dances, in which the author, herself a Swedish tango dancer who has been on a dance holiday in Buenos Aires, critiques the suggestion that (dance) tourists in Africa and Latin America are looking for sex.

> In his novel, *Platform*, Michel Houellebecq is wrong when he lays out the plans for sex tourism in Cuba. The tourist visiting Cuba is not looking for sex. But dance. [. . .] The German man does not dream of sexual intercourse in a *casa particular*. He is dreaming of becoming one of the dancing ones at the local salsa club. Letting his hand rest against a woman's groin, swinging his hips together with hers, putting a spin on her feet and creating a swirl of arms above their heads. [. . .] The climax for most of us is not a kiss or sex in an obscure corner. It is when someone reaches out their hand and makes you become one with those dancing at the dance club. (Holm 2004: 27, my translation)

Accounts like this might be read as a way of protecting not solely the tango but dance journeys at large from the potentially harmful associations with other kinds of intimacy tourism. In addition, the historical accounts referring to sublime tango and profane sexual lust remind us of the sacred objectives ascribed to tango voyages as distinct from a tourist vacation serving trivial recreational aims (such as meeting bodily needs). However, we might notice that the quote above—just like many accounts reflecting on actual dance experiences—is infused by a rather erotically charged vocabulary. Although an erotic discourse pervades dancers' lived experiences and tango culture at large, several dance tourists, for reasons partly having to do with respectability politics, engage in boundary work in order to discursively separate the tango from sex and dance tourism from sex tourism.

Consequently, one way of making the relation between tourists and local dancers intelligible as potentially "authentic" is by framing Argentine men as economic equals. This might be illustrated by the following account from two French women who hired a private teacher during their three-week-long tango holiday. They quickly became friends with José and spent more and more time together dancing in their apartment and out at the clubs. In addition, Valérie once indicated that something more than dancing was going on between Chloé and the dance teacher. "They *really* like each other", she said. Although they had signed an economic contract with José, exchanging money for his dance services, their view on the living conditions of Argentine dancers suggests that the relation is equal—and hence distinct from the manufactured intimacy found in sex tourism.

Maria: I noticed how I became rich once I got here. At home I am quite a poor researcher living off of grants. What were your experiences?

Valérie: I didn't feel that way. The world of tango is a pretty wealthy world if you compare it with many other worlds. Most dance teachers earn more money than ordinary workers. A couple of classes render the same money as an ordinary worker makes in one month. [. . .] In such a world you don't have to feel too rich, I didn't feel that way. (Valérie, 55-year-old, France)

Chloé: Most people in these *milongas* showed a good standard. They were well-dressed, looking good. (Chloé, 56-year-old, France)

Valérie: You wonder whether the really poor people even dance tango.

Demographically true or not, the construction of local tango dancers as wealthier than other Argentines makes romantic sense of the French women's relation with their dance teacher. By emphasizing the relatively good salaries of tango workers, the potentially questionable consequences of an economic imbalance between romantically involved—or at least intimately dancing—counterparts are downplayed. This shows how the category of social class intertwines with the framing of transnational heterosexual romance. In addition, feelings are here used as a further way of legitimating acts and relations that might touch upon questionable terrain, in this case the associative link between tango tourism and sex tourism.

RACIALIZED GENDER REGIMES

Although tango tourism is not restricted to female dancers, much of the romantic illusion spread in popular representations of Buenos Aires targets female dancers—as do many services within the tourist market. Furthermore, and in contrast to the production of erotic imaginaries of Asian countries such as Thailand as a sexual paradise for western men (O'Connell Davidson 1995), Latin America and Argentina are often portrayed as a resort for western women who are romantically and sexually "dried out" at home (Meisch 1995; Sanchez Taylor 2006). When looking at the world through such glasses, we find that it is divided into transnational zones of gendered desire. Different regions and entire continents are coded with a feminine and/or masculine sexual appeal (see Törnqvist 2010b). There are several accounts of how Argentina and Buenos Aires are conjured up as "sexy places" in which western women might be romanticized and offered sexual recognition. One such example is found in the following story told by Sybil, from the U.S., who speaks about a tango-dancing friend of hers who came to Buenos Aires to "have an affair".

> The tango was an excuse. It could have been any Latin city. But she came to have an affair. Because of the fact that her husband has had an affair for years and finally she just wanted to create some distance emotionally. [. . .] She is not gonna find happiness, we all know that. But she came here to have that experience and she has absolutely no shame in admitting that that is why she is here. She is having a great time with these amazing looking men who are ten years younger than her. [. . .] And I think a lot of western women do that, travel because they are not getting used up the way they are used up emotionally, sexually, in their lives at home. So you hear of Latin countries and Latin men and you come here for that experience. (Sybil, 51-year-old, U.S.)

In this account, Buenos Aires, and particularly the dimly lit *milongas* in which people dance their nights away in the close embraces of strangers, is portrayed as the perfect place for a sexual adventure. Argentina is furthermore described as a particularly interesting site for romance as Argentine men are believed to know how to treat a woman. In Buenos Aires "emotionally dried out" women from Europe and the U.S. can expect sexual confirmation and pleasurable adventures. The story about Sybil's friend is significant also in its combination of romantic dreams with a straightforward analysis that borders on cynicism.[6]

Sex, Romance and Tango 189

In my informants' accounts, as well as in popular representations found in tango novels, travel magazines and tourist pamphlets, Argentine men are often construed as a mixture of "white"/"European", given the national history with recent ancestors from Italy and Spain and the strong impact of urban European city life, *and* overtly sexual "Latin Lovers", much like the hypersexual "black male stud" in tourist representations of local men in the Caribbean (Nagel 2003; Kempadoo 2001; Said 1995; Sanchez Taylor 2006; Segal 1997).[7] One consequence of representing male Argentine tango dancers as "flirty" and "always sexually willing" is, as in women's romance tourism in other parts of the world, that it is difficult to imagine (tourist) women as sexual exploiters (Sanchez Taylor 2006). There are various stories being told of Argentine men doing everything to flirt with western women. In a blog diary of Canadian Emma on tango holiday in Buenos Aires, for instance, she describes how Ruben, a local dancer, tries to get intimate on the dance-floor. During a dance set, he attempts to "cuddle" and whisper flirty words although she assures him that she is married. "Ruben: and where is he? Far away. Me: but he is close to my heart. Basta. Bailamos. (nice try.)"[8] Another account, demonstrating how a racialized and sexualized male Argentine comes to fore in the representations of tango in Buenos Aires, is the endnote of Marina Palmer's autobiographical novel *Kiss & Tango*. Having lived through various heartbreaking relationships with Argentine lovers/dance partners, she ends her tango adventure in Buenos Aires in the arms of a "sexy", yet emotionally safe, Argentine dancer. A couple of days before leaving town she spends a night in a *telo*, a cheap "love hostel" renting rooms by the hour, with Javier.

> Javier's talent, as I discovered last night, is not the tango. I've never been with anybody whose sexuality was so pure, so raw, so exciting, and so unadulterated by feelings. [. . .] He took me to the threshold of pain and then beyond it to find pleasure on the other side, completely unravelling my body so that its secrets lay out on open display. [. . .] In two hours, Javier made up for all the bad or nonexistent sex I've had to endure the last three years. He has single-handedly put Buenos Aires back on the map as the World Capital of Latin Lovers. At the Eleventh hour, Argentina's reputation has been saved! For some reason, this makes leaving Buenos Aires less difficult. (Palmer 2006: 318–320)

Although the sexual experience with Javier is described as breathtaking and a true rollercoaster, the dancer/author Palmer leaves both him and Argentina without heartbreak. This, we might suggest, is because the sexual and bodily experience has been separated from her emotional self. She is ready to take off just when Argentine men finally conform to her initial fantasy, as Latin Lovers who can be enjoyed physically—but at an emotional distance. This story might be put in dialogue with the existential terrain of tango travels and the interaction with risk management discussed in Chapter 4.

Like Palmer, some women who did get involved romantically with local dance partners stated that they did not want to be heartbroken. Like Sybil's friend, they wished to have a pleasant adventure—not to put their entire existence at stake in the arms of an Argentine stranger.

However, tango in Buenos Aires also provides a rather different case. Also, the problem with romantic affairs in the context of tango tourism is linked to the nexus of race, gender and sex. In fact, the (moral) evaluation of sexual practices in tango involves racial scrutiny of the romantic counterpart, in this case local male dancers. As shown in this study, local men are at times desired romantically when acting against the racial stereotypes of savage and exotic men constituted by an aggressive sexuality—and economic subordination. We find one example of this in the following discussion between the two Swedish friends Magdalena and Elisabeth, who make romantic judgments about Argentine men based on their interaction styles and bodily approach.

Elisabeth: There were these men, these *porteño* men [men from Buenos Aires] and it was all clear what they wanted. You could feel it pretty quickly. They were out picking up women. (Elisabeth, 48-year-old, Sweden)

Magdalena: You could feel the difference in their way of dancing. (Magdalena, 50-year-old, Sweden)

Elisabeth: The attention towards me as a follower.

Magdalena: But this man who danced with us all the time, he was different. He said: "It's so nice around your table". In general he was like that. He was a fine dancer. He invited us up, one at a time. A real gentleman. It didn't feel like he was making any moves towards us but he was always very attentive and kind of gently flirting. Kissing us on the cheek when we arrived and taking care of us when we left. I mean he didn't ask for anything, he was just nice. But perhaps he was a little bit more European because he was married to a German woman and had moved to Germany. He had learned. And he wanted to live more passionately once he was here in Buenos Aires.

Magdalena's and Elisabeth's portraits of vulgar *porteño* men—only out for casual sex—as a contrast to the "nice" and "more European" Argentine man who took turns dancing with them reflect a vision of a controlled civilized intimacy. They express appreciation for his gentlemanly manners (flirtatious behavior but no sexual invitations) and limited physical closeness (dancing heart-to-heart and kissing on the cheek, but no further approaches). In other words, they appreciate a masculinity among their dance partners, offering recognition and comfort through carefully restricted verbal and bodily closeness. In their reflection on the Argentine man married to a German woman, race is explained as a matter of cultural degrees. Local men can climb the "cultural ladder" through European refinement and hence become romantically desirable, in this case by virtue of the performance of a restrained sexuality.[9] Following Savigliano's study of Argentine tango history, we might suggest that this framing of Argentine men reflects a dichotomy separating civilized western men from Latin-American "machos". The Spanish word "macho"—originally meaning "man"—is actually being used to describe a "barbaric, uncivilized 'virility' attributed to Latinos. It is used not for the purpose of destabilizing the category of maleness but rather to contribute, by way of contrast, to the consolidation of manliness—a 'civilized' bourgeois maleness that is universally supremacist over all other class, racial, and national gendered identities around the globe" (Savigliano 1995: 46–47). This way, the sense-making of Argentine men as amazing lovers, machos and rundown swindlers serves an ongoing shaping and editing of "other" men as well as men at home. The (future) husbands and boyfriends, are constituted not as "exciting and passionate" (Rebecca, 43-year-old, Australia) as the Argentines but as civilized, trustworthy and equal and hence men which the women will eventually return to.

CONCLUSION: NEGOTIATING SEX, ROMANCE AND TANGO

Throughout this chapter we have explored the ways in which the relation between sex and tango is negotiated within the context of an Argentine dance holiday. The relation is partly (re)produced in terms of a distinction between sex and dancing, which frames the travels as part of a culturally refined artistic commitment rather than a "cheap" search for recreational needs. Within the symbolic tango economy, dancing skills and "sophisticated" tango manners are partly separated from—and held to be more sublime and sacred than—sexual acts linked to putatively low bodily needs (the profane).

It is suggested, though, that the distinctions drawn between sex and tango—as well as the division between affective and economic relations—cannot be explained only in relation to the intimate tango economy. Approaching sexual affairs within the context of tango tourism from a *gendered* perspective, partly discussed in Chapter 3, we have seen how some female dancers engage with a risk evaluation involving a fear of sexual offense and stigma. In fact a gendered perception of physical and moral dangers when taking tango intimacy outside the dance venues makes up an important element of tango-sex negotiations. As suggested in the discussion of *class* and the financial status of potentially romantic counterparts, some dancers negotiate their experiences using a distinction between commercialized and authentic romance. This partly relates to a moral class regime based on normative heterosexuality and maintained through respectability politics. In fact, tourism and transnational intimacy seem to be reproduced along a binary opposition between tango and sex, "civilized" culture and "vulgar" economics. Tango dancing is constructed as a refined form of intimacy—not sex—and the dance voyages as a refined cultural exploration—in contrast to cheap beach-affairs. Such boundary work involves the *racial* framing of Argentine men. Among the women who did engage romantically with their dance teachers and local dance partners we find two types of narratives. The first one sexualizes Argentine dancers. In this framing, Argentine men (and possibly women) come across as "amazing" lovers (Rebecca) and carriers of a "pure", "raw" and "exciting" sexuality (Palmer). The second narrative offers quite an opposite framing, inscribing at least some Argentine men as "European" and hence as a white, wealthy and civilized class of South-Americans (Magdalena and Elisabeth). Both of these narratives suggest that Argentine men can hardly be sexually exploited by western women.

The examples discussed in this chapter might suggest that in order to make transnational romance intelligible as authentic, potentially provocative differences must be downplayed. Making the Argentine lovers intelligible as white, European and "pretty wealthy"—in contrast to other Latin-American people and poorer sectors of the Argentine population—appears to be a way of legitimating romantic involvement between tourists (women) and locals (men). This implies that tango dancers weave a notion of equality and sameness into their understanding of authentic romance. However, there is one exception. When it comes to gender, difference—at times framed as a power imbalance—is not only naturalized but sometimes even asked for. Tango dancers like Rebecca seem, in fact, to wish for acknowledgement not only as dancers instead of tourists, but also as women (and men) instead of markers of economic class ("walking wallets"). Although it would seem difficult to add a global class-position to the image of a pure self, loved for who she or he is, gender makes up the erotically charged divide in heterosexual romance. This implies that it is as women or men that tango tourists can come into existence as loveable subjects. This evokes questions concerning the cultural production of romance. Which differences do we accept as a legitimate basis for romantic love and sexual desire, particularly in the context of encounters across a Global South–Global North divide? And which opposites are supposed to attract?[10] Such questions might shed light on the spectacular heterosexual play in tango and the staging of a drama of gender difference through which women and men are positioned on opposite sides of the dance-floor. By engaging in such play, dance tourists can actually avoid being identified as part of a wider global landscape of unjust living standards where tourists are simply people with money—and not primarily tango dancers or (heterosexual) women.

These negotiations must be related to the fact that the categories of gender, race and class hold different romantic status. Whereas both gender and race can be translated into a language of desire and sexual attraction, although race is sometimes framed as a "questionable" fetish, class differences constitute a reason to suspect that a relationship is not based on "real love". As illustrated in the story of Rebecca and her date, the underlying romantic question is the implication of the date's socio-economic status. Rebecca rejects him not primarily as a racialized subject (a "Latin Lover"), or in terms of his gender (a man), but as *a poor man*. His performed poverty—real or not—undermines his legitimacy as a romantic subject. In addition, for Rebecca it poses the risk of breaking both her heart and finances, but more importantly, it threatens to place her in the role of an unrespectable and non-authentic romantic subject. In part, this must be understood in relation to a more general conflict between the value spheres of economy and love, associated with rather contrasting logics, rationales and values. In addition, the broken romantic expectation expressed in Rebecca's story demonstrates that this is also a case of postcolonial anxieties expressed as a fear of being fooled by the other. Referring to the title of a classic piece by bell hooks (1992), the wish to "eat the other"—or be eaten—is limited to situations in which people conceive of themselves as in charge. From the examples brought up in this chapter it seems as if romantic affairs in tango tourism might be pursued as long as the frontiers between the "civilized" and "exotic" worlds are kept intact, and as long as the biographical construction of self can be liberated from questionable associations with commercialized affect and sex tourism.

To sum up, this chapter has wished to provide yet another terrain for exploring the diffuse and contested terrain of tango tourism. As shown, the nexus between tango dancing and sex is negotiated in relation to class, race and heterosexuality . Instead of a one-dimensional representation of tango as synonymous with—*or* strictly separated from—sex, the intimate dancing seems to offer a floating terrain inside which dancers can participate in various kinds of feelings and types of intimate engagement with temporary dance partners. As discussed in Chapter 2, the dancing experience allows for a particular attraction, though it is restricted to the dance-floor and the walls of the *milonga*. Like scholars who recognize the multilayered nuances of intimacy in other arenas of social life (cp. Jamiesson 1998), I suggest that we reflect on intimate dance voyages in terms of various emotional expectations and bodily practices that might—but do not necessarily—involve an erotic or romantic dimension. The various understandings and configurations of dance journeys suggest that we use a language that gets beyond the simple metaphors of tango as sex—and tango tourism as sex tourism.

However, this chapter also suggests that various restrictions on how to engage in romantic affairs on holiday are addressed—restrictions which seem to sharpen the divides between relatively wealthy westerners and relatively poor Argentines, tourists and locals. Returning to the discussions in Chapters 6 and 7 regarding the gap between discourse and practice, we might assume that something similar is going on in the rapport between tango tourism and sex. For reasons having to do with tango culture, with respectability politics and with norms surrounding heterosexuality, we might suppose that dancers have reasons for concealing the stories of their romantic lives on holiday. One example of this is the Swedish dancer Anna-Lena, who corrects her own recalling of a "passionate" dancing experience with an Argentine dancer much younger than herself. At stake in the narrating of a tango romance in the Global South is not only tango honor, but the making of "real women" and respectable—and lovable—selves. What tango tourists are actually doing off the Argentine dance-floors might be more questionable—and more radical—than what we get to hear about in interview situations and public blog posts.

9 Dancing Geographies

INTRODUCTION

It may be that the group of listeners who most strongly identify with the words of the well-known tango song *Mi Buenos Aires Querido* has shifted. As a consequence of the last decade's dramatic spread of tango throughout the western world, the nostalgia over Buenos Aires speaks to the heart of Norwegian, French and Australian dancers. When leaving their tango hostels in taxis and jet aircrafts to soon be in tango exile far from the Argentine dance-halls, they sing along with the love song directing its words to the city:

> My beloved Buenos Aires, the day I see you again, there will be no more sorrow or forgetfulness. My Buenos Aires, land full of flowers, my final hours will be spent here. No disappointments under your sky. The years go by and we forget the pain. I will have you know that just thinking of you makes all my heartaches scatter away.[1]

As tango historian Julia Taylor writes rather poetically, Argentina "seems more a state of mind than a country" (1998: 54). A similar approach is noticeable among dancers from all over the world who identify Buenos Aires as an emotional "home". Argentina lives through its music, language, poetry, food and manners among people who never put their feet on Latin-American soil but who spend a great number of hours enclosed in the cultural universe of Argentine tango. Buenos Aires is the natural advisory reference point, helping to explain the origin of steps, the logic behind particular dancing rules and how to be successful "living the tango". At times the importance of certain practices, such as adapting to the "line of dance" counterclockwise, is stressed with references to the crowded dance-floors of *El Beso, El Niño Bien, La Confitería Ideal* and other clubs in Buenos Aires—rather than with examples found in the local tango scene. "Over there", European and North-American dance teachers explain, people have embodied the knowledge of how to navigate the tango. Moreover, the dancing vocabulary, hardly ever translated from Spanish, functions as a constant reminder of the Argentine origin. Concepts such as *sacada*, *cortina* and *tanda* come with the syntax and sound of the Spanish-speaking continent. In addition the vocabulary provides symbolic linkages between early twentieth-century Buenos Aires and today's institutionalized dancing practices. At other times the city is appealed to as a standard when changes are brought forward in local tango communities. When traditional rules are softened up—as when same-sex dancing is accepted and brought forward—legitimizing examples from clubs in Buenos Aires are often mentioned.

Although Buenos Aires seems the confident capital of tango, the global spread of the culture has made geography a contested matter. The Argentine dance has in fact made itself at home in various European capitals and even in sleepy coast towns in Spain (Sitges) and Sweden (Tylösand). Some invested and recognized dancers within tango communities throughout the world do not bother to visit Buenos Aires as they claim that the city is overloaded with tango kitsch and tourist commercialization. What is advertised as an authentic place by Argentine tango schools, tourist agencies and the Argentine Ministry of Tourism is by certain non-Argentine dancers approached as a manufactured place—shaped to suit tourist imaginaries about tango.

Throughout this chapter we will explore the negotiations and struggles over the meaning associated with Buenos Aires as the capital of tango. Whereas the previous chapters looked into the production of authenticity in relation to various practices and identities related to tango tourism, this chapter revolves around the negotiations of space. We will look into discourses and practices performed by the people who make up the lived geographies of tango tourism—local dancers, temporary tourists and actors within the tango market. Through various empirical examples, three contested terrains will be explored. First, we will interrogate *the anchoring of cultural art forms within geographic spaces*.[2] Buenos Aires still holds a unique position in relation to tango. In fact, the context of dance voyages makes the significance of the Argentine capital—its nostalgic past and present magnetism—hard to exaggerate. The streets, sounds and smog of the city—experienced through an actual visit or with the help of textual and visual representations—make up a seductive imaginary of tango for most tango dancers throughout the world. The city is also advertised as the dancers' Mecca—a place to approach with curiosity and hopefully visit. In addition, the global spread of tango has made Buenos Aires a lived reality in places far from the Argentine national borders through the adoption of Argentine manners, food, drinks, movements, rituals and aesthetics. Also, those dancers who are not particularly interested in visiting the city are faced with references and anecdotes from Buenos Aires together with imported Argentine customs and vocabulary. This implies that the notion of a foreign place—Buenos Aires—is a lived reality in local dancing communities all over the world.

In this chapter we will also explore the dialectical relation between material spaces and their multiple lived and imagined realities, involving projected fantasies, feelings and commercialized representations (cp. Lefebvre 1991: 184). It is implied that people often embody one and the same place from within different *mindscapes* (Löfgren 1999: 22). This suggests that the nexus of expectations, experiences, embodied memories, life phases and moods comes together in affecting people's actual experiencing—sensing and sense-making—of a particular place. This complexity is crucial for understanding the emergence of tourist destinations and the rather different sets of living conditions linked to such places. A second contested terrain explored in this chapter is hence *the relation between the lived realities of Buenos Aires and the city's imaginative framing* and will be discussed primarily under the heading "Conflicting Realities". At times these two dimensions go hand in hand, as when everyday poverty among local people is exoticized and turned into a tourist attraction (see Frenzel, Koens and Steinbrink 2012 for examples). At other times the actual living conditions significantly deviate from the promises cultivated by tourist bureaus or—as in the context of tango voyages—the local dancing communities throughout the world. As we shall see, the tension between the tango imaginaries and the lived Argentine realities creates a number of dilemmas facing both temporary visitors and tango residents. Buenos Aires comes to the fore as a geographic other—a place desired, longed for and yet feared.

A related concern has to do with the *significance of physical places in global times*. Scholars such as Manuel Castells (1996) have argued that globalization and the development of the digital net have reduced or at least changed the significance of actual places. Moreover, Castells, together with Bauman (2011) and Negri and Hardt (2008), claims that today's economic and political life primarily takes place in anonymous spaces of flow, far from scrutinized practices and social responsibilities. Financial transactions with implications for millions of people occur in a second, far from national borders and outside national regulations. But what about culture? How does the globalization of cultural art forms such as tango affect the constitution of a place? The kind of globalization at stake in this book is not so much about the impact of IT and the fast movement of capital. Rather, tourism is an example of the kinds of global movements which have been around for much longer. People crossing national borders for the sake of adventures, knowledge and business dates to long before the invention of the concept of globalization. However, tango tourism is bound up with some of the dilemmas regarding space which appear in the globalizing processes central to our time. In the third part of this chapter—"Reterritorializing Argentine Tango"—it is suggested that globalization has enforced the emergence of cosmopolitan tango networks and the appearance of new tango sites outside of Argentina. Instead of travelling to faraway Buenos Aires a younger crowd of skilled European dancers go on tango holiday wherever other "good dancers" go—crowded Berlin or festivals in rural communities throughout Europe. As the dance culture spreads throughout the world it partly detaches from Argentina.. But what does this imply? Is tango culture reterritorialized, but elsewhere? And what is the significance of such shifts in relation to the body-centered practice of dancing, which implies that the tango requires bodies as well as geographic terrains in order to be practiced? In the third part of this chapter we will also inquire into the forces as well as the political and economic implications of geographic detachment. In relation to the fragile Argentine economy, the struggles over tango geography prove to be a matter of survival—for the Argentine nation, as well as for individual actors within the dance market.

These questions are explored from various perspectives and through a variety of empirical examples. The chapter starts off with a discussion of the attempts to assure the linkages between tango and the city of Buenos Aires. In the spatial representations produced by tourist agencies, the national Ministry of Tourism as well as local actors within the dance market, tango is brought forward as a deeply Argentine matter. In fact a mutual reinforcement of the territorializing of tango unites the tourist place marketers and many visitors. However, Argentine tango proves to partly escape the attempts to tie it to Buenos Aires. In the last two sections of the chapter we will look into the many and partly conflicting geographies of tango dancing. Due to the global spread, the dance culture and Buenos Aires itself live in places far away from their actual geographic placement. To sum up, Argentine tango comes to the fore as a destabilizing tourist geography and, moreover, a contested terrain of ongoing spatial negotiations.

BUENOS AIRES AND TANGO PLACE MARKETING

Marks of authenticity, bound up with spatial experiences of characteristic *milongas* and Argentine neighborhoods, are partly what attract foreign dancers to Buenos Aires. As one Swedish dancer puts it: "I was curious about the essence of tango. What is this?, you know, what's really going on in Buenos Aires? It all sounded so exciting, the ways in which the men ask you up to dance, I just had to see it. And then the occasion turned up" (Elisabeth, 48-year-old, Sweden). As Elisabeth's curiosity indicates, the reason thousands of dancers from all over the world travel to Buenos Aires each year—instead of other places known for their high level of dancing and their exciting *milongas*—is a belief in the cultural, historical and symbolic impact of the city. The promises of Buenos Aires' sensuality, its smells, sounds and tactile experiences, trump the fantasies associated with European and North-American dance-halls. Hence, far from being solely a projection screen viewed in faraway places, Buenos Aires is wished to be encountered directly—through the bodily, sensual and emotional presence of everything that is associated with the city. This implies that some dance voyagers hope the city will leave bodily and emotional marks. Dancing the tango in one of the recognized *milongas* is anticipated with the hope that it will transmit the heart and soul of Argentine culture.

Hence, for obvious reasons the marketing of tango travels emphasizes a strong embeddedness of the dance culture within the city of Buenos Aires. The tango is made synonymous—or at least deeply infused—with the spaces of the Argentine capital: its old-fashioned cafés, the harbor areas and famous avenues. It is not a coincidence that agencies addressing dance voyagers offer not only dancing events but also city tours. As one tourist agency, particularly targeting North-American dancers, advertises in a flyer: "Buenos Aires, being a big city, requires special guidance in navigating and experiencing its many charms. Experience the feeling of being 'porteños'" (*Tango-All-Inclusive*). In fact, Buenos Aires is stated to be part of the complete tango experience. When marketers trade on the city's urban heritage, they point to the impact of actual buildings, worn-out dancefloors and remaining décor such as bar disks and old-fashioned toilets, as intensifying the tango experience. Some of these places achieve an almost religious status as they provide and produce icons which materialize the belief system of tango.

In addition, tango plays an important role in promoting Buenos Aires as an exciting destination for all kinds of travelling—holiday journeys as well as international conferences.[3] The tango metaphor transmits some of the general values market actors associate with the city. Just like the tango, the Argentine capital has rather successfully been packaged as the perfect mixture of the civilized and savage world. In magazine articles and tourist destination marketing the city is represented as a blend of Europe and Latin America, wealth and poverty and the nostalgic past and cosmopolitan present. Buenos Aires is said to offer "first class shopping" as well as a charming roughness in the form of a "taste of Latin America" (*Dagens Nyheter*, 23 October 2011). In addition, it attracts North-American tourists with a more exotic—and both a geographically closer and cheaper—version of Europe. In fact, Buenos Aires comes to the fore as foreign and familiar at the same time. As one travel agency puts it: "Dance, drink and eat your way around the most sophisticated, European city in South America—Buenos Aires. Get to know the city everyone loves to love. [. . .] Enjoy a tango show before a free day to explore the 'Paris of the Americas' on your own, or dance the night away in the smoky Milongas (tango houses)".[4] In fact, Buenos Aires appears as yet another plastic city, possible to associate with all kinds of contradictory meanings. Like the cities of Venice and Paris represented in various simulated forms in Disneyland and the casinos of Las Vegas, Buenos Aires is as real to people in its representational as in its actual form (cp. Baudrillard 1994; Cohen 2011). In fact, the symbol "Buenos Aires" is strong enough to carry other trademarks. This is how might understand that the city, along with the tango, is being used by various companies and brands in their advertising of perfumes, watches and shoes.

The importance of advertising tango as a unique culture intimately linked to the city of Buenos Aires actually has to do with the increasing importance for cities throughout the world to be staged as unique. As Monica Degen writes in her book on what she labels the "sensing cities" of Barcelona and Manchester: "Similar to the fashion cat-walk, cities now contend with each other by parading made-up images of different areas of the city which advertise these spaces as favorable and appealing environments for business and leisure. Cities proudly display their new styles and designed environments on the global cat-walk" (Degen 2008: 27). This partly has to do with the economic rewards connected with the "collective symbolic capital" of cities, to use the words of David Harvey (2002: 9). In a piece targeting monopoly rent he discusses how cities like Barcelona have accumulated symbolic capital through successful staging of creativity and the celebration of distinctiveness. The values generated as a consequence of a particular "architectural heritage, distinctive marks of lifestyle and literary traditions" (ibid) have had a significant drawing power upon capital flows. In relation to Buenos Aires, the process of making the city a popular urban holiday destination—not only among tango dancers—is bound to a similar staging of the city as a unique place. The city is advertised in terms of its particularity: its unique tango, soccer teams, gauchos, wines, *parilla* restaurants serving the well-known beef, even the bloodstained history with its left-open wounds from the junta dictatorship (as the Mothers of Plaza de Mayo[5]) is marketized as a unique Argentine flavor. In that sense the country and the city itself—the mythologies, artifacts and painful collective memories ascribed to it—are made objects of cultural consumption.[6] In the attempts to attract tourism, also the financial collapse and the continuous economic hardship are managed to be brought forward as a potential advantage. One example of this is found in the Ministry of Tourism's call for international tourist investors. On their official home page, a photographic mosaic portraying various landscapes of Argentina embraces an advertisement for foreign capital to be invested in the tourism sector. The national economic decline is here promoted as a "competitive advantage".[7]

CONFLICTING REALITIES

The recent increase of foreign visitors has placed Buenos Aires at a dramatic intersection. As in other holiday destinations in Latin America and Africa, the hardship on the side of local people—who are making a living out of tourism—exists side by side with the exotic and carefree representations produced by travel agencies that wish to turn geographic places into seductive tourist fantasies. Turning to the first dimension of this intersection, Buenos Aires might be approached in terms of an economic landscape. Argentina used to be one of the most economically powerful countries in Latin America, apparent in the capital architecture's impressive monuments and broad avenues. However, things have drastically changed as a consequence of the financial crisis in 2001. More than ten years later a development is slowly emerging, yet the unemployment rates are still high, as are the migration streams to Europe and the poverty rates. Everyday life for average Argentine people is still under financial pressure, forcing many to take several jobs in order to pay for food and housing. This has consequences for the spatial relations of the city. The economic decline leaves visible marks on streets, buildings and infrastructure and shapes the inhabitants' navigation throughout the city. Certain areas are becoming "sketchy" and are hence avoided by the upper middle classes. This enforces additional spatial segregation, as when wealthy and poor neighborhoods are kept relatively far apart. However, one might also notice that poverty, as a result of the crisis, has spread out in ways that make it impossible to fully dissociate the marks of scarcity from average city life.

When it comes to the impact of tourism, the streams of international visitors—and the flow of foreign capital—have partly enforced a similar segregation. One aspect of this is the evolution of restricted tourist enclaves, as discussed in Chapter 6. Tourism has also enforced processes of gentrification to offer comfort and safe shopping areas (cp. Zukin 2010). As is often discussed in urban geography, the "cleaning up" of shabby neighborhoods to suit the demands of middle- and upper-class inhabitants and tourists risks taking away the flavor that actually gives the area its "value" (authenticity, artistic flavor, factory aesthetics etc.). This kind of dilemma undergoes an additional twist in relation to nostalgic tango voyages. The neighborhoods that achieve an almost religious tango aura are not posh Recoletta and Palermo (where most tourists live) but rather the poor harbor district and the far-off *barrios*—the aspects of the city that come across in tango poetry. Poverty and hardship are part of the seductiveness and actually create tourist value as the marks of scarcity become marks of authenticity.

As the destination marketing campaigns mentioned above indicate, the successfulness of attracting temporary visitors and foreign capital depends on various political and economic factors—such as the financial crisis together with current national attempts to make tourism a policy sector. There are, however, other factors present in the making of a tourist destination. In fact, the attractiveness of cities like Buenos Aires has largely to do with informal markets and, moreover, the everyday services and life of ordinary people outside tourism. As Elin, a Swedish dancer on a two-week stay, states, her first tango experience did not take place in any of the fancy *milongas* but in one of the characteristically worn-out and rather scruffy city taxis: "I thought it was just amazing to be in that first cab and realizing that they are actually playing tango on the radio. Being the most natural thing!" (Elin, 35-year-old, Sweden). Seemingly everyday experiences like this, yet with an exotic touch, are what enrich the slogans of tourist companies and ultimately what make cities like Buenos Aires tourist magnets, attractive to foreign capital. However, the distribution of rewards tied to the collectively generated symbolic capital of cities is a rather selective matter. As David Harvey rhetorically asks: "which segments of the population are to benefit most from the collective symbolic capital to which everyone has, in their own distinctive ways, contributed both now and in the past?" (2002: 10). Based on her work on female sex tourism in Jamaica and the Dominican Republic, Jacqueline Sanchez Taylor makes a similar point. "The tourist industry sells long haul holidays as 'an experience', and as such, it relies on local people to provide a face and character to what would otherwise be a standardized hotel, beach and holiday for western tourists. It therefore depends on the informal tourist sector, which operates alongside the formal industry, to provide the 'local color' that cannot be supplied by hotel employees and tour representatives", she writes (2006: 55). In the context of Buenos Aires, the ordinary people walking the crowded streets together with the marks of poverty and the military dictatorship are part of what constitutes the complete holiday experience. Knowing that "rough" life goes on out there, implying a "flavor of *real* Latin America", as the tourist advertising puts it, lends meaning to the trip (cp. Frenzel et al. 2012). Although many visitors expect this to be part of their travel experience—at least as "décor"—the average Argentine rarely gets a share of the attracted foreign capital. In fact the poverty and roughness of Buenos Aires produce a symbolic—and economic—tourist value, at the same time that they create a tourist fear which cuts the city off from certain groups of residents as a "safety" measure. As discussed in Chapter 6, this fear actually seems to favor foreign actors within the tourism sector. Hence it seems as if the (economic) *realities* of cities like Buenos Aires transform into tourist value when experienced at distance, rather than a reality affecting temporary tourists themselves.

For some dancers, the actual marks of economic reality are perceived as errors, not corresponding to the imagined city. Anna-Lena, for instance, speaks of the city as "terribly dirty and shabby. There are cracks in the pavement which make you stumble and dog poo everywhere" (Anna-Lena, 58-year-old, Sweden). Some visitors had imagined a much more picturesque and "charming" city, with outdoor cafés in sunny squares and colorful buildings, as shown in the postcards from the touristy area of La Boca. Instead they found themselves confronted with a metropolitan city, overloaded with traffic, smog and people. For some dance tourists the expectations of a relaxing vacation with red wine and tango was even replaced with the rather frightening challenge of surviving the city. Buenos Aires appeared as the contemporary Latin-American metropolis it actually is. In the following account by the Swedish dancers Elisabeth and Magdalena, the expected and experienced city actually divides in two.

Magdalena: My experience when I got there was that it was much bigger than I had expected. I kind of hadn't created that image from home, that it was so swarmingly big. I believe I had been thinking tango, not the city, so for me it was like it came all towards me, a big traffic chaos. It was pretty tough

	in the beginning, hard to understand. I wasn't feeling all that happy the first week, I was feeling very disoriented map-wise and so on. (Magdalena, 50-year-old, Sweden)
Elisabeth:	And all that traffic. (Elisabeth, 48-year-old, Sweden)
Magdalena:	And it was very messy and so, you know, well after a while I got used and it felt pretty ok. [. . .] But it strikes you that it's not very beautiful. Well there are some beautiful buildings but . . .
Elisabeth:	It was a lot of dirt and just grey and garbage. Cars that broke down in the street, one motorcycle that collapsed in two in the middle of the street.

Similar comments can be found in relation to the interior design of the milongas. Recently arrived dancers often comment on the old-fashioned buildings, the worn-out furniture and the filthy bathrooms with broken lockers. Some dancers speak of this as taking them back to the forties. This, in fact, reflects an ambiguity having to do with the symbolic time travel of tango. On the one hand tourists wish the journeys to Buenos Aires—a spatial movement—to represent a nostalgic travel back in time, to the golden years of the tango orchestras and the tango cafés. On the other hand, the actual concrete marks of old times—for instance, dirty and broken furniture and buildings—symbolize a poverty equivalent to risk and danger for European and North-American tourists. In that sense dance journeys struggle with a more general paradox of tourism: the "over there" reality rarely conforms to the imagined reality. In other words the material and imaginary spaces of Buenos Aires partly conflict. Some dancers explain the conflict in terms of a tension between the city and the tango life, like Magdalena in the passage quoted above: "I was thinking tango, not the city". The fact that the city is partly constructed from the horizon of a cultural investment in tango simply affects how it is being made sense of. This makes the representational spaces of Buenos Aires revolve around the emotional and sensual experiencing of tango, together with its mythical past. In that sense, these travels actually shed light on the ways we think about the material and imaginary aspects of a place. Rather than portraying the city in terms of its streets and buildings, dancers like Magdalena imagine it as a feeling. Once she connects with that particular sentiment (sensually transmitted through music, poetry, aesthetics and touch), she is in the capital of tango. Which is to say: once the feeling escapes she is no longer in the Buenos Aires she knows of.

A somewhat related aspect has to do with the construction of tango and the tango capital as a symbolic—and geographic—space for escapist adventures, as discussed in Chapter 4. As Carolina, a Swedish dancer in her fifties, originally from Bolivia, comments, this might also be what some tourists practice out on the Argentine dance-floors. In her account, Buenos Aires is packed with foreigners who are using the ambiance and the geographic—as well as cultural and economic—distance to break away from their everyday lives: "Who are the women who close their eyes during the dance? The Argentines? No. The Europeans. They love to dream, they wish to be somewhere else and they use Buenos Aires to do that" (Carolina, 53-year-old, Sweden). However, the hectic and invasive city life—its six-lane highways running across town and the perceived risk of being robbed—makes the same foreign place a reality imposed on the tourists, a reality that forces them to keep their eyes open. This is illustrated in an account by Swedish Daniella in which she describes how she wished to do what Carolina suggests, use tango as "an escape from reality", but how the Argentine reality—described as "you are under attack"—enforced her to be "tough".

Daniella: That is what the tango has been for me, an escape from reality, because I don't want to deal with the ice cold truth out there and life itself [going through a difficult divorce]. It becomes a drug, sure it is, besides a genuine interest. [. . .] When you go far abroad you can let go of yourself, get rid of some ballast. Once you have distanced yourself so much geographically it might be even more of a trip out of reality. (Daniella, 50-year-old, Sweden)
Maria: And then you are facing another reality . . .
Daniella: Yes, you have to get on with the new reality. You cannot just play around in Buenos Aires. It's pretty tough out there, you are under attack, you have to make it . . . just the fact of not speaking Spanish . . . you need to be tough, you need to communicate with the people, in their way, make place for yourself, grab what you want. [. . .] That's how it is in Argentina, you win or you lose.

As a result of the conflicting realities—based on economy and sentiment– some visitors leave the city with a feeling that "real" tango slipped through their fingers: "real" tango both as a transcendent dancing experience allowing them to find a greater sense of meaning and as a sense of connection with the everyday life of the place they are visiting. In a conversation, North-American Monique and Steve together with Argentine Allan, discuss the fact that the impossible search for the "real thing" might function as an implicit engine behind the expanding tango market. This is what leads people to come back, take more classes, visit more *milongas*. As Monique says, it might even be that the projection screen—in the form of an escapist imaginary—is more valuable than the actual experiences of tango in Buenos Aires.

Steve: People are coming here, looking for something. But they are not going to find it. (Steve, 58-year-old, U.S./Argentina)
Monique: No. (Monique, 56-year-old, U.S./Argentina)
Steve: They are not going to find it but their dreams of it will be there and they will think that they might be able to find it

	and the fact that they come back here once every two years keeps it going. As soon as they really connect with what tango is and what the culture is really about they will realize that it's no different here than over there, it's just a set of different taboos ...
Allan:	The foreigners will not get what they search for but they can touch an idea. (Allan, 22-year-old, Argentina)
Monique:	Yes, by coming back they keep the dream alive.

These examples stress the ambiguous significance of materializing belief systems into concrete geographic spaces and objects. On the one hand, the worshipping of actual places—such as the Argentine milongas and cafés—and certain objects—such as the local tango shoe brands—demonstrates that materialized places and objects are important in (re)producing tango as a unique culture. Without Buenos Aires, both as a mythical projection screen and a lived everyday reality, the tango would be something quite different—in Argentina and elsewhere. On the other hand, the tension between the mythical inscription of a place and its lived everyday realities (materiality) puts dance voyagers such as Elisabeth and Magdalena in dialogue with other travelers deeply invested with an imaginary place. At times the prior knowledge actually gets in the way when experiencing iconic sites. As a Freud states in an anecdote about his encounter with modern Athens, he could not believe that he had actually seen the Acropolis. For him the Acropolis was a product of literary experience in his childhood and hence associated with a magnitude which was stronger for being imagined (Travlou 2002: 16–17). Another example is the accounts of Christians going on pilgrimage to Jerusalem in search of spiritual fulfillment. Several depictions of holy journeys to the biblical city during the nineteenth and twentieth centuries convey a clash between the mythic construction of Jerusalem, a place with divine associations, and the realities of a remote dusty terrain (Kärnborg 2003; Lagerlöf 1901/2007), a clash quite similar to the one that occurs when tango lovers encounter Buenos Aires. The examples of the Argentine capital as an ambiguous carrier of values beyond the actual streets, smells, sounds and aesthetics not only point to the dilemmas arising from a gap between imagined and *in situ* experienced spaces. They also indicate that the imaginative and emotional investments in a place are decisive, both for people's actual navigation within geographic spaces and for the creation of so-called tourist value, serving to attract foreign capital.

RETERRITORIALIZING ARGENTINE TANGO

As illustrated throughout this book, the cultural production of tango as linked to a particular geographic place revolves around an intriguing ambivalence. On the one hand the dance comes with a strong geographic identity.

The nationality is even stressed in the name: Argentine tango. On the other hand its diffusion to countries all over the world implies that the tango has successfully been detached from the geographic anchoring suggested by the name (cp. Manning 2007: xvii). The dancing culture has in fact become subject to a universalization of the particular, making local customs originating in the city of Buenos Aires general and culturally translatable to other places and cultures. One consequence of this is that the dancing culture is being disconnected from the Argentine capital and from Argentine dancers. For some dancers, particularly the recognized dancers, the nobility of tango, the educational and artistic objectives ascribed to the journey, makes Argentina a platform not primarily for discovering Argentine culture and the making of Argentine friends—but for practicing and experiencing tango dancing. In fact, some dancers declare that their three-week-long dance holiday could have been placed anywhere in the world as long as the quality of teachers and other dancers was guaranteed and the *milongas* offered dancing till dawn. In such accounts, Buenos Aires is yet another backdrop for an international dancing holiday, although with its particular flavor. For some of these dancers, a voyage to Argentina is actually not that different from travel to one of the many international tango festivals throughout the world or a dancing weekend in Berlin or Barcelona. What attracts dancers to various places is the level and number of "good dancers". In fact, there are many committed and well-recognized dancers who have never even taken a trip to Buenos Aires, but who have been to several European tango sites known for their good dancers and ambiance, especially during festivals. Such are the cities of Istanbul, Nijmegen in Holland and the Spanish coast town Sitges. However, Buenos Aires is present during these festivals in the form of star Argentine dancers who perform and offer dance workshops. That is to say, that European and North-American dancers are not forced to travel to Buenos Aires to participate in an Argentine tango experience—Argentina has made itself accessible outside of Argentina. Some dancers perceive this tendency as mostly positive, as for instance the tango teacher Linn.

> This is kind of good. For a Swedish dancer who doesn't have the time and money [to travel to Buenos Aires] but who is able to go to Tylösand over a weekend with good dancers and invited teachers from Argentina. Perfect! But you can never take away the origin of tango and its life in Buenos Aires. It will always be Argentine tango, it can never be Swedish tango. Even if they find good dancers in Tylösand and even if that is enough for some dancers there will always be those who wish to go to Argentina to see what it's like. That is at least what I believe. (Linn, 21-year-old, Sweden/Argentina)

In Linn's account, the reason some dancers chose other destinations, closer to home, is partly explained by the money and time a journey to Argentina requires. The Argentine presence within these more proximate places and venues makes tango festivals a "perfect" compromise. Swedish Daniella, who herself has been both to Buenos Aires and several tango festivals, marathons and dance weekends throughout Europe, comments on the fact that some dancers chose not to visit Argentina, partly by offering the same explanation as Linn (money and time restrictions) but also by adding a dimension. She approaches the choices of destination partly as a matter of tango-related identity work, fuelled with the impact of social networks as well as symbolic capital.

Daniella: There is a trend once you are frequenting this subculture frenetically, as I have done for the past five years. You find that those dancers who are really hooked, who are constantly striving for better dancing experiences, better dancers, do not go to Buenos Aires but rather go to tango marathons[8] and festivals in Europe. They need new blood, to get away from the home communities and the tango-family incest but they wish to stay within their European network. The older ones go to Buenos Aires, the young ones go to marathons. (Daniella, 50-year-old, Sweden)
Maria: Why don't they go to Buenos Aires?
Daniella: It is partly a money matter, it's far away. [. . .] But it is also a social thing. They have gotten to know each other, it's a click, a small tango nobility. A tango Versaille, a club for mutual admiration. [. . .] The layers of really good dancers in Europe, they go to marathons, they don't go to Buenos Aires.

We might argue that the possible reterritorialization of Argentine tango has to do with the strong focus on the dancing element and the detachment from or rather downplaying of other aspects of the culture. Although tango dancing is symbolically associated with the city of Buenos Aires, the non-verbal dancing communication has successfully dispersed into a growing cosmopolitan culture. (Those expressions more closely associated with the Spanish language—such as the poetry, literature and music—as well as Argentine history are qualities strongly linked to actual places and possibly harder to dissociate from Argentina.) Over the past twenty years, we have seen how the dancing movements are stretching out into global spaces and how tango is forming itself into networks of primarily Europeans and North-Americans, who share the transnational and crosscultural body language of tango dancing. In addition, we might suggest, these clusterings of non-Argentine dancers are brought together by the dancers' sharing of similar economic and cultural backgrounds. Among other things, this implies a financial condition which enables them to travel and meet other similarly tuned dancers in various European and North-American cities and festivals offering dancing till dawn as well as arenas for social networking.

This trend is noticeable also among tourists in Buenos Aires. As discussed in Chapter 6, certain dance voyagers tend to spend more time with dancers from their home community or certain European or North-American tango "crowds" than with Argentine dancers. When it comes to the actual dance-floor experiences, many visitors report that they dance more with other Europeans and North-Americans than with locals. This can be explained partly by the international networks in tango, which connect dancers across national borders—but within European or North-American clusters.

Returning to Daniella's account, which places negotiations of the tango geography within the framework of the intimate dance economy and dancers' "feel for the game", we might notice that the selection of dance partners and holiday destinations is part of the status play within tango. Rejecting Argentine dancers—and Buenos Aires in favor of other tango destinations—is not necessarily an "inappropriate" thing to do; under certain circumstances such choices even function to legitimize dancers. This is particularly true for a younger European and North-American crowd of tango inheritors—dance teachers, *milonga* organizers, tango DJs—who are inventing and developing new dancing styles (such as "organic tango"), pedagogies (queer tango dance schools with their "own" pedagogy) and aesthetic ideals (adapted to the social context, often involving fewer slit skirts and tango suits), and who intend to make the tango part of "their culture". The symbolic mastery of tango by non-Argentine actors acting outside Argentina, and the attempts to create alternative dance destinations outside Buenos Aires, requires an emphasis on new characteristics. In this making of authenticity values, originality and creativity are more important than traditional anchorage (cp. Andriotis 2011: 1621). Instead of copying the styles of Buenos Aires these venues attempt to offer something quite different; they are aspiring to create new origins and sites of tango. In their attempts to do so, some of the tango inheritors apply feminist ideas and notions from the queer movement. In addition they use other kinds of music than traditional tango and they make use of their knowledge and contacts within other physical and artistic cultures when developing their tango, such as theater, contact improvisation, lindy hop, circus, yoga, African dancing etc. For some of them, one aspect of distinguishing their dancing styles and pedagogical devices is actually to position themselves against traditional tango life in Argentina. For instance, some tango inheritors criticize the argument that the right "blood" (being Argentine) facilitates access to tango and that only those who strictly conform to the many Argentine rules will get to the "real tango". Rather than looking back into tango history, these dancers make a point of their break with the "old", "essentialized" and "commercialized" culture.[9]

To sum up, we might approach the growing international tango scene as a possible example of a fluid cosmopolitan culture in which dancers (tourists) pick and choose the destinations of their tango voyages in accordance with what a place has to offer. In this evaluation, the actual place is of less importance than its temporary visitors, activities and attached symbolic credentials. This means that even Argentina can be phased out as the number one destination for experiencing Argentine tango. In contrast to ecotourism in the Amazons and history travelling to the Berlin Wall, the physical terrain of Argentina and its capital is not decisive for experiencing tango dancing. Although the embodied nature of dancing requires an attachment to a place, a terrain where the dancers can put their feet and execute their movements, the actual places for dancing practices might shift. In fact, the spatial significance of Argentine tango is part of an ongoing struggle and negotiation among those dancers who make up the geographically diffused culture of tango dancing.

CONCLUSION: NEGOTIATING TANGO GEOGRAPHIES

The case of tango tourism illustrates that the relation between cultural art forms and geographic places is far from given. In fact, the examples brought forward in this book constitute a case against a somewhat common understanding that cultural expressions, such as Argentine tango, are rooted in particular places. It is true that the movements of tango, captured in the slow walk of the dancers, take place in actual places. However, it is equally true that those places are manifold and shifting. In addition, the relation between an art form and a place—in this case tango and the city of Buenos Aires—is often subject to ongoing negotiations and symbolic struggles. Examples from the past illustrate that the tango has nostalgically been annexed by nationalist interests for the sake of uniting people—as well as for the sake of creating new dividing lines. Currently, a tourist industry is making use of the linkages between tango and the city of Buenos Aires for the sake of attracting foreign capital. Buenos Aires as well as its tango is advertised as an instance of "raw" and exotic Latin America—a place where Europeans and North-Americans get a taste of nostalgia and have passionate encounters.[10] In that sense, the relations in tango tourism evoke questions concerning the significance, interests and cultural struggles involved in the imposing of territorial visions.

However, we also find a rather opposite tendency as the Argentine tango is appreciated not primarily for its exotic flavor but rather because of its fairly uncomplicated adaption to local habits in the places where the dance is being practiced—wherever that might be. Many dancers stress that the beauty of the movements and the distinctive communication lie at the heart of their interest, and acknowledge the interrelations between tango dancing and other kinds of physical cultures and intimate relations present in their daily lives—rather than the Argentine connection. In fact, the tango makes up a symbolic geography through which different places are evaluated, negotiated and inscribed with meaning. The different rankings of these places are partly linked to the different notions of authenticity in tango. As the discussions in various chapters of this book have suggested, authenticity involves a multilayered and partly conflicting set of values. Although most tango dancers wish to experience "genuine tango" as they travel with dancing aspirations to Buenos Aires or elsewhere in the world, the actual significance associated with authenticity differs. For some dancers the old Argentine dance-halls represent authenticity; for others they are signifiers of "kitsch" and commercialized tango. To put the issue somewhat simply, two general notions of authenticity with consequences for how dancers make sense of Argentina and Buenos Aires can be identified. The first one, which we might call a *modernist* authenticity discourse, frames tango dancing as one of many expressions of Argentine culture. Connecting with the tango involves entering into a dialogue not only with dance movements but with a broader spectrum of cultural expressions such as tango music, Argentine history, the Argentine lifestyle, the tango vocabulary (*el lunfardo*) and the presumed tango sentiments. This clearly connects the tango with the city of Buenos Aires and its history. Exploring authentic tango hence implies a total Argentine experience, which—for obvious reasons—is believed to go deep into the psyches of dancers as they walk the famous avenues of Buenos Aires and as they dance their nights away in classic Argentine venues. A *postmodernist* take on the meaning of authenticity in tango, on the other hand, offers a rather critical approach to the attempts to link the contemporary dance scene to Argentine history and the Argentine capital through the use of traditional tango ideals. Those dancers who approach the tango from within what I call a postmodernist frame acknowledge primarily the dancing experience and place it at the center of tango culture. This emphasizes the dancing as it is experienced by those people who make up the present tango scene, Argentines and others, in Argentina and elsewhere. Rather than celebrating historical knowledge, such as detailed familiarity with the classic tango orchestras from the 1930s and 1940s, a postmodernist take on tango rather encourages a tango knowledge relating to the present challenges and prospects of the dancing and its particular form of communication. Tango authenticity is here bound up with a notion of artistic expression and cultural development which evaluates new forms of dancing styles rather than the adoption of traditional practices and rules. In this view, authentic tango does not depend on the national or cultural origin of the dancers (Argentines or Swedes) or the actual places of the dancing (Argentina or Sweden). In fact, many practitioners who recognize this mode of authenticity criticize the traditional dance venues for essentializing tango through its dated rules and heterosexual organizing of the dancing.[11]

To sum up, a *modernist* discourse on tango ties the quest for authenticity to a particular place, the city of Buenos Aires, whereas a *postmodern* framing recognizes tango authenticity as linked to a particular way of relating to the dancing and hence a bodily and emotional practice which might as well be executed in the community halls of Stockholm or on the beaches of San Francisco. An additional difference between the two perspectives regards the definitions of acknowledged tango. As discussed in Chapter 6, a modernist perspective recognizes only those expressions strongly connecting with the traditional ways of dancing and organizing *milonga* life as "real tango". According to a postmodernist view, all kinds of dancing styles and all ways of communicating with others, both bodily and musical, can be tango, if the practitioners make sense of them as such. This implies a larger spectrum of practices, involving for instance the use of musical genres not found in traditional tango, alternative body styles and movements found outside the tango scene and various ways of organizing the social life of tango, for instance inspired by feminist and queer ideals, in place of traditional tango manners.[12] Putting these different takes on tango in dialogue with the topic of tango tourism, we might find that a postmodernist framing conceives of tourism as part of the definition of contemporary tango, whereas a modernist view conceives of (tango) tourism and the impact of globalization as a symbolic threat to Argentine tango culture. Ironically though, mostly those dancers who aspire to encounter "real" Argentine tango in the shape of an Argentine dancer or an ancient Argentine dance-hall are keen to embark on a journey to Buenos Aires, and hence add to the imprints of tourism.

This implies that the ongoing struggle over the definition of "real tango" partly involves boundary work engaging not only with notions of space but also with temporality. In fact, tango, just like other cultural phenomena, is characterized by a continuous struggle in which temporal distinctions are at stake. As Bourdieu writes, the "pushing back" of traditional advocates and the "dating" of their knowledge are part of a struggle over recognition: "As the newcomers come into existence, i.e. accede to legitimate difference, or even, for a certain time, exclusive legitimacy, they necessarily push back into the past the consecrated producers with whom they are compared, 'dating' their products and the taste of those who remain attached to them" (Bourdieu 1980: 289). Following Bourdieu, we might conclude that certain associations with the past might function discrediting also in tango. However, recognizing the specificity of the sentimental tango, we also find that dancers who are associated with the history of tango are often acknowledged as carriers of deep tango *connaissance* and authenticity.[13] Being a carrier of traditional values and a place offering access to traditional venues helps to constitute Buenos Aires as an attractive tourist destination, particularly for tango dancers. However, like other cultural pursuits, also the tango is affected by a play of status in which the new, the latest style around, the *à la mode* dancing, is valued. In fact, the play surrounding temporality shows that the historical inscription of symbolic capital—the cultural heritage and historical roots—at times become a problem for the city. In a particular framing, the construction of Buenos Aires as a "dated" tango city, offering nothing but manufactured dancing suited for tourists, cuts off the interest for some tango dancers.

Negotiating time and space is a matter of redefining and destabilizing culture. Although a majority of the dancers I met in Buenos Aires—for obvious reasons—and many of the dancers in Stockholm and San Francisco stress the Argentine impact on tango, the examples discussed in this chapter suggest that the Argentine "origin" is being challenged and that the significance of being Argentine is not solely a credential for local dancers. In fact, even the name—*Argentine* tango—might turn into a conflicting subject. Visiting dancers, as well as market actors and the Ministry of Tourism struggle to make sense of Buenos Aires and tango culture along such negotiations: a balancing act that moves between the past and the present, nationalist nostalgia and elusive cosmopolitanism. This chapter suggests that the interlacing of geography and temporal distinctions, together with various notions of authenticity, is part of creating the unsettled spaces of tango tourism.

Part IV
Conclusion

10 Tango Tourism
Between Market Adaption and Cultural Resistance

INTRODUCTION

In this last chapter of the book we will explore the relation between market forces targeting tango tourists,[1] on the one hand, and tango as an art form making up its own intimate economy, on the other hand. The argument put forward is that tango has never—and probably will never—be free from economic interest and the logic of market forces.[2] As this book shows, however, the impact of tourist markets on cultural art forms is constituted through ongoing negotiations which turn, in this case, tango tourism into an unsettled arena of commercialized and affective relations. This implies that those forces which try to annex tango are linked to a number of conditions partly dictated by the culture itself. This is to say that there are limits to the commercialization of tango. Without the values associated with the culture, the dance-floor dramas and the close-embrace dancing, the sweat and tears of the Argentine *milongas*, the market would have nothing to offer. In that sense a Disneyfication or McDonaldization of tango is impossible. Or rather, it is impossible within the realm of tango tourism. Disneyfied tango would simply not be recognized as tango by those dancers dedicated enough to undertake a journey to Buenos Aires. In the context of the academic debate on global capitalism, tango tourism is a case which demonstrates that commercialized exploitation is possible only as long as market forces can make use of and profit from values other than economic ones (values which might in fact clash with the logic of a capitalist *modus operandi*). In that sense a capitalist expansion involving new markets—be they cultural art fields or entire cities—depends on and is delimited by the capacities and nature of non-capitalist values (cp. Brown 2008; Harvey 2002, 2005; Tornhill 2010; Törnqvist 1995). Throughout this final chapter we will apply this argument to the micro-politics of the Argentine dance-floors, exploring how a culturally embedded market operates and how the belief system of tango enables as well as blocks a commodification of tango.

In this chapter we will also address the impact of globalization. Let us start by declaring that the fact that a large proportion of dancers in most tango clubs in Buenos Aires nowadays are Europeans, North-Americans,

Australian and Japanese is not by definition "bad for tango", as suggested by certain dancers. Rather, we should ask *how* the tango and the city of Buenos Aires are being exposed to the increasing number of people coming from all over the world and *how* the streams of tourism are related to a commercialization of tango and shifts in everyday Argentine life. The examples brought forward in this book suggest that the tango is both shaping and being (re)shaped in various social, economic and political geographies, some of which are formed inside the tourist-dense dance-halls of Buenos Aires. Moreover, these examples show that places and cultures are rarely fixed entities; rather, they are shaped—and reshaped—by the people who embody them: residents as well as temporary visitors, market actors and clients. However, there are different points of entrance and for obvious reasons very different ways of navigating throughout these geographies. Hence, when exploring the imprints of globalization and market forces on local cultures, we must address more detailed questions regarding the consequences of a "resistant" culture and the conditions enforced by the negotiations of values.

This concluding chapter builds upon the analyses conducted in previous chapters and is organized into three sections. The first one addresses the actual values at stake in the negotiations and boundary work involved in tango tourism. The second part enquires into the conditions shaping these negotiations. In this section we will explore the significance of symbolic tango capital and discuss the implications of a culturally embedded market. In the third part we will discuss the critique against commercialization from a somewhat different angle. We will relate this to tourist identity work carried out by the visiting dancers as well as with focus on the everyday consequences for the people living in the holiday site, those who are making a living from tango-tourism dollars. The relations explored in this book come across not only as constitutive for dance voyagers' holiday experience, but as intimately bound up with a larger realm of economic and political matters in Argentina, as well as in tourists' home countries.

NEGOTIATING TANGO TOURISM

This book provides several examples of how tango culture meets the forces of commercialization and the impact of globalization with resistance. However, rather than stating that resistance lies within the dancing *as such*, the kinetic and intimate connection—the politics of touch—together with the improvised nature of the dance form, as claimed by some dance scholars (Olszewski 2008: 64; cp. Manning 2003; Turner 2005), I suggest that it should be approached in terms of an ongoing negotiation and balancing act which must be understood in relation to tango as a

Tango Tourism

value system with its internal belief structure and economy. In order to approach what might be described as a form of cultural resistance, we must return to the field of tango with its implicit regime of justification and the ways in which the logic of the field is interpreted, incorporated and reproduced by dancers. However, in order to understand the intersection of tango and tourism we must also recognize that the market space of tango, with its various offers for tourists, is associated with values attractive to foreign dancers on a two-week tango holiday. In order to present this relation in visual form, the chart below maps out some general values and capacities associated with tango and tourism, respectively. On the side of the tango, we find values such as dancing skills, authenticity and tango honor, whereas the aspects of the tango market which primarily target dance tourists are associated with tourist values such as safety and accessibility to the culture.

TANGO	TOURISM (MARKET)
Tango economy (meriting values)	Capitalist market (purchasing values)
Dancing skills, tango honor, gender difference	Economic capital
Mystification (taboo of making things explicit)	Demystification (the price tag)
Gift economy (discourse on mutuality, free will, spontaneity)	Contracts based on commercial transactions
Risk taking, uncertainty, vulnerability	Purchasing safety measures
Proximity	Distance
Sacrifice, existential stakes, pain	Recreation, comfort, leisure
Originality	Reproduction
Exclusivity	Accessibility
Slow, embodied knowledge, internalized culture	Fast-track, transitory, visitor
Permanent	Temporary
Sacred	Profane

As this chart suggests, there are several conflicting dimensions within the intersection of tango and tourism. Some of them revolve around the ways in which dance voyagers are addressed: as culturally embedded tango dancers in touch with their inner selves *or* as tourist consumers operating in a shallow market space. This relates to the interference of a *capitalist logic* with the *honor code* of tango. In short, an honor code partly revolving around the *sacrifice* can be described in opposition to the qualities associated with *capitalist markets* and the use of *economic capital*. As discussed throughout this book, the symbolic economy of tango requires values to be *merited* through *dedication, bodily training* and passage through *transformative rites*, whereas the tourist market is bound up with values such as *comfort* and *risk-reduction* (regarding emotional vulnerability implicit in tango dancing and the risks associated with a journey to Buenos Aires). One example of this is the *price-setting* of dance-floor accessibility and the transmittance of dancing skills, which helps tourists—as well as Argentine dancers—access the culture through *monetary means*—rather than striving for its values through the use of *symbolic tango credentials*. For such reasons, money is partly perceived as providing illegitimate *shortcuts* and hence to interfere with the intimate tango economy. This potential conflict reflects the function of *justification principles* in tango. In fact, the reactions against commoditized tango—for instance in the form of taxi dancers—imply that the tango constitutes a validation order based on its own moral system, which assigns its members rewarding credentials or, on the contrary, disqualifying labels, as a function of their incorporation of legitimate values.

Implicit in this clash are also two different *temporalities*. Tango is often represented as an *embodied knowledge* and way of being in the world which takes years to fully master. What tango tourists are being offered in the form of private dance teachers and taxi dancers is a *shortcut* to tango *connaissance*, a *fast track* available for money. As one tango-tourist agency writes, they provide "the fast, authentic and fun way to dance tango in Buenos Aires" (a *Tango-All-Inclusive* flyer). Other market actors wish to help tourists "speed things up", i.e. to avoid losing time on bad dance partners and *milongas*. Hence tourist services offer easy *accessibility*, whereas the tango is associated with the *slow* and *viscous* body movements of the dancing, together with a notion of deep cultural knowledge calling for temporal investments to be made.

One aspect of this is the organizing of time in relation to the significance of *uncertainty*. Whereas tourism offers *safety* and *comfort*, tango is believed to require *ambiguity* and *risk-taking*. As discussed in Chapter 3, gift economies such as tango revolve around the absence of collectively agreed-upon "prices" for the values at stake—although its members embody a sense of fair trades. This might be exemplified by the comparison made by some dancers between taxi-dancing and prostitution. This comparison reveals, among other things, that economic transactions bring a formal contract situation to the dance-floor, which deemphasizes the impact of the actual dancing experience and the potential level of intimacy between two dancers. Economic transactions impose a regulation on a relation which should not be restricted beforehand. It is believed that part of the magic disappears when two dancers know beforehand that they will dance a number of *tandas* together. In that sense the intersection of tango and tourism involves a conflict between two social forms: a *spontaneous* and a *regulated* sociality. In some dancers' views, the commercialization of tango thereby also threatens a notion of *liberty* and *individuality*, implicit in tango dancing. Offering an avenue out of unexpected and uncertain shifts in the gift economy, the market is said to turn dancers into *passive consumers*, cutting them off from the *transcending* promises of tango. Subjecting the tango to upfront economic deals through which a *price tag* is put on the experiences also conflicts with the *taboo of making things explicit*, the *mystification* and the *myth-making* central to the tango culture. Ultimately, and in the words of Mary Douglas, the worries about "dirty" tourist dollars invading the intimate dance embrace include a fear of contamination from an economic logic. Money, and the cultural shifts implied by a tourist adjustment process, is simply believed to threaten to corrupt the *emotionality* of tango with a *cold* profit *rationality*, stemming from the logic of an economic sphere. This would not only challenge certain tango values but also the *autonomy* of the field. This, we might suggest, risks taking away the transformative capacities associated with tango.

Based on these discussions, we might understand the chart above as an attempt to visualize the struggle between market forces and the field of tango dancing. On the right side of the chart we find those values which the market attempts to trade, and which revolve around the accommodation of tourists within the world of tango. On the left side we find the conditions imposed by the world of tango. Visualized this way, the conflicting relations in tango tourism reflect a clash between value spheres. Whereas the tourist market trades comfort and accessibility, the tango economy revolves around the play of rather opposite values, such as uncertainty and sacrifice. From this perspective, the configuration of tango tourism might be described in terms of a collision between two belief systems and sets of practical reasons with their own associated credentials, rewards and logics.[3] This is to say that the tango is not very easily subjected to a market logic and to values associated with tourism. However, as follows from this book, it is equally true that certain market values seem attractive to large groups of dancers, locals as well as tourists. In fact, throughout the chapters we have explored the conflicting values and identities emerging through tango tourism as subject negotiable to conversion. Hence, rather than being interpreted as a conflict between fixed value spheres, tango tourism appears to cover a rather destabilized set of relations. This suggests that the chart above should not be approached as a list of absolute dichotomies, but rather as a continuum illustrating the spectrum of values at stake. Moreover, the list should be read as an effort to temporarily fix an ongoing struggle. As discussed throughout this book, tango—as well as tourism—should be approached as a set of embodied practice and negotiated meaning systems which undergoes shifts and dislocations. However, these processes can be captured at particular moments in time. One aim of this study has been to detect and describe tango tourism as it comes across at a specific point in time, using a particular set of questions and analytical perspectives.[4]

Contested Authenticity

Following from this discussion, we might conclude that it is not the intersection of tourism and tango *as such*, or the commercializing of tango *as such*, which creates concerns among visiting and local dancers. To a large extent dance voyages include various forms of legitimate consumption which put tango dancers in dialogue with other tourists. Just like holiday travelers around the world, they purchase airplane tickets, nights at hotels and guided city tours. Most tango tourists are also happy clients within the market space of tango, consuming diverse dance services and tango items. In fact, the educational objectives of dance journeys force many dancers to purchase dance classes and hire private teachers, in addition to the consumption of tango goods such as dancing shoes, particular clothing and music recordings. As discussed in Chapters 6 and 7, it is rather when certain aspects of the belief system of tango are challenged that the tango market is made sense of as a provocation. Returning to the chart above, we will find that most tango voyagers end up neither as total believers in the transformative capacity of an "authentic" tango voyage nor as mere tourist consumers. In order to visualize this, we must break the chart down in order to convey more detailed information about the values at stake. The following continuum aims at illustrating how a limited number of practices, places and market services are associated with various degrees of authenticity. The chart should be read as an approximate visualization which primarily serves to offer an illustration of how we might link tango and tourism, respectively, to presumed authenticity values. This entails that the distance between the different *milongas*, market actors, tango services and frequent visitors is not exact, but rather aspires to indicate that these elements are inscribed with meaning *in relation* to one another—and according to their associative constitution in relation to the continuum.

Visualizing tango tourism this way makes a number of things obvious. First of all, it shows that authenticity is a continuum interrelated

	TANGO High degree of authenticity			**TOURISM** Low degree of authenticity
Venues	Out-of-town *milongas* Sin Rumbo	Inner-city neighborhood *milongas* Yira-Yira	Large and well-known inner-city *milongas* Confitería Ideal	Inner-city tango-show restaurants Rojo Tango
Items	Regular clothing stores, not branded for tango	Tango dancing stores (targeting both local and visiting dancers)	Tango dancing stores (primarily targeting dance tourists)	Tango items in souvenir shops
Dance services	Community-center classes	Acknowledged tango schools, private dance classes with recognized dancers	Tango taxi dancers	Dance classes and tango escort offered by tourist agencies, hotels and restaurants
Audiences	Majority of Argentines	Argentine and foreign dancers	Foreign and Argentine dancers	Foreigners with no or limited tango knowledge

with commercialized practices. This suggests that commercialization is not equivalent to the destruction of authentic meaning, but rather that this relation is one target of the sense-making practices. The chart also implies that the level of authenticity associated with various tango venues, items and services is not guaranteed by the Argentine framing, i.e. by being offered in the capital of tango. Instead the production of authenticity is linked to a number of factors, such as urban location (inside/outside the city center), degree of commercialization (high/low) and ethnic inscription (Argentines/foreigners). Secondly, it becomes clear that most tango tourists avoid the tourist pole of the scale. Throughout the previous four chapters we have investigated how dance tourists distance themselves from places, services and people associated with "touristy" commercialization, such as tango-show restaurants. More surprisingly, though, those venues and services associated with a high level of authenticity, by virtue of their anchorage within the Argentine (tango) culture and society, are also rejected by most foreign dancers. Such are the local neighborhood *milongas* outside of the city center as well as those *centros culturales* which offer tango classes primarily for Argentine dancers and for free or at reduced prizes. Although many tango tourists aspire for "genuine" tango and to have the same experiences as local dancers, the values associated with Argentine authenticity seem to be downplayed in favor of comfort, geographic proximity and safety. We might also add that the presence of other tourists actually seems to render certain places attractive, as long as these dancers represent a certain dancing level as well as status within the world of tango. We might even suggest that some visitors wish to explore a tango characterized by its adaption to foreign dancers. This is indicated by the success of those tango schools with a high level of English speaking teachers, as well as those offering dancing styles and pedagogics resonating with what the dancers are familiar with from their home communities.

It seems, in other words, that authenticity is an important yet stretchable value at stake in tango tourism, shifting in meaning and significance.[5] When dancers make sense of the motives behind their journeys to Buenos Aires, the aspirations for "real" tango are often put center stage. However, the quest for authenticity is presumably not as decisive for their actions and everyday practices in Argentina, or rather the meaning and significance associated with "real" tango shift once they plunge into the dance-clubs in Buenos Aires. Visiting dancers seem rather happy to occupy the middle of what is here visualized as a continuum ranging from local Argentine tango life outside the city center, on the one hand, to tango as a mere tourist attraction, on the other. We might also notice, drawing on the discussions in Chapter 6, that authenticity becomes more important the closer to the tango scene dance tourists get. Although most visiting dancers hire rooms and apartments in tourist-dense areas and although they are happy to consume tourist services and items unrelated to tango, they do not wish to identify themselves—or to be identified by others—as tourists and clients within the *milonga*. Another way to put it is that they combine elements and attempt to find a middle ground between the two poles, neither getting caught in a superficial tourist experience nor plunging too deeply into a world which does not offer the desired comfort and safety. This implies that the distinction between commercialized services and authentic experiences, made by certain tango dancers as well as by some academic scholars (Crick 2005; Greenwood 1982; Turner and Ash 1975) should be approached with concern (cp. Bruner 1991: 240–241; Bernstein 2001; Cohen 1988).

However, there are certain consequences of tourists' divided take on authenticity. The fact that many tourists tend to spend most of their time in Argentina with other Europeans or North-Americans has to do with the limited time-frame, linguistic barriers and clustering of tango events in wealthier inner-city areas. This might also be related to the romantic and economic framing of Argentine people—and particularly men—as unreliable. Still, many dance tourists wish to experience the tango with local dancers. As discussed in relation to several empirical accounts in this book, Argentines are appreciated for qualities having to do with their supposed cultural heritage and knowledge basis. In statements and narratives they are framed as "native guides" and "forays" to "real Buenos Aires". However, because they are appreciated on premises linked to authenticity values and at times mere exoticism, Argentine dancers are rarely the objects of long-term friendship among the tourists.[6] The average tango tourist adds more Europeans and North-Americans than Argentines as new friends on her or his Facebook account during a tango holiday in Buenos Aires. Rather, Argentine dancers at times end up as educational means and souvenir experiences, for use back home.

One additional consequence of the negotiated authenticity is that the critique of commercial forces seems to leave out the economic giants within the tourism industry—the airline companies together with multinational hotel chains. This has to do with the fact that the fear of a loss of aura is not associated with Argentine culture and the city of Buenos Aires at large, but primarily with tango dancing. This implies that most dancers do not consider the purchase of hotel rooms to be an economic transaction which interferes with their identity as tango dancers or adventurous voyagers. Neither do they regard the consumption of exclusive shoe brands and dance classes in internationally well-known tango schools as part of a problematic consumption practice conflicting with the goals of their journey. On the contrary, these examples represent a mainstream pattern of consumption within tango tourism and as such are assumed to help deliver the complete Buenos Aires experience. In that sense, tango tourism seems to support a trend in international tourism. Also in relation to the intimate dance journeys, it is likely that a large proportion of the average traveler's expenses does not end up in the country she or he is visiting but rather with international firms such as aircraft companies and tourist agencies (Urry 2002: 57; cp. Dielemans 2008).

Reterritorailized Tango and the Loss of Aura

The significance of these negotiations is related to the values at stake— values connected both with tango as an autonomous art form and the rewards related to an Argentine tango journey. In this section we will address some possible outcomes of these negotiations. We should be careful to note, however, that the following discussion is not an empirical conclusion, describing the state of affairs in contemporary Argentine tango, but rather an attempt to sketch potential consequences of a value negotiation. The overall argument is that tango culture cannot embrace all kinds of translations and stretching of values without losing something on the way. If the negotiations between tango and tourism are taken too far, with the consequence that a comforting and risk-reducing tourist market is all there is, the values associated with tango dancing in Buenos Aires would diminish. As David Harvey writes: "the more easily marketable such items become the less unique and special they appear" (2002: 12). In that sense, and rather ironically, an excessive commodification of tango might put an end to market expansions.

The potential loss of aura is particularly noticeable in relation to the contested geography of tango tourism. As discussed in Chapter 9, the city of Buenos Aires is still the number one holiday destination for Argentine tango dancers. Its future hold, however, seems in fact to depend on developments regarding the commercialization of tango and further tourist adaption. If the negotiations go too far right on the authenticity continuum, with the consequence that tango life in Buenos Aires would consist mostly of tourist dancers and *milonga* dance escorts in the form of taxi dancers, the most dedicated dancers would probably choose other destinations for their dancing holiday. This has to do partly with the delicate production of authenticity in relation to actual places and can be related to a study by Erik Cohen on so-called dark tourism in the Holocaust museum in Jerusalem. At the center of his investigation is the relation between authenticity and location, and the distinction between what he calls *in situ* sites, the actual place of an historical event—such as Auschwitz—and *in populo* sites, such as the Holocaust museum (2011: 194). This is one example of how the cultural significance connected with a particular place can be separated from that place. Using Cohen's terminology, the primary site in tango is Buenos Aires whereas the secondary sites are all those other places around the world where the tango is being danced and practiced, such as the European tango festivals and dance marathons. What motivates dance voyagers to travel to Buenos Aires instead of to these other sites are the cultural, historical and artistic promises associated with the city. If those values are threatened, it is likely that some potential tango tourists will choose other destinations.

What is somewhat neglected in Cohen's study, however, is the fact that the negotiations surrounding authenticity and places are often infused with symbolic struggles involving economic interest and political prestige. The attempts to link the tango to the city of Buenos Aires might be interpreted in terms of a response to a possible reterritorialization. In fact, the more diffused the tango gets, geographically and in relation to its various cultural forms, the more important it becomes for Argentine actors—individual tango teachers as well as the Ministry of Tourism—to try to tie the dance more strongly to the Argentine culture and economy. However, such attempts might have quite the contradictory effect, at least when the tango is advertised through what some tango aficionados would criticize as a rather stereotypical language. Although the slogans advertising "the tango capital" as a "passionate city" might attract certain kinds of tourists, such advertising will also, due to the logic of exclusivity in tango, lead certain groups of potential tango tourists—for instance the European *avant-garde*, the "tango nobility"—to continue developing their tango outside Argentina.

The possible loss of aura not only regards the marketizing of Buenos Aires, but covers also other aspects of tango culture, such as the promise of transcendence. In a pioneering study in tourism research, Dean MacCannell (1976) portrays the driving forces behind people's wishes to travel abroad as the anomalies of modern life. People go on holiday to foreign countries as a response to alienation growing out of industrialization and social fragmentation, he claims. Similar ideas are present among the tango dancers in this book. In several autobiographies written by tango dancers, and in academic work on tango, the interest in the Argentine culture is partly described in terms of a silent protest against what the writer/dancer perceives of as some depressing features of the early twenty-first century (Cusumano 2008; Olszewski 2008; Palmer 2006; Taylor 1998). Whereas society is described as increasingly artificial and commercialized, the tango is said to offer artistic exploration and genuine connection with others. Whereas the nuclear family is facing validity and sustainability problems, the tango is said to offer new arenas in which people can live intimate lives. Whereas intense processes of rationalization and techno-scientific discoveries are rapidly advancing, the dance is said to constitute a culture which provides spaces for emotional ties with history. And as the gap between the rich and the poor world increases, some dancers insist that the tango floor is a place where people meet across social barriers.

These imaginaries form a backdrop for some dancers' critique of the commercialization of tango and the expanding streams of (other) dance tourists. As discussed throughout this book there are examples of dancers, Argentines and others, who fear that the accommodation of tango to the demands of foreigners on a dance holiday risks undermining the "radical" heart and soul of tango. One concern is that the influences from the outside world—the impact of money as well as "postmodern" values—will eventually colonize tango and destroy its cultural depth and transformative capacities. Such a fear represents a context for understanding the negotiations in tango tourism. On the one hand, the visiting dancers wish to consume tango in the form of certain services and items, such as private dance classes with famous teachers and Buenos Aires–branded tango shoes. Some visitors also wish to buy into the safety measures and comfort that tourist agencies offer. In other words, a certain degree of commercialization and interference of a tourist logic within the tango is appreciated. On the other hand, it is feared that if the negotiations along the tango-tourism continuum are taken too far, the magnetism of tango in Buenos Aires will eventually be lost. If tango is reduced to only show-tango in expensive hotel restaurants and tango kitsch, i.e. stereotypical postures, fishnet stockings and slit skirts, the values that dancers from all over the world come looking for might disappear.

This touches upon a more general paradox within many streams of tourism. Exploiting places for tourism is ultimately what risks taking away the values that attract tourism. By travelling to a place wished to be discovered as untouched ground, visitors put the uniqueness of that place at risk. This is sometimes framed as "imperialist nostalgia" or even "tourist nostalgia" (Bruner 1991: 246; Jonsson 1993). As Coleman and Crang write: "such activity bears with it the ironic seeds of its own destruction, as the very presence of the tourist corrupts the idea of reaching an authentic and totally different culture. Paradoxically, a nostalgic semiotic economy is produced, one that is always mourning the loss of that which it itself has ruined. [. . .] The really authentic unspoiled place is always displaced in space or time—it is spatially located over the next hill, or temporally existed just a generation ago" (2002: 3).[7]

The negotiations pointed to in this book must also be related to the values and transformative capacities bound up with tango as a cultural art form. In order to function as a powerful and seductive belief structure for its aficionados, the field of tango must maintain a certain degree of autonomy from other cultural spheres. To make tango "magic" and its acts of consecration possible, the accessibility of the world is regulated according to its own logic and its own symbolic values. This is important also in order for the value system to be powerful enough to tie people together, and impose a practical reason which enables the formation of social groups. The *illusio*, the tango belief embodied as a set of practices and mental dispositions, is ultimately the condition for shaping local and global tango communities. One consequence of this relative autonomy is that the field is able to create a particular social stratification based on the values at stake. In fact, the shared belief paves the way both for social bonds and legitimate stratification layers. People are not supposed to- and rarely do—become dance partners out of professional interest or similarities regarding social background or political ideology, but rather due to factors such as dancing style and level of commitment together with musical preferences and status within the world of tango dancers. This means that the logic of the field dominates dancers' perception and behavior, at least once they enter the *milonga*. One of the sacrifices required to become a tango dancer is accordingly that dancers leave behind the habits, relationships and social identities they form and cultivate outside of tango. This implies that status credentials in other social fields, such as money or a high-skilled professional position, cannot—and should not—be recognized as values within the *milonga*.[8] This strengthens the bonds among the insiders and is also what makes possible a transformative capacity: the transgression of values and hierarchies acknowledged in other spheres of life.

TANGO RECOGNITION AND TOURIST IDENTITY WORK

In this section we will set aside the actual values at stake and move on to discuss a number of conditions which shape the negotiations. It will be argued that the encounter between tango and tourism is not solely a clash between abstract value spheres, but also a set of human relations involving those people who embody the everyday life of Argentine tango: dancers and service providers within the market space of tango. In order to understand the negotiations and their possible imprints, we must situate these actors—and their acting—within a social field of relations. In regard to the object of study, this includes the structuring and positioning of tango dancers according to the intimate dance economy. It matters, so to speak, if those dancers who choose to leave Buenos Aires for other tango destinations are beginners or well-recognized dancers. The same is true regarding dancers' likelihood of buying into the market services and tango goods. Rather than being an economic matter, conditioned primarily by dancers' economic status and purchasing capacities,[9] it seems that the rejection of market services is related to the intimate tango economy and the possession of tango credentials. Using such a terminology, we might argue that only some dancers can afford to reject the accommodating market services; i.e. only some dancers can afford *not* to purchase those services.

In the present section we will discuss how different groups of dancers relate to and engage with the ongoing negotiations based on their position within the field of tango dancers. As discussed in Chapter 3, the possession of symbolic capital—i.e. the legitimate tango credentials acknowledged as such by other dancers—is crucial in these processes. In the second part of this section we will explore the impact of symbolic capital from the angle of a group of dancers who prove to be weak in relation to the tango economy—but powerful in regard to financial status. Through a discussion of middle-aged female tango tourists we will reflect on the relation between economic and symbolic vulnerability, i.e. the relation between an economic logic based on economic capital and an economy acknowledging tango credentials. In the third part of this section we will look into the impact of symbolic capital on the market space. We will explore a culturally embedded market and address the question of how service providers' close relation with the culture—which is a condition also for economic success—affects the level of market adaption in tango.

Let us start by saying that it is not so much a matter of whether dancers consume tango or not; most dancers, both locals and tourists, actually do. Rather, what is significant is dancers' level of *illusio* together with their possession of tango credentials decisive for the kind of consumption they engage with. On the one hand, dancers like North-American Emma and Swedish Daniella, who are "down with the tango" and have been to Buenos Aires several times, are not in need of the services offered by many tourist agencies. Dancers like them are, in fact, keen to escape the associations linked to tourism and reject offers which are perceived as "too touristy". They are asked to dance out in the *milongas* and have been around long enough to have their own networks, both of foreign dancers and Argentine professionals. Rather than paying for tango *taxistas*, these dancers purchase the latest models of tango shoes and take private classes with up-and-coming Argentine star dancers. On the other hand, we find beginning dancers with neither sufficient dancing skills and cultural knowledge, nor sufficient networks and travelling experiences, to feel comfortable on their own. Dancers like North-American Pam (discussed in Chapter 6), a beginner in tango, have good reasons for buying into the comforting tourist services involving taxi dancers and accommodating city tours. At large, this group of dancers is also more rewarded by the price-setting of symbolic goods in tango, as this provides accessibility (to dance partners and the culture) without the risks involved with playing the game of uncertainty based on credentials acknowledged by the intimate dance economy.

It seems, in other words, that dance travelers enter the tango-tourism intersection from different positions, depending on their various tango resources and to some extent their travelling experiences, which involve language skills and social abilities. The embodied credentials also interrelate with how dance tourists make use of consumption as part of their identity work in tango. This is partly related to dancers' level of tango *illusio* and their ability to "sense" the rules of the game. *Beginning dancers* like Pam sometimes convey a certain unawareness regarding the cultural "right" and "wrong". This implies that these dancers are probably less concerned than others about cultural distinctions in tango regarding the latest trends in dancing shoes and the up-and-coming stars. The next level of dancers on the scale of *illusio* and tango recognition, which we might call the *tango middle classes*, actually seems to show some similarities with middle classes elsewhere. They exhibit greater concerns and anxieties over positions and credentials—doing things the proper way and manifesting good taste, i.e. reproducing cultural distinctions—than both the elite and the lower-ranked groups. *Experienced dancers* like Daniella, who have many years of practice and who are recognized in their local dancing communities, have sufficient tango credentials both to avoid the comforting services offered by the market and to consume them when wanted—confident enough not to feel threatened in their tango identity. What brings different groups of dancers together, however, is that they all reflect and negotiate meaning along the tango-tourism continuum. All of them may not end up watching show-tango in "touristy" restaurants, but they all reflect upon the significance and social impact of (not) doing so.[10]

When evaluating the impact of the behavior of these various groups of dancers, we should take the significance of symbolic capital into account. In fact, the recognition and status that the dancers transmit to their acts is decisive for their effect on the tango scene. If top-ranked dancers start avoiding certain *milongas*, dance schools or tango-shoe models, these services and items will lose status and become less desirable for other dancers as well. In that sense, what become successful services within the market space of tango and additionally how the negotiations over tango tourism develop, is not only a matter of what individual market actors are able to offer, but also a response to the structuring of the field of dancers. Conversely, the actions of beginning dancers in tango are clearly important for the market—as they make up a significant client group. However, their symbolic impact is rather limited. In that sense, the negotiations over authenticity, intimacy and commercialization are intertwined with the field of tango dancing and the level of symbolic capital embodied by different groups of dancers. This turns out to be important also in relation to larger trends within tango, such as the reterritoralization previously mentioned. Such a development is apparently connected with the choices of the "tango nobility". If the "good dancers" leave Buenos Aires for other tango destinations, other dancers might join them.

Intimate Vulnerabilities

One factor which deserves a bit more attention is how these negotiations reflect the degrees of vulnerability in tango. This focus paves the way for a discussion of how the gendered and heterosexualized framing of tango affects market forces. In previous chapters we have discussed the gendered impact of safety measures on tourist practices. In this section we will look particularly into a gendered kind of emotional vulnerability and explore how the heterosexualized play in tango creates different kinds of bargaining positions and makes certain groups of dancers more likely to accommodate market services. Let us start by suggesting that the global networks of dominance and dependency addressed in this study involve several aspects, only a few of which are economic. As the Swedish dancer Daniella puts it, foreigners use the tango to manage an emotional vulnerability, whereas Argentine dancers use the tango as an avenue for lifting themselves out of economic vulnerability.

> The Argentines grow up with poverty but they can work themselves upwards, by becoming really good dancers, that way they can reach a position, become famous, become someone. This is a total contrast to us westerners who are materially safe but carry an existential pain. I came to the tango to get the strength to survive a divorce. This was my therapy. I put up a shelter through tango. [. . .] I was extremely vulnerable when I came to Buenos Aires the first time. But I was kind of tough on the outside and I was not interested in having a romantic affair or to be robbed of my money, unless I decided to. (Daniella, 50-year-old, Sweden)

Rather than stating that one or the other kind of vulnerability is better or worse—or more or less "real"—we might propose that the hardships managed in tango (tourism) are different for different groups of dancers. This book demonstrates that gender is one such component. The study of tango tourism entails exploring a gendered terrain which involves a range of existential risks closely related to the gendered project of making oneself respectable (cp. Skeggs 2005) and lovable (cp. Butler 1990/1999). Although defining themselves as economically powerful and independent, often with successful professional careers and strong social networks, some women who embark on a tango journey to Buenos Aires claim to be subjected to a particular vulnerability due to their gender and age. The fact that the tango world is heavily invested with a heterosexual matrix and highly preoccupied with gender difference makes this an emotionally high-risk enterprise, not least for middle-aged women. Some of these women report that they are rejected more often than other dancers, and that a constant process of bodily evaluation (by other dancers) is devastating for their self-image. This has to do with the intimate economy of tango, with the strict dancing hierarchies and exclusionary practices which partly reinforces ideals of femininity linked to the worshiping of young, "capable" bodies.

This vulnerability should be put in relation to the objectives ascribed to the journeys and the economic, social and emotional investments made in order to realize them. Some dancers ascribe transformative capacities to travel to Buenos Aires: at times they hope the journeys will provide a new sense of meaning after a life crisis. This implies that the disappointment of being rejected, with its implicit notion of failure, is related not only to tango dancing but to life at large. For some dancers the tango letdown becomes a life defeat. These examples show that, in addition to categories such as gender and class, life trajectory and turns in life, such as divorces or a close relative's death, are important when making sense of tango tourism. In fact, life situation appears to be decisive in relation to the choices with which dancers are confronted.

Moreover, the gendered play in tango imposes expectations on the body, particularly on women's bodies, in addition to what they actually do and express on the dance-floor. Being recognized as "beautiful" and "sensual" functions to reward practitioners in tango as elsewhere. Although such acknowledgements also reward men with credentials, they are not subject to the same sort of requests to adapt their bodies and emotional selves according to the ideals (partly because of the male shortage of dancers). The context of global tourism enforces this tendency. As discussed in Chapter 8, regarding the production of authentic romance as intertwined with a notion of gender difference—not differences based on class–, the tourist context and the associative linkages with "questionable" forms of intimate tourism enforce the creation of "lovable" bodies. It is as women—or men—that tango tourists can engage on equal terms with local dancers in the Argentine tango—in intimate dancing relations as well as in romantic endeavors off the dance-floor. This is how we might understand the mixture of market offers, ranging from dancing escorts to body modification particularly addressing female dance tourists. Besides pictures of women's legs carried up by different models of high-heeled dancing shoes and "sexy" female clothing, the advertising pages in the Argentine tango magazines feature agencies which offer make-up classes and plastic surgery. In the context of tango, such consumption is not an expression of superiority, but rather of weakness and lack—lack of the right kind of embodied femininity as well as of legitimate tango qualifications. To sum up, we might claim that the market for these kinds of body-centered services emerges partly from a gendered vulnerability connected with ideals of femininity, in tango and elsewhere. Somewhat ironically, though, rather than criticizing the underlying gender structures, the questioning of these services often addresses individual women.

One could argue that this particular form of vulnerability—and the consumption patterns it evokes—is a privilege of a western mobile middle class, wealthy and safe enough to travel to places which put them in edgy situations which they are able to manage through the help of commoditized measures. Rather than dismissing these experiences as crocodile tears of the privileged, however, I suggest that they add complexity to the understanding of power and emotions in a globalized world. Through an exploration of vulnerability, expressed primarily by female tourists, the emotional embodiment of recognition becomes crucial when investigating how various power regimes operate. The case of tango tourism indicates that economic equality between men and women—and even cases in which women are economically superior—may not remove the impact of ideals of femininity requiring bodily adjustments and emotional conformity. As the case of tango tourism indicates, a gendered coming-into-being intersects with class, age and racialized discourses. Moreover, this leads us to ask how intimate vulnerabilities in tango and elsewhere target certain groups more intensely than others and how this interrelates with commercial forces. Hence, this study contributes an example to research showing that consumption is a highly emotional enterprise, serving to comfort and provide a sense of meaning, rather than being strictly a matter of purchasing goods. This argument is often made with reference to the chimerically positive impact of shopping, which is apparent, for instance, in the way western consumption culture serves to fill up a sensed gap of meaning (Bauman 2007). The phenomenon of tango tourism illustrates that fear, shame and vulnerability are present as emotions in consumption, reinforcing as well as blocking markets.

In addition, the case of economically powerful women with few tango resources illustrates the clash between two types of justification regimes. For this group the tourist market offers not only safety measures and comforting shortcuts, but also (gender) equality. With the help of economic capital temporary visitors can partly transgress the heterosexualized hierarchies within the Argentine world of tango and pay for male dancers to invite them up to dance. Through the purchase of a taxi dancer, accessibility is secured; moreover, expensive private classes with recognized dancers promise to improve tourists' dancing skills within a short time-frame—and hence increase their chances of getting to participate in the dancing. As already discussed, however, certain shortcuts to tango—accessed through the use of economic capital—partly imposes a tourist shame on its purchasers, marking them as outsiders and potentially digging them deeper into the exclusion and vulnerability they sense within the world of tango.

This calls for a comment regarding a tendency in globalization and intimacy studies to privilege economic explanations and modes of domination. In research on sex tourism, for instance, material factors are often placed center stage in the analysis and framed as a political matter, whereas emotional aspects are downplayed as private matters (cp. Sanchez Taylor 2006: 56). For understanding the relations in tango tourism, such a bias is rather limiting. In the market space of tango tourism, many Argentine tango workers engaged in intimate body labor—such as certain exclusive private dance teachers—are recognized as the expertise and nobility within the culture. "We are the stars", as one tango teacher puts it (Linn, 21-year-old, Sweden/Argentina). In other words, the power relation between tourist clients and service providers in holiday sites is far from one-dimensional and is determined only in part by economic factors. However, rather than creating a hierarchy between two sets of conditions—or vulnerabilities—I suggest that we take the messy intersections between different structuring conditions, including negotiations of commercialization, into account when exploring the relations in globalized intimacy.

A Culturally Embedded Market

As follows from this study, there are good reasons to avoid a binary divide putting the tango on the one side and the market on the other. Also those market actors who attempt to trade tourist values such as accessibility and comfort are part of the culture. Rather than representing an outside force distanced from the goods they are trading and aiming to appropriate "the creativity embedded in the web of life" (Harvey 2005: 71), many service providers are themselves deeply invested with the culture. Just like other dancers, they pursue dance enjoyment, tango recognition and they embody the belief system as well as the intimate dance economy. As discussed in Chapter 5, the market is primarily made up of Argentine dancers who are trying to make a living out of their passion and skills in tango. The agencies are mostly small-scale and often operate on the hazy border between professional work and leisure activity. In fact, the tango market can be related to what professional musicians, artists and dancers in other cultural fields experience as a conflict between economic necessity and creative freedom (cp. Aspers 2005; Bourdieu 1993, 2000; Galli 2012; Larsson and Svensson 1992).

This indicates that the commercial forces in tango do not simply subject the dancing culture to market adjustments. Because of the culturally embedded market, we might actually assume that the meaning-world of tango creates conditions for how such adjustments can be brought about.[11] Just like other markets of symbolic goods, the trading of tango is closely bound up with the logic and values of the field. As in the world of literature or ecological gardening, those market actors who try to make a living out of tango dancing are required to accept the belief system of tango, including the discourses and practices which define the world. Also, in tango the "practical master of the law of the functioning of the field" and *illusio* (embodied conviction) are necessary features for those who wish to be successful actors within the market (Bourdieu 1980: 262). This implies that symbolic tango capital is decisive also for market actors and made a requisite for economically profitable outcomes. The tango, just like other spheres in which a pre-capitalist logic exists, is partly organized through the collective disavowal of narrow economic interest. This implies that the rejection of economic motives at times even functions to reward dancers. Those behaviors and choices which seem to lie outside the realm of rational action embody a sense of rationality that conforms to the intimate dance economy.

Returning to the successful tango schools and *milongas*, we find that economic disinterestedness helps them to accumulate symbolic capital, which in turn helps to create a profitable business. In the case of the *milonga*, the successful organizers (in terms of recognition and estimated number of visitors) take pride in delivering "quality tango", i.e. services and goods recognized as high in quality by the acknowledged members of the world of tango dancers. This general guidance is apparent in the forming of an audience. The goal for most club organizers is not only to attract as many visitors as possible, i.e. as many entrance fees as possible, but also to attract the *right* audience: a crowd that confirms the club's profile and helps to create an ambiance that combines excellent dancing, important social networks and charisma with a distinctive tango atmosphere (warm, friendly, traditional, underground, sexy etc.). In that sense the club organizer perceives the audience not as a one-dimensional economic value, but rather as the prime symbolic value for making a *milonga* successful, symbolically and economically.

This suggests that in order to understand why certain services, goods and values become tradable and others not, we must turn to the social and moral world in which the trades take place. This becomes apparent in the case of taxi dancers, who offer a service that many dancers objectively need: a guaranteed dance partner with decent dancing skills. However, as this study indicates, the structuring of the field of tango, together with dancers' aspirations for particular emotionality, mutual agreement and individuality, partly blocks the market of dance-partner services. Hence, market success not only depends on the objective demands within a client group, but also has to do with moral conventions and cultural legitimacy. This suggests that, when inquiring into the imprints of commercialized forces on local cultures, we must ask more detailed questions regarding the nature of the market as well as the actors' relations to the values being traded. This involves questions about the driving forces behind commercialization, together with questions regarding the organizing of the market and its logic, values, actors and motivations. In that sense, the case of tango tourism suggests that markets are emotionally and socially invested worlds which need to be studied and conceptualized as such, rather than being addressed merely in terms of strictly rational and profit-maximizing structures (Bourdieu 1998; Aspers and Beckert 2011; Zelizer 2005; Weber 1965, 1995).

Because tango tourism is a culturally embedded market, the market actors have to manage the inherent conflicts within it. Ultimately they are asked to make business out of symbolic goods which some of their presumed clients wish to experience outside the realm of commercialization. One example of the difficulties this creates is the trading of authenticity values. The delicate task involves managing a value conflict between accessibility, on the one hand, and exclusivity, on the other. A related concern for the market actors touches upon the relation between authenticity and exoticism. The tango services and products must be advertised as Argentine, i.e. as impossible to purchase anywhere else in the world, but the overly exaggerated expressions of Argentine culture, the so-called "tango kitsch", must be avoided. This requires a balancing act. Dance teachers, hostel managers and city guides face the task of offering authentic experiences with an exotic touch, i.e. of delivering "non-touristy" services and experiences to tourists on tourists' conditions. The market actors are forced to strike a balance between values associated with the accessible and those associated with the unreachable, between tango kitsch and presumably refined exclusive art expressions, between stereotypical projections and authenticity values. One example of a successful balancing act is performed by *DNI Tango*, discussed in Chapter 5. This dance school has clearly distanced itself from "tango kitsch" and even traditional tango. *DNI* promotes itself as exclusive and concerned with refined artistic qualities. This "elite" approach, potentially distancing for beginning dancers coming for their first Argentine experience, is balanced with a "friendly" and service-minded atmosphere, stressing each student's "individual capacities". Hence, the school appeals both to tango values such as authenticity and artistic quality and tourist values in the form of comfort and accessibility.

Turning to an apparently contrasting example, that of taxi-dancing, a phenomenon which actually borders on the illegitimate commercialization of tango, we find that there are layers of meaning also to this service and that the taxi dancers themselves negotiate meaning along with legitimate tango narratives. For instance, Ezequiel, the manager of a taxi-dancing agency, claims—for quite obvious reasons—that the purchase of taxi dancers is not an inauthentic way of experiencing tango. To the contrary, he expresses certainty that the taxi-dancing service, because it supplies a dance partner who takes you "as you are", creates a friendlier and more accepting atmosphere for exploring the depth of tango culture. He uses the analogy of the nursing profession, which aims to accommodate all kinds of patients based on their specific needs, when he describes the ethics behind the taxi-dancing business. He also explains that he came up with the idea as a response to the discriminatory world of tango, in which certain groups of dancers have few chances of discovering the culture. This suggests, once again, that we abandon the dichotomy between commercialization and authentic values. Trading a service for money, and primarily to tourists, is not necessarily made sense of as a "selling out", either by the service provider or the larger cultural scene. A similar argument is made by Yvonne Payne Daniel (1996), who has studied tourist-oriented dance performances in Haiti and Cuba. She explores how spaces of creativity and artistic development appear also in those performances which target tourists. Tourism replicates dance traditions in the form of "staged" culture, but in doing so tourism also offers new spaces for artistic development and cultural change (cp. Coleman and Crang 2002: 10). This illustrates that the ways in which the relation between commercialization and authenticity values comes to the fore depend on a number of factors, among them the play of status and recognition within the field of dancers. Returning to the discussion of symbolic capital, we might propose that the imprints of such negotiations also are related in part to the status of market actors. Whether or not taxi-dancing will gain recognition among larger groups of tango dancers depends on taxi dancers' anchorage within the field of tango—which is partly conditioned by the recognition associated with the service as such as well as with individual taxi dancers. If recognized star dancers would offer their service in the shape of exclusive paid-for dancing sessions out in the *milongas*, taxi-dancing would probably find new groups of purchasers.

DANCING SOCIAL BARRIERS AWAY?

As discussed throughout this book, dancing across continents and socio-economic dividing lines is partly romanticized in tango, at times narrated in the form of a voyage out-of-the-ordinary. The dancers create a world in which the structuring principles and hierarchies outside of tango are temporarily erased. This endeavor aims at purity and autonomy and can be summarized in the postulate that "all that matters is tango". In this section we will argue that such a break with social barriers serves certain worldviews and the interests of certain groups of dancers. Although the negotiations of values in tango tourism must be related primarily to the intimate dance economy and dancers' various degrees of symbolic capital, the field of tango dancing needs to be situated also within a larger economic and political terrain. This is to say that there are economic and political consequences of the symbolic negotiations in tango that fall outside the reach of tango culture. In this section we will provide a materialist framing of the negotiations of symbolic values, partly arguing for the consequences this might have on the local job market. This involves exploring some possible imprints of the embracing of authenticity values and the actual effects a rejection of market forces might have on everyday life in the tourist site. Secondly we will argue that some of the negotiations in tango tourism might be read as attempts to negotiate away the impact of class. Not being a tourist is a way of staging oneself as outside the influence of global capitalism. Thereby, this section addresses the economic and political imprints of an emotionalized tango mythology. In the third part we will integrate a class-analysis with a gendered perspective, arguing that several vulnerabilities and lines of conflict are present within the intersection of tango and tourism.

This book suggests that the incitements for certain services—but not others—are produced according to dance tourists' sense-making of authenticity. It follows that this brings about consequences for the Argentine job market surrounding tango. The negotiations pave the way for those services which can be conceptualized as operating outside of a "touristy" commercialization and, moreover, a commercialized intimacy. In addition, dance tourists not only negotiate tango values such as emotionality and authenticity but also relate to traditional tourist values such as safety and comfort in their choices of what to purchase and from whom. As discussed in Chapter 6, at times this actually seems to favor non-Argentine actors within the Argentine tango market. We might also notice that the authenticity claim tends to lead tango tourists to reject small-scale tango actors (such as taxi dancers and certain kinds of private dance teachers) in favor of large-scale tourist actors, and to reject street vendors selling artistic tango "reproductions" in favor of mass-produced posters sold by the well-known tango stores. In that sense, tango tourism is an illustrative case of how symbolic negotiations affect economic structures.

Turning to a claim made by one dance scholar, we might actually suggest that it is likely that tango dancing probably can survive "global wayfaring and hybridization" (Olszewski 2008: 64). The tango seems capable of mutating into new dance forms and finding new social arrangements as it moves to new places, without losing some of its characteristic features, such as the level of intimacy in the dance connection and the improvised dancing style. In that sense the tango aura seems to be able to re-create itself. A more troubling concern is what such a development implies for Argentina and the city of Buenos Aires. In what follows we will address the economic and everyday consequences of giving up on an authenticity discourse that ties important tango values to the city of Buenos Aires. Not only is the tango an important national hallmark, but the culture has also created an important job market which might end up moving with the tango, wherever it goes. If recognized dancers—Argentines and others—choose to leave Buenos Aires for Berlin, a steady group of dancers will follow them; as a consequence, this is also where job opportunities, PR advertising and economic capital will go. In that sense, the dance-floor micro-politics—in Buenos Aires as well as in Sweden—contributes to the shaping and reshaping of the Argentine job market. Moreover, the negotiations over authenticity are decisive for whether the symbolic and economic values linked to contemporary Argentine tango life will escape the city and leave it only with the museal attraction power associated with historical tango markers. This implies that although many tourists perceive themselves as vulnerable in relation to the Argentine tango world, they actually appear to be powerful actors when it comes to influencing present and future tango life in Argentina. The increasing number of temporary visitors in Buenos Aires has an impact on the city's economy, as well as its cultural life, urban planning, risk measures and aesthetics.

Although tango culture is still strongly embedded within the Argentine capital and although Argentina has the "copyright" on tango, by the recognition of Argentine tango as a world cultural heritage, we might actually already find traces of the development sketched above. In one sense it seems that this happens when star Argentine performers leave Argentina to go on tour—and in some cases settle down—in Europe, North America, Japan and Australia. Providing dance classes in places far away from Argentina is more profitable—economically and symbolically—than running a similar business in Buenos Aires, where there is tough competition with other star Argentine dancers and lower wages. In that sense, the contemporary globalization of tango paves the way for migratory streams and takes with it the knowledge, cultural heritage and symbolic capital associated with the city. This suggests that spatial negotiations are important also with respect to globalization. No matter how the tango twists and turns as it moves around the globe with its aficionados, places remain, to freely quote Lefebvre, "a matter of life and death".[12] This is true for certain parts of the tango-dancing culture, for the local dancers who pay their food and housing bills with foreign capital and for the dance tourists who locate their existential and emancipatory fantasies in the city of Buenos Aires.[13]

Tango Tourism and the Making of a Classless Class

In the previous section we have explored the imprints of authenticity values in relation to the economic geography of tango tourism. In this section we will look into the impact of emotions in tango—as discourses and driving forces—from a similar perspective. We will contextualize the problem of market forces and tourist adjustments in tango, as ascribed by some dance tourists, within a larger political terrain. This puts a finger on the actual questions and dilemmas bound to the commercialization of tango. Is the perceived problem that global inequalities are putting obstacles in the way for human relations to develop—or is the problem that hindrances are created for tourists' to experience so-called genuine cultures and intimate connections outside of market interests?

When approaching the various accounts of "tango magic", "deep intimacy", "real feelings" and the sentiment that "all that matters is the dance connection" appearing throughout this book from the perspective of the unequal living conditions implicit in tango tourism, the emotionalized mythology appears rather cynical. Dance magnetism is far from all that matters in tango tourism. Foreign and local dancers do bring similarly tuned bodies—adapted for tango dancing—to the dance-floors of Buenos Aires, together with similar clothes, musical references and historical knowledge and a common dedication to the culture. However, they also bring their distinct living conditions, their class positions in a global world and their different relations to Argentina—as a home and workplace or a holiday destination.

One possible way of understanding emotionality as a central value in tango is that the dancers—locals and tourists—use the dancing as an escapist avenue to actually overcome such class divisions and power inequalities. Such an interpretation might be put in dialogue with Octavio Paz, who, in his book *The Double Flame* (1996), describes sexuality as subversive and dangerous because it does not recognize class or social hierarchy. This, he argues, is why there have been immense social regulations against various kinds of sexual practices and relations. In tango, a similar idea is present. In several accounts discussed in this book, tango dancing is approached in terms of its transcendent and transgressive qualities. The dance-floor is said to bring people together who would not meet elsewhere, who would not recognize each other as possible friends or lovers elsewhere. When tango strikes, the social barriers of the outer world are believed to shatter.[14]

Rather than evoking subversive transformations, however, it seems as if the view of dancing as a practice removed from social and economic factors has partly become a discourse in itself, downplaying—rather than radically breaking with—the categories and hierarchies at stake. Aspiring to identify oneself as a tango dancer, instead of a tourist, a foreigner, a wealthy westerner or a client—and hence the claim that local dancers should do the same—is linked to a number of (supposedly unconscious) consequences. One interpretation is that this might be a way for the visitors to manage the social stratification and dilemmas arising from the unemployment and hardship present in the holiday site. The investments in a discourse of feelings might be interpreted as a kind of protection, a means to buy oneself free from an economic and political reality in which a phenomenon such as local dancers for rent for tourists is partly an answer to global inequality. Seen in this light, the critique of certain forms of commercialization—such as the taxi-dancing service—might be interpreted as a way of protecting not tango *per se* but rather the notion of tango as a set of relations far removed from hostile everyday life in the global village. Buying into such an imaginary, intimate voyagers can avoid identifying themselves as part of a wider global landscape of unjust living standards in which tourists are simply people with money—instead of primarily tango dancers. Hence, the discourses on authenticity and emotionality might serve to (re)produce the illusion of international tourists as part of a *classless class*, geographically and socially mobile, and outside the reach of unequal living conditions.[15]

Based on this interpretation, the concerns regarding "questionable" tango services might be approached not only as a protest against commercialization as such, but also as a protection of a particular worldview and a particular set of rights for middle-class Europeans and North-Americans on holiday. Such a claim must be related to the tango-tourism dilemma as it is addressed in some of the accounts in this book. The problem is not so much that racialized and sexualized bodies in the Global South are being put on sale, but rather that a "wrong" kind of commercialization might affect the "right" feeling in tango. This might be illustrated with an example of how dancers who have been to Buenos Aires share recommendations with future voyagers on how to avoid the negative impact of commercialization for the sake of a better holiday experience. As one female dancer on the Swedish webpage Tangoportalen states: "Of course we are walking/dancing dollar bills for some people, that you have to live with and learn to neglect because in the larger picture it is very nice in Buenos Aires and at the *milongas*" (Patricia). To some extent, this is ultimately also what tourist agencies are offering: safe and comforting avenues away from a disturbing poverty in holiday destinations—whether that poverty takes the form of local street vendors or taxi dancers trying to attract clients out in the *milongas*.

Returning to Octavio Paz, we might conclude that the wish to experience tango and tango dancing outside of commercialization and unequal living conditions involves an aspiration to temporarily transcend the social categories of the outer world. The construction of an imaginary classless class fits the tango mythology and its startling anecdotes of pure encounters. In fact the notion of "real" tango is equivalent to a romantic idea of social purity, in the sense of ideal encounters taking place outside the impact of economic and social boundaries. However, the wish to dance social barriers away proves to be restricted in time and space. As several accounts in this book indicate, the wish to "melt in" and pass as a local dancer and have experiences outside the "tourist décor" is limited to the tango context. The downplaying of visible markers related to social class and ethnicity (being a European or a North-American in Latin America) is restricted to the dance-floor. In that sense, tango dancers wish to erase the impact of class—or rather, they wish to access the privileges when needed but not when they get in the way of realizing a tango adventure. The wish to escape a client and a tourist identity—as categories defined primarily in relation to class and ethnicity—does not imply a desire to leave the high-standard housing in the inner city for a room in one of the suburbs. In that sense the movements across social and economic borders are part of the tourist experience and represent a temporary shift in perspective—serving to add knowledge appropriate to (middle-class) tastes and lifestyle—rather than a stepping-stone for social transformation. A more radical abandoning of privileges would ultimately render impossible the journeys to Argentina and tango tourism as such. Hence, outside of the tango economy and its symbolic sense-making of money, most visiting dancers—like a majority of privileged people throughout the world—do not wish to dance social barriers away.

Drawing on this discussion, this book offers no celebration of emotions, but instead wishes to take seriously the significance and impact of feelings or, in a more exact formulation, the impact of certain discourses of emotionality. One answer to the question "what do emotions do?" (Ahmed 2004: 4) within a repeated narrative revolving around "chemistry", "tango magic", "falling in love" and "authentic and auratic character" is that they produce and legitimate blindness in relation to larger political and economic structures. The strong idea of feelings as evolving from within the dancing body promotes a culture in which explanations bound to (psychological) emotional structures are privileged over those associated with global class politics.

Gendered Class Politics in Tango

In order to understand this we might consult dance historian Martha Savigliano's fascinating work on the birth and rise of tango culture. According to her, heterosexuality was foregrounded as the main script in tango during the turn of the last century. Her empirical subject is the poor and newly established nation-state of Argentina, a melting pot of people from all over the world trying to live side by side, among them slaves from the African colonies, indigenous groups and recently migrated Europeans. As an alternative to letting the tensions between different social groups erupt, however, tango became a cultural expression whereby antagonisms based on class position and racial hierarchies were channeled through the emotional language of heterosexual romance. In many tango songs of the time men cry over women who left them for other men. What is not made explicit, though it rests between the lines, is that the men involved belonged to different classes. Translating the social tensions into a heterosexual drama, however, simplified and depoliticized the class conflicts. As Savigliano writes: "In the micropolitics of tango, all social tensions are simmered in the sexual cooking pot—a pot in which sexuality seems to be a male concern over questions of maleness" (1995a: 40). She continues: "gender conflicts were interpreted as given, universal, unavoidable dilemmas. The problem was reduced to mere sentimental banality and to the terrain of the apolitical" (1995b: 84).

It is possible to see similar front- and backstage acting in various aspects of the contemporary Argentine melting pot. Tango is no longer a concern only for the Argentine nation; rather, it is a global expression which embraces all those anxieties surrounding class, national honor, race and gender which have evolved in postcolonial times. The framing of these anxieties, however, is similar to what Savigliano identified. Just as in the past, it is only the drama between women and men, staged as a romantic scene of intimacy and flaming passion, which is allowed to play out in all the registers. When Judy from Portland hides her face in her hands, crying, we say that the reasons are jealousy and a broken heart. When Guillermo leaves the dance-floor in anger we refer to a machismo culture. And as Swedish Peter and Argentine Lucia turn their bodies into one in the dance embrace and execute a power play with their legs and feet, we glorify the passionate tango. But maybe we are wrong. The emotional outbursts and presumed dance-floor romances might also be cries and responses to a nostalgic imperialism, reflecting the fact that authenticity, seen up close, tends to slip every tourist's grasp. We say that the quarrels in the dance clubs stem from the complicated communication demanded in tango, but these could also be signs of a global frustration with deeper cultural and political roots. Looking closer, we might actually find the unsettled accounts of an ongoing class struggle. The taxi dancers who engage in sexual affairs with their clients might not be attempting to make money—but rather attempting to break with an economic matrix, using the subversive capacity implicit in sex, its absolute uncertainty and possible break with routinized identities and performances, to create a state of human relations outside of the manufactured comfort offered through the service work in tango. Watching the dramas through such a lens, the tango songs shift meaning one more time. They were never simple poems of love but always melodies speaking of a wounded world and our desires to make it complete.

This book is actually putting forward the argument that class is a significant dimension of tango tourism. Economic resources, together with the degree of tango *illusio*, function as a selection principle for the forming of a group of dancers who are able to undertake travel to Buenos Aires. The privileges inscribed in tourism are, however, associated with ambiguous concerns and responses. As discussed throughout this book, most dancers do not wish to conquer the world of tango on behalf of their global class position. Rather, they wish to become one with the world they are visiting without using money as a "shortcut". This is not to say that tango tourism is played out in a class-free zone. On the contrary, class and the impact of economic capital are highly present in shaping contemporary Argentine tango. In addition, the economic promises implicit in tourism function as an engine behind parts of the dance market. In other words, no matter whether tango tourists are perceived as wealthy in their home countries—or whether they wish to come across as wealthy westerners when visiting Argentina—they represent a global class bound up with the privileges of foreign capital.

An additionally important class-related ingredient in tango tourism is the economic vulnerability on the side of some of the Argentine dancers. The Argentine crisis, together with the expanding number of Europeans and North-Americans travelling to Buenos Aires to dance tango, has intensified a form of emotional consumption in which Argentine dancers' bodies are for sale in the form of private tango classes and escort dancing. In that sense tango tourism might be approached as another example of how today's Global South constitutes a space for emotional consumption and intimate body work. However, tango tourism comes across as quite a contrasting case in relation to the literature on postcolonial power relations. Many studies in the crosscutting fields of globalization and intimacy studies actually provide rather neat cases in which the intersection of class, gender and racial regimes results in a united stratifying force. Poor women from Third World zones are used as cheap labor in markets suited for wealthy westerners, often men. In the cases of both sex tourism and migratory care labor, these women are exploited in terms of their economic vulnerability (class), in terms of being women (gender) and as racialized subjects associated with "natural" caring talents or a "sexy" aura (race). These dimensions actually often reinforce each other in ways that dig these women deeper into dependency and restricted agency (Ehrenreich and Hochschild 2003; Gavanas 2009). Rather than constituting a case of how economic power is used by white western men, the relations emerging on the Argentine dance-floors are less clearly defined. As in examples of women's so-called romance tourism in Jamaica and Ghana, in tango tourism the market of intimate services primarily targets women as clients and men as providers (Kempadoo 1999; O'Connell Davidson and Sanchez Taylor 2005; Sanchez Taylor 2006), and in that sense turns a traditional gender order upside down. However, as this book suggests, the intricate dance economy, together with the (hetero)sexualized organizing of the tango, actually downplays some of the economic privileges held by western women on tango holiday.

What makes the case of tango tourism intriguing is that it allows for various modes of domination to intersect. Female tourists' relative economic privilege might be used to further reproduce certain social hierarchies—or as a means to radically break with them. In fact, the (hetero)sexualized gender play in tango actually proves to contain material much more explosive than love, attraction and intimacy (as suggested by the early aficionados in Savigliano's work). We might actually approach some of the tango dramas discussed in this book as narratives of a silent war—not only between the Global North and South—but also between men and women. Drawing from such a perspective, we could reinterpret some of the stories, such as the accounts of Susanna, who paid for a tango escort, and Rebecca, who despised her Argentine date because he let her pay the café check. We might read Susanna's choice of dance partner as an attempt to temporarily buy herself free from a (hetero)sexualized gender order. Susanna's activation of her financial superiority can be interpreted as a way to downplay the negative effects of being a woman in the world of tango. Rebecca's reaction might be interpreted as resistance to male domination. Her refusal to accept her date's behavior can be read as a way of marking agency in a context where women are required to await men's recognition.

In other words it is not in any way evident how intimacy, as a set of discursive scripts and embodied and emotionally invested practices, operates in a global world. On the one hand, intimate relations between the Global North and South can be perceived as the ultimate expression of cynical power relations, whereby material goods and promises of a better life are exchanged for pleasure and comfort. On the other hand, intimate cross-continental relationships—expressed through close-embrace dancing in the framing of tango tourism—might also constitute a radical resistance to racist decrees of social segregation. According to such a view, we could describe intimacy as a potentially powerful and subversive force which might enable people to transcend material and symbolic borders and engage in the empathic and political enterprise of acquiring new perspectives on the world (see Törnqvist 2010b for further discussion). In her book on the history of tango, Marta Savigliano describes the tango as a site for impossible—and hence possibly subversive—encounters in the following words.

> The history of the tango is a story of encounters between those who should never have met or between those who, having met, will remain forever disencountered. Brewing resentment, it is a stubborn story of impossible but fatal encounters, like the matching of pieces or mating of species that do not fit but will stick together. The tango is both a product and a promoter of these hybrid events. Black and white, rich and poor, men and women, colonizer and colonized—each is brought much too close to the other; the tango embrace is dangerously tight. It proposes the violation of critical distances in such a way that the experience of tension and conflict becomes unavoidable. (Savigliano 1995: xiv–xv)

Today's close-embrace dancing in the crowded halls and cafés of Buenos Aires involves a critical dynamic which has similarities with what Savigliano is describing. The level of intimacy brings people "who should never have met"—"black and white, rich and poor, men and women"—dramatically close to one another. Close enough to draw power plays onto the dancefloor—and close enough to allow people to let go of differences in class, race and age. Even though this appears most often as an unused political potential, the *milongas* offer spectacular sceneries that allow us to see the various ways in which intimacy and sensual pleasures interweave not only with market forces, but also with radical promises of another world.

CONCLUSION: LOCALIZING GLOBALIZATION

The Argentine tango proves to be another example of the local embeddedness of global processes. In fact, one central claim following from this book is that the consequences of globalization should be studied in its local contexts, meaning in the local worlds, relations, embodied practices and identities negotiated by people in their everyday lives, at home as well as on holiday. As many scholars have pointed out, the vast and dispersed processes of globalization can only be grasped and fully understood in their lived realities. As Ulrich Beck argues: "Globalization—which ostensibly is about the Great patterns, about the exterior, about what eventually adds and extinguish everything else—is touchable in the small, the concrete, in place and site, in the own life, in cultural symbols which all carry the signature of the 'glocal'" (2000: 73).

As shown in this study, the influence of tourist streams slowly changes tango in Buenos Aires. New markets, professions, cultural rules and emotional repertoires appear. However, it is not in any sense given what these shifts signify and how they come about. When turning to the tango-related market forces motivated by tourism, we find that the ambiguous significance of economic capital in tango and the questionable tourist identity help to place obstacles in the way of full-scale commercialization. This suggests that we take seriously the values at stake for the people who embody market adjustment processes and the effects of globalization. Economic structures on a macro level—such as tourism—actually seem to depend on the micro-politics of local communities, in this case the world of tango dancing. Local places and locally defined relations prove to be important sites for what we might approach as a sort of cultural resistance. Hence, in order to approach the relation between intimacy and globalization, this book argues for the importance of recognizing the belief structures as well as the conflicting lines of divergence making up the everyday life of those people who embody the object of study. Money does not rule all worlds and the supposedly cold logic of market forces is at times forced to adapt to the specificities of local cultures.

In that sense this study ascribes the strengths of ethnographic fieldwork to its means of entering the embodied and emotional processes of globalization, located within individual actors and sets of social relations in specific places. However, we should also note the importance of exploring conflicting discursive practices through which the world of Argentine tango tourism—as well as other forms of tourism—comes into existence. This book illustrates that dancers, rather than inhabiting a world embodied and lived solely in the close-embrace dancing of the *milongas*, engage in rather complex discursive practices through which the bodily experienced dancing is made sense of in ways that must be related not only to the belief system of tango, but also to more general discourses of sex, money and tourism. Through negotiating and sense-making processes, the dancers are part of shaping the world of tango tourism, and moreover Argentine tango.

This book does not glorify the radical promise of intimacy in tango; neither does it offer a dystopic vision. Instead it seeks to take seriously the search for sensual communication and human bonds in the geopolitical context of postcolonialism. What makes tourism a distinctive dimension of global mobility is its double nature of providing both promises and threats. Many dance travels to Buenos Aires are part of a sincere search for affection, even as the very same trips are invested with exoticized discourses about Latin America and the consumption of local body work. The landscape of tango tourism is made up of dance steps, existential dwelling and dollars. Hence, tango tourism is an intriguing case for exploring an ambivalent time of shattered and reinforced national borders. It dramatically shows intimate spheres to be a global matter as they allow a flourishing of people, money, and fragile dreams. Moreover, tango tourism provides an intriguing case for exploring the relation between economic and emotional vulnerability, in which the body is the prime locus. Ethnographic examples have been brought forward to discuss how gendered subjectivities not only intersect with social class, ethnicity, age and (hetero)sexuality but also negotiate modalities of power differently under conditions of emotional vulnerability. In one sentence, this book has wished to theorize the intimate journeys and their interplay of emotional orders within economic realities, to the heart of the promises and dilemmas of our globalized world.

Appendix

NOTES FROM A DANCING RESEARCHER

A Sensing Sociology: Notes on Embodied Ethnography

This study is influenced by what ethnographic researchers in the various fields of "physical cultures," such as dancing, boxing and stage acting, have called "carnal ethnography" (Wacquant 2004, 2005; cp. Lande 2007), "full-contact sociology" (Øygarden 2000), "emotional participation" (Bergman Blix 2010: 61), "embodied autobiography" (Olszewski 2008: 67) and "embodied ethnography" (Wade 2011: 228).[1] In his book on boxing, Loïc Wacquant theorizes the "moral and sensual conversion" of the researcher as a sociological imperative, aiming for the "inner depths" of the "cosmos under investigation".

> To accomplish that, there is nothing better than initiatory immersion and even *moral and sensual conversion* to the cosmos under investigation, construed as a technique of observation and analysis that, on the express condition that it be theoretically armed, makes it possible for the sociologist to appropriate in and through practice the cognitive, aesthetic, ethical, and conative schemata that those who inhabit that cosmos engage in their everyday deeds. If it is true, as Pierre Bourdieu contends, that "we learn by body" and that "the social order inscribes itself in bodies through this permanent confrontation, more or less dramatic, but which always grants a large role to affectivity," then it is imperative that the sociologist submit himself to the fire of action *in situ*; that to the greatest extent possible he put his own organism, sensibility, and incarnate intelligence at the epicentre of the array of material and symbolic forces that he intends to dissect; that he strive to acquire the appetites and the competencies that make the diligent agent in the universe under consideration, so as better to plumb the inner depths of this "relation of presence to the world, and being in the world, in the sense of belonging to the world, being possessed by it, in which neither the agent nor the object is posited as such". (Wacquant 2004: viii)

Taking on an embodied ethnography of tango tourism implies that I have made myself accessible to the physical repetition which not only shapes the body with the appropriate dispositions for dancing tango, but also conveys a set of knowledges, tastes, aesthetics, competencies and ways of perceiving the world, including a sense of justice. This suggests that I have aimed to shape not only an analytical but also a bodily and emotional avenue through which I am approaching the field. My field-notes are often written out of my own bodily and emotional responses to a tango-related situation and first later on analyzed and deconstructed. This implies that the study inquires not only into the practices and institutionalized regulations activated when dancers, for instance, have their invitations turned down, but also into *how it feels* to be turned down: how the body responds to a dance rejection and how the emotional response interacts with the field of relations in tango, i.e. how rejections are mirrored by the other dancers' actions. When it comes to matters of taste and aesthetics, this study contains field-notes regarding my own shifting preferences concerning clothing, body styles, haircut, accessories, makeup: all those external signifiers which mark one's belonging to a cultural field. My notepad includes descriptions not only of the content of my "new" wardrobe, but also of what a particular skirt or dress signifies within the world of tango. I have intended to address why *it feels* good to wear this skirt, but not that one, and how qualities of design, fabric, color and length make certain outfits comfortable and others not. In the analytical process I have returned to my field-notes and explored them in search of what these emotional responses can tell us, not only about tango dancing, but also about femininity ideals and the ambiguous identity work in tourism. In that sense, my own bodily and emotional experiences are used as critical points of departure for conceptual explorations.

The fieldwork in Buenos Aires was carried out during the Argentine summer—October 2007 to January 2008—and hence the peak point for tango tourism. It involved an intense participation in tango life at a range of venues and tango-related spots. In order to plunge into a twenty-four-seven tango-tourist life, I decided to stay at a so-called "tango hostel". I rented a five-square-meter room without windows in the centrally located *Congreso* neighborhood. The room was one of several habitations rented out by a European tango dancer who had settled down in Buenos Aires some years ago to make a living out of her passionate interest in tango. Besides offering rooms for visiting tango dancers, the two-floor apartment contained a dancing studio which the landlord used for dance classes as well as for practicing tango herself. She also organized *milongas* in a recognized tango venue and was a well-known figure in the Argentine tango community. After having my breakfast, at times with other tango lodgers or the landlord, I spent my days at various dance schools, *practicas* (dancing events focusing on practice, often occurring during midday), in shoe and clothing stores, at festival sites, at cafés and restaurants with other dance tourists as well as attending tango-related events (such as a trainee day for taxi dancers). The evenings were spent at the *milongas*.[2] Recognizing that dancing itself makes up an important source of knowledge, I spent my days and nights actively engaging in the spectacular social play, on and off the dance-floor. Besides being part of dancing practices, I spent significant time chitchatting with other dancers at the tables surrounding the dance-floor, hanged out in the *milonga* bars, spoke with club organizers, dance teachers, taxi dancers, tango-DJ's, managers and workers within diverse tourist agencies. Later on, when the *milonga* closed for the night, I took a taxi—or on rare occasions a bus—with dancers living in my area, sharing the evenings' excitements and frustrations. During the tango-intense days, I tried to make as many primary field-notes as possible, quickly sketching down a situation or particular dialogue as soon as it occurred. However, in order not to lose sight of all the experiences and information, I took some "days off" from the tango. On those days I normally went to a "tango-free" spot, normally the café around the corner, to write down notes from memory and enrich the short comments with more details and information. I also used the hours at the café to formulate new research questions and rewrite the interview guide. Some of these "tango-free" days I used for carrying out interviews and listening to and process previously conducted conversations.

The analytical focus has shifted throughout the research process. At times I have made an effort to capture the general patterns regarding how to behave in order to harmonize with the dancers at a certain *milonga* or how to engage in a service purchase in order to keep the face and protect the dancing identity of both service provider and client (myself). At other times I have tried to capture the exceptions and those situations and phenomena which seem to diverge from everyday Argentine tango life. This might convey up-front provocations and reactions, stemming from "out-of-the-script" actions. As is discussed in several passages in this book, exceptions are interesting as they stress the general features of the culture. Rather than pointing towards the center, however, they often indicate the borders and limits of a sanctioned and legitimate way of acting.

Embodied ethnography puts the researcher into concrete everyday situations in which a sociological reflexivity is enforced (Woodward 2008; Bourdieu and Wacquant 1992). Clearly, my encounters with the world I am studying are shaped not only by the fact that I encounter it dancing and on high heels, but also by the fact that I, as a white, European woman with limited knowledge of the Spanish language, represent a larger stream of tourism in Argentina. Being a tango dancer and a tourist myself implies that I have been viewed—and acted upon—as a dancer and a tango tourist by other dancers. Within the encounters with other tourists, it is possible that the supposed shared experiences of being an "outsider" in the Argentine tango community have created a sense of intimacy. I have also been recognized as a possible client for market actors. The fact that I carried out most of the ethnographic fieldwork with my tango shoes on and with the look of a typical "tourista", fairly blond and with clothing and manners indicating another cultural background, has allowed me insights into the tourist experience—not least regarding the ways I have been approached by dance teachers, taxi dancers and representatives from tourist agencies. This has resulted in a number of intriguing encounters and has pulled me into the material in unexpected ways. One example of this is how I was invited to a "special tango party", offering a mixture of dancing adventure and consuming practices in a spectacular Argentine building. As is described in detail in Chapter 5, the fact that I was asked to dance with the manager of this clothing store—for reasons most likely having to do with my tourist appearance—provided me with an invitation to the event. At other times, I have exposed myself to various tango-tourist situations in order to access experiences and knowledge. This involves going alone to *milongas* known for being spots to which taxi dancers and private tango teachers go to find clients.

Living the tango, which involves incorporating the dancing into daily routines and, moreover, making tango a practical guideline in life, has provided me not only with an embodied knowledge, but also with a social position which facilitates access to certain kinds of information. In almost all fields of investigation there are topics which are rather sensitive and for this reason difficult to ask people about. This implies that formal interviews might not always be the frame best suited for accessing reflections and accounts. Ethnographic work, allowing for a closer relation to the empirical area of study, provides the researcher with a greater sensitivity towards the precarious and charged topics within the field. In addition, it provides access to all those situations and places in which "it happens", in which everyday patterns are consolidated and in which extraordinary things occur. In addition, some reflections will arise only out of emotional responses and are seldom captured within the rather formal interview-situation. Examples of this is bitterness over "failed" dancing promises or bliss regarding an "amazing" dancing evening. This implies that the places for accessing knowledge are often rather informal spaces such as late-night taxis taking the dancers back to their hostels, the ladies' room in a *milonga* or the obligatory chat with a dance partner between two dance sets. As a non-dancing researcher, without tango shoes on my feet, I would not have had access to these situations and the kind of emotionalized information that active participation in a community makes available. Living the tango simply allows for an exploration of lived tango.[3]

However, ethnographic work in Buenos Aires is not sufficient to capture the dance voyages to Argentina. As argued in this book, I acknowledge that tourism takes place as much "at home" as "over there". Negotiating tango tourism as well as shaping images and expectations of Argentine tango occurs in local dancing communities throughout the world. Moreover, the home communities are important points of reference and hence implicitly present in the dance voyagers' everyday holiday life. Experiences made in Buenos Aires are reflected through the dancers' various nexus of belonging at home. In addition, the holiday experiences are at times transformed into values and credentials for use in the dancing community back home. For instance dancers narrate and stage their travels through public storytelling, the showcasing of Argentine shoe models and "imported" dance steps, as well as through enlargement of social networks to include new tango friends made in Buenos Aires. This has prompted me to add fieldwork in two of the tourists' home regions, the Bay Area of Northern California (San Francisco and its surroundings) and the Swedish capital area (including Stockholm, Uppsala and Örebro). The observations made in the tourists' home communities are restricted to six-month (Sweden) and four-month periods of time (U.S.).[4] This fieldwork has not been as intense as the ethnography in Argentina, partly due to the fact that my life in Sweden and the U.S. has been bound to other work tasks.

The ethnography in this study is a knowledge-generating methodology that wishes to make use of my personal involvement in the field, without being entangled in the narrow biographical tradition of reporting on the personal queries and crises of the author, what is sometimes called "diary disease" (Barthes 1982: 480–481; cp. Ambjörnsson 2004: 46–48; Geertz 1988: 90). In order to avoid getting caught in such a narrative, the writing style in this book is not particularly "personal". For example, my own field-notes serve primarily as a methodological basis for the analysis. Instead of overexposing my own voice, using the field-notes as first-hand quotes, I am primarily referring to other voices from the field, generated through interviews and blog-post readings. For those who wish to access my field-notes, part of them are accessible in the book *Tangoexperimentet* (2010). As a somewhat polished notepad, collecting and bringing order to my reflections, that book covers accounts of my bodily and emotional transformations as well as thoughts on the intimate knowledge process, including the challenges and vulnerabilities present in an embodied ethnography.

Voices from the Field: Notes on an Interview-study

In order to capture the ongoing negotiations in tango tourism and, moreover, to make them accessible and illustrative for the reader of this book, the ethnographic fieldwork is combined with an interview-study. The interviews have been carried out primarily with Swedish and North-American dance tourists (primarily from the dancing communities which are part of the field-study), but have been conducted with tourists from other countries as well. I have also carried out interviews with a few Argentine hobby dancers and actors within the market space of tango involving dance teachers, taxi dancers and managers of travel agencies.[5] Starting with the tourists, the primary focus of this study, a typical dance traveler is a hobby dancer with between six months and ten to fifteen years of tango experience. Some dancers return to Buenos Aires on a yearly basis, others visit the city once and never go back and a few decide to move to Argentina for reasons having to do with tango. The restricted world enforces certain similarities among the tourists. Only those with a strong enough motivation for exploring the tango, its dance elements and surrounding culture, will use up their vacation weeks to go to Argentina instead of visiting friends and family closer to home. Moreover, the selection process depends on dancers' previous tourist experiences, as well as their capability and willingness to travel without a comforting tourist package. Although such possibilities are offered by tourist agencies, most dancers wish to make the Buenos Aires experience different from a regular charter vacation. The selection also has to do with economic resources. Just buying a flight ticket to Argentina is a rather large expense for most Europeans and North-Americans. Adding to this cost is payment for housing and food along with tango-related expenses (*milonga* entrances, dance classes, tango shoes etc.). Hence, it is symptomatic that the tango travels appear to attract primarily an economic middle class from the larger cities throughout North America, Europe, Australia and Japan. Work-wise, the voyagers can be found within the middle-class professions of academics, teachers, nurses, medical doctors and engineers, but also within art-related professions such as photographers, health consultants, artists, gardeners and yoga instructors. In regard to their cultural preferences, the strong interest in tango brings them together in regard to aspects related to cultural class (a somewhat common taste and lifestyle regarding the consumption of music, food and other leisure activities).

Taking these factors together suggests that not all dancers with a strong commitment to tango can afford traveling to Argentina. Neither is the average tango tourist any dancer wealthy enough to afford the trip economically. Rather, the selection seems to be based on a mixture of these elements, blending economic resources with tango conviction and travelling commitment. This being said, we should be sensitive to the variations and differences in the ways the dance tourists live and make sense of their journeys. There are various ways of embodying and doing tourism, and the people travelling to Buenos Aires to dance tango are not just tourists and tango dancers, but also embedded in various social settings such as gendered structures, each of which lend meaning and contours to the travel. Both men and women embark on these journeys, but just as the percentage of women is larger in the dance scene in general, it is larger also among dance tourists. The age group varies from twenty to seventy years of age, with a majority in their thirties to late fifties.[6] The dancers come from different parts of the world and they travel with various expectations and life trajectories under the skin. Moreover, they have different routines and standards regarding travel and consumption in general, and distinct preferences as to what they wish to experience in Buenos Aires and how they wish to experience it, partly due to their level of cultural belonging in tango. Hence, in order to understand the practices and significance of tango tourism, we need to take seriously the various contexts of the travels as well as the various objectives ascribed to dancing holidays.

The selection of informants has been conducted with the aim of capturing some diverging lines regarding age, national belonging and level of tango experience. When it comes to class, the selection suggested by the nature of the phenomenon implies that all informants are economically stable enough to spend two to four thousand U.S. dollars on a dancing holiday. The informants are mainly white European and North-American women, with the exception of two male tango tourists, and two female tango tourists originating from Latin America (not Argentina). This selection partly mirrors the gender and ethnic bias in tango dancing and partly relates to a decision made at an early stage—and later on abandoned—to study only female tango tourists. In addition an absolute majority of informants define themselves as heterosexual, although some suggest that tango dancing has made them sensitive to sensual and sexual feelings towards the same sex. At the time of the interview, a majority were singles, some of whom had just ended a marriage or a long-term relationship. In addition, one important demarcation of this study is that it targets people who come to Buenos Aires specifically to dance tango, i.e. not the larger groups of tourists who wish to explore the tango culture during their holiday visit. This study focuses primarily on tourists who are visiting Buenos Aires for two to three weeks. However, I have also interviewed a few foreigners who have stayed longer as well as dancers who have settled down in Buenos Aires and now work as dance teachers or managers of their own tango-tourist agency.

Regarding the selection of market actors, discussed in detail in Chapter 5, I wish to mention the focus on tango taxi dancers. As is addressed in several chapters in this book, the taxi-dancing service—particularly Argentine men offering their dancing company to tourist women—is an intriguing example pointing at the ambiguous function of the tango market. The character of what we might call a border phenomenon, which occurs at the line between legitimate and illegitimate purchases in tango, makes escort dancing a methodological detector. Exploring the ways in which not only taxi dancers themselves, but also dance voyagers make sense of this partly questionable service reveals how central discourses in tango, particularly on intimacy and authenticity, clash with the services offered by a tourist market (such as safety and accessibility to the culture). By studying this service and the tourists' sense-making of it, we are also able to investigate how border phenomena can be made legitimate through various discursive acts, redestabilizing and renarrating the significance of an intimate purchase.

Throughout the book we will repeatedly return to a selected group of dancers; they are quoted at greater length and more background information about them is presented. This so-called "in-group" consists of dancers whom I have been following more closely and involves five tourists (Daniella, Margareta, Elisabeth, Susanna and Kate), three market actors (Ezequiel, Steve and Monique) and one local dancer (Allan). I have conducted several interviews with some of them, both in Buenos Aires and in their home communities (in the cases of the tourists), and I have spent time together with them outside of the interview situation. With some of them I have been out dancing, and we have shared dance-floor experiences in hostel breakfasts and out at city tours. Although the "small talk" off the record is not represented as quotes in the study, the richer contours of these dancers and their sense-making of tango and tourism infuse the material with more angles and dimensions, sometimes rather contradictory, and thereby provide a deeper understanding of possible objectives behind the voyages and the ongoing negotiations. These circumstances may have affected the interviews. The fact that I have had more information about these informants—and that they have had substantial information about me—has allowed for more intimate interview situations which tend to turn to the "core" topic at once. In addition it should be mentioned that that the fact that I myself was a tango dancer and a tourist in relation to the informants probably affected the interview situation with all informants. The interviews mainly took the form of a conversation, directed through my questionnaire but with a large degree of openness in relation to topics and turns occurring throughout the discussions (for instance I choose to add personal reflections and experiences from tango dancing during the interviews). The risks associated with such an "interview style" have been balanced by the advantages, which are—to my mind–livelier and more sincere conversations.

The selection of informants entails a number of limitations. As already mentioned, male dance tourists are downplayed, partly due to a set of research questions which were important at the first stage of this study (at an early stage, one focus was to explore similarities with women's so-called romance tourism in Africa and other parts of Latin America). Also, the perspectives of local dancers in Buenos Aires are downplayed in this study. This has to do with the focus on the target group of tango tourism: the tourists themselves. We might also note that from the point of view of the methodological approach of this study, an embodied ethnography, it would be difficult to write the "local" story about tango tourism. Such stories, however, need to be told and will hopefully find their storytellers before long. An additional limitation has to do with sexuality and implies that the significance of the queer tango movement—which for instance includes the tourist streams to Buenos Aires during the yearly queer tango festival—is neglected in this study.

Narrating Tango Tourism: Notes on Textual Analysis

This study also addresses textual narratives and representations of tango tourism found in novels, documentary books, movies, blog pages covering travel diaries written by tango dancers in Buenos Aires, discussions on virtual home pages for tango dancers and advertisements found in the Argentine tango magazines as well as in flyers distributed in the *milongas*. Although this is a limited part of the study, I wish to discuss three pieces of material in larger detail. *First*, I wish to mention the autobiographical books and movies covering the author's or director's process of becoming a tango dancer, partly through realizing a ritualized journey to Buenos Aires. More and more such narratives appear on the market, and they have come to constitute their own genre. The books being read within the scope of this study are *Pardans* (by Birgitta Holm 2004), *Kiss & Tango. Diary of a Dance-Hall Seductress* (by Marina Palmer 2006), *Tango: An Argentine Love Story* (by Camille Cusumano 2008), *Long after Midnight at the Niño Bien* (by Brian Winter 2008) as well as the movies *Taxidancing* (by Jessika Karlsson, Annica Karlsson and Emilia Ramsin Barlas 2012)[7] and *The Tango Lesson* (by Sally Potter 1997).[8] As these titles suggest, the narratives cover the Argentine experience, often in a rather romanticized and emotionalized language. Analyzing these books and movies aims at tracing those stories which are repeated over time, suggesting that they represent significant building blocks in the construction of a tango tourist narrative. This kind of material is also interrogated in search for the contested terrains and conflicting relations in tango, and moreover in tango tourism. Implicit in this is the ongoing identity work revolving around the public shaping of a tango dancer.

Secondly, I wish to bring up the Argentine tango magazines *El Tangauta*, *B.A. Tango*, *La Milonga Argentina*, *Tango Map Guide* and *La Porteña Tango*, which contain the latest news, interviews with star performers, photo galleries of well-known *tangueras* and *tangueros* and advertisements for dance schools, freelance tango escorts and tango guest houses.[9] These magazines are distributed for free in most well-known *milongas* and dance schools and have both Spanish and English versions. The magazines make up an important ingredient in the Argentine tango scene as they call attention to dancing trends, upcoming—and declining—stars (the front page normally displays studio photography of a young, upcoming dancer or dancing couple), rumors and gossip about celebrity birthday parties and festivals as provided through the photo gallery section as well as events celebrating the history of tango, not least through extensive memorial articles about deceased dancers and musicians. Moreover, they are important in relation to the expanding streams of tango tourists. The magazines specifically target this group of readers through the translated English section, as well as through the extensive advertisement section. To a certain degree the publicity section targets tango tourists particularly (as in adverts for airport transfers, Spanish language classes and tango hostels). The publicity section is what finances the magazines and supports their free distribution throughout various tango venues. The methodological significance of this material primarily lies within the social function of the magazines. They are actually an important actor within the Argentine tango world, mapping out the world through a selection of which dancers to portray and represent, not least for the prestigious cover photograph and main interview article. In addition, the rich publicity section makes these magazines important for the analysis of values traded in the Argentine market space for tango dancing.

Thirdly, I wish to mention the Swedish webpage *Tangoportalen*, formed in 2005 and closed in 2010. Besides offering schedules for dancing events and buy-and-sell pages, the webpage provided a virtual community through which the members could send each other messages and communicate in discussion threads about various tango-related topics. In this study, *Tangoportalen* is primarily interesting for the elaborate discussions between dancers, which provide significant keys to how various conflicts and dilemmas within the nexus of tango tourism are approached and managed. This material is used primarily to analyze the construction of taxi-dancing as a partly illegitimate market service. When used, this material is made anonymous for ethical reasons. As *Tangoportalen* is now closed, the discussions being referred to are no longer accessible to the public.[10]

In general, I conceive of the various empirical materials covered in this study as making up equally important—yet differently shaped—pieces of knowledge. Practices and small talk recognized in the ethnographic work, interview accounts and autobiographical narratives, together with the discussions on webpages for tango dancers, all provide accounts which show—in their own specific ways—how tango, dancing, tourism, sex, money and authenticity are constituted through negotiating processes. However, these kinds of accounts represent different genres which—to a certain degree—are bound to distinct logics. Most of the voyage documentaries, for instance, follow a similar plot, starting with dance classes at home, reaching a potentially emancipatory climax as the dancer/author travels to Buenos Aires and conveying a rather nostalgic and sensual framing of the tango-tourist experience (Cusumano 2008; Palmer 2006; Potter 1997). By and large, the stories for public display often reflect a more romantic view of tango, revolving around the deep communication and the nostalgic longing for the past, than do the interviews in this study or the small talk addressed in the ethnographic work.

We might also notice some diverging lines whose directions depend on the different kinds of readers and audiences involved. In those webpages particularly targeting other tango dancers, such as the former Swedish tango site *Tangoportalen*, the accounts are rather specific and reflect the ongoing boundary work with a subtlety that makes them accessible primarily for other tango dancers. Some of the novels aspiring to reach a broader circle of readers, on the other hand, provide more exotic and "sexy" stories that have a possibly lower degree of legitimacy among dancers. Common to all of these publicly exposed travel accounts is that they are part of an ongoing storytelling process shaping and reshaping the boundaries of tango dancing and Argentine dance journeys. The narratives are important creators of a contemporary tango mythology, shared and negotiated particularly by other tango dancers. The publicly disseminated and well-known tango tales conjure up important points of reference that dance tourists use to assign meaning to their experiences. For instance, the book by Marina Palmer, *Kiss & Tango* (2006), was a frequent point of reference in some of my interviews, particularly with North-American dancers. Such narratives shape the horizons of expectation for future tango tourists and provide material used by dancers to constitute their own tango identity by negating others' experiences.

Notes

NOTES TO CHAPTER 1

1. Argentine tango is a music style aligned with nostalgic poetry and a social dance that originated in the area around Rio de la Plata (Buenos Aires and Montevideo) during the early twentieth century.
2. Although the tango is often framed within a heterosexual gender regime, revolving around honor and the worshiping of bodies perceived according to traditional ideals of femininity and masculinity, dancers describe how the dance breaks down into a multitude of interpretations and performances. Many practitioners perceive the tango as a movement across gender lines and have experienced a sensual intimacy that diverges from norms around heterosexuality.
3. Whereas Edward Said (1993) describes how the Orient has been portrayed as a feminine continent ready to be unveiled by the western eye, Argentina and much of Latin America is often represented as a male part of the world (Archetti 1999; Savigliani 1995a). In contrast to images of white western middle-class men, Argentine masculinity is construed as "macho" and at the same time "romantic" and "soft" (cp. Segal 1997; Yuval-Davis 1997).
4. Similarities and diverging lines between different groups of tango tourists are discussed in Appendix: "Notes from a Dancing Researcher".
5. For pedagogical reasons, I will continue to use the term "tango tourism", aware of its conflicting and negotiated meaning. I will also use the terms "voyager" and "traveler", realizing that those terms have more positive connotations. They imply a greater degree of mobility and are less intertwined with the notion of a tourist industry; rather, they presuppose that the "traveler" is free, undertaking her or his journey outside of constraining structures.
6. The impact of the "body-turn" in the field of dance research, which can be seen in the focus on the kinetic and artistic aspects of dancing, seems to have evoked a bias also towards emancipatory promises, through the bodily presence and expression of the dancers (Manning 2003; Olszewski 2008; Wade 2011). Like these researchers I acknowledge a radical potential in tango dancing, not least in relation to sexuality and intimacy (Törnqvist 2010a; Törnqvist 2010b). However, this is not all there is. Tango, and possibly other dance cultures as well, are also social communities made up by hierarchies and competition together with traditional gender and class regimes.
7. Viladrich has studied the tango scene in New York and the ways in which immigrant tango artists "trade" their dancing skills and company for medical assistance and other services which are hard for them to afford. Hence,

260 *Notes*

        she conceptualizes the tango as a social field in which a play with symbolic goods takes part.
8. The concepts of *field* and *habitus* will be discussed in more detail in Chapters 2 and 3.
9. However, prostitution and the global care chain, with a new kind of labor force giving up homes and families in the Global South to work for families in the North, show that intimacy still makes up profitable markets for consumption, offering services and (mostly female) bodies in exchange for money.
10. This description departs from Mats Franzén's reading of Lefebvre in which he notes a dialectic taking on space in terms of a *scale* ranging from the "micro-spaces in which our bodies and their measurements constitute our departure into the world, through streets and squares, neighborhoods and cities, to the urban net in the global space which today's capitalism presupposes and creates" (2004: 57, my translation).
11. In fact, the tango and tango dancing might be used as a metaphor for both modern and postmodern city life. The intimate embrace between strangers in the hallmark venues of an urban lifestyle, the cafés and dance clubs, makes up an image of the fragile collective in anonymous cities (Cressey 1932; Simmel 1907/1971). With the processes of globalization, however, the nature of Argentine tango is put in dialogue with other hybrids. Similar to cities like New York and Tokyo, Buenos Aires comes across as a cultural cross-section.
12. On the one hand, we find the tradition following the ethnographic accounts of Georg Simmel and the Chicago school, which approaches the city as a material and relational space made up of perception and practice (Jacobs 1961; Park 1925/1984; Simmel 1907/1971). On the other hand, postmodern scholars have taken an interest in cities like Los Angeles, which are explored as an urbanity of floating signs and medial representations (Baudrillard 1989).

NOTES TO CHAPTER 2

1. We should note, though, that there are important differences between the belief systems of various religions and that of tango dancing—not least in relation to the kinds of issues they deal with. Although tango culture provides a mythology and a poetry which touch upon existential questions, it lies beyond the scope of the tango to address questions such as "What happens when people die?, Is there a life after this? etc.".
2. www.tangoinspiration.com (accessed 2012–08–15)
3. In her book on the trajectory of Argentine tango dancing, Christine Denniston frames it as a development of a common language: "The reason I could dance with all of these people, even when they led steps that I had never seen before, was that fundamentally they were all speaking the same language. Some chose to speak it simply, others created complex poetry with our feet, but once I had learned the language I could understand them all" (Denniston 2007: 2).
4. For analytical reasons this chapter provisionally reduces tango dancing to a number of common denominators. However, we should not neglect the variety among dancers and the many ongoing struggles over meaning and interpretation. The motives for dancing shift between individual dancers and collective communities, together with the role that the tango gets to play in individual dancers' lives, and those motives determine the exact meaning

they assign to it and the various practices that tango enforces. For obvious reasons, the tango is not the same for a beginning dancer taking her or his first steps in the dance studios of Stockholm as it is for those Argentine dancers who lived with the tango throughout its golden age (1935–1952), when orchestras flourished in the cafés of Buenos Aires, and experienced both tango censorship during the military regime and the comeback in the eighties and nineties. Accordingly, the exact role that the tango gets to play in individual dancers' lives partly differs due to the dancers' situatedness within a gendered class structure fuelled by racialized and sexual markers. The impact of these dividing lines will be given more attention in subsequent chapters.
5. This field-note is also used in a book chapter by the author and Kate Hardy entitled "Taxi Dancers: Tango Labour and Commercialized Intimacy in Buenos Aires", in K. Hardy, S. Kingston and T. Sanders (eds.), *New Sociologies of Sex Work*, Surrey: Ashgate.
6. This suggests that the gender implications of the actual dancing are rather complex. Actual dancing is far from the stereotypical art reproductions of tango couples in dramatic postures. Also, the tango vocabulary is somewhat misleading. The actual communication is more complex than being a play of leader and follower, in which the active role is played by a man and the passive role by a woman. The so-called leader normally suggests a movement which is interpreted by the follower in her or his way. In addition, it is worth mentioning that the gender roles are being transformed and played with. In more and more dance schools both women and men are taught to "lead" and "follow", and in more and more *milongas* same-sex dancing is encouraged.
7. Peter Bengtsson: "Tango: något för riktiga Män och Kvinnor, eller en intrasexuell dragshow?", posted 18 January 2006.
8. Although the queer tango movement is evolving and although many dancers make sense of the dance-floor experiences across normative heterosexuality, heterosexual romance is still a strong codex for shaping relations and producing order within the world of tango dancing.
9. The particular examples brought forward in this illustration cover the year of my fieldwork (2007) and will probably change over time (some venues will most likely be phased out to make way for new clubs). I also wish to mention that there are venues, such as *La Viruta* and *Salon Canning*, which attract people from different age groups and with different dancing preferences.
10. This is encouraged by tango teachers and more experienced dancers. Practicing and dancing with different partners is often said to help dancers cultivate the skill of being present in the moment instead of routinely following the patterns of one partner. Some dancers explain the constant shift of partners as a function of the wish to improve their dancing. As dancers become more advanced and take interest in new styles and techniques they are urged to move on to partners who fit their objectives better. Others talk of the difficulties of handling the emotional bonds created by the close-embrace dancing; they say that when expectations of involvement in more than tango appear, it is time to move on.
11. www.totango.net (accessed 2009-10-22). Elsewhere, the bodily and emotional tango intimacy is similarly described in the language of sex and romance. As the following passage from a blog written by a Canadian woman on tango holiday in Buenos Aires illustrates, sex can be used as an up-front metaphor for describing dancing experiences: "I had a fabulous dance (*bueno como orgasmo*) close to the end with Scott (an Australian) and then was quite happy to sit and watch" (www.emmaholder.com, accessed 2009-11-02).

262 *Notes*

12. There are exceptions to this description, not least the growing scene of so-called gay or queer tango, with festivals, schools and practitioners all over the world. It is also necessary to comment on the situation for immigrant Argentine tango artists, mostly teachers and professional performers, who are trying to make a living in Europe and the U.S. out of their dancing skills and Argentine identity (normally believed to bring authenticity and cultural knowledge). This group differs from dancers that belong to the majority of the non-Argentine dance scenes, partly because of their economic and legal situation. Many work low-paying restaurant jobs during the day and try to eke a living out of tango at night (see Viladrich's 2005 study of tango immigrants in New York City).
13. www.tangonoticias.com (accessed 2008-12-04)
14. www.totango.com (accessed 2009-10-22)

NOTES TO CHAPTER 3

1. Wacquant continues: "Human beings become such by submitting to the 'judgment of others, this major principle of uncertainty and insecurity but also, and without contradiction, of certainty, assurance, consecration' [Bourdieu 1997/2001: 237]. Social existence thus means difference, and difference implies hierarchy, which in turn sets off the endless dialectic of distinction and pretention, recognition and misrecognition, arbitrariness and necessity" (Wacquant 2008: 265).
2. In this particular study, with its focus on tango tourism, the empirical field in question is primarily limited to the tango-dancing community in Buenos Aires. However, the aim of this study is not to describe this field in all its complexity, but rather to focus on those relations which are addressed by the impact of increasing streams of dance tourists. However, as will be discussed later on, this implies that the communities in dancers' home countries are also significant for defining the Argentine field of tango dancing. In addition, although various practices and narratives regarding tango differ between various local dancing communities, certain aspects discussed in the previous and the present chapter, such as the belief system and the function of an intimate dance economy, bring dancers from different dancing communities together and form tango dancing into one cultural field. Approaching tango dancing in such terms, we find that entire dancing communities are ascribed different degrees of recognition, primarily depending on their artistic and cultural development. On such a relational chart, Buenos Aires comes out strong, with its numerous venues and many acknowledged star dancers. This is indicated, not least by the fact that tango dancers from all over the world still chose Buenos Aires as the number one destination for a tango journey.
3. The notion of a *tango economy* is derived from the work of Pierre Bourdieu on economies of symbolic goods. This includes his anthropological work on Kabylian farmers (2001), his studies in the field of art and literature (1984, 1991) and his attempts to bring these studies together in order to "extract the general principles of an economy of symbolic goods" (1998: 93; cp. 1984). These principles are the gift exchange, the function of recognition, the taboo of calculation and a distinction between the sacred (pure) and the commercial (1998: 93; cp. 1984). In this chapter, we will find examples of all these principles.
4. We should also note that the tango obviously allows for individual evaluations of these resources. For one dancer musicality is decisive in the partner-selection, whereas others emphasize the embrace, the body size of a partner

and a friendly manner. Although personal preferences differ, most dancers are capable of recognizing generally acknowledged values in tango.
5. Most people who undertake a journey to Buenos Aires save money in order to spend it on expensive flight tickets, housing, dance classes and tango shoes. In addition, the travel involves a social sacrifice. The Argentine tango holiday appropriates vacation weeks for tango dancing instead of social activities with family and friends outside of tango.
6. http://www.tejastango.com/ (accessed 2012-05-27)
7. Although the values at stake are recognized by dancers in the form of an embodied knowledge, to some extent the dance economy is characterized by the lack of collectively agreed-upon "prices". As Bourdieu writes on the gift exchange of symbolic economies: "This consensus regarding the exchange rate is also present in an economy of symbolic exchanges, but its terms and conditions are left implicit. In the exchange of gifts, the price should be left implicit: I do not want to know the truth of the price, and I do not want the other person to know it either. Everything occurs as if there were an agreement to avoid explicitly reaching an agreement about the relative value of the things exchanged, by refusing all prior explicit definitions of the terms of exchange, that is, of the price" (Bourdieu 1998: 96).
8. Catherine Hakim speaks of erotic capital and erotic power as a fourth capital form in addition to economic, cultural and social capital. In her view this is a "combination of aesthetic, visual, physical, social and sexual attractiveness to other members of your society, and especially members of the opposite sex, in all social contexts" (2010: 3). Hakim claims this is an increasingly important asset in late-modern societies, potentially decisive not only in dating markets but also in media, politics, sports and the labor market.
9. In Buenos Aires and mostly in the traditional venues, men are still in formal charge of asking up—although women engage in the invitation play called *el cabeceo* with eye-glances and body language. In most dance scenes outside Argentina both women and men are allowed to ask up but men are still predominantly the active party in the process.
10. There are, however, exceptions to this tendency of negative impacts due to age. One is the example of 58-year-old Anna-Lena, who danced with a man thirty years younger on her first day out in Buenos Aires. "It was an afternoon *milonga* at La Confitería Ideal, with a lot of old men. I was seated at one of the sides with only one dancer at each table. So I was sitting all alone. Three tables away there was this young guy with whom I made eye contact. He was like twenty-two and a half, or twenty-five. And we danced and he was a terrific dancer. I didn't quite understand what he said but I think he was a tango teacher or was from a tango family. He danced like a God. We danced four *tandas*. That saved my evening. Some kind of connection appeared between us, in spite of the fact that he was so much younger" (Anna-Lena, 58-year-old, Sweden). Drawing on the logic of the intimate economy generates additional readings of Anna-Lena's experience. The fact that they met in a tourist-dense *milonga*, known to be a market space for all kinds of advertising teachers, taxi dancers and clothing vendors,—and the dance partner's comment about being a teacher, indicates that he might have had an interest in turning Anna-Lena into a dance student, which is not to say that he did not also enjoy her dancing company.
11. However, we might also note that the process of *becoming* a tango dancer, the bodily adaption implicit in this process, implies that the body is also a carrier of possibilities of radical breaks, not least with limited ideals of femininity ideals. In a piece on a lindy-hop community, Lisa Wade (2011)

explores the emancipatory promises of the dance and shows how the dancers make use of their bodies in order to transgress gender normative ideals.
12. www.kissandtango.info (accessed 2008–01–15)
13. When reading Palmer's book more carefully one discovers that sexual affairs across the tango hierarchies are more complex than only being about the trading of sex for dancing credentials. The fact that well-recognized dancers are more often approached, for both dancing and sex, than others, might be understood as a delicate mixture of physical attraction through intimate dance communication and the appeal of charisma. As Bourdieu writes, relations of domination often transform into affective relations, at times within the language of charm and romantic promises (1998: 102). The same seems to be true within the intimate economy of tango dancing. It is apparent, though, that the recognized male dancers in similar kinds of stories are not understood as acting immorally.
14. We should also be concerned with the representations of Latin-American men as always "sexually willing". As elsewhere, gender in Argentine society is a diverse category. See Chapter 8 for a more detailed discussion.
15. Interestingly, though, as Jaquee Sanchez Taylor writes, there is a parallel discourse of heteronormativity which imputes dishonor to those women—and men—who are not sexually desireable to the opposite sex (2006: 47).
16. Ethnographic studies of the queer tango world would provide some interesting and provocative additional cases. These dancers clearly reject the heterosexual organizing of the *milonga*, but are reducing the negative sanctions of such out-of-script acting by forming their own dance scene with its particular rules and regulations.
17. As already touched upon, in tango as elsewhere, aging seems only rarely to function as a credential for women. The traditional gender norms rather make age a problem for female dancers.
18. www.emmaholder.com (accessed 2009–11–02)
19. The heterosexual order—and the struggle over scarce resources (male dancers)—might serve as an explanatory context for the harsh words at times spread by female dancers about other female dancers. Given the discussions in this chapter it might not be a coincidence that age is a basis for making fun of other women, as in the following statement from a Canadian blog post reporting on life in Buenos Aires: "Some characters: Desperately Seeking Something woman (in her 60s)—permanently stuck in the eighties with weird tattered lace and extremely bad hair (looked like she was wearing a hair-dye cap with tufts pulled out of it. ACK! Although not a bad dancer, just made us cringe to look at her" (www.emmaholder.com, accessed 2009–11–02).

NOTES TO CHAPTER 4

1. We should notice that most of the interviews referred to in this chapter took place during dancers' visits in Buenos Aires or in their home countries upon their return. This is to say that their sense-making partly looks back on how they conceived of the journeys before actually going to Argentina.
2. Paula Bialski (2008; 2012) uses the term "intimate tourism" to explore online hospitality exchange systems as a new form of tourism, found for instance in so-called couch surfing. Drawing on a notion of intimacy similar to Jamieson's (1998), focusing on dialogue, individuality and "personal growth", Bialski shows how visitor and host create intimate relations within a short time frame. The relation between tango tourism and other kinds of intimate travel will be discussed in more detail in Chapter 8.

3. In movies such as *Dirty Dancing 2*, the interference of class and romantic feelings is relocated to the Global South as upper middle-class Katey Miller from the U.S. accompanies her family to Havana and explores the salsa with the help of Javier, a young Cuban man. As Katey enters the local club, La Rosa Negra, with her quite boring and overprotective North-American date, we understand from her way of looking at the provocatively intimate dance-floor couples that she is taken by the dance, its rhythms and movements. Whereas her strikingly white date sees only sex and the need to protect her from it, she sees dancing and the need to break with uptight family morals. Later on, as Katey gets closely involved with Javier and caught in a moral family dilemma, she explains: "When I danced with him, I became the woman I wanted to be."
4. However, male tango dancers also travel to Argentina although female tango travelers represent the majority. Furthermore, the expectations and public mirroring of the trips vary according to gender. Additional examples are romance and sex tourism, dealt with in more detail in Chapter 8.
5. We should notice, however, that tango voyagers also conceive of the risks in tango as hindrances that must be avoided. We might in fact notice two different approaches to this kind of uncertainty: a positive one, through which risk is approached as a means to achieve possible benefits, and a defensive one, which conceives of risk as pervasive (Lupton and Tulloch 2002). This might be captured in the description of the tango journey as an "emotional rollercoaster", a simile which stresses both the positive and negative impacts of a manufactured risk-situation.
6. In Chapter 10 we will explore these different kinds of vulnerability in larger detail.

NOTES TO CHAPTER 5

1. We should notice that this book addresses primarily those services, attractions and items which target tango tourists. These services and items are, however, often also purchased by Argentine dancers.
2. A study focusing on the working conditions and various actors as well as their diverse experiences and sense-making of the market would require a more comprehensive interview-study with workers and managers within different sectors of the market space of Argentine tango.
3. www.turismo.gov.ar/eng/menu.htm (accessed 2012–02–13).
4. As the *Argentine SEC Informa* (Sistema Estadístico de la Ciudad) reported in April 2009, almost three hundred hotels and three hundred hostels and bed-and-breakfasts were licensed. Among such businesses, half the rooms available were in four-star establishments or higher.
5. www.wttc.org (accessed 2008–03–10)
6. www.travelandleisure.com (accessed 2008–03–10)
7. Whitson defines informal work as "work that deals with legal products or services, although the production or distribution of these is either unregulated or illegal" (Whitson 2007: 124).
8. One characteristic of the informal market is the coteries of small-scale entrepreneurs, helping each other out. One example of this is a Dutch woman who works as a landlord, offering rooms in her apartment to tango tourists, as well as a dance teacher and organizer of tango clubs and parties. At the time of my fieldwork she was working together with a mobile clothing store, among other collaborations. She describes the cooperation as beneficial both to her and the store owner; she gave dance performances during certain store

events and thereby provided a good ambiance and publicity both for him and her.
9. Advertisement regarding workshops offered in Stockholm, 8–9 September 2012 (www.tangonorte.com, accessed 2012–08–30).
10. Parts of this discussion can be found in a book chapter by the author together with Kate Hardy entitled "Taxi Dancers: Tango Labour and Commercialized Intimacy in Buenos Aires", in K. Hardy, S. Kingston and T. Sanders (eds.), *New Sociologies of Sex Work*, Surrey: Ashgate. However, the main focus of the present chapter—the values associated with accessibility—is not the focus of the joint book chapter.
11. The ambiguous reception of taxi dancers among the tourists will be discussed in more detail in Chapter 7.
12. www.tangopasional.com/TEST_JS/ba.html (accessed 2011–12–03)
13. According to Hochschild's own definition, emotional labor is "the management of feeling to create a publicly observable facial and bodily display; emotional labor is sold for a wage and therefore has exchange value. I use the synonymous terms emotion work or emotion management to refer to these same acts done in a private context where they have use value" (Hochschild 1983/2003: 7).
14. In fact it seems that tango was part of the trafficking of women. An official police report from 1927 states that "a man was arrested at Florence who was about to take eighteen girls to Buenos Ayres where they were engaged to dance. This man was the brother of a brothel-keeper at Buenos Ayres" (Guy 1995: 149). However, as an American study from 1932, *The Taxi-Dance Hall*, demonstrates, the concept of dance escorting might actually also stem from an institution found in some larger North-American cities during the depression. Paul Cressey (1932/2003: 3) describes the taxi dancer in the U.S. as "like the taxi-driver with his cab, she is for public hire and is paid in proportion to the time spent and the services rendered". So-called "dance hosts" also appear today, for instance as a service on cruise ships. For example, The Gentlemen Hosts agency offers "goodwill ambassadors" and dance partners to "women travelling independently" on cruise lines and river boats. The hosts are promoted as "Single men, 40 to 70 years old, who are still young at heart. Always dancers! [. . .] Kind, honorable and smiling community-minded volunteers" (www.theworkingvacation.com, accessed 2011–02–03).
15. www.tangopasional.com/TEST_JS/ba.html (accessed 2011–12–03)
16. When exploring the other party in this market transaction, the presumed clients, the attempts to trade cultural authenticity through the use of highly sexualized and racialized images do at times evoke rather the opposite reactions than expected. Although some visitors enjoy the colorful and "sexy" representations of tango, many reject this aesthetic—so-called tango kitsch—as vulgar and "cheap" copies. Some tourists actually dismiss entire dance schools as carriers of fake authenticity because of their attempts to attract tourists with the help of a charming outdoor patio and the helping hands of young "charming" Argentines, features that are perceived by some dancers as "Argentine décor".
17. One such example is found on a North-American tango webpage under the heading "Where to buy tango shoes in Buenos Aires" (www.tejastango.com, accessed 2012–05–27).
18. www.niptucktravelbuenosaires.com/ (accessed 2010–10–24)
19. www.tangowithjudy.com/HOW%20IT%20WORKS.htm (accessed 2012–08–15)
20. For obvious reasons such definition power is of greater significance in Buenos Aires, the capital of tango, than elsewhere in the world. Appointing "real

maestros" is a national concern in a country where tango attracts news value in daily papers.
21. www.dni-tango.com (accessed 2012–05–29). The discussion of *DNI Tango* is based on participant observation at the school as well as information provided on their home page. Hence the analysis primarily targets the school's *staging* of artistic excellence and recognition.
22. Success in launching a new shoe brand, particularly for those actors who are not in the position of exerting absolute symbolic power, i.e. who are not absolute trendsetters, requires knowledge about and insight into the tango scene. This involves knowledge of recent trends—what are the dancing styles *à la mode*, who are the up-and-coming stars and the declining ones, where do people go dancing etc.? When it comes to the competing shoe labels, the most successful ones are those able to claim that their models are adjusted to current dancing trends and those that manage to get well-recognized dancers to use their shoes. In this way, different labels offer very different shoe models with an advertisement that actually targets one and the same client group. For instance, models with extremely high heels—and extremely low heels—have been advertised to suit the trend of *tango nuevo* which attracted a large group of younger dancers during the first decade of the twenty-first century.
23. Here we might point out that the global melting pot of Buenos Aires not only fosters startling anecdotes about Argentina but also harbors exotic representations of life in wealthier countries far North. Stories about adventures and everyday life in Paris, Stockholm and San Francisco flourish not only among the tourists themselves but also among local dancers and professional tango workers.

NOTES TO CHAPTER 6

1. In addition, we might notice that non-Argentine actors within the Argentine tango market have some advantages also in relation to the language barrier. As some non-Argentine dancers who offer tango classes state in their adverts, they are "English speaking".
2. Such a view might put the expanding streams of tourists coming to Buenos Aires for tango in dialogue with histories of the unsettled origin of tango. As suggested by tango historians, the tango was never a local custom with culturally defined roots, but was always transformable and unsettled (Savigliano 1995a). According to such claims, the impact of temporary visitors might be described as a continuation of an already existing trajectory in tango and an inherent dynamic of a cultural expression that never belonged to anyone and was never fixed in space and time.
3. It can be mentioned, for instance, that a Japanese couple won the international world competition in Argentine tango dancing in 2009.
4. www.emmholder.com (accessed 2009–11–02)
5. www.tejastango.com/money_matters.html (accessed 2012–05–27)
6. This is reflected in historic accounts of the origin of tango in the poor, violent harbor neighborhoods of Buenos Aires. Protecting one's honor, and not making a fool out of oneself, is often stated to have been a matter of life and death. As suggested by the lyrics of one famous tango song, *En la Buena y en la Mala*, the theme of honor also relates to the problematic presence of money in intimate relations: "I met you during good times and lost you when times got bad. My innocence was so white and your insensibility dark. [. . .] My wallet was a magnet that made it your ambition to create a

simulacrum of passion." My translation. Original lyrics: Enrique Cadícamo; music: Domingo Scarpino (1940).
7. Furthermore this quote shows how nationality is played out in the distinction play around tourism.
8. In relation to the discussions in Chapter 1, this is another argument for providing a full-bodied analysis, bringing embodied ethnographic work together with interrogations of the discursive sense-making offered from within the field.
9. However, as noted in this chapter, there are also accounts of how Argentina and its capital contribute to the makeup and staging of the tango experience. As discussed in relation to the blog post by Canadian Emma, "penetrating the real city" is used as a signifier of authenticity and tango depth.

NOTES TO CHAPTER 7

1. www.tangoportalen.se (accessed 2007–09–20). This discussion was carried out between March 24, 2006, and April 2, 2006, and had 51 posts.
2. The relation between tango tourism and various forms of sex tourism will be further explored in Chapter 8.
3. It can be noted that the romantic engagement with an Argentine functions as a symbolic ending to the journey also in certain popular narratives. In her autobiographical book *Kiss & Tango*, Marin Palmer—the author and main character—says farewell to Buenos Aires in the arms of a "sexy tango partner" named Javier (Palmer 2006: 319–320).
4. "Only transactions for money have that character of a purely momentary relationship which leaves no traces. [. . .] Money is never an adequate means in a relationship between persons that depends on duration and integrity—like love, even when it is only of short duration. Money serves most matter-of-factly and completely for venal pleasure which rejects any continuation of the relationship beyond sensual satisfaction: money is completely detached from the person and puts an end to any further ramification" (Simmel 1907/1971: 121).

NOTES TO CHAPTER 8

1. In an interview she declares that "tango is very romantic, just having that face to face contact and the leading from the chest. You're sharing your axes, that's extremely beautiful and you can fall in love very easily. When you dance with someone who has that passion and understands the tango then you can become very emotional. [. . .] It's all about chemistry I think. But—hey—you can fall in love on the beach, you don't have to do it while tangoing. I know it happens a lot in tango but it actually happens everywhere" (Susanna, 50-year-old, U.S.).
2. There are also cases of long-term relationships between Argentines and foreigners initiated on the dance-floors of Buenos Aires. Some of these relationships involve marriage and children and constant travelling back and forth between Argentina and the country of origin of the partner (Sweden, France, Germany, U.S.). These relationships, however, are not the focus of this chapter.
3. Still others stress that the confusion of dancing intimacy with love and romance makes life at the *milonga* difficult. One example of this is how the Swedish dancer Lasse experiences a failed love affair he had with a dance

partner. "You don't want to have love relations inside tango, it gets too complicated. Once I made the mistake, I started dating a dance partner and it ended badly. We confused the connection you might feel with someone in tango with real love and attraction but we were actually not meant to be lovers. That's fair enough but in tango it means that you lose a dance partner so I'm continuing as a bit of a loner, separating my tango life from my love life" (Lasse, 58-year-old, Sweden).
4. Parts of this and the following two sections are based on an article published in the *Feminist Review* (2012) entitled "Troubling Romance Tourism. Sex, Gender and Class inside the Argentinean Tango Clubs".
5. This narrative includes classic stories such as *Romeo and Juliet*, and more updated ones like *West Side Story*, *Dirty Dancing* and *Pretty Woman*. In all these examples obstacles come between the protagonists—in some cases socio-economic divisions, in others family traditions. What they all have in common is that the obstacles help to make the attraction stronger. Not least as a dramaturgical effect, the differences are used as a thrilling device to maintain the excitement.
6. We might notice, though, that the story is not told in the first person, but by her friend Sybil. The fact that I never got to hear about such straightforward motivations in relation to sex can be put in dialogue with the earlier discussion of the sex-related shame experienced by dancers when sexual intimacy is not managed in correct ways.
7. Stereotypical tango masculinity is framed as both macho and feminine. The Argentine *tanguero* is said to care about his looks; he is vain, urban, verbal and emotional—and yet he is a macho man, sexually charismatic and known for his skills in conquering women (Archetti 1999). Drawing on tango history, he is also a modern man, a man of good taste and manners, clearly distinguished from the rural *gauchos* (the farmers). Feminized tango masculinity in a country made up of a large percentage of rural farm workers might create a problem involving honor (Savigliano 1995a; 1995b).
8. www.emmaholder.com (accessed 2009-11-02)
9. Similar mechanisms, bound up with class, are at work when it comes to the regulation of women's sexuality. As Beverley Skeggs (2005: 969–970) argues, the moral borders around the vulgar and too overtly exposed female (hetero)sexuality has become more ambiguous with cultural representations such as the ones found in the HBO series *Sex and the City*. As long as the outspoken and raw sexuality is embodied by economically and culturally esteemed women—performing an upper middle-class lifestyle and boasting an adequate set of bodies—potentially vulgar situations are understood as romantic.
10. In the Hollywood storylines, a key dramatic element is the image of love as a force strong enough to bridge social differences. However, the beauty of the "impossible love" narratives does not stem from differences as such, in the sense of an attraction based on diversity; rather it climaxes at the point where social differences are transgressed. It is in that sense that the movies tell a story about the power of love. It is when Baby and Johnny in the movie *Dirty Dancing* throw themselves in each other's arms in the public dance-room, thereby showing that their will to be together is stronger than traditional family norms and socio-economic differences, that we applaud. Moreover, love conquers when superficial differences (economic ones) are erased by strengthening desired differences, which is to say those between the sexes. It is as a woman and a man that Baby and Johnny unite on the dance-floor, not as a poor worker man and an upper-class tourist rich enough to buy his services.

NOTES TO CHAPTER 9

1. My translation. Original lyrics: Alfredo Lepera; music: Carlos Gardel (1934).
2. It should be mentioned that the tango lives primarily in the Rio de la Plata region, which includes the Uruguayan capital Montevideo as well as Buenos Aires. However, Buenos Aires is the number one target for dance tourism.
3. The significance of tango as a general tourist magnet was further stressed when the dance was declared part of the world's cultural heritage by the United Nations (UNESCO) in 2009.
4. www.gadventures.com (accessed 2012–02–03)
5. This is a group of Argentine mothers whose children were murdered during the military dictatorship (1976–1983). Until January 2006 they convened every Thursday afternoon at Plaza de Mayo wearing white head scarves, embroidered with the names of their children.
6. This also shows in the real estate businesses entered by foreign investors during the Argentine crisis. Some of the North-American and European investors were tango dancers who bought cheap flats and apartment complexes to rent—and eventually sell—to tango tourists. Although they were mostly located in the upper-class area of Recoletta, the presumed customers were not primarily attracted by the neighborhood as such, but the larger scenery of Buenos Aires.
7. www.turismo.gov.ar/eng/menu.htm (accessed 2012–02–13)
8. The marathons are a kind of intensified form of dance festival, normally held over a weekend and with a strong focus on the dancing. At certain of these marathons, the music keeps playing throughout the weekend and the dancers take breaks only for eating and resting.
9. It should be noticed, however, that Argentine dancers and dance schools are also part of this development. See for instance the discussion of *DNI Tango*, Chapter 5.
10. We actually find a rather similar development in tango history. In the 1920s the tango was exported to the fine cafés and ballrooms of Paris and other European cities (Savigliano 1995a: 100–135). Geographic anchoring was a contested matter at that time as well. The successfulness of the global exporting of Argentine culture partly had to do with its exoticized status: the tango was made desirable by virtue of its geographical and cultural estrangement.
11. In the following statement, for instance, Elin answers my question about whether she experienced "tango euphoria" in Buenos Aires by recalling dances not with Argentines but with "a French guy and a Dutch". In her view tango is not so much about the particularity of Argentina or the cultural belonging of the dancers ("the blood") as about finding those similarly tuned "souls" who respond similarly to the music.
    Elin: I did have some dances which were like: shit this is it. [. . .] For me it's about those moments of total communication with your dance partner, time stops and it's us and the music but it doesn't have to be defined as you and I, it's more like a unity moving to the music. There were some occasions like that and it was amazing. (Elin, 35-year-old, Sweden)
    Maria: How was this affected by you being in Buenos Aires?
    Elin: Well, it was with a French guy and a Dutch. It is such a huge arena. All good dancers, all dancers, go there [to Buenos Aires]. But tango is all about two souls who are on a quite similar frequency at the same time.
12. Translating this to other cultural art forms, we might see how a postmodernist take on art expands the reach of artistic expressions to cover more varied art projects, including those artistic endeavors which explore artistic borders

themselves by offering "non-traditionalist" artistic works, whereas a modernist definition implies the subordination of certain aesthetic rules.
13. In practice, though, these discourses are not as competitive with and strictly divided from one another as described here. In fact, they often overlap, as shown in the many examples of dancers—such as Daniella—who travel both to Buenos Aires in search of Argentine culture and to marathons and festivals throughout Europe with the aim of accessing fine dancing experiences.

NOTES TO CHAPTER 10

1. This implies that the notion of a market elaborated on in this book primarily covers those services, attractions and items which target dance tourists. At times these services and items are purchased also by Argentine dancers; at times they are meant only for tourists, as when tourist agencies accommodate dance tourists with a package of services.
2. When looking at this relation historically we find that economic transactions have been part of the tango for long time. From the presumed early days at the brothel around the turn of the last century, throughout the so-called "golden age" of the forties when tango orchestras flourished in the cafés and dance-halls, artistic skills in the area of dancing and music have been traded for money (Guy 1995; Savigliano 1995a). However, the impact of a money market within tango has shifted and possibly grown with the economic crisis and the expanding number of foreign dance tourists.
3. In order to theorize this further, we might acknowledge previous work on value spheres (Weber 1915/1995) and regimes of justification (Boltanski and Thevenot 2006; cp. Dahlberg 2010). Turning to Bourdieu and his notion of habitus as corresponding with the structuring of a field, its rewarding logic and relational chart, we find that the embodying of a particular cultural world—such as tango dancing—creates a particular vision, an evaluating and justifying vision. As Bourdieu writes: "Habitus are also classificatory schemes, principles of classification, principles of vision and divisions, different tastes. They make distinctions between what is good and what is bad, between what is right and what is wrong, between what is distinguished and what is vulgar, and so forth" (Bourdieu 1998: 8–9). Using the vocabulary of Bourdieu, we might approach these cognitive frames as "dispositions of the body" (Bourdieu 1998: 54), a claim which is striking in the heavily body-oriented world of tango dancing.
4. Regarding the chart, we should be careful to note that the qualities associated with tango and tourism, respectively, are related to the main object of this study.
5. This book conducts a critical analysis of those values, such as authenticity, to which legitimizing power and transformative capacities are ascribed. Authenticity functions as a potent discourse and is used as a legitimating key concept in several tango-related debates. Moreover, claims for authenticity are sometimes bound up with a conservation of value systems. The defenders of traditional gender ideals in tango regarding partner constellation, dress codes and general manners, for instance, often refer to same-sex dance partners as a threat to "real" tango. At times this claim is brought forward with arguments suggesting that such a turn in tango is imported from abroad—and hence represents a danger for Argentine tango. In such a framing, authenticity values and the significance of manners associated with a particular place—Buenos Aires—are used to promote sexist and homophobic ideas.

6. This tendency comes across in some of the accounts reflecting on romantic relations in tango. In Chapter 8, we encountered Rebecca who has had several sexual affairs during her tango visit, some of them more serious than others, and she describes them all as "amazing" and as "exciting and passionate". However, the economic differences between her and her Argentine romantic partners get in the way of long-term relations. As she puts it: "If I would engage with someone from here seriously, it would basically be me supporting them, and I'm not ready to support a man. [. . .] I want someone who is my financial equal and unfortunately these *porteño* men are not". This might also be exemplified by Marina Palmer (2006), who wishes to have sexual adventures with Argentine "Latin Lovers"—but without being heartbroken.
7. In one sense, we might suggest that such nostalgia is already present in the tango. Argentine as well as foreign dancers look back yearningly into the history of the tango. However, this nostalgia is not evoked by tourist exploitation and has managed to be made part of contemporary Argentine tango life, a sentiment associated with "an authentic and totally different culture".
8. However, it should be noted that status credentials such as "looks", youth and social abilities are also rewarding in the world of tango.
9. Still an economic analysis is relevant. When looking at the authenticity continuum from a class perspective, we find that it implies different levels of costs, notable particularly for Argentine dancers but also for certain groups of dance tourists. Going for a tango show might be ten times the price or more to a *milonga* exhibition far away from the city center. The same is true for the purchase of tango goods, ranging from the expensive shoe- and clothing brands particularly targeting tourists and those everyday Argentine clothing stores with prices adapted to Argentine salaries. In fact, the relation between exclusivity (expensive) and authenticity is rather ambiguous in tango tourism due to the fact that it is mostly tourists who can afford those items advertised as exclusive. In fact, it happens that signifiers of Argentine culture—i.e. cultural marks embodied by Argentine dancers—are not always recognized as authentic by temporary visitors. Such is the case of a tango aesthetic which stresses a gender divide and involves slit skirts and the generous exposing of naked skin. Although such an aesthetic is part of the everyday Argentine tango life, in the sense that many local dancers appreciate it and for the fact that such clothes are accessible in fairly discounted clothing stores, it is at times despised by dance tourists as "cheap" and moreover as fake tango reproductions.
10. We might also comment on some possible national patterns in relation to the dancers view on the intimate services offered on the tango market, such as taxi dancing. The choices of what to consume and how—if at all—seem to follow, not only the dancers experiences in tango, but also some diverging lines following different service cultures. Looking at the international visitors being the main focus in this study, the North-American dancers are more service friendly than the Swedes. Some of these variations might be explained by the function of the two welfare regimes. In a society like Sweden, characterized by a traditionally strong welfare state and a social liberal ideology, the question of house hold services—for instance—has (at least during the 1990s) evoked a massive public debate, whereas the North-American organization of family life to I much higher degree leans on the provision of service work such as nannies and domestic services (Nyberg 1999; Wouters 2004).
11. This shows similarities with a study on the Stockholm advertising world in which Raoul Galli claims that advertising "primarily reflects the social world that creates it, i.e. the advertising world" (2012: 1), rather than society at large or even the principals and clients.

12. In Lefebvre's own words: "groups, classes or fractions of classes cannot constitute themselves, or recognize one another, as 'subjects' unless they generate (or produce) a space. Ideas, representations or values which do not succeed in making their mark on space, and thus generating (or producing) an appropriate morphology, will lose all pith and become mere signs, resolve themselves into abstract descriptions, or mutate into fantasies. [. . .] Long-lived morphologies (religious buildings, historical-political monuments) support our antiquated ideologies and representations. [. . .] Space's investment—the production of space—has nothing incidental about it: it is a matter of life and death" (Lefebvre 1991: 416–417).
13. In the words of Simon Coleman and Mike Crang, I suggest that we "understand tourism as an event that is about mobilizing and reconfiguring spaces and places, bringing them into new constellations and therefore transforming them. [. . .] We would argue that tourist places and performances are about admitting the incompleteness of experience and places. We want a sense of performativity of place rather than just performance in place" (2002: 10).
14. This is a common theme also in classic and popular culture. The power of love as a subversive force threatening social stability is dealt with in well-known books and movies such as *Romeo and Juliet*, *West Side Story*, *Dirty Dancing* and *Pretty Woman*.
15. One further key to the significance of an imaginary classless class of dance voyagers draws on the larger spectrum of tourism as a field of taste and class-related lifestyles. The significance of tango journeys might be framed in relation to an implicit set of class-cultural distinctions. In pointing to the cultural aim of their journey, dancers often define themselves as different from other kinds of tourists. As discussed in an earlier chapter, they distance themselves from the kind of mass tourism to "cheap" beach resorts that originates in the recreational needs of an expanding group of wealthier working-class families. In this context the touristy commercialization of tango becomes an element that creates associations with others kinds of tourism. Recognizing tourist practices as class markers, destabilizes the dividing line between refined culture travelling and recreational journeys of the masses.

NOTES TO THE APPENDIX

1. Ethnography is a strong methodological tradition within the research field of dancing that often generates rich descriptive analyses based on the practices of a particular dance world and hence results in well-informed and fascinating studies (see Olszewski 2008; Parviainen 2002; Skinner 2008; Urquía 2004; Wade 2011; Wulff 2008). However, we should also acknowledge other types of analyses, such as Savigliano's deconstructivist research based on historic material (1995a; 1995b) and those projects using dance videos and choreographies as material for exploring gender and spatiality, as in the case of Valerie Briginshaw's (2001) work on contemporary dance.
2. Regarding the Argentine *milongas*, the ethnographic fieldwork primarily covers four selected inner-city dance clubs with a mixed crowd of local dancers and tourists: *Confitería Ideal*, *Niño Bien*, *Salon Canning* and *Práctica X*. They are different in profile and target group. *Confitería Ideal* is a fairly "touristy" venue, as it is an historic site and a well-known tango spot—also among regular tourists visiting Buenos Aires. The dancing style is mostly traditional and the average age among the dancers around fifty. This club offers afternoon *milongas* and live concerts and is hosted in a beautiful fin de siècle building with lush velvet curtains and marble pillars. *Práctica X*,

by contrast, targets a younger group of dancers with various dancing styles (for instance, the so-called *tango nuevo*) and is profiled as an underground venue, hosted in a rough industrial space without traditional interior design such as tables. The two additional clubs can be situated between these two poles, although *Salon Canning* is more casual and offers a more varied range of club organizers than *Niño Bien*. It should be noted that the scene is undergoing changes, with new clubs and crowds emerging, especially as a consequence of the increasing number of visitors coming to town. Therefore, the empirical descriptions of the specific characteristics of clubs and tango schools should be read in the context of the time limits of my field-work.
3. In addition, the fieldwork and the participation in various activities have allowed me to access important additional material, such as formal interviews and material useful for the textual analysis. This involves Argentine tango magazines, of which only a few are available on the net, and the distribution of flyers and brochures aiming at attracting clients to a particular dance school or *milonga*.
4. Moreover, I have been using my own five years of tango dancing—on and off—and my experiences in different tango communities around the world as a basis for discovering and articulating the practices, belief system and embodied regulations making up the world of tango dancing. In addition to the tango scenes of Buenos Aires, San Francisco and Stockholm, this involves experiences in the tango communities of Barcelona, Paris, Lisbon and various Swedish cities as well as the social life associated with tango festivals in Buenos Aires, Sweden and Spain.
5. The interview study consists of twenty-eight informants, of which a few have been interviewed on several occasions. Nineteen tango tourists have been interviewed; of these, eight are North-American, seven Swedish, two French, one Australian and one Belgian. Among the tourists, a majority of the informants are women (sixteen interviewees). In addition, two male Argentine hobby dancers have been interviewed. When it comes to the market actors, seven interviews have been carried out with taxi dancers, dance teachers, tourist agency managers and *milonga* organizers. They cover three Argentines, three North-Americans and one Swede. The interviews have been conducted in the interviewees' native language, i.e. Spanish, English and Swedish, respectively (informants with other native languages have been interviewed in English), and have been translated into English when used as quotes in this book. It might be noted that the stated age in the quotes refers to the age of the informant at the time of the interview. The fact that the interviews were carried out between 2007 and 2012 entails that some informants are presently five years older today than what is stated in the book. In three cases the informants are named with two countries—for instance, "Sweden/Argentina". This indicates that the informant is Swedish but currently working and living in Argentina. The interviews have been carried out in Argentina, the U.S. and Sweden and have lasted between one and three hours. Most of the interviews were conducted in one-to-one situations, although a few were carried out in group settings. It should be mentioned that, on a few occasions, I use quotes stemming from the context of the ethnographic fieldwork and not from the formal interviews. Those cases consist of a sentence or a couple of words—no more—that I have written down during an informal conversation. Such quotes are used primarily to provide the study with voices from the field, and to give the reader a richer sense of how the dancers speak in their own words about the issues at stake. All informants are made anonymous for ethical reasons and have been informed about the aim of the study and the conditions inscribed in their participating.

6. The same is true for the Argentine audience and those dancers who are working as dance teachers or performers and run their own schools and dance companies. At large the tango attracts middle-class Argentineans primarily from Buenos Aires. Some dancers belong to the old generation of *milongueros* who grew up during the so called "golden-age" of tango, whereas a younger crowd recently picked up on the culture and is now part of transforming the music and the dancing scene (for instance through *tango nuevo* and electronic tango music).
7. The framing of this movie being a documentary short-film (14 minutes long), makes it diverge from the other popular narratives in composition and plot, not the least by providing quite brief information about the two main characters.
8. Whether it is academic writhing, novels or documentary books on tango history, personal anecdotes (in academic writing, these take the form of ethnographic notes) often blend with analyses of the culture. An absolute majority of the academic studies—and movies, such as *The Tango Lesson*—I have encountered are carried out by researchers who have also been dancing or have in other ways been "down with" the tango. It might not be a coincidence that the Swedish literature professor Birgitta Holm, also a tango dancer, has written a beautiful and poetic book on her encounter with the tango. The fact that the tango literature transgresses the borders of various genres complicates our reading and use of it. In this book I have attempted to make a distinction between those books and articles with an academic profile and those books which target a broader audience. The first category will primarily be approached as research literature, being quoted and referred to as research, whereas the more popular tango literature will be approached primarily as material. As suggested by the diffuse nature of the genre as a whole, however, such a distinction is not fully satisfactory.
9. A selected number of issues of these magazines, from the year 2007 and 2012, have been analyzed.
10. When it comes to the other key group of tango tourists in this study, the North-Americans, I have primarily interrogated a number of webpages and blog posts created by individual dancers (some of which have given rise to comments by and discussions with other dancers).

References

LITERATURE

Aalten, A. (2007) 'Listening to the Dancer's Body', in C. Schilling (ed.) *Embodying Sociology: Retrospects, Progress and Prospects*, Oxford: Blackwell Publishing.
Abadi, S. (2003) *Milongan: Omfamningarnas basar*, Stockholm: CKM.
Ahmed, S. (2004) *The Cultural Politics of Emotion*, Edinburgh: Edinburgh University Press.
Alexander, J. (1997) 'Erotic Autonomy as a Politics of Decolonization: An Anatomy of Feminist and State Practice in the Bahamas Tourist Economy', in M. J. Alexander and C. T. Mohanty (eds.) Feminist Genealogies, Colonial Legacies, Democratic Futures, New York: Routledge.Ambjörnsson, F. (2004) *I en klass för sig. Genus, klass och sexualitet bland gymnasietjejer*, Stockholm: Ordfront.
Ander, G. och N. Hansson (2005) *Tango: återkomsten*, Stockholm: Ordfront.
Andriotis, K. (2009) 'Sacred Site Visitation: A Phenomenological Study', *Annals of Tourism Research*, 36(1): 64–84.
———. (2011) 'Genres of Heritage Authenticity: Denotations from a Pilgrimage Landscape', *Annals of Tourism Research*, 38(4): 1613–1633.
Archetti, E. P. (1999) *Masculinities: Football, Polo and the Tango in Argentina*, Oxford: Berg.
Aspers, P. (2005) *Markets in Fashion: A Phenomenological Approach*, London: Routledge.
——— and J. Beckert (2011) 'Value in Markets', in J. Bekert and P. Aspers (eds.) *The Worth of Goods: Valuation and Pricing in the Economy*, New York: Oxford University Press.
Baerenholdt, J. O., M. Haldrup, J. Larsen and J. Urry (2004) *Performing Tourist Places*, Aldershot: Ashgate.
Barthes, R. (1982) 'Deliberation', S. Sontag (ed.) *A Barthes Reader*, New York: Hill and Wang.
Baudrillard, J. (1994) *Simulacra and Simulation*, Ann Arbor: University of Michigan Press.
Bauman, Z. (1998) *Globalization: The Human Consequences*, London: Polity.
———. (2003) *Liquid Love: On the Frailty of Human Bonds*, Cambridge: Polity Press.
———. (2011) *Times of Interregnum*, Lecture at Södra Teatern, Stockholm, August 17, 2011.
Bawin-Legros, B. (2004) 'Intimacy and the New Sentimental Order', *Current Sociology*, 52(2): 241–250.
de Beauvoir, S. (1949/1995) *Det andra könet*, Stockholm: Norstedts.
Beck, U. (1992) *Risk Society*, London: SAGE.

———. (2000) *What Is Globalization?*, Malden, MA: Polity Press.
Beedi, P. and S. Hudson (2003) 'Emergence of Mountain-Based Adventure Tourism', *Annals of Tourism Research*, 30(3): 625–643.
Bergman Blix, S. (2009) 'Emotional participation—The Use of the Observer's Emotions as a Methodological Tool When Studying Professional Stage Actors Rehearsing a Role for the Stage', *Nordic Theatre Studies*, 21: 29–38.
———. (2010) *Rehearsing Emotions: The Process of Creating a Role for the Stage*, Stockholm: Stockholm University.
Bernstein, E. (2001) 'The Meaning of the Purchase: Desire, Demand and the Commerce of Sex', *Ethnography*, 2(3).
———. (2007a) *Temporarily Yours: Sexual Commerce in Post-Industrial Culture*, Chicago: University of Chicago Press.
———. (2007b) 'Buying and Selling the "Girlfriend Experience": The Social and Subjective Contours of Market Intimacy', in M. Padilla et al. (eds.) *Love and Globalization: Transformations of Intimacy in the Contemporary World*, Nashville: Vanderbilt University Press.
Bialski, P. (2008) *Intimate Tourism: Enquete dans un reseau d'hospitalite*, Limoges: Solilange.
———. (2012) *Becoming Intimately Mobile*, Frankfurt am Main: Peter Lang.
Boissevain, J. (2002) 'Preface', in S. Coleman and M. Crang (eds.) *Tourism: Between Place and Performance*, New York: Berghahn Books.
Boltanski, L. and L. Thévenot (1991/2006) *On Justification: Economies of Worth*, Princeton: Princeton University Press.
Bordo, S. (1993) *Unbearable Weight: Feminism, Western Culture, and the Body*, Berkeley: University of California Press.
Borges, J. L. (2007) *Fiktioner*, Stockholm: Bonnier.
Bourdieu, P. (1980) 'The Production of Belief: Contribution to an Economy of Symbolic Goods', *Media, Culture & Society*, 4(2): 261–293.
———. (1984) *The Field of Cultural Production: Essays on Art and Literature*, New York: Columbia University Press.
———. (1990) 'Fieldwork in Philosophy', in *In Other Words: Essays Towards a Reflexive Sociology*, Cambridge: Polity Press.
———. (1998) *Practical Reason: On the Theory of Action*, London: Polity Press.
———. (1991) 'Några egenskaper hos fälten', in *Kultur och Kritik: Anföranden av Pierre Bourdieu*. Göteborg: Bokförlaget Daidalos.
———. (2000) *Pascalian Meditations*, Cambridge: Polity Press.
———. (2001) *Male Domination*, Cambridge: Polity Press.
——— and L. Wacquant (1992) *An Invitation to Reflexive Sociology*, Cambridge: Polity Press.
Briginshaw, V. (2001) *Dance, Space and Subjectivity*, New York: Palgrave.
Britton, S. (2005) 'Tourism, Dependency and Development: A Mode of Analysis', in Y. Apostolopoulos, S. Leivadi and A. Yiannakis (eds.) *The Sociology of Tourism: Theoretical and Empirical Investigations*, New York: Routledge.
Broady, D. (1991) *Sociologi och epistemologi. Om Pierre Bourdieus författarskap och den historiska epistemologin*, Stockholm: HLS Förlag.
Brown, W. (2008) 'En befriad feminism? Revolution, sorg, politik", in *Fronesis*, 25–26: 191–209.
———. (2010) *Walled States, Waning Sovereignty*, New York: Zone.
Bruner, E. (1991) 'Transformation of Self in Tourism', *Annals of Tourism Research*, 18: 238–250.
Butler, J. (1990/1999) *Gender Trouble: Feminism and the Subversion of Identity*, New York: Routledge.
———. (1997) *Excitable Speech: A Politics of the Performative*, New York: Routledge.

Castells, M. (1996) *The Information Age: Economy, Society and Culture. Vol. I, The Rise of the Network Society*, Malden, MA: Blackwell.
Cohen, E. (1988) 'Authenticity and Commoditization in Tourism', *Annals of Tourism Research*, 15(3): 371–386.
———. (2005) 'The Sociology of Tourism. Approaches, Issues and Findings', in Y. Apostolopoulos, S. Leivadi and A. Yiannakis (eds.) *The Sociology of Tourism: Theoretical and Empirical Investigations*, New York: Routledge.
———. (2011) 'Education Dark Tourism at In Populo Site. The Holocaust Museum in Jerusalem', *Annals of Tourism Research*, 38(1): 193–209.
Coleman, S. and C. Mike (2002) *Tourism: Between Place and Performance*, New York: Berghahn Books.
Collins, R. (1992) *Sociological Insight: An Introduction to Non-Obvious Sociology*, New York: Oxford University Press.
Cressey, P. (1932/2003) *The Taxi-Dance Hall: A Sociological Study in Commercialized Recreation and City Life*, New York: Routledge.
Crick, M. (2005) 'Representations of International Tourism in the Social Sciences: Sun, Sex, Sights, Savings and Servility', in Y. Apostolopoulos, S. Leivadi and A. Yiannakis (eds.) *The Sociology of Tourism: Theoretical and Empirical Investigations*, New York: Routledge.
Cusumanu, C. (2008) *Tango: An Argentine Love Story*, Berkeley: Seal Press.
Dahlberg, C. (2010) *Picturing the Public: Advertising Self-Regulation in Sweden and the UK*, Stockholm: Stockholm University.
Daniel, Y. P. (1996) 'Tourism Dance Performances: Authenticity and Creativity', *Annals of Tourism Research*, 23: 780–797.
Davis, M. (1990) *The City of Quartz: Excavating the Future in Los Angeles*, New York: Verso.
Degen, M. M. (2008) *Sensing Cities: Regenerating Public Life in Barcelona and Manchester*, New York: Routledge.
Denniston, C. (2007) *The Meaning of Tango: The Story of the Argentinian Dance*, London: Portico.
Dielemans, J. (2008) *Välkommen till paradiset: Reportage om turistindustrin*. Stockholm: Atlas.
Douglas, M. (1966) *Purity and Danger: An Analysis of Concepts of Pollution and Taboo*, London: Routledge.
Durkheim, E. (1893/1994) *The Division of Labour in Society*, London: The Macmillan Press Ltd.
Ebron, P. (2002) *Performing Africa*, Princeton: Princeton University Press.
Ehrenreich, B. and A. R. Hochschild. (2003) *Global Woman: Nannies, Maids, and Sex Workers in the New Economy*, New York: Metropolitan Books.
Elsrud, T. (2001) 'Risk Creation in Traveling: Backpacker Adventure Narration', *Annals of Tourism Research*, 28: 597–617.
Evans, M. (2003) *Love. An Unromantic Discussion*, Cambridge: Polity Press.
Fanon, F. (1952/1986) *Black Skin, White Masks*, London: Pluto.
Featherstone, M. (1999) 'Love and Eroticism: An Introduction', in M. Featherstone (ed.) *Love and Eroticism*, London: SAGE.
———. (2010) 'Body, Image and Affect in Consumer Culture', *Body & Society*, 16(1): 193–221.
Fletcher, R. (2008) 'Living on the Edge. The Appeal of Risk Sports for the Professional Middle Class', *Sociology of Sport Journal*, 25: 310–330.
Fourcade, M. (2007) 'Theories of Markets and Theories of Society', *American Behavioural Scientist*, 50(8): 1015–1034.
Franzén, M. (2004) 'Jane Jacobs och den urbana offentligheten' and 'Rummets tvära dialektik—notater till Henri Lefebvre', in T. Johansson and O. Sernhede

(eds.) *Urbanitetens omvandlingar: Kultur och identitet i den postindustriella staden*, Göteborg: Daidalos.

———. (2005) 'Mellan stigma och karisma: Stureplan, Sergels torg och platsens politik', *Fronesis*, 18: 136–152.

Frenzel, F., K. Koens and M. Steinbrink (eds.) (2012) *Slum Tourism: Poverty, Power and Ethics*, New York: Routledge.

Galli, R. (2012) *Varumärkenas fält:* Produktion av erkännande i Stockholms reklamvärld, Stockholm: Stockholm University.

Gavanas, A. (2009) 'Äkta sex på kommersiella villkor?', *Framtider*, 4: 18–20.

———. (2010) *Who Cleans the Welfare State? Migration, Informalization, Social Exclusion and Domestic Services in Stockholm*, Stockholm: Institute for Futures Studies.

Geertz, C. (1988) *Works and Lives. The Anthropologist as Author*, Cambridge: Polity Press.

Giddens, A. (1991) *Modernity and Self-Identity: Self and Society in the Later Modern Age*, Cambridge: Polity Press.

———. (1992) *The Transformation of Intimacy*, Stanford, CA: Stanford University Press.

Goertzen, C. and M. S. Azzi (1999) 'Globalization and the Tango', *Yearbook for Traditional Music*, 31: 67–76.

Goodwin, D. (1998) *Tango! A Story of Sacramento's Argentine Tango Community*, Master of Arts Project, California State University.

González, A. (2000) *Surviving in the City: The Urban Poor of Santiago de Chile 1930–1970*, Uppsala: Uppsala University.

Gotfrit, L. (1988) 'Women Dancing Back: Disruption and the Politics of Pleasure', *Journal of Education*, 170(3): 122–141.

Guy, D. J. (1995) *Sex and Danger in Buenos Aires: Prostitution, Family and Nation in Argentina*, Lincoln: University of Nebraska Press.

Habermas, J. (1992) *The Theory of Communicative Action*, Cambridge: Polity.

Hakim, C. (2010) 'Erotic Capital', *European Sociological Review Advance Access*, published April 10, 2010.

Hall, M. C. (1996/2005) 'Gender and Economic Interests in Tourism Prostitution: The Nature, Development and Implications of Sex Tourism in South-East Asia', in Y. Apostolopoulos, S. Leivadi and A. Yiannakis (eds.) *The Sociology of Tourism: Theoretical and Empirical Investigations*, New York: Routledge.

Hannerz, E. (2012) 'Punk and the Mainstream Other', Conference Paper at the Swedish Sociology Association conference, March 16, 2012.

Hardt, M. (1999) 'Affective Labor', *Boundary* 26(2): 89–100.

Harvey, D. (2002) 'The Art of Rent: Globalization, Monopoly and the Commodification of Culture', *Socialist Register*, 38: 93–110.

———. (2005) *Spaces of Neoliberalization: Towards a Theory of Uneven Geographical Development*, Stuttgart: Franz Steiner Verlag.

Hellum, M. (2002) *Förförd av Eros: Kön och moral bland utländska kvinnor bosatta på en grekisk ö*, Göteborg: Göteborgs Universitet.

Hemmings, C. (2005) 'Invoking Affect: Cultural Theory and the Ontological Turn', *Cultural Studies*, 19(5): 548–567.

Hess, R. (1998) *Les Tangomaniaques*, Paris: Anthropos.

Hochschild, A. (1979) 'Emotion Work, Feeling Rules, and Social Structure', *Journal of American Sociology*, 85(3): 551–575.

Holm, B. (2004) *Pardans: Med fragment av en kavaljersröst*, Stockholm: Bonniers.

Holyfield, L. (1999) 'Manufacturing Adventure: The Buying and Selling of Emotions', *Journal of Contemporary Ethnography*, 28(1): 3–32.

―――. (1983/2003) *The Managed Heart: Commercialization of Human Feeling, Twentieth Anniversary Edition, With a New Afterword*, Berkeley, CA: University of California Press.
Holbrook, M. and E. Hirschman. (1982) 'The Experiential Aspects of Consumption: Consumer Fantasies, Feelings, and Fun', *Journal of Consumer Research*, 9: 132–140.
hooks, b. (1999) 'Eating the Other: Desire and Resistance', in S. Hesse-Biber, C. Gilmartin and R. Lydenberg (eds.) *Feminist Approaches to Theory and Methodology: An Interdisciplinary Reader*, Oxford: Oxford University Press.
Hughson, J. (2008) 'Ethnography and "Physical Culture"', *Ethnography*, 9(4): 421–428.
Illouz, E. (2007) *Cold Intimacies: The Making of Emotional Capitalism*, Oxford: Polity Press.
Jacobs, J. (1961) *The Death and Life of Great American Cities*, London: Pimlico.
Jamieson, L. (1998) *Intimacy: Personal Relationships in Modern Societies*, Cambridge: Polity Press.
Johansson, T. (2004) 'Den frånvarande staden?', in T. Johansson and O. Sernhede (eds.) *Urbanitetens omvandlingar: Kultur och identitet i den postindustriella staden*, Göteborg: Daidalos.
Jonsson, S. (1993) *De andra: Amerikanska kulturkrig och europeisk rasism*, Stockholm: Norstedt.
――― and J. Syssner (2011) 'Postkolonialism', in J. Syssner (ed.) *Perspektiv på turism och resande*, Lund: Studentlitteratur.
Kempadoo, K. (ed.) (1999) *Sun, Sex, and Gold: Tourism and Sex Work in the Caribbean*, Lanham, MD: Rowman & Littlefield.
Knorr Cetina, K. (2012) *The Synthetic Situation: Interactionism for a Global World*, Lecture at the Swedish Sociology Association conference, March 17, 2012.
Kärnborg, U. (2003) *Stjärnfältet*, Stockholm: Bonniers.
Laclau, E. and C. Mouffe (1985) *Hegemony and Socialist Strategy: Towards a Radical Democratic Politics*, London: Verso.
Lagerlöf, S. (1901/2007) *Jerusalem*, Stockholm: Bonniers.
Laing, J. H. and G. I. Crouch (2011) 'Frontier Tourism: Retracing Mythic Journeys', *Annals of Tourism Research*, 38(4): 1516–1534.
Lande, B. (2007) 'Breathing like a Soldier: Culture Incarnate', in C. Schilling (ed.) *Embodying Sociology: Retrospects, Progress and Prospects*, Oxford: Blackwell Publishing.
Larsen, S., T. Øgaard and W. Brun (2011) 'Backpackers and Mainstreamers: Realities and Myths', *Annals of Tourism Research*, 38(2): 690–707.
Larsson, T. and G. Svensson (1992) *Twilight Time: Studier i svenskt dansmusikliv*, Uppsala: Samhällsvetenskapliga forskningsinstitutet SAMU.
Lefebvre, H. (1991) *The Production of Space*, Oxford: Blackwell Publishing.
Lepp, A. and H. Gibson (2003) 'Tourist Roles, Perceived Risk and International Tourism', *Annals of Tourism Research*, 30(1): 606–624.
Lévi-Strauss, C. (1976) *Tristes Tropiques*, Harmondsworth: Penguin Books.
Lewis, J. (2001) *The End of Marriage? Individualism and Intimate Relations*, Cheltenham: Elgar.
Lindholm, C. (1999) 'Love and Structure', in M. Featherstone (ed.) *Love & Eroticism*, London: SAGE Publications Ltd.
Lois, J. (2001) 'The Gendered Emotional Culture of Edgework', *Gender & Society*, 15(3): 381–406.
Lupton, D. and J. Tulloch (2002) 'Risk Is Part of Your Life: Risk Epistemologies among a Group of Australians', *Sociology*, 36(2): 317–334.

Lundström, C. (2006) 'Svenska latinas: Rasifierade diskurser om femininitet och representationer av latinidad i Sverige', in K. Sandell and D. Mulinari (eds.) *Feministiska interventioner: Berättelser om och från en annan värld*, Stockholm: Makadam.
Lyng, S. (1990) 'Edgework: A Social Psychological Analysis of Voluntary Risk Taking', *The American Journal of Sociology*, 95(4): 851–886.
Lyng, S. (2005) 'Edgework and the Risk-Taking Experience', in S. Lyng (ed.) *Edgework: The Sociology of Risk-Taking*, New York: Routledge.
Löfgren, O. (1999) *On Holiday: A History of Vacationing*, Berkeley: University of California Press.
MacCannel, D. (1973) 'Staged Authenticity: Arrangements of Social Space in Tourist Settings', *American Journal of Sociology*, 79(3): 589–603.
———. (1976) *The Tourist: A New Theory of the Leisure Class*, New York: Schocken Books.
Malki, L. (1995) *Purity and Exile: Violence, Memory, and National Cosmology among Hutu Refugees in Tanzania*, Chicago: Chicago University Press.
Manning, E. (2003) 'Negotiating Influence: Argentine Tango and a Politics of Touch', *Borderlands*, 2(1): e-journal.
———. (2007) *Politics of Touch. Sense, Movement, Sovereignty*, Minneapolis: University of Minnesota Press.
Mauss, M. (1923/1997) *Gåvan*, Lund: Arkiv.
McRobbie, A. (1984) 'Dance and Social Fantasy', in A. McRobbie and M. Nava (eds.) *Gender and Generation*, London: Macmillan.
Meisch, L. A. (1995) 'Gringas and Otavaleños: Changing Tourist Relations', *Annals of Tourism Research*, 22(2): 441–462.
Merleau-Ponty, M. (1945/1999) *Kroppens fenomenologi*. Göteborg: Daidalos.
Mishra, R. (1999) *Globalization and the Welfare State*, Northampton: Edward Elgar.
Mjöberg, J. (2011) *Innerlighetens tid: En sociologisk undersökning av intimitet och senmodernitet*, Uppsala: Uppsala University.
Moaz, D. (2007) 'Backpackers' Motivations. The Role of Culture and Nationality', *Annals of Tourism Research*, 34: 122–140.
Mohanty, C. T. (2003) *Feminism without Borders. Decolonizing Theory, Practicing Solidarity*, Durham: Duke University Press.
Morin, E. (2008) *Seven Complex Lessons in Education for the Future*, Paris: UNESCO.
Mowatt, R. A. and H. C. Charles (2011) 'Visiting Death and Life: Dark Tourism and Slave Castles', *Annals of Tourism Research*, 38(4): 1410–1434.
Nagel, J. (2003) *Race, Ethnicity and Sexuality: Intimate Intersections, Forbidden Frontiers*, Oxford: Oxford University Press.
Negri, A. and M. Hardt (2008) *Samtal om makt och en framtida världsdemokrati*, Lecture at Södra Teatern, Stockholm, September 18, 2008.
Nilsson, Å. (2012) 'Risk and Control in Adventure Sports', Conference Paper at the Swedish Sociology Association conference, March 16, 2012.
Nyberg, A. (1999) 'Hemnära marknadstjänster—kvinnors befriare?,' *Kvinnovetenskaplig tidskrift*, 3: 57–61.
O'Connell Davidson, J. and J. Sanchez Taylor (1999) 'Fantasy Islands: Exploring the Demand for Sex Tourism', in K. Kempadoo (ed.) *Sun, Sex, and Gold: Tourism and Sex Work in the Caribbean*, Oxford: Rowman and Littlefield.
———. (2005) 'Travel and Taboo: Heterosexual Sex tourism to the Carribean', in L. Schaffner and E. Bernstein (eds.) *Regulating Sex: The Politics of Intimacy and Identity*, London: Routledge.
Olszewski, B. (2008) '*El Cuerpo del Baile:* The Kinetic and Social Fundamentals of Tango', *Body & Society*, 14(2): 63–81.

Opperman, M. (ed.) (1998) *Sex Tourism and Prostitution: Aspects of Leisure, Recreation, and Work*, New York: Cognizant Communication Corporation.

Palmer, M. (2006) *Kiss & Tango: Diary of a Dance-Hall Seductress*, New York: HarperCollins Publishers.

Park, R. E. and E. W. Burgess (1925/1984) *The City: Suggestions for Investigation of Human Behaviour in the Urban Environment*, Chicago: The University of Chicago Press.

Parviainen, J. (2002) 'Bodily Knowledge: Epistemological Reflections on Dance', *Dance Research Journal*, 34(1): 11–26.

Pateman, C. (1988) *The Sexual Contract*, Cambridge: Polity Press.

Paz, O. (1996) *The Double Flame: Love and Eroticism*, San Diego: Harcourt Brace & Company.

Plummer, K. (2003) *Intimate Citizenship: Private Decisions and Public Dialogues*, Seattle: University of Washington Press.

Pruitt, D. and S. LaFont (1995) 'For Love and Money: Romance Tourism in Jamaica', *Annals of Tourism Research*, 22(2): 422–440.

Riley, D. (2005) *Impersonal Passion: Language as Affect*, Durham: Duke University Press.

Ritchie, B. W. (2003) *Managing Educational Tourism*, New York: Channel View Publications.

Rivero, C. (2004) *Argentinsk tango: Berättelser från queertangoscenen*, Uppsats påbyggnadskurs i genusvetenskap, Stockholm: Stockholm universitet.

Romano, C. (2005) *Argentinian Tango: A History*, Buenos Aires: Editora AC.

Roseneil, S. and S. Budgeon (2004) 'Cultures of Intimacy and Care Beyond "the Family": Personal Life and Social Change in the Early 21st Century', *Current Sociology*, 52(2): 135–159.

Roseneil, S. (2007) 'Queer Individualization: The Transformation of Personal Life in the Early 21st Century', *NORA: Nordic Journal of Women's Studies*, 15(2–3): 84–99.

Rypka, D., E. Cukierman and G. M. Sanchez (2005) *Buenos Aires Off: Emociones, pasiones y tango*, Buenos Aires: Cukierman Editores.

Said, E. W. (1995) *Orientalism: Western Conceptions of the Orient*, London: Penguin.

Sanchez Taylor, J. (2006) 'Female Sex Tourism: A Contradiction in Terms?', *Feminist Review*, 83: 42–59.

Sassen, S. (1999) *Globalization and Its Discontents: Essays on the New Mobility of People and Money*, New York: New Press.

Savigliano, M. E. (1995a) *Tango and the Political Economy of Passion*, Boulder: Westview.

——. (1995b) 'Whiny Ruffians and Rebellious Broads: Tango as a Spectacle of Eroticized Social Tension', *Theatre Journal*, 47(1): 83–104.

Sawyer, L. (2006) 'Racialization, Gender and the Negotiation of Power in Stockholm's African Dance Courses', in K. M. Clarke and D. A. Thomas (ed.) *Globalization and Race: Transformations in the Cultural Production of Blackness*, Durham/London: Duke University Press.

Segal, L. (1997) 'Competing Masculinitites: Black Masculinity and the White Man's Black Man', in L. Segal (ed.). *Slow Motion: Changing Masculinities, Changing Men*, London: Virago.

Selwyn, T. (1996) 'Introduction', in T. Selwyn (ed.) *The Tourist Image: Myths and Myth Making in Tourism*, Chichester: John Wiley & Sons.

Shilling, C. (2004) 'Physical Capital and Situated Action: A New Direction for Corporeal Sociology', *British Journal of Sociology of Education*, 25(4): 473–487.

Simmel, G. (1907/1971) 'Prostitution', in D. N. Levine (ed.) *Georg Simmel: On Individuality and Social Forms*, Chicago: The University of Chicago Press.

———. (1911/1971) 'The Adventure', in D. N. Levine (ed.) *Georg Simmel: On Individuality and Social Forms*, Chicago: The University of Chicago Press.
Sistema Estadístico de la Ciudad. (2009) *SEC informa*, April 2009.
Skeggs, B. (1997) *Formations of Class and Gender: Becoming Respectable*, London: SAGE.
———. (2005) 'The Making of Class and Gender through Visualizing Moral Subject Formation', *Sociology*, 39(5): 965–982.
Skinner, J. (2008a) 'Women Dancing Back—and Forth: Resistance and Self-Regulation in Belfast Salsa', *Dance Research Journal* 40(1): 65–77.
———. (2008b) 'Emotional Baggage: The Meaning/Feeling Debate amongst Tourists', in H. Wulff (ed.) *Emotions: A Reader*, Oxford: Berg.
———. (2009) 'Leading Questions and Body Memories: A Case of Phenomenology and Physical Ethnography in the Dance Interview', in A. Gallinat and P. Collins (eds.) *Keeping An Open 'I': Memory and Experience as Resources in Ethnography*, Oxford: Berghahn Books.
Soomägi, J., L. Breitner and P. Syrjänen (2002) *Om tango*, Helsingborg: P. Syrjänen.
Spivak, G. C. (2002) 'Kan den subaltern tala?', in *Postkoloniala studier*. Skriftserien Kairos number 7. Stockholm: Raster förlag.
Stoller, L. A. (2002) *Carnal Knowledge and Imperial Power: Race and the Intimate in Colonial Rule*, Berkeley: University of California Press.
Strain, E. (2003) *Public Places, Private Journeys: Ethnography, Entertainment, and the Tourist Gaze*, New Brunswick: Rutgers University Press.
Søndergaard, D. M. (1999) *Destabilising Discourse Analysis: Approached to Poststructuralist Empirical Research*, Copenhagen: Copenhagen University.
Takeyama, A. (2008) *The Art of Seduction and Affect Economy: Neoliberal Class Struggle and Gender Politics in a Tokyo Host Club*, Champaign, IL: University of Illinois Press.
Taylor, J. (1976) 'Tango: Theme of Class and Nation', *Ethnomusicology*, 20(2): 273–291.
———. (1998) *Paper Tangos*. Durham, NC: Duke University Press.
Thomas, H. (2003) *The Body, Dance and Cultural Theory*, New York: Palgrave Macmillan.
Thompson, R. F. (2005) *Tango: The Art History of Love*, New York: Pantheon Books.
Tomkins, S. (1963) *Affect, Imagery, Consciousness. Vol. II: The Negative Affects*, New York: Springer Publishing.
Tornhill, S. (2010) *Capital Visions: The Politics of Transnational Production in Nicaragua*, Stockholm: Stockholm University.
Travlou, P. (2002) 'Go Athens: A Journey to the Centre of the City', in S. Coleman and M. Crang (eds.) *Tourism: Between Place and Performance*, New York: Berghahn Books.
Turner, B. (2005) 'Introduction—Bodily Performance: On Aura and Reproducibility', *Body & Society*, 11(4): 45–62.
Tönnies, F. (1887/2001) *Community and Civil Society*, New York: Cambridge University Press.
Törnqvist, M. (2006) *Könspolitik på gränsen: Debatterna om varannan damernas och Thamprofessurerna*, Lund: Arkiv.
———. (2010a) *Tangoexperimentet*, Stockholm: Ruin förlag.
———. (2010b) 'Love Impossible: Troubling Tales of Eroticized Difference in Buenos Aires', in A. Jónasdóttir, V. Bryson and K. Jones (eds.) *Sexuality, Gender and Power: Intersectional and Transnational Perspectives*, New York: Routledge.
———. (2012) 'Troubling Romance Tourism: Sex, Gender and Class inside the Argentinean Tango Clubs', *Feminist Review*, 102: 21–40.

―――― and K. Hardy (2010) 'Taxi Dancers: Tango Labour and Commercialized Intimacy in Buenos Aires', in K. Hardy, S. Kingston and T. Sanders (eds.) *New Sociologies of Sex Work*, Surrey: Ashgate.

Törnqvist, T. (1995) *Skogsrikets arvingar. En studie av skogsägarskapet inom privat, enskilt skogsbruk*, Uppsala: Samhällsvetenskapliga forskningsinstitutet (SAMU).

Urry, J. (1990) *The Tourist Gaze: Leisure and Travel in Contemporary Societies*, London: SAGE.

――――. (2002) 'Mobility and Proximity', *Sociology*, 36(2): 255–274.

Urquía, N. (2004) '"Doin' It Right": Contested Authenticity in London's Salsa Scene', in A. Bennett and R. A. Peterson (eds.) *Music Scenes: Local, Translocal and Virtual*, Nashville: Vanderbilt University Press.

Viladrich, A. (2005) 'Tango Immigrants in New York City: The Values of Social Reciprocities', *Journal of Contemporary Ethnography*, 35(4): 533–559.

Wacquant, L. (2004) *Body and Soul: Notebooks of an Apprentice Boxer*, Oxford: Oxford University Press.

――――. (2005) 'Carnal Connections on Embodiment, Apprenticeship and Membership', *Qualitative Sociology*, 28(4): 445–474.

――――. (2008) 'Pierre Bourdieu', in R. Stones (ed.) *Key Sociological Thinkers*, New York: Palgrave Macmillan.

Wade, L. (2011) 'The Emancipatory Promise of the Habitus: Lindy Hop, the Body and Social Change', *Ethnography*, 12(2): 224–246.

Wang, N. (1999) 'Rethinking Authenticity in Tourism Experiences', *Annals of Tourism Research*, 26(2): 349–370.

Ware, V. (1997) 'Purity and Danger: Race, Gender and Tales of Sex Tourism', in A. McRobbis (ed.) *Back to Reality? Social Experience and Cultural Studies*, Manchester: Manchester University Press.

Weber, M. (1915/1995) 'Religious Rejections of the World and Their Directions,' in H. H. Gerth and C. Wright Mills (eds.) *From Max Weber: Essays in Sociology*, London: Routledge.

――――. (1930/1965) *The Protestant Ethic and the Spirit of Capitalism*, London: Allen & Unwin.

Weenink, D. (2008) 'Cosmopolitanism as a Form of Capital: Parents Preparing their Children for a Globalizing World', *Sociology*, 42(6): 1089–1106.

Weaver, D. and M. Oppermann (2000) *Tourism Management*, Milton: Jacaranda Wiley.

Wettergren, Å., B. Starrin and G. Lindgren (eds.) (2008) *Det sociala livets emotionella grunder*, Malmö: Liber.

Whitson, R. (2007) 'Beyond the Crisis: Economic Globalization and Informal Work in Urban Argentina', *Journal of Latin American Geography*, 6(2): 122–136.

Winter, B. (2008) *Long after Midnight at the Niño Bien*, New York: Public Affairs.

Wolkowitz, C. (2006) *Bodies at Work*, London: SAGE.

Woodward, K. (2008) 'Hanging Out and Hanging About: Insider/Outsider Research in the Sport of Boxing', *Ethnography*, 9(4): 536–560.

World Tourism Organization. (1995) *Collection of Tourism Expenditure Statistics*. Technical Manual, No. 2.

――――. (2011) The UNWTO edition 2011 'Tourism Highlights'.

Wouters, C. (2004) *Sex and Manners: Female Emancipation in the West, 1890–2000*, London: SAGE.

Wulff, H. (2008) 'Ethereal Expression: Paradoxes of Ballet as a Global Physical Culture', *Ethnography*, 9(4): 519–536.

Young, I. M. (2005) *On Female Body Experiences: "Throwing like a Girl" and Other Essays*, New York: Oxford University Press.

286 *References*

Yuval-Davis, N. (1997) *Gender and Nation*, London: SAGE.
Zelizer, V. A. (2005) *The Purchase of Intimacy*, Princeton: Princeton University Press.
Zukin, S. (2010) *Naked City: The Death and Life of Authentic Urban Places*, Oxford: Oxford University Press.
Øygarden, G. A. (2000) *Den brukne neses estetikk: En bok om boksing*, Uppsala: Uppsala Universitet.

OTHER SOURCES

Newspaper Articles

Dagens Nyheter (2011) 'Buenos Aires—staden som har allt', 23 October.
Ottawa Citizen (2007) 'Sex tourism: When women do it, it's called 'romance travelling'', 27 January.

Movies

Karlsson, J., A. Karlsson and E. Ramsin Barlas (2012) *Taxi-dancing*, Barlas Productions.
Potter, S. (1997) *The Tango Lesson*, Sony Picture Classics.

Tango Magazines

Selected issues of the following Argentine tango magazines from the year 2007 and 2012:
B.A. Tango
El Tangauta
La Porteña Tango
La Milonga Argentina
Tanguata, BsAs
Tango Map Guide

Webpages

www.dni-tango.com Webpage for the tango school *DNI Tango* in Buenos Aires
http://www.emmaholder.com Blog of a Canadian tango dancer, including a tango diary from Buenos Aires
www.gadventures.com Webpage for tourist agency "Adventure Travel and Tours" offering tours to Buenos Aires and other places
http://www.kissandtango.info Webpage for the bestselling book *Kiss and Tango* by Marina Palmer
http://www.lptango.com.ar Online edition of *La Porteña Tango*
http://www.sonypictures.com/classics/tango/thetango.html Webpage about the movie *The Tango Lesson*, by Sally Potter (1997). This page covers information about the movie, featuring the Argentine star dancer Pablo Veron and Sally Potter, as well as information about the tango.
http://www.tangodanza.de A monthly German tango magazine, the *Tangodanza*, which offers not only a dance and events calendar for Germany and Europe, but also articles on Argentine politics and contemporary history

http://www.tangofocus.com/holidays.php Tourist agency for tango dancers and other tourists in Buenos Aires, offering "exclusive tango tours"

www.tangoinspiration.com Webpage for Uruguayan–Swedish tango dancing couple Cristina Ramirez and Tommy Persson, offering dance classes and including covering Cristina's tango diary from Buenos Aires

www.tangomango.org Webpage for North-American tango dancers, primarily covering schedules and upcoming events

www.tangonorte.com Stockholm-based Swedish-Argentine tango association

www.tangonoticias.com North-American tango webpage

http://www.tangopasional.com/TEST_JS/ba.html Tourist agency offering a full-package program for visiting tango dancers in Buenos Aires

www.tangoportalen.se Webpage for Swedish tango dancers, covering schedules and upcoming events and offering an interactive forum

www.tangowithjudy.com Webpage for North-American tango teacher and tourist agency based in Buenos Aires, offering—among other services—"cosmetic surgery travel" to Argentina. This webpage was formerly http://www.niptuck-travelbuenosaires.com/

http://www.tejastango.com/ Tango Argentino de Tejas, North-American webpage created by Stephen and Susan Brown, teachers and tango organizers partly based in Dallas and Las Vegas. The webpage covers various kinds of information on tango, partly related to a tango holiday in Buenos Aires.

www.theworkingvacation.com The Gentlemen Host Program webpage

www.totango.com Canadian webpage, primarily covering tango music but also offering information on the dancing and dance culture

http://www.turismo.gov.ar Webpage for the Argentine Ministry of Tourism

http://www.welcomeargentina.com Webpage for tourists in Argentina, with a page devoted to tango-related venues and events: tango-shows as well as *milongas*

www.wttc.org Webpage for the World Travel and Tourism Council

Index

A
Abadi, S. 82[1]
accessibility 217–218
adventure 17–18: existential 95–97; liminal 102; manufactured 15: tango 101–103
Ahmed, S. 41, 240
artistic exploration 93–95
autobiographical novels 14, 25, 158–159, 254–255
Argentina 3–4, 195–212: capital (see Buenos Aires); economic crisis 4, 17, 106–110, 201; people 142–147, 223
Aspers, P. 21
authenticity 15–16, 140–141, 147–156: and distinction 174; and space 206–212, 223–224; as symbolic capital 79–82; contested 220–226; -ic places 91; modernist and postmodernist discourse 210–211; negotiating 156–161; quest for 90–93
Azzi, M. S. 7

B
Bauman, Z. 4–5
de Beauvoir, S. 99
Beckert, J. 21
belief: embodied 55–57; production of 31–34
Beck, U. 244
Bernstein, E. 173
body 24–5, 263, 271: and space 22–23; -centered services 230–231; dispositions of 31; economy of the 23–24; in tango dancing 34–39; mind dichotomy 180; sacrifices 64; turn 5, 259

boundary work 24, 140, 155–157
Boissevain, J. 13, 15
Bourdieu, P. 20–21, 24, 31, 59–63, 211, 233, 262–264, 271
Bruner, E. 16
Buenos Aires 11, 18, 142–147, 195–212, 224, 236–237: fieldwork in 248–251; marketing 198–200, 224–225; *Mi Buenos Aires Querido* 195; sexualizing 188–189

C
cabeceo 35, 54, 69
capital: emotionality as 76–79; economic 62 (see money); sexual 69–72; social 67–69; symbolic 61, 64–67, 217–218, 227–235
capitalism 19, 215, 217–218, 260
Castells, M. 21
class 17: and gender 269; distinctions 140–141; constructions of 192, 240–243; making of a classless 237–240; social 182–185; middle 186–188, 228, 252; working class culture 153
care chain 260
city: modern and postmodern 260; mythmaking of 23
Cohen, E. 13, 16, 224
Coleman, S. 226, 273
commercialization 215–226: -ized hospitality 13; -ized intimacy. *See* intimacy
consecration 66, 127, 226, 262
consumption: and authenticity 151–152; and emotions 231; cultural 6
cortina 50, 118

---

1. The selection of references in the index is based on works being quoted in the book.

290   Index

Crang, M. 226, 273
Cressey, P. 266
culture: -al art form 196; -al expropriation 17; -al resistance 19, 215–217; -al theory 5; physical 5, 247; and national identity 7
Cusumano, C. 98

D
dance: economy (see intimate tango economy); escort (see taxi dancing); lindy-hop 5–6; salsa 5; skills 64–65; studies 5–6; trading dancing skills 110–113
discourse 7, 10, 16, 18, 25, 31: -iv practice 24; -iv struggle 175
Douglas, M. 180, 219

E
economy: and risk 86–88; conflicting 19–21; disavowal of economic interest 19, 134–136; embodied 84–85; gift 67–69; -ic conversions 20, 63; -ic hardship 6; -ic sociology 21; informal (see market); intimate tango 19–21, 58, 226–232; of the flesh 64; landscape 200–205; symbolic 60–61, 262
educational: exploration 93–95; values 110–113
Elsrud, T. 18
embodied: ethnography (see ethnography); practice 20, 24, 33
emotion: and power 231; -al edgework 99–101; -al imperative 76–77; -al labor (see labor); -al space 20; as discourse 237–240; as objects of consumption 15; in tourism 14–15; management 78–79; negotiating 174; work (see work); in tango 40–43, 172
ethnography 23–26, 247–251
exotic: attributes 81; -icizing the tourist 82–84; othering 10–12, 81–82; places 11

F
Featherstone, M. 69, 77
feeling. See emotions
femininity ideals 98, 182–185
feminist studies 5–6, 12
field 20, 60, 216–217, 226–235, 262: autonomy 219, 226

Franzén, M. 260

G
Galli, R. 60, 272
gender 11–12, 20: and age 230–231, 263–264; -ed class politics 240–243; -ed vulnerability 69–72, 229–232; in tango dancing 261; racialized gender regime (see race)
gentrification 201
geography: deterritorialized 10; emotional 22–23; negotiating 209–212; place marketing 198–200; reterritorialized 205–209, 223–226
Giddens, A. 4–5, 168
gift exchange 67–69: globalized 132–133
globalization 10–12, 17, 215–216, 242–243: and geography 197–198; and tango 6–8; localizing 243–245
Global South: exploitation of 11–12; Global North divide 192
Goertzen, C. 7
Gotfrit, L. 5
Guy, D.J. 43, 266

H
habitus 56–57, 271
Hakim, C. 69, 263
Harvey, D. 17, 200, 224, 232
heterosexuality 20, 83, 264: in tango dancing 259, 261; romance 182–185, 240–241; play with 87, 229–231
Hochschild, A. 117, 266
Holm, B. 163–164, 186
honor 20, 60, 217–218: dance-floor 53–55
holiday. See tourism
hooks, b. 193
Hughson, J. 5

I
identity work 13, 18, 126, 140, 255
illusio 21, 59–60, 226
individuality 155–156, 217, 219
individualism: discourse on emotionality 168–169
interview-study 24, 26, 251–254, 274
intimacy: commercialized 162–163; global 10–12, 242–243; in late-modern societies 9–10, 168;

J
Jamieson, L. 264
justification: principles 217–218; regime of 231–232, 271

L
labor: body 21; emotional 11, 266; informal (*see* work)
Latin America 4, 11, 82, 199
Lefebvre, H. 22, 197, 237, 273
Lévi-Strauss, C. 13
Lyng, S. 100
Löfgren, O. 197

M
MacCannell, D. 15–16, 225
Manning, E. 7
market: adaption 215–216; conversions 135; culturally embedded 232–235; impact of market forces 19; informal 265–266; -izing symbolic values 133–136; of tango 19–21, 104–106; tourist 152
masculinity: Argentine 179, 259, 269; negotiating 171–172; sexualizing Argentine 188–191, 264
Mauss, M. 67
McRobbie, A. 23, 47
method 23–26, 247–257
methodological: detector 162; embodiment 23–26; mobility 26; reflexivity 249–250
mindscape 197
milonga 4, 34–35, 47–49, 273–274
milonguero 34, 46
Mjöberg, J. 10
mobility 17, 22, 102, 155, 259
modernity 13–15, 101
money: and honor 152–155; and intimacy 173–174; (mis)use of 174; negotiating 174, 239–240
manufactured 166–169; negotiating commercialized 174–176; restricted 49–51; tourism 97–99, 264; trading 117–120

N
narrative 8, 18, 20: analysis 24–25, 254–257; narrating practice 18; sexualized 43–44
negotiation 8, 19, 21–22, 27, 61–62, 66
neo-liberalization 17
nationality 14: negotiating 205–209, 268

O
Olszewski, B. 19, 236

P
Palmer, M. 73–74, 189–190, 268
Paz, O. 238
pista 48
Plummer, K. 9
practical reason 55–57, 219
practice 7, 10, 18, 25, 31
politics: -al act 154; class (*see* gender); of touch 7; of pleasure 5; respectability 185–188
porteño 171, 190
postcolonialism 5–6, 12, 244

R
race: -ialization 81; -ialized gender regime 188–191, 242
recognition 20, 58–63, 90, 226–232
risk-management 99–101, 217–218, 265
romance 177–194

S
sacred 32, 56, 61, 179–180, 187
sacrifice 63–67, 218–219
Sanchez Taylor, J. 12
Savigliano, M. 6, 179, 240, 243
sex: and tango 177–194; as metaphor 261; labor 11–12; negotiating 191–194; play with 72–76; tourism (*see* tourism); -uality and class 185–188; -uality studies 5–6; -ualization 8; -ualized metaphor 181; -ualizing tango 43–47; -ualizing tango work 120–123
Simmel. G. 13, 15, 17–18, 101–102, 173, 268
Skeggs, B. 186, 269
Skinner, J. 5
social form 9–10, 15
space: in late modern societies 21–22; *in situ* and *in populo* 16, 205, 224; negotiating 209–212; safe 144–147
Spanish: language 207, 249

T
tanda 34, 50

tango: aesthetics 80; club (see *milonga*), cosmopolitan 207–208; export- 7; institutionalized 47–49; *Kiss and see* Palmer, M.; family 51–53; fin de siècle 179; history 267, 270; kitsch 266; magazines 255–256; -portalen 165, 256; queer 46, 254, 261–262, 264; schools and teachers 110–113; shoes 131–132, 267; studies 6–8; trademarks 130–132; webpages 256, 286–287
tango tourism: theorizing 5–8; negotiating 216–226
taxi-dancing 12, 113–115, 162, 233–235, 253: as means 169–170; as shortcut 163–166; legitimating 169–174; negotiating 174–176
taxista. See taxi dancing
Taylor, J. 6
temporality 211–212, 218
terrain *see* geography
text-analysis 25–26, 254–257
tourism: and traveling 259; as practice 17–18; agencies 115–116; conceptualizing 13–18; conformity 155–156; cultural production of 156–161; definition 13–14; dark 13; history of 14–15; imaginary 200–205; impact of 16–17; in Argentina 3–4, 106–110; intimacy 97–99; mass 15; minister of 17; negotiating 156–161; package 4; romance 12; sex 11–12, 99, 186–188, 232, 242; shallow 147–151
tourist: identity 13–18, 139–141; identity work 226–232; nostalgia 226; shame 232; tango 251–252
trading: aesthetics 125–127; accessibility 113–116; artistic values 110; authenticity 123–125; emotions 116–123; knowledge 110–113; recognition 127–133
transformation: capacities 226; of self 13, 16; rites 218
traveling. *See* tourism

U

urban geography 22, 201, 260
Urry, J. 15, 17, 22, 102

V

value 20–21, 58–63: negotiation 223–224; spheres 19, 181, 193, 219–220, 227, 271
verso 88
Viladrich, A. 7, 259–260
voyage: into the ordinary 141–147; out of the ordinary 7, 89, 101–103
vulnerability 229–232: economic 229, 241–242; emotional 229–232; gendered (*see* gender)

W

Wacquant, L. 25, 60, 247–248, 262
Wade, L. 5–6
Whitson, R. 265
Winter, B. 35
Wolkowitz, C. 110–111, 117
work: body 110–111, 114, 122; emotional 78–79, 266; informal 106–110, 265
World Tourism Organization 107
Wulff, H. 36–37, 100

Y

Young, I. M. 71–72

Z

Zelizer, V. 21

Ø

Øygarden, G. A. 25–26, 36